Charles Morris

Our Island Empire

a Hand-Book of Cuba, Porto Rico, Hawaii, and the Philippine Islands

Charles Morris

Our Island Empire
a Hand-Book of Cuba, Porto Rico, Hawaii, and the Philippine Islands

ISBN/EAN: 9783743306981

Manufactured in Europe, USA, Canada, Australia, Japa

Cover: Foto ©ninafisch / pixelio.de

Manufactured and distributed by brebook publishing software (www.brebook.com)

Charles Morris

Our Island Empire

CONTENTS.

★ ★

SECTION I.
CUBA.

SECTION		PAGE
I.—Historical Sketch		7
II.—Physical Conditions		15
	Extent and Situation	15
	The Mountain System	17
	Plains and Rivers	21
	The Coastal System	23
	The Forest Region	25
	Geology	26
	Climate	28
III.—Natural Productions		32
	Forest Trees	32
	Food Plants and Fruits	34
	Animals	38
	Metals	41
	Minerals	44
IV.—Civil and Political Relations		48
	Governmental Organization	48
	Divisions of Territory	50
	Abolition of Slavery	51
	Religion	52
	Means of Communication	53
	Population	57
	Education	60
V.—Centres of Population		62
	Havana, the Capital City	62
	Matanzas	77
	Cardenas	80
	Other Northern Ports	81
	Santiago de Cuba	83
	Trinidad	88
	Cienfuegos	89
	Inland Cities	91
	Health Resorts	94

CONTENTS.

SECTION	PAGE
VI.—MANNERS AND CUSTOMS	96
City Life	96
Food and Beverages	104
Street Scenes	108
The Gambling Propensity	112
Rural Life	116
VII.—AGRICULTURAL PRODUCTIONS	124
Coffee	124
Tobacco	132
Sugar	136
Live-Stock	144
VIII.—MANUFACTURES AND COMMERCE	149
Cigars	149
Commerce	151
Finances	156
The Future Outlook	159

★ ★

SECTION II.

PORTO RICO.

I.—HISTORICAL SKETCH	165
II.—PHYSICAL CONDITIONS	171
Size and Situation	171
Rivers and Lakes	173
Islands	174
Harbors	175
Geology	177
Climate	178
III.—NATURAL PRODUCTIONS	181
Plant Life	181
Animal Life	183
Minerals	184
IV.—CIVIL AND POLITICAL RELATIONS	186
Government and Religion	186
Roads and Railways	187
Population	189
Education	192
V.—CENTRES OF POPULATION	194
General Conditions	194
San Juan	194

CONTENTS.

SECTION		PAGE
	Ponce	199
	Mayaguez	200
	Other Seaports	201
	Inland Towns	202
VI.—MANNERS AND CUSTOMS		205
	The Spanish Class	205
	The Peasant Class	206
VII.—AGRICULTURAL INDUSTRIES		210
	Fertility of the Soil	210
	Farm Crops	212
	Live-Stock	217
VIII.—MANUFACTURES AND COMMERCE		219
	Articles of Manufacture	219
	Commerce	219
	Finances	223
	Future Prospects	225

★ ★

SECTION III.

HAWAII.

I.—HISTORICAL SKETCH		228
II.—PHYSICAL CONDITIONS		237
	Geographical Relations	237
	Geological Formation	239
	Mountain System	240
	Volcanoes	241
	Plains and Valleys	245
	Harbors	247
	Climate	248
	Rainfall	250
	Diseases	251
III.—NATURAL PRODUCTIONS		253
	Forest and Fruit Trees	253
	Useful Plants	258
	Native Animals	261
	Introduced Animals	263
IV.—CIVIL AND POLITICAL RELATIONS		266
	Territory of Hawaii	266
	Population	267

SECTION		PAGE
	Education	270
	Religion	271
	Public Works	273
V.—Centres of Population		278
	Honolulu	278
	Hilo	283
	Lahaina	285
	Kailua	285
VI.—The People of Hawaii		287
	The Native Population	287
	Dwellings and Food	293
	Inhabitants of Foreign Origin	295
VII.—Agricultural Industries		299
	General Conditions	299
	Sugar Production	300
	Coffee Culture	306
	Other Agricultural Products	309
	Grazing Industries	312
	Bird Products	314
VIII.—Manufactures and Commerce		317
	Mechanical Industries	317
	Commerce	318
	Shipping	320
	Finances	321

★ ★

SECTION IV.

THE PHILIPPINE ISLANDS.

I.—Historical Sketch		323
II.—Physical Conditions		334
	Geography	334
	Geology	337
	Volcanoes	339
	Luzon	342
	Mindanao	343
	The Smaller Islands	344
	Harbors	347
	Climate	349
	Diseases	352

CONTENTS.

SECTION	PAGE
III.—NATURAL PRODUCTIONS	356
Forest Trees	356
Fruit and Food Plants	361
Animal Life	362
Metals	367
Minerals	371
IV.—CIVIL AND POLITICAL RELATIONS	373
Government	373
Religion	376
Public Works	381
Population	384
The Civilized Natives	386
The Wild Tribes	393
Education	396
V.—CENTRES OF POPULATION	399
Manila	399
Iloilo	410
Cebu	411
Other Towns	412
VI.—THE PEOPLE OF THE PHILIPPINES	416
Character of the Natives	416
Dwellings, Food, and Dress	423
Popular Amusements	428
The Mestizos	434
The Moros	436
The Wild Tribes	439
The Aetas, or Negritos	440
VII.—AGRICULTURAL INDUSTRIES	443
Manila Hemp	443
Sugar	446
Tobacco	450
Rice	451
Coffee	453
Other Vegetable Products	455
Live-Stock	458
VIII.—MANUFACTURES AND COMMERCE	460
Cigars	460
Other Manufactures	461
Commerce	463
Finances	467
The Future Outlook	469

PREFACE.

The United States of America, after more than a century of continental growth and development, has, upon the threshold of the Twentieth Century, taken a new and radical step forward in its national career, having added to its dominions a large number of tropical islands, situated on the opposite sides of the earth, and inhabited by peoples strikingly distinct from those of the great republic of the West. The question, What shall we do with them? is one which necessarily arises, but which only time and experience can answer. Some of these islands have been accepted as territorial acquisitions of the United States; others stand at present as wards of the republic, their future status left open to the decision of events. In the new and untried situation into which this country has entered, any hasty settlement of these momentous problems would be unwise and might prove disastrous. A period of watching and waiting is what wisdom dictates,—of drifting on the tide of events until circumstances shall point the way and judgment grow mature. This is not as many would have it. There are numbers eager to settle all questions in a breath, ready to adopt the first half-considered decision—and repent at leisure. Fortunately, this is not the sentiment of those into whose hands this problem has fallen, and who are feeling their way with commendable slowness and grave consideration to a judicious solution of each question as it arises.

The decision rests not alone in the hands of the legislative and executive branches of the government, but in those of the people as well. An enlightened public opinion is an important element in the situation, and to the formation of such a just conception of the circumstances some degree of acquaintance with the conditions of these island acquisitions is highly important. It is for this purpose, in part, that the present work has been prepared,—to give the people of the United States a general knowledge of the problem they have taken in hand, through a succinct description of these new island dominions, their natural conditions, physical resources, and the character and modes of life and thought of their populations, as a guide to an enlightened decision as to what had best be done with them.

This is only one of the purposes—and not the main one—that the author has had in view. There is a natural feeling of interest concerning these islands, based partly on the usual desire to know, partly on more personal motives, which it is important to gratify. There are some who have it in view to visit one or more of these islands, for business or observation, or for permanent residence; others who desire to enter into business relations with their merchants or producers; and many others who are moved by the natural thirst for information, which recent events have directed strongly towards these oceanic lands.

"Our Island Empire" is designed to cover all the points here adverted to, and to give in a single volume of moderate size the information which elsewhere would need to be sought in many distinct works. It embraces a comprehensive description, from various points of view, of Cuba, Porto Rico, and the Hawaiian and Philippine Islands, including their extent and situation, natural and industrial productions, governmental conditions, public works, population, commerce and manufactures, and all other matters of general interest concerning them, being prepared with the view that, from this one work, the reading public may obtain an intelligent and satisfactory acquaintance with the leading facts concerning these new wards and colonies of our home country.

In gaining these tropical islands, the United States has entered into a new and important business and political relation with the nations of the world. Widely separated as they are, they possess a remarkable similarity in production, to which a brief allusion may here be made. Sugar is the leading product of most of them and an important product of them all. Coffee and tobacco form other valuable crops. The only vegetable product of mercantile importance special to any one of them is the Manila hemp of the Philippines. In their great variety of tropical fruits they present a like similarity. By their acquisition, this country adds widely to the scope of its vegetable productions, gaining a leading place among the sugar and tobacco producers of the world, and a very prominent one among the producers of coffee and various other food substances. Its commerce with these countries bids fair to gain a great development, and their productiveness to be enormously enhanced under the stimulus of American capital and enterprise.

Politically, the outlook may prove a similarly broad

one. This country has lifted the anchors which hitherto held it fast to the American continent, and has drifted far over the seas into that arena of colonial international relations from which it has heretofore striven to keep clear. What the result will be no man can predict. We have primitive populations to civilize, indolent populations to stimulate, hostile populations to pacify, ignorant populations to educate, oppressed populations to lift into manhood and teach the principles of liberty and the art of self-government. And we are thrown suddenly into the turbid maelstrom of the Eastern Question, with its impending problem of the possible partition of the ancient empire of China among a host of land-hungry applicants.

Whether or not the United States will be forced to take a hand in this great game, or what controlling influence in the direction of justice and discretion it may exercise over the result, are subjects with which the writer of this work does not undertake to deal. It has been his object simply to present the elements of the situation; to give readers some definite general idea of the character and conditions of the new acquisitions of the United States; to offer the facts of the case and leave to them the forming of what they may consider the just and proper conclusions from these premises. There are two sides to this as to every question; but the wise man will take neither side until he has learned all that the question involves, and in acquiring such information it is hoped that he will find this work of practical value.

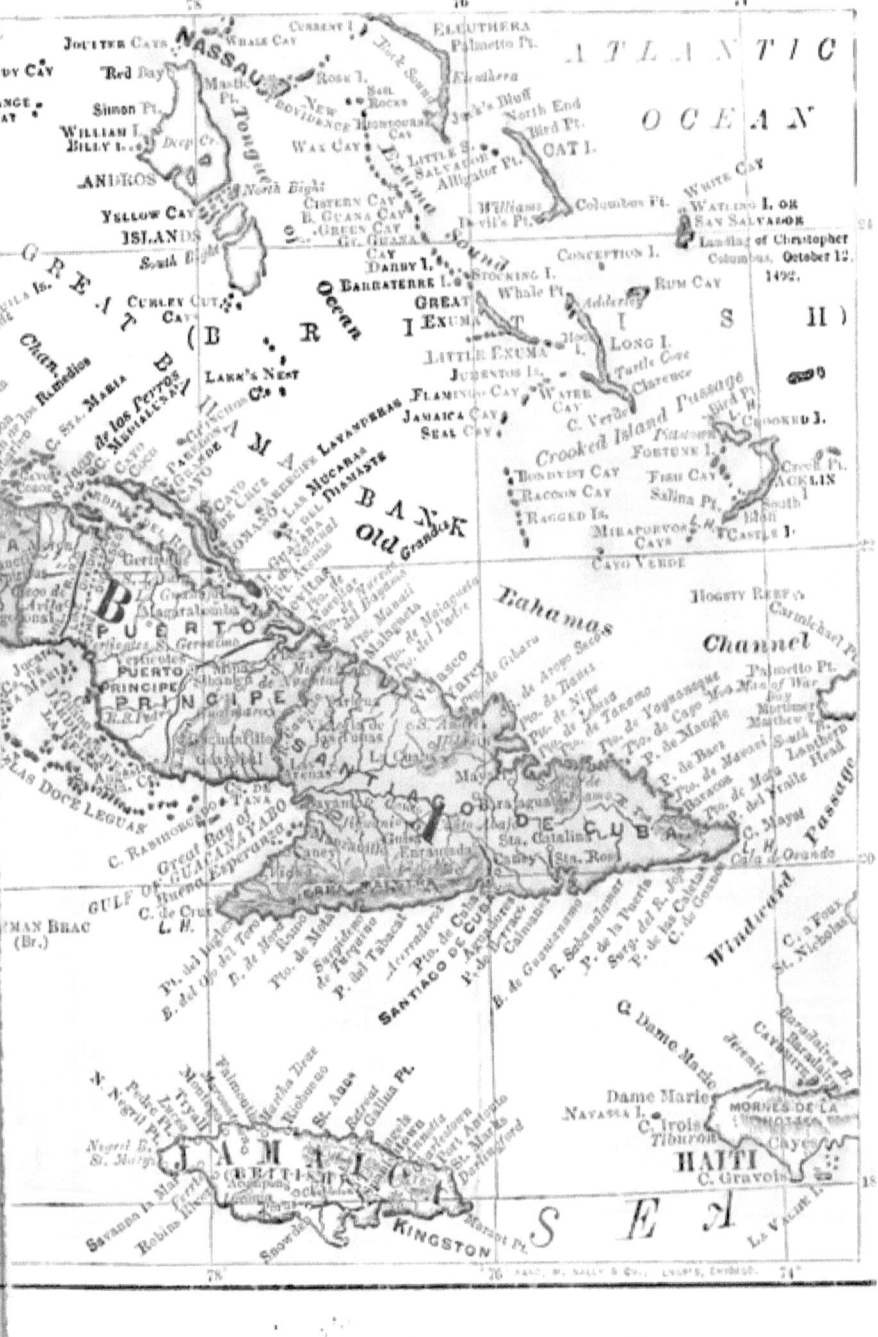

OUR ISLAND EMPIRE.

⋆ ⋆ ⋆

SECTION I.

CUBA.

⋆ ⋆ ⋆

I. HISTORICAL SKETCH.

It was on the 28th of October, 1492, that the eyes of white men first fell upon the green shores of Cuba, the largest, richest, and most important of that tropical island group since known as the West Indies. Columbus was enchanted by its verdant charm and designated it as "the most beautiful land that eye ever saw." He named the island Juana, in honor of Prince Juan, son of Ferdinand and Isabella of Spain. After the death of Ferdinand the name was changed to Fernandina. It was afterwards named Santiago, from the patron saint of Spain, and subsequently Ave Maria, in honor of the Virgin. But all these names have given way to that of Cuba, the title applied to it by its native inhabitants.

Columbus made two other visits to this newly discovered land, in 1494 and again in 1502. It was first circumnavigated and proved to be an island in 1508, and in 1511 Diego Columbus, the son of the discoverer, fitted out an expedition for its colonization.

The first settlement was made at Baracoa. In 1514 Santiago and Trinidad were settled, and in 1515 a town named San Cristoval de la Havana. This is now known as Batabano, the name Havana having been in 1519 transferred to the site of the present capital, which was founded in that year.

The Indian inhabitants of Cuba are described as a tranquil and happy people, living in peaceful enjoyment of their rich island, and welcoming the whites as a superior race. Only one of their chiefs opposed the invasion of the island, Hatuey, a fugitive from Hispaniola, whose people had been treated with shameful cruelty by the Spanish settlers. He was repaid for his patriotism by being burned alive as a fugitive slave. His fellows soon followed him to the grave. The population of the island at that time has been estimated at three hundred thousand. Few of these survived at the end of the century. Enslaved and forced to severe and unaccustomed labor, they died rapidly under the lash of their heartless masters, while their occasional insurrections were quelled with a sanguinary cruelty that aided greatly in their disappearance. Their place was taken by negro slaves, who grew numerous after 1580, at which period the cultivation of tobacco and sugar-cane became active industries. The rearing of cattle had previously been the principal occupation of the settlers.

The Spaniards did not find Cuba a haven of peace. As early as 1538 Havana was attacked and burned by a French privateer, and in 1554 it was again taken and destroyed by the French. The first invasion led to the building, by the famous Fernando de Soto, of the fortification known as the Castillo de la Fuerza, and the second to the erection of the Morro and the Punta, ancient works of defence which still exist.

For nearly two centuries subsequently the people of Cuba were kept in a state of dread by the privateers and freebooters who infested its waters, and at intervals invaded its shores. The daring mariners of England, France, and Holland held the Spanish galleons to be free spoil, and the buccaneers of the West Indies added to their piracy on the high seas the capture and sack of the cities of New Spain.

These minor acts of hostility were succeeded, in 1762, by an invasion in force,—a British fleet and army under Lord Albemarle making a vigorous assault on the harbor and city of Havana. The fleet consisted of nineteen ships of the line, six frigates, and nearly two hundred transports; the army of about fourteen thousand men. The walls of Havana were manned by a Spanish force of nearly double this strength, mainly volunteers, who made an obstinate defence. For two months of the sickly summer season the siege continued, disease proving a far more deadly foe to the besiegers than the guns of the enemy. The affair was decided by a reinforcement of twenty-three hundred men from Connecticut, New York, and New Jersey, led by Generals Putnam and Lyman, heroes of the French and Indian War. Their coming gave heart to the British and discouraged the Spaniards, and the city, vigorously assailed, surrendered on August 14. The terms of surrender included about one-fourth of the island, and the whole of Cuba might readily have been made British territory; but it was restored to Spain by treaty in the following February.

The only advantage to the victors of this futile conquest was a fleet of Spanish ships taken in the harbor, and a spoil in gold and silver to the value of about $3,600,000, which the invaders, like so many freebooters, divided among themselves. There were comparatively few to share this rich booty. The deadly climate had swept off the invaders in hosts. Of the Americans, Trumbull tells us that "scarcely any of the private soldiers, and but few of the officers, ever returned. Such as were not killed in the service were generally swept away by the great mortality which prevailed in the fleet and army."

The prosperity of Cuba under the Spaniards dates from this period. The first census, taken in 1773, yielded a total population, black and white, of only 171,620. It has increased nearly tenfold since that date, the latest census giving a population of over 1,600,000. Luis de Las Casas, who became captain-general in 1790, was indefatigable in his efforts for the advancement of the island. He introduced the culture of indigo, did his utmost to remove the restrictions upon commerce, and promoted a series of highly useful public works. His wise administration kept Cuba tranquil during the revolution in San Domingo, and the French emigrants from that island introduced into Cuba the culture of coffee, which became a flourishing industry.

The reign of oppression in Cuba became pronounced after 1825, in which year King Ferdinand of Spain, incensed by the loss of his dominions upon the main-land, issued a decree which gave the captain-generals almost absolute authority over the island, bestowing on them the powers "which by the royal ordinances are granted to the governors of besieged cities." They were given "ample and unbounded power" to exile from Cuba any official of whom they disapproved, and to suspend, at their own free-will, the execution of any order or provision concerning the administration.

The effect of such a decree, giving autocratic power to a succession of men chosen for political reasons, none of them natives of the island, and many of them seeking it with the purpose of acquiring a fortune by any available means, may be imagined. Some of these men have acted honorably; others have made for themselves a record of infamy. Not only were the captain-generals, but practically all the officials of the island, sent from Spain; the people of Cuba being excluded from office, exposed to illegal exactions of all kinds, heavily taxed to support a standing army and navy, and deprived of civil, political, and religious liberty.

The result of this method of colonial government has been a bitter and intense hatred of the Spanish officials by the native population, and a series of insurrections and filibuster invasions, occurring at intervals until 1868, in which year began a rebellion of ten years' duration. For the suppression of this formidable revolt, Spain sent more than 150,000 soldiers, commanded by her ablest generals, to Cuba; but in the end, hopeless of success, was forced to offer favorable terms to the insurrectionists and promise the people a series of reforms. These terms the Cubans, equally hopeless of success, accepted; but their leaders took care to leave the island, having no great faith in Spanish honor.

The promised reforms did not touch the office of the

captain-general, who retained his autocratic power and his absolute control of the administration. The island was divided into its present provinces, provincial assemblies were instituted, and representation in the Spanish Cortes was granted. But these reforms were manipulated in the interest of the Spanish party; taxation continued as heavy as ever, the officials as corrupt, frauds as prevalent, salaries and perquisites as high, and the restrictions on commerce as severe, while the debt of the island grew with a discouraging rapidity in view of the fact that hardly a dollar of it was spent in the interest of the islanders.

This state of affairs had its natural outcome in a new insurrection, which broke out in February, 1895, and which for three years Spain sought in vain to suppress, though she sent 200,000 men to the island, and used measures whose barbarity aroused a wide-spread sentiment of indignation. Imprisonment of terrible severity, massacre of non-combatants, and similar atrocities did not suffice. Under the administration of Captain-General Weyler the country people were driven in multitudes from their homes, their houses and crops destroyed, and they concentrated around the cities and forts, where it is estimated that more than 200,000 of them died miserably of disease and starvation.

This frightful cruelty aroused an irrepressible indignation in the United States, in which country sympathy for the suffering Cubans had for many years prevailed. Earnest efforts were made by the charitable to feed the starving, and a strong sentiment in favor of warlike aid to the insurrectionists arose. All hopes of a peaceful solution of the difficulty vanished in February, 1898, when the United States battle-ship Maine was blown up by a submarine mine in Havana harbor and sent to the bottom with three-fourths of her crew. This fatal act, to whomsoever due, put an end to hesitation. Congress reflected the warlike sentiment of the people; all efforts to avert hostilities proved futile; and on April 21 war between the United States and Spain began, the American fleet being sent to blockade the port of Havana and the adjoining portion of the Cuban coast.

Within four months thereafter the war was at an end and Cuba was free, the Spanish fleet having been destroyed off Santiago harbor, the Spanish army defeated in a severe engagement, and the city and garrison of Santiago de Cuba, with the neighboring territory, surrendered to the United States army. By the terms of the peace protocol, signed August 12, 1898, Spain agreed to remove all her forces from Cuba, to whose people the United States Congress had guaranteed an independent government, and the century of oppression was at an end. Subsequent negotiations fixed the 1st of January, 1899, as the date of final evacuation of the island by Spain, and on that day the United States entered into temporary military occupation, to be continued until a stable government of the island should be established by the Cubans.

This rapid historical review is offered as preliminary to our main purpose of description, with the purpose of showing in general outline the causes leading up to the present condition of affairs in the island of Cuba. Some such result as that which has occurred was inevitable, sooner or later. The colonial policy of Spain was so irritating to all right-thinking nations, and in particular to the American people, as to grow yearly more difficult to endure, and her methods of warfare became in the end so intolerable that the United States could not avoid coming to the aid of the oppressed. What will be the final result it is too soon to say. The Cubans may prove capable of self-government, and they may not. In the latter case, the only solution of the problem seems to be the absorption of Cuba by the United States.

II. PHYSICAL CONDITIONS.

EXTENT AND SITUATION.

Cuba, the Queen of the Antilles, as it is frequently called, lies wholly within the tropics, and not far south of the main-land of the United States, the channel separating it from Florida being 130 miles wide. A second channel, of somewhat less width, divides it from the nearest portion of Yucatan. Narrower channels lie between it and the neighboring islands of the Bahamas, Jamaica, and Hayti. It is bathed on the south by the waters of the Caribbean Sea, on the north by the Atlantic Ocean, and on the northwest by the Gulf of Mexico, its nearest United States neighbor being the island of Key West, eighty-six miles distant.

Cuba is a long, narrow, crescent-shaped island, its convex side turned to the north. It has been compared in shape to a bird's tongue, and also, in view of its peculiar eastern expansion, to a hammer-headed shark. It extends through eleven degrees of longitude (74° to 85° W.), and through about four degrees of latitude (19° 50′ to 23° 10′ N.); it is crossed by the meridian of Washington about 200 miles from Cape Maisi, its eastern extremity. The length in a direct line is about 760 miles, but following a curved line through its centre it may measure more than 800 miles. It averages about eighty miles in width. Near its eastern end, on the meridian of Manzanillo, it attains a width estimated at from 125 to 140 miles, while in the vicinity of Havana it narrows to about thirty miles, and at Mariel, its narrowest point, to twenty-four miles. To gain a conception of its size as compared with American distances, it may be said that if laid down on our northern States it would extend from New York to the vicinity of Chicago; while its width near Havana would stretch about from Baltimore to Washington; near Santiago, from New York to Albany.

In actual dimensions Cuba approaches closely to the State of Pennsylvania (45,215 square miles), its area, including its coastal islands, being given as 45,883 square miles. South of its western section, crossed by the meridian of Havana, lies the Isle of Pines (Isla de Pinos), of 1214 square miles area, while the many small islands have a combined area of about 1350 square miles. The coast line is about 2200 miles in length, or nearly 7000 miles if all its numerous indentations be included.

The island, through much of its extent, possesses a low, flat coast, subject to frequent floods, and containing many large lagoons, especially on the north, their only commercial use being their yield of salt. A screen of islands, keys, banks, and reefs, grouped into four archipelagoes, extends along much of the coast, rendering navigation difficult and dangerous,—in many places impossible. Yet this is by no means wholly the case, about half the coast line being free from these obstructions, while no island, in proportion to its extent, surpasses Cuba in harbors, many of them accessible to the largest ships. These generally have narrow entrances, but open into spacious bays within, and offer commodious shelter and easy defence. Of those on the north may be named the ports of Bahia Honda, Mariel, Havana, Matanzas, Cardenas, Nuevitas, and Nipe; on the south are the spacious harbors of Guantanamo, Santiago de Cuba, Trinidad, and Cienfuegos. The island in all is said to have fifty-four ports, fifteen of which are open to commerce.

Cuba occupies a very favorable position for commerce, lying, as it does, at the mouth of the Gulf of Mexico, the northern and southern entrances to which extend past its shores, and being in such close proximity to the United States, Central America, and South America. Its capital, Havana, has in consequence been designated the "Key to the New World."

THE MOUNTAIN SYSTEM.

Cuba has a backbone of highlands, rising in the east to mountainous elevation, and extending from end to end of the island, while from their northern and southern slopes plains stretch to the bordering seas. They now approach the north coast, now the south, and now follow the centre of the island, but are not continuous, being broken into groups, between which lie rolling uplands, or in some regions low plains only a few hundred feet above sea level. Extending, of varying height, from Cape San Antonio in the west to Cape Maisi in the east, the chain here turns westward again, and follows the southern coast line past Santiago to Cape Cruz. This extension causes a marked widening of the province of Santiago de Cuba, to which it gives a triangular form. The total length of the highlands approaches 1000 miles, and they occupy about one-fourth of the total area.

It may give a wrong impression to designate this

as a mountain range, as is ordinarily done, it being more correct to speak of it as a watershed, out of which, or adjacent to which, rise mountainous peaks or short independent ranges, but whose ordinary height is from 100 to 400 feet, and occasionally less. In the east it rises into a complex mass of mountains with fertile valleys between their heights.

The coast range between Cape Maisi and Cape Cruz, known through much of its length as the Sierra Maestra, or Master Mountains, contains the highest elevations on the island, its loftiest summit being the Pico de Turquino, 8320 feet or more in height, and lying midway between Cape Cruz and Santiago. Between Turquino and the city of Santiago the range takes the subordinate name of Sierra de Cobre, or Copper Mountains, from their containing the copper mines of the Santiago district.

From Santiago eastward the southern and central ranges are joined by lateral spurs, the whole forming an intricate series of elevations, forest clad, and cut into sharp ridges known as *cuchillas*, or "knife-edged" crests, as distinguished from the *sierras*, or "saws." These connecting ridges break up the country into a maze of precipitous elevations, which render the eastern half of the province of Santiago de Cuba a country very difficult to traverse and little known. In this district, with its few and poor roads, its dense forests, its sudden ascents and descents, its pathless intricacies, the insurrection long held its own, its numerous lurking places, caves, and defiles enabling the insurgents to defy pursuit.

This broken and rock-bound country is, in diversity of products and beauties of nature, one of the most attractive in the world. Its many changes of elevation, with the consequent rapid variations in climate, people it with a remarkable variety of plants,—orchids, palms, and others,—many of them bearing rich-hued tropical flowers, while insect life may be seen here in its gayest colors and greatest abundance. Add to these features of attraction the frequent cascades due to the numerous streams and abundant rainfall, the richness of the verdure, the striking rock portals and other forms of mountain architecture, and we have in the cuchillas a varied array of nature's charms which few other localities present.

The central chain displays near its eastern extremity, back of the port of Baracoa, a striking peak over 3000 feet high, long known to navigators as El Yunque de Baracoa ("The Anvil of Baracoa"). As the harbor of Nipe is approached the mountains decrease considerably in height, and by the time the bay of Nuevitas is reached they vanish as a range, only detached groups appearing at intervals. One of these, the Sierra de Cubitas, north of the city of Puerto Principe, has been long noted for its great caves, and came into prominence during the recent insurrection as the place of retreat of President Cisneros and his cabinet, the officials of the insurgent government. Between the Cubitas group and that of Bamburanao, in the province of Santa Clara, the island narrows to a width of less than fifty miles, and sinks nearly to sea level. Across this region extended the first military trocha, a line of forts, wire fences, and timber breastworks established for the purpose of checking the movements and dividing the forces of the rebels.

Farther west the highlands approach the southern

shore, the Sierra de San Juan y Trinidad extending from Trinidad to Cienfuegos and beyond. Immediately back of the harbor of Trinidad rises the peak of Potrillo, an elevation of about 3000 feet altitude. As Matanzas is approached the northern highlands rise into the Pan de Matanzas (1300 feet), a sugar-loaf peak famous among mariners, as enabling them to get their bearings off a dangerous coast.

Westward from Matanzas the mountain ridge grows more continuous, culminating in a peak 2000 feet high, beyond which it gradually sinks and finally disappears in the sandy and marshy region of Cape San Antonio. The flatness of this end of the island is in marked contrast to the lofty elevations with which it terminates at Cape Maisi in the east. At Mariel, west of Havana, is the narrowest part of the island, a depressed region across which General Weyler built his celebrated trocha in 1896.

As may be seen, the ridge varies greatly in height, now attaining considerable elevation, now descending almost to sea level. The only continuous chain is the Sierra Maestra, in the extension to Cape Cruz. This southeastern sierra forms a great calcareous mass, its summits usually naked and rocky. The central and western mountains are largely composed of compact limestone, which has been excavated by subterranean waters into numerous caverns, some being of great extent and striking beauty. These were utilized by the insurgents during the insurrection as places of shelter and concealment. Some of the mountain peaks, such as that of Turquino, show indications of former volcanic action, though no active volcanoes now exist. Earthquakes occasionally occur, Santiago de Cuba province being their chief location. Those of 1776, 1842, and 1852 were of great severity.

PLAINS AND RIVERS.

Occupying the spaces between the isolated mountain groups, and extending in rolling slopes from the mountains to the coasts, lie the fertile plains of the island, a productive region of lowlands which comprise much the greater part of the area of Cuba, and whose richly fertile soil, under the stimulus of a tropical sun and frequent rains, has immense powers of production. These lowlands, gently undulating and rising only from eighty to one hundred feet above sea level, form a practically continuous belt around the island, in which are to be found the great sugar plantations. Above these and on the lower slopes of the central range lie the grazing and farm lands, whose products include the famous Cuban tobacco. The highlands are, as a rule, covered with dense forest.

Of the fertile lowland districts the most celebrated are those of Jagua (Cienfuegos), Trinidad, Mariel, and Matanzas. The provinces of Matanzas and Santa Clara contain at once the best and the worst lands of Cuba, well watered and highly fertile soil occurring side by side with districts noted for sterility. Regions of marsh land extend along much of the coast, and the flat southern coast lands are subject to overflow.

As regards the watercourses of the island, the rivers, flowing from mountain to coast, are necessarily short. They are, however, very numerous, and in the rainy season swell into deep and wide floods. The Cauto, the largest stream, drains the long valley between the Sierra Maestra and the main mountain ridge, and is navigable for small vessels for sixty miles inland. Its navigation, however, has not always proved safe. The bar at its mouth was shifted by a heavy flood in 1616 so as to imprison all the vessels in the stream, one of them a Spanish man-of-war. They were held beyond escape and had to be abandoned.

On the north side the largest stream is Sagua la Grande, ninety miles long and navigable for about twenty miles. Among the streams navigable for shorter distances are the Sagua la Chica, the Jatibonico of the South, the Sasa, the Agabama, and the San Juan, the last of which flows into the bay of Cienfuegos. The island possesses few lakes, most of which lie near the coast marshes. There are some, however, in the mountain region, of which much the most interesting is Ariguanabo, about twenty miles southwest of Havana. Walled around with rock ridges, this attractive body of water is about six square miles in area and thirty feet deep, and is rich in finny wealth.

What is said above does not tell the full story of the rivers, nor its most interesting feature. The limestone which forms the mountain masses of Cuba and extends in a thick layer down their slopes to the marsh region or the sea is permeable to water, and has been dissolved away so as to form great caverns and long underground tunnels, into which many of the streams plunge and disappear. Some rise to the surface again, others flow under the sea, through which their waters are often forced upward in glistening springs. Elisée Réclus remarks that " in the Jardines, so named from the verdure-clad islets strewn like gardens amid the blue waters, springs of fresh water bubble up from the deep, flowing probably in subterranean galleries from the main-land."

Of these disappearing streams one of the most remarkable is the Rio San Antonio, which drains the lake of Ariguanabo, and which, after passing through the town of San Antonio de los Baños, sinks into the earth at the foot of a spreading ceiba tree, and fails to reappear. Various similar streams might be named, among them the Jatibonico of the North, which, after vanishing, rises again in a series of tumbling cascades. The short stream called the Moa forms a superb cascade 300 feet in height, and disappears in a cavern to reach the surface again at a lower level.

The Falls of the Rosario, in the province of Pinar del Rio, are notable for their beauty. In the same province the excavating waters have given rise to an imposing natural bridge. Elsewhere these waters have left evidences of their former labors in large caverns, of which Cuba has a remarkable number, many of them with magnificent stalactites. These include the cave of Cotilla, near Havana, the celebrated caves of Bellamar, near Matanzas, of San José de los Remedios, of Monte Libano, north of Guantanamo, and many others of less celebrity.

THE COASTAL SYSTEM.

Around great part of the circumference of Cuba extends a series of thickly grouped islets and reefs, estimated at 1300 in all, which stand decidedly in the way of easy navigation, and cut off about half the coast from free access. These are of coral origin, being due to the same class of minute creatures that has covered the mountains and plains of Cuba with a thick layer of limestone. They constitute four distinct groups, two on the north and two on the south. From Cape San Antonio to Bahia Honda extends the Guaniguanico archipelago, which includes the dangerous Red Banks. Farther east, stretching from Cardenas to Nuevitas, lies the Sabana Camaguey, composed of a multitude of keys and reefs, whose eastern section was named by Columbus Jardin del Rey (King's Garden). This title of Jardin has been given to both the southern groups. Extending from Cape Cruz to Trinidad lie the Jardines de la Reina (Queen's Gardens), and from Cienfuegos nearly to the western end of the island extends the archipelago of the Canarreos, which includes the large Isla de Pinos and the Jardines and Jardinellos (Little Islands), that group of green islets in whose midst the sunken waters from the far-off highlands rise in fresh springs, which bubble up through the salt waves.

Amid this host of islands there is only one of importance for its size, the Isla de Pinos (Isle of Pines), to which Columbus gave the name of Evangelist Island. This measures about sixty miles in its greatest length from east to west, and fifty-five miles in maximum breadth. It lies about sixty miles from Batabano, the nearest port on the main-land of Cuba. In the north its surface is mountainous, rising to a considerable height and thickly wooded, while the soil is of high fertility. In the south it is low and barren. Between the two sections extends a swamp, across which sweep the tides, dividing the island practically into two. These sections are connected by a stone causeway built on some rock ledges at the water level.

While the portions of the Cuban coast free from

island screens present bold, high outlines, broken by the narrow entrances to many capacious harbors, the sections sheltered by the archipelagoes are usually low and marshy, and thickly covered by mangrove and other water plants of the tropics. The Zapata, a great shoe-shaped marsh on the southern coast, is more than sixty miles long, its flat surface being at sea level and most of its extent consisting of impassable quagmires, though here and there the surface is firm enough to support a grove of trees. Winding through its mangrove thickets may be seen the channels of former rivers, and in its depths lie numerous lakes, some open to the sun, while the surface of others is covered with the leaves and flowers of innumerable tropical lilies. Breakwaters of sand, thrown up by the waves, here and there enclose the stagnant marsh waters, and off the coast the coral animals are busy building a wall which will in time shut in this broad expanse from the sea.

THE FOREST REGION.

Much the greater part of the island of Cuba is covered with forest of the most tropical luxuriance of growth. Innumerable vines bind tree to tree with their tough cordage, and passage can be made only by constant use of the ever-present machete, that invaluable implement of the rural Cuban. Outside the range of virgin forest are extensive regions covered with stunted trees and lofty grasses, whose shelter was abundantly made use of during the insurrection for concealment and ambush.

Of the area of Cuba nearly 20,000,000 acres, about two-thirds of the whole, remain in a state of unoccupied wildness, nearly 13,000,000 acres of this extensive territory being covered with primeval forest. These broad woodlands contain numbers of trees of high economic value, of which we shall speak later. The dominating plant is the royal palm, found not only throughout the forests, but in all parts of the island, to whose landscapes its columnar trunk and gracefully spreading leafy top give an ever-present charm. Nature showers beauty on a Cuban landscape, and over all its lower forms towers the royal palm, usually from fifty to seventy feet in height, but occasionally gaining an altitude of more than 100 feet. Planted alternately with the mango and other tropical trees, these palms compose on the *cafetales*, or coffee estates, avenues miles in length, forming aisles of surpassing beauty, in which, " overtopping the other trees, their sweeping noble arches do not exclude the sunlight, which pours through the intervals as through the windows of a cathedral and illuminates the green solemnity of the majestic colonnades."

GEOLOGY.

There is excellent reason for the belief that Cuba was at one time connected with the neighboring mainland, since fossil animals of a recent geological period, such as the megalonyx, mastodon, etc., are found both here and in the United States. It is believed that these animals made their way into Cuba by the route of Florida, to which the island was then connected. Fernandez de Castro, a geologist of experience, concludes that all the great geological divisions are represented in Cuba, though the best marked strata are those of the tertiary period, all of whose formations are abundantly represented by fossil species. Still later are the post-pliocene beds, containing the fossils above mentioned as similar to those found in the United States, and argillaceous and calcareous deposits whose fossils represent species still living. To the same late period belong the very abundant conglomerates of lime, iron, and metamorphic rocks, and the shell deposits which exist in considerable abundance in certain localities.

Most valuable of the deposits is the external layer of vegetable mould known as *Tierra Colorado* (red earth), which contains much iron and forms an admirable soil for the culture of tobacco and sugar-cane. In Pinar del Rio and some other localities are silicious alluvial deposits, of the greatest value in the tobacco culture. The limestone deposit, of which we have spoken as composing mountain masses and forming a layer over the plains, is being added to steadily along the coast, whose numerous islets and keys are the work of myriads of coral animals. These creatures are still actively at work building new reefs and joining adjacent islets by bridges of coral rock.

Through this wide-spread layer of limestone the older formations frequently protrude,—granites, sienites, diorites, serpentines, and other ancient rocks being so abundant as to create the impression that they form the basis upon which all the later formations of the island are laid. Of these the serpentine is the most abundant, covering large areas, and attaining in some localities a thickness of 600 feet. In it are rich mines of copper, and in some places petroleum runs out of its clefts. In eastern Cuba abundant springs of this valuable mineral oil are found.

CLIMATE.

The climate of the low coast lands of Cuba is that of the torrid zone, whose northern boundary runs just north of the island. In the higher interior the torrid heats decline, and the climate is more in accordance with that of the temperate zones. As is general in countries on the borders of the tropics, the year is divided into a wet and a dry season, so called, though rain falls in every month of the year. The insular situation causes much precipitation, and at all seasons the humidity of the atmosphere averages over eighty degrees.

The specifically hot and wet season extends through half the year, from the beginning of May to the end of October, during which thunder-storms are of almost daily occurrence, and the downpour of rain is at times of great violence. Throughout this period the temperature is high and varies little day or night, the mean temperature of Havana in August being about 82° F. In some districts it reaches 90°. The only alleviation is the refreshing sea breeze, which rises daily in the afternoon, and redeems, in a measure, the great warmth and humidity of the atmosphere.

During the remaining six months of the year, called the dry season by contrast, the rains are moderate and the temperature considerably reduced, Havana having a mean, during this period, of about 70° F. In the interior, at elevations of 300 feet or more, the temperature is considerably lower, and occasionally falls to the freezing point, while in the highlands frost is not uncommon. Yet the average temperature varies only about eleven degrees between the hottest and the coldest months. The mean annual rainfall is nearly fifty-two inches, of which the eastern section of the island receives somewhat the greater portion.

The prevailing winds are the easterly trades, though cool north winds visit the western section in the dry season, lasting for forty-eight hours or less and causing a marked decrease of temperature. Hurricanes are occasionally disastrous, but are less frequent in Cuba than in the islands farther south, five or six years sometimes passing without such a storm. That of 1846 caused great destruction in Havana, and in 1894 the fruit industry in the northeast section was almost exterminated.

Cuba has no diseases peculiar to itself, but shares with the American tropics generally their scourge of yellow fever; which makes its appearance annually during the wet season in the seaports and coast regions, where it rages with virulence, causing great loss of life. It is, however, unknown in the interior; and there is excellent reason to believe that its prevalence in the coast cities is the fault of the people themselves,—a natural result of their lack of sanitary care. With cities properly cleaned and with due attention to the laws of health this dread disease might quite disappear.

Malarial fevers and dysentery are very common in many parts of the island, and great care is needed by visitors to Cuba to avoid getting the clothes or the body wet, or sleeping out of doors without protection from the night dews. Of course, care is requisite in drinking only pure water, against over-indulgence in some of the island fruits, and in personal cleanliness. Leprosy is probably more common in Cuba than in the Hawaiian Islands, but the leading physicians say that there is no danger of a clean white man being affected. In the Cuban hospitals, however, the idea of separation of patients affected with contagious diseases from others does not seem to exist, a state of affairs which must lend much aid to the propagation of disease.

The dangerous result of unacclimated people from the north visiting Cuba in the wet season was strikingly shown in the war of 1898, the deaths in the American army from malarial and yellow fever and other diseases far exceeding those from battle. This was, no doubt, in considerable measure due to unsanitary conditions. In Santiago and its vicinity the very idea of sanitation had not been born. Since then this city, under American control, has, for the first time in its existence, been thoroughly cleaned. The effect of this new state of affairs upon its health conditions remains to be learned, but can scarcely fail to be highly advantageous.

In conclusion, it may be said for the climate of Cuba that on an average rain falls on not more than ten days in the month, and rarely on more than twenty days in the rainiest month, while an all-day rain occurs on only seventeen days in the year. The rains are generally in the afternoon, the mornings being usually sunny.

The abundant rains in the warm season, the occurrence of sunshine on almost every day, and the plenitude of refreshing breezes give Cuba a remarkable exuberance of vegetation and a climate unsurpassed in the tropics. The great transparency of the atmosphere adds much to the beauty of the landscapes, and yields a peculiar brilliance to the starlight and a soft, mellow glow to the sunsets, whose only fault is their tropical brevity. The surrounding seas are of unusual beauty, with their deep green color variegated with shifting opaline lustres, presenting gleams of such rich and varied hues as are never seen in the waters of the north.

III. NATURAL PRODUCTIONS.

FOREST TREES.

The vast forests of Cuba, so dense as to be almost impenetrable, many of their deep recesses having never been traversed, contain numerous species of valuable trees, frequently luxuriant in growth and magnificent in dimensions. Hard-wood trees, of high value for cabinet work and other purposes, are very abundant, including the mahogany, ebony, cedar, logwood, iron-wood, lignum-vitæ and various other species. It is said that there are in all more than forty varieties of fine cabinet woods. The palm, with more than thirty species, is everywhere present. The ubiquitous and useful cocoa-nut palm extends its realm from mountain to coast-lands, and the stately royal palm (*Palma real*) is found in all localities, especially in the west. This queen of the south is associated in the Isle of Pines with a tree characteristic of the north, the pine, so common there as to give its name to the island, in which it shares the surface with the mahogany and the palm. Something peculiar in the soil causes this tree to flourish here, so far from its native regions. It also occurs in Pinar del Rio, whose name likewise is derived from it.

All the majestic trees of the Mexican lowlands, so famous for the beauty of their foliage and the splendor of their flowers, give grace and charm to the Cuban coasts; while in the forests, in addition to the useful trees named, are various dye-woods, an abundance of ferns, and vines in great variety, some of these of such strength as to strangle the trees which they clasp in their insinuating embrace. It is the intricacy of these clinging vines, or lianas, that renders the forests impossible to traverse without the constant aid of the machete. "Only those who have seen a tropical forest can form an idea of these dark woods, with their giant trees, thorny bushes, cactus plants, and trailing lianas, gracefully pendant, swinging from branch to branch, and wound around trunk and limb of trees in most wonderful tracery, beautiful to the view, but almost impossible to pass through." Troublesome as they are, the splendor of their foliage and flowers gives rich warrant for their existence to the lover of beauty.

Among the most stately and striking of the trees of Cuba is the ceiba, or silk-cotton tree,—the latter name being derived from its large seed-pod, which is packed with cotton-like fibre of a soft, silky texture. This imposing tree often attains a height of a hundred feet, its massive trunk, with its buttress of exposed roots, reaching upward for fifty feet without a branch, while its dense canopy of foliage affords complete protection from the sun. A smaller tree, but one of marked attraction, is the tamarind, with its delicate, deep-green foliage and the chocolate-colored pods which hang in thick loops from every branch.

Eminent among the trees of Cuba, alike for beauty and utility, are the palms, which give a tropical tone to every landscape. And chief among the numerous species of these is the royal palm, a tree native to the island, and everywhere present with its trunk like a Corinthian column and its plume-like crown of verdant foliage. Here it stands in solitary dignity, there clusters in shady groves ; now grouped in the valley, now rising above the trees of the forest, now lifting its plumed crest upon a wooded mountain summit, now rising in long avenues like the stately pillars of some grand temple. It is as useful as beautiful, there being no part of it that is not adapted to human purposes. The wood yields boards excellent for building purposes, the hard outer shell of the trunk being readily split into strips. The roots are claimed to possess medicinal properties. The leaves are used for thatch, and their long, semicircular stem, which embraces the trunk of the tree, has a variety of uses. It becomes pliable when soaked in water, and may be shaped into a water-bucket, a wash-basin, or other receptacle. The bud of the central spire, from which the leaves expand, consists of a tender substance which is very palatable as a food, either raw, cooked as a vegetable, or made into a preserve with sugar.

FOOD PLANTS AND FRUITS.

Food plants exist in the greatest abundance and variety. Much the most important of alimentary plants is the plantain, with the choicest variety of whose fruit we are so familiar in the banana. Next in order of usefulness comes the cassava or manioc, with its sweet and bitter varieties. Of these the root is used,—the sweet being eaten as a vegetable, and the bitter, after its poisonous juice is extracted, being converted into bread. The sweet root is as mealy as the potato when boiled, while the bitter is the source of the well-known starchy food known as tapioca.

Other farinaceous roots include the sweet potato

and the yam, though these are less used than in other West India islands. Maize or Indian corn is indigenous, and is grown in considerable quantities,—the green leaves being employed as fodder and the grain as food for man and beast. The cacao-bean plant is also grown and rice is extensively cultivated. Very little attention, however, is paid to horticulture, and the ordinary garden vegetables are little used except in the dry season for the supply of Havana and the other large cities. There is cultivated, however, a variety of beans, the favorite being known as the *garbanzo*.

Cuba is rich in fruits, possessing almost all those of tropical and subtropical lands. The most esteemed among these are the pine-apple and the orange, the latter in several favorite varieties. To the orange may be added the lime and the lemon, bearing blossoms, green and ripe fruit at the same time, and filling the air with their fragrance. The banana grows everywhere and bears with prodigal profuseness, its great bunches of green fruit ripening as well off the tree as on it. Other well-known fruits are the fig, the pomegranate, the tamarind, and the guava,—the last being converted into a highly esteemed jelly or preserve, eaten everywhere in Cuba and famous all over the world. The tamarind is universal on the island; a tall and handsome tree, the acid pulp of its bean-like fruit, when steeped in water, yielding a cooling and delicious beverage, much used in the tropics. Another fruit tree, equally wide-spread, is the cocoa-nut palm, which grows to the height of fifty feet or more; its long drooping leaves revealing beneath their bases the great bunches of nuts weighing as much as three hundred pounds. When nearly ripe, the nut yields a pleasant, cooling, and healthful beverage, much used in Cuba.

There are many other delicious fruits, too perishable to be transported from the island. These include the mango, zapota, rose-apple, mammee, sapotilla, custard-apple, and others. The mango, an exotic, yet nearly as abundant as the banana, grows upon a handsome tree, with shining, dark-green foliage; its yellow fruit, about three times the size of an egg-plum, growing in long pendant bunches. It is very juicy when ripe, and is an especial favorite with the negroes. Growing wild in the forest about Santiago, it formed a somewhat perilous addition to the diet of our troops during the recent campaign. The sapotilla is a tree of attractive aspect, its leaves being glossy and feathery, its blossoms white and bell-shaped, with a perfume like that of the apple-blossom. It bears a round fruit of about the size of a peach, with a rough, dark skin. It is delicious when fully ripe, the pulp melting in the mouth like a custard. The custard-apple has a tough skin and a subacid flavor, its pulp being full of little black seeds. It weighs a pound or more, is soft and juicy, and is much used for flavoring purposes. The star-apple is so named from the star-like figure shown by its centre when cut through. It has a green interior even when ripe, but is exquisite in flavor, being eaten with a spoon out of the outer rind. The rose-apple grows on a handsome, symmetrical tree, with oval glossy leaves, and large, white, fragrant blossoms. The fruit is of the size and shape of a large peach, smooth of skin, and cream-colored throughout. Its pulp is firm and has so strong a flavor of attar-of-rose as to render it somewhat unpalatable. It is much used to flavor soups and puddings. The mammee is a large fruit growing on high, umbrageous trees, solid in texture, and with a flavor approaching that of the peach, though less delicate. When ripe, it is light yellow in color.

While many of these fruits grow on more or less lofty trees, the pine-apple, one of the best of them all, is the humblest in its manner of growth,—a field of pine-apples being little more attractive than a field of cabbages. It grows single upon a low stem, reaching some twenty inches in height. The plant bears but one apple at a time, but will yield an annual crop for three or four years. Cuba possesses, according to a recent botanical catalogue, a total of 3350 indigenous species of flowering plants, in addition to the many that have been introduced.

The chief cultivated plants of the island are three in number,—sugar-cane, tobacco, and coffee. Of these tobacco is a native, the others have been introduced. The cultivation of only one of these plants is to-day in a promising condition. Coffee, introduced in the eighteenth century, and cultivated largely after the revolution in Hayti, has greatly fallen off, and now makes a very small figure in the exports. The demand for sugar has also largely declined, in consequence of the competition of beet-root sugar; while the destructive activity of the insurgents has, for the time being, ruined the plantations. Tobacco is at present the only flourishing product, its superior quality making a steady demand for it in all parts of the world. Under new conditions, however, the profitable culture of sugar is likely to be restored.

Cotton was at one time a product of importance, and new attention was paid to it during the American civil war, but its culture met with no great success, and it is now but little grown.

ANIMALS.

Cuba possesses only two indigenous quadrupeds, one a rodent of about the size of a rabbit, being from twelve to eighteen inches in length; it resembles a rat in general appearance. This is known as the agouti (*jutia* or *hutia*), is black in color and makes its home in hollow or cleft trees, on whose leaves and fruits it feeds. Its flesh formed part of the diet of the Cubans during their insurrection, though it is insipid in taste. The other native mammal is one of the insectivorous class, the solenodon, the other representatives of whose family are confined to Madagascar. The swamps contain a few deer, but these are thought to be the descendants of animals introduced from the continent. The flying squirrel, the dormouse, and various other quadrupeds add animation to the landscape.

There is no lack of reptiles. Lizards are abundant, of various species, the large iguana being common. The dangerous crocodile and cayman occur, and turtles are numerous along the coasts, frequenting the reefs and shallows and the sandy beaches. Serpents are not numerous. One of these, the *maja*, is of large size, attaining a length of twelve to fourteen feet and a circumference of eighteen or twenty inches. It is harmless to man, and is said to lodge in the roofs of country houses and prey on the poultry. The *juba*, a species about six feet in length, is more vicious in disposition, but there are no venomous snakes. The manatee, known familiarly as the sea-cow or cow-whale, is found in the waters of Cuba, as in the tropical waters of the Atlantic in general. Land crabs are so common as to be something of a nuisance, appearing frequently in large numbers, and crossing the island in troops from north to south every spring at the opening of the rainy season. Bats, some of them huge in size, form an occasionally unpleasant element of the fauna.

Cuba is abundantly provided with birds, there being more than 200 species indigenous to the island, many of them of great beauty of plumage. They include only a few birds of prey, important among which are the vulture and the turkey-buzzard. These are the licensed scavengers of the island, and are protected in their useful labors by the law, paying for their immunity by their services in the removal of putrefying flesh. But for them, the death-rate of Cuba might be much higher than it is, the people being ignorant or heedless of the first laws of health.

Of the more familiar birds may be named the bluebird, cat-bird, and robin, while wild pigeons are present in great variety, blue, gray, and white of hue. By the waters of the lagoons patiently watches the red flamingo; the gaudy paroquet makes his harsh voice heard in the forests: here is the brightly variegated English lady-bird, the golden-winged woodpecker, the indigo-bird, and many others, most brilliant among them the tiny humming-birds, of which some sixty species are found, of every variety of metallic hue.

The small streams of the island, as well as the bays

and inlets, are well supplied with fish, but food-fish are not abundant off the Greater Antilles, though they thrive in the Bahamas. Shell-fish are numerous, the oysters, which cling to the branches of the mangrove trees, being abundant but small, and lacking the delicious flavor of those of northern seas. Insect life occurs in the ordinary tropical exuberance, and embraces a number of those pests that go to render life an annoyance. These noxious forms include the everywhere-present mosquito, the sand fly, the chigoe or jigger, a biting ant called the vivajagua, spiders whose bite produces fever, and scorpions. The last are less malignant than those of Europe. Chief among the useful insects is the bee, whose wax and honey are products of considerable commercial value. Fireflies are numerous and of various species. Of the large *cucujo*, a dozen placed in a wicker cage are said to afford light enough to read by; while a calabash pierced with holes and containing from fifteen to twenty of these insects often serves the poorer people as a sort of lantern. They are easily kept by feeding them on the soft pulp of the sugar-cane, being very fond of sweets. The belles of Cuba do not fail to employ these brilliantly luminous insects as ornaments, wearing them in their hair, in necklaces, or attached to their dress, which can be readily done without injury to the insect. Butterflies, many of them of great beauty, are very numerous, there being not less than 300 distinct species.

Among the wild animals are two escaped from domestic service, the dog and cat, which in their feral state form staple annoyances of the island. The wild dog, known as the *perro jibaro*, has regained its native fierceness and carnivorous habits, though it is less dangerous than the wolf, since it never attacks man unless pressed in the chase. These dogs, whatever their original color may have been, uniformly become of a dirty black hue, with a very rough coat. They lurk in the forests and do much damage among the cattle. Earnest efforts have been made to extirpate them, but in spite of this they increase in numbers. The cat, known in its wild state as the *gato jibaro*, pays its chief attention to the poultry yard.

Of domestic animals, the ox, horse, and pig are the most numerous, cattle-raising being one of the leading industries. Horses are bred largely in certain localities. Sheep, goats, and mules are less numerous, though of late years the great Spanish jackass has been introduced with some success for the purpose of breeding mules. Of domestic birds may be named the common fowl, the goose, turkey, peacock, and pigeon. Of these the first named is everywhere raised; in city and country alike.

METALS.

It was the hope of finding rich deposits of the precious metals that first attracted the Spaniards to Cuba. Gold was sent to Spain by the early settlers, with no statement as to its source; but it is now believed to have been the accumulated wealth of the natives, wrung from them by violence and torture, since no important source of this valued metal has since been discovered. Gold-bearing sands are found in the rivers Holguin, Escambray, and others, and gold has been obtained from the workings of Agabama and Sagua la Grande rivers; but the cost of obtaining it exceeds its value, and Cuba gives no promise of importance in its yield of this metal.

Silver has been found, in conjunction with copper, at Villa Clara; specimens of the ore, worked in 1827, yielding more than seventy-five ounces to the ton of ore. Yet despite this promising show, the mining of silver here has not been a success. Silver, associated with mercury, has also been found in the Isle of Pines. For a long period in the past copper continued the most important of Cuban metals. It exists in several sections of the island, the most valuable deposits being in Santiago de Cuba. The rich veins at Cobre, near the city of Santiago, were opened in the seventeenth century and continued to yield until late in the eighteenth, when they were abandoned. Their lack of profit was due to the imperfect methods of working the ore, for the heaps of refuse material, when examined by English mining experts at a later date, proved so rich in metal that they were sent to England to be smelted, and the old workings were reopened. From 1828 to 1840, copper to the value of from $2,000,000 to $3,000,000 was shipped annually from this district to the United States; and the mines continued profitable until 1868, when the outbreak of the insurrection put an end to operations. The shafts, from 900 to 1200 feet deep and extending below sea-level, subsequently filled with water, which has effectively stopped operations. Much copper remains, as may be judged from the fact that it has proved profitable to pump the mine water into sluices containing scrap iron, upon which the copper held in solution is deposited.

One of the largest veins of copper in the world is

said to exist in this district, in which shafts were formerly sunk to the depth of over 1100 feet. It is believed to be still very rich, and, despite the troubles from water, is likely again to be opened through the aid of American capital. There are a number of other mines, nearly all of which have been worked in the past, and most of which offer good prospects to future operators.

Iron exists in considerable abundance in several sections of Cuba, in some of which it is profitably mined. One of the richest localities is said to be the Cubitas Mountain region,—the seat of government of the recent insurrection,—in which iron ores of several kinds occur in enormous quantities. Also along the route surveyed for the designed railway from Santa Clara to Santiago almost inexhaustible beds of chromic iron ore exist. It is said, also, that copper, nickel, and cobalt exist in large deposits in the province of Puerto Principe; but this remains to be proved. The Cubitas mines would probably now be worked but for the insurrection, an American company having been formed for that purpose. They promise well, and the necessary railway connections can be easily made.

At present the only important workings are those in the Sierra Maestra Mountains, near the city of Santiago de Cuba. Here the metal exists in great and promising abundance. Two American associations—the Juragua and the Spanish-American Iron Companies—are here engaged in mining, employing from 800 to 1400 men. The ores, of mixed brown and red hematite, are of unusual richness, yielding from sixty-five to sixty-eight per cent. of metal, and this of superior quality, being very free from sulphur and phosphorus. From 30,000 to 50,000 tons of ore are shipped monthly to the United States, where the iron is used in the manufacture of steel, much of it for armor-plate. There are numerous undeveloped veins of equal richness in the vicinity of Santiago, several of them belonging to the Sigua Iron Company, a Philadelphia organization, not now in operation.

The Sierra Maestra Mountains also contain manganese ore, various deposits existing between Santiago and Manzanillo. The veins are large and the ore promising, yielding in some cases fifty-eight per cent. of metal of superior quality. A recent statement reports for the island one hundred and thirty-eight mining claims of iron, eighty-eight of manganese, fifty-three of copper, five of gold, three of zinc, two of lead, two of mercury, one of chrome iron, and one of antimony. But these exist largely on paper, and while many of the properties covered are rich in metals, the value of others remains in doubt.

MINERALS.

Various opinions exist concerning the presence of coal, which has been claimed to occur in abundance in many localities, alike in the mountains and in the lowlands. A deposit near Guanabacoa, in the vicinity of Havana, which has been mined to some small extent, indicates under analysis a very inferior quality of coal, and is probably merely asphaltum. The large deposits stated to exist in Santiago province await investigation, and it is very doubtful if they are not rather lignite than true coal.

Much of what has been claimed as coal is evidently

asphaltum, which near the coast often becomes semi-liquid, resembling naphtha or petroleum. This native bitumen was used by the discoverers of the island as pitch to repair their ships. Asphaltum occurs in all the provinces of the island with the exception of Pinar del Rio. Considerable deposits of it exist near the cities of Villa Clara and Cardenas. The Villa Clara bed is some twelve feet in thickness and resembles lignite. For forty years past it has furnished the material for the gas supply of the city, and shipments of it have been made reaching 10,000 tons per year.

The Cardenas deposits exist in a peculiar situation, lying at the bottom of the bay, covered by a considerable depth of water. There are four of these deposits near the city, one of which yields a very fine grade of the material, used for varnish-making in the United States. The water is from eighty to one hundred and twenty-five feet in depth, and the asphaltum is obtained by dropping on it a long iron bar from a moored vessel, the pieces broken off being brought up by naked divers, who gather them into scoop-nets. More than a ton is thus obtained daily, the substance being replaced from below as mined.

There are three other deposits of lower grade, suitable for paving or roofing. The largest of these is near Diana Key, fifteen miles from Cardenas, at a depth of twelve feet. During the past twenty-five years it has yielded more than 20,000 tons, and shows no signs of exhaustion, the holes made in it constantly filling up from beneath. Petroleum exists in a similar manner under Havana harbor, through whose waters it bubbles up. It is found to trickle freely from the rocks at a point thirty-three miles east of Manzanillo, and even to appear at points in the streets of that city. It occurs similarly in other localities, though no borings or other tests of its quantity have been made.

Cuba is rich in marbles of excellent quality, varying considerably in color and frequently susceptible of a rich polish. These are found in the provinces generally, but most abundantly in the Isle of Pines, which yields many varieties noted for their beauty. A thick slate, suitable for floors and pavements, is obtained in quarries near Havana, and slate of finer quality in the Isle of Pines. The true mineral wealth of the island of Cuba is yet unknown, through lack of sufficient interest in and knowledge of mineralogy among the inhabitants, and future exploration may develop rich deposits in unsuspected localities.

Mineral springs are numerous, and those of San Diego, Madringa, and Guanabacoa have attained some degree of celebrity. The last named, being within a few miles of Havana, is a place of common resort, but difficulty of access stands in the way of the others becoming popular. The hot springs of the Isle of Pines are rapidly growing famous, and the village of Santa Fé, where they are situated, yearly attracts many health seekers to its curative waters. The number of cures claimed for these waters is surprisingly large.

Salt is obtained in quantities from the bordering keys or islets, along whose margins are many natural *salinas* (salt pans). These are shallow depressions which retain the salt water, to be evaporated by the sun. Many hundreds of tons of salt are annually obtained from the salinas along the inlet of Majana and those of Chaco.

The richest of the provinces of Cuba in mineral wealth is Santiago de Cuba, which embraces the most mountainous districts of the island. Its hills yield gold, iron, copper, manganese, mercury, zinc, alabaster, marble, rock crystal, and asphalt; while its caverns often contain beautiful stalactites. As yet the mineral riches have been developed chiefly in the immediate vicinity of the capital city of the province, and little is known regarding the possible wealth in minerals of the intricate system of the cuchillas and the interior sierras.

IV. CIVIL AND POLITICAL RELATIONS.
GOVERNMENTAL ORGANIZATION.

The close of the insurrection of 1868-78 was followed by a series of so-called reforms, one feature of which was the division of the country into the six provinces whose names we have already given. Each of these provinces has for capital the city whose name it has taken, the whole being divided into a number of judicial districts, twenty-six in all. As these are frequently spoken of without mention of the province in which they are situated, it is desirable to specify them.

Beginning at the west, we find in the province of Pinar del Rio the districts of Pinar del Rio, Guanajay, Guane, and San Cristobal; in that of Havana the districts of Havana, Bejucal, Guanabacoa, Guines, Jaruco, Marianao, and San Antonio de los Baños; in that of Matanzas those of Matanzas, Alfonso XII., Cardenas, and Colon; in Santa Clara those of Santa Clara, Sagua la Grande, Cienfuegos, and Juan de los Remedios; in Puerto Principe those of Puerto Principe, and Moron; and in Santiago de Cuba those of Santiago de Cuba, Baracoa, Guantanamo, Holguin, and Manzanillo. In each of these districts, named from its central city, justice has been administered, under the Spanish system, by an *alcalde mayor*, in association with the ordinary *alcaldes* or local judges.

The "reform" of 1878, under which the insurgents

CIVIL AND POLITICAL RELATIONS. 49

were induced to enter into a treaty of peace, contained measures which would have been of considerable benefit to the island if properly carried out. They included suffrage under a property qualification, representation in the Cortes at Madrid, elective assemblies for the provinces and boards of aldermen for the cities, and other features which we do not need to mention, since they existed only on paper. Any possible benefit to the people from these changes in the political status was hindered by the maintenance of the captain- (or governor-) general in his absolute authority. The representation in the Cortes was in a hopeless minority, the elections were manipulated in the interest of the Spanish party, and the captain-general could suspend any legislative body or remove any mayor at will, so that he had complete control of the situation. The judicial system was similarly held in leading strings, since this powerful functionary had the power to overrule the decisions of any court, and even to suspend the execution of an order coming from the government of Spain itself.

When in 1895, as a new measure of "reform" in response to the insurrection of that year, a "council of administration" was appointed seemingly as a check on the captain-general, the fatuous government of Spain took special pains to rob this council of even the shadow of power. The captain-general was given authority to suspend fourteen of the thirty members at will, and if the remaining sixteen proved troublesome he could set aside all their acts and do as he pleased. Such a system held the very essence of despotism, and as regards the Spanish system of colonial administration it will suffice further to quote the ancient adage, "Whom the gods wish to destroy they first make mad."

DIVISIONS OF TERRITORY.

The island of Cuba is divided in popular acceptation into four *regions* which do not agree very closely with the political districts. These are the Vuelta Abajo (the lower turn), Vuelta Arriba (the upper turn), Los Cinco Villas (the five towns) and Tierro Adentro (the interior). Of these popular divisions the Vuelta Abajo extends from Cape San Antonio to the meridian of Havana, the portion between this meridian and San Cristobal, in Pinar del Rio, being specially known as Los Partidos. Within this district lies the great tobacco region of Cuba, which yields the finest leaf in the world. The Vuelta Arriba lies between Havana and Cienfuegos, and Los Cinco Villas between the latter city and Puerto Principe. The five towns (now cities) are Santa Clara, Sagua la Grande, Cienfuegos, Trinidad, and Remedios. This district is variable in its borders, being extended by some as far east as Holguin. Between it and the eastern end of the island lies the Tierro Adentro, which includes the chief mountainous regions.

Other boundaries might be given for these districts, which are far from well defined and often overlap; but this is a matter of no special importance, while the frequent use of these popular terms renders an acquaintance with their meaning desirable.

In addition to the popular division, there are ecclesiastical and political divisions of the island. For religious convenience Cuba is divided into two dioceses, the bishopric of Havana and the archbishopric of Santiago de Cuba. The bishop and archbishop divide the island about equally between them, the line of delimination crossing the province of Puerto Principe near its western boundary.

The political division of the island is into six provinces, each of which bears the name of its capital city. These are, beginning at the west end, Pinar del Rio, Havana, Matanzas, Santa Clara, Puerto Principe, and Santiago de Cuba. They are further subdivided into judicial districts and municipalities. Camaguey, often spoken of in accounts of the insurrection, and still in popular use, was the former name of the territory now officially known as Puerto Principe.

ABOLITION OF SLAVERY.

The insurrection of 1868-78 did one good work, it enforced the abolition of that system of slavery which had existed in the island since its original settlement by Spain. Many slaves from the plantations had joined the rebels in arms, and, probably to prevent a continuance of this and to enlist the negroes in the Spanish cause, a law was passed on July 4, 1870, giving freedom to all slaves who had served with or assisted the troops. It was further enacted that all children of slaves born after that date should be free, and all slaves who had reached or should subsequently reach the age of sixty years.

In the capitulation of 1878 the insurgents stipulated for the freedom of those slaves who had served in their ranks. This was agreed to, and the government of Spain, in its desire to pacify this considerable class of the population, went further, and on February 13,

1880, passed a law abolishing slavery, the slaves to remain under a system of "patronage" until 1888. Two years before that period expired, on October 7, 1886, a decree was promulgated declaring the patronage at an end and the slaves free. Thus ended a system which had existed in Cuba for nearly four centuries.

RELIGION.

Religiously, Cuba, under the tutelage of Spain, was a true son of the mother country, intolerance being maintained in the colony as strictly as it had for many centuries been maintained at home. No religion but the Roman Catholic was permitted to exercise its rites upon the island. The Protestant, the Jew, the member of any Christian or non-Christian sect might live and breathe upon Cuban soil, but he must avoid any expression of religious opinion not sanctioned by the Church of Rome, and from end to end of the island could find no place of worship devoted to his special form of faith. The state religion was sustained at state expense, its costs being met out of the revenues of the island. It cannot be said that it was well sustained in any other way, the religious indifference of the people being evident to every traveller. The rites of the Church seem to have been little understood and less cared for by the easy-going population, while the priests troubled themselves not a whit about the spirit, so that the form of worship was observed and the revenues were duly paid over.

Originally there was but one diocese in Cuba, that of Santiago, which included also Florida and Louisiana. The diocese of Havana was not constituted until 1788. In 1804 the bishop of Santiago was elevated to the dignity of archbishop, an honor which has not been conferred upon the prelate at Havana. The ecclesiastical government of the island is divided between these two dignitaries of the Church, as already stated, and the minor clergy are appointed by them.

The salaries of these prelates, under the old *régime*, were $18,000 annually. What they are likely to be under the new *régime* cannot now be stated. With the passing of Cuba from under the dominion of Spain the existence of a state-supported church in that island reached its end, and the intolerance that forbids any other form of worship can no longer be sustained. Politics and religion are alike in a transition stage, from which radically new conditions promise soon to emerge.

MEANS OF COMMUNICATION.

Cuba is very poorly provided with roads, the most of those dignified with the title being rude trails, which can rarely be traversed with comfort in the dry season and are in a deplorable state during the rainy period. Over these roads merchandise is transported in heavy carts drawn by oxen or mules, or on the backs of pack mules where the roads are, as usual during the rainy season, impassable to wheeled vehicles. For passenger travel, outside the cities and off the lines of railway, the two-seated *volante* (flyer) has long been a favorite vehicle, and a very comfortable one considering the state of the roads, with the added advantage that it cannot be overturned. This is due to the great height of its two wheels, six or even seven feet, their wide distance apart, and the lowness of the carriage, which is slung from the axle by leather straps. The shafts are fifteen feet long, one horse being harnessed in them and the postilion riding a second, which is attached by traces to the carriage. A third horse is sometimes harnessed on the other side of the shaft. This carriage is peculiar to Cuba, and is very well adapted to its roads, though it has vanished from the cities. As formerly used in city streets, the volantes were often very expensively ornamented by wealthy owners, with trimmings of silver and sometimes even of gold, while the negro postilion was attired in a scarlet jacket profusely decorated with gold and silver braid, high jack-boots with big silver buckles at the knees, and huge spurs, cutting a figure that must have made him the delight of small boys. At present it has been completely replaced by the victoria, now so abundant in the streets of Havana.

Of the highways, the longest and best known is the Camino Central (central road), which extends from Havana to Santiago, passing through the intermediate interior towns. There are in all some two hundred and fifty miles of turnpikes or paved roads, known as *calzadas*. Of these the longest is that extending from Havana to San Cristobal and thence to Pinar del Rio. There are a few others varying from twelve to thirty miles in length, and a considerable number of short ones in and adjoining towns and cities. With these exceptions, the roads of the island are largely left to nature, and are rarely in condition for rapid and agreeable travel.

The fact that most of the large towns of Cuba are seaports, and readily reached by water, has stood in the way of active railroad construction on the island. The total length of track is something over a thousand miles, made up principally of comparatively short lines connecting important places. The most populous districts of the island are traversed by the lines of the United Railways Company, four in number, which run from Havana respectively to Matanzas, Batabano, La Union, and Guanajay. At these places connections are made with other roads. The Western Railway extends from Havana to Pinar del Rio, traversing the Vuelta Abajo tobacco country. Railways run to inland cities from the several ports to the eastward, including Matanzas, Cardenas, Sagua la Grande, Nuevitas, Caibarien, and Cienfuegos. Santa Clara, for instance, is connected with Cienfuegos on the south and Cardenas on the north by rail, Puerto Principe with Nuevitas, etc. One line, the Jucaro-Moron, built for military purposes, crosses the island in the province of Puerto Principe, following the course of the trocha which extended here from Jucaro in the north to Moron in the south. The Santiago Railway extends about thirty-three miles inland, winding through the mountain valleys and gradually ascending, its terminus being at San Luis. There are short roads at various points, as at Guantanamo, from Havana to adjoining towns, etc., and with the main lines are connected many private roads, mostly narrow gauge, built by the sugar planters for convenience in moving their crops. Street railways also traverse the streets of Havana and some other cities. It can scarcely be doubted that American enterprise will, before many years, extend railway communication from Pinar del Rio to Santiago de Cuba along the axis of the island, passing through all the important intermediate towns and connecting by branches with the principal places off the main line.

Steamboats connect the coast ports, running with some regularity between Havana and all the principal places on the north coast and reaching Guantanamo and Santiago on the south. There are southern lines which ply east and west from Batabano, touching at all the ports of the south coast, and extending southward to the Isle of Pines. The railway from Havana to Batabano offers ready connection from the capital with these lines, so that Havana has water communication, direct or indirect, with all the ports of the island.

The Cuban coast towns have frequent communication by steamship lines with Europe and the United States, there being lines from Havana to Spanish, French, and German ports and a monthly steamer from Vera Cruz to Southampton, touching at Havana. Key West is in semi-weekly communication with Havana; there are lines from New York to all the important Cuban ports, north and south, and mercantile lines from Philadelphia, New Orleans, and other cities to various Cuban ports.

Havana, Santiago, and Cienfuegos have submarine telegraph connection with various countries, while wires run from these cities to all the towns and villages of any importance on the island, and a submarine cable connects Cienfuegos and Santiago. The International Ocean Telegraph Company connects Havana by cable with Florida; the West India and Panama Telegraph Company with Santiago, Jamaica, Porto Rico, the Lesser Antilles, and the Isthmus of Panama; and the French Submarine Cable Company with Santiago, Hayti, San Domingo, Venezuela, and Brazil. The extent and good service of these cable lines was shown by the great difficulty experienced in attempts to cut off telegraph communication with Spain during the recent war.

The Cuban telegraph system is the property of the government, and the same is the case with the telephone system, which is widely in use in Havana, connecting with all the public and most of the private buildings in the city and suburbs. The island possesses a total of about 2300 miles of telegraph line.

POPULATION.

Cuba is rather sparsely peopled, considering its fertility and abundant capacity for food production. At the last regular census, that of 1887, the total population was 1,631,687. The estimated population in 1894 was 1,723,000. Since that date, as a result of the insurrection, with its fatal accompaniments of disease and starvation, there has been a marked decrease, several hundred thousand of the population having perished. The State of Pennsylvania, of practically the same area, has a population which may be estimated at 5,500,000, more than three times that of Cuba. But this is in great part a result of its manufacturing interests and large city population. Virginia, rural like Cuba, and closely approaching it in area, has approximately the same population.

The population of Cuba has been steadily growing during the century. In 1787 it amounted to 176,167. From that date there was a rapid increase, the total reaching 635,604 in 1817, thirty years later. It reached the million mark in 1841. In 1867, just before the outbreak of the rebellion, it was 1,426,475. Its subsequent increase was for years checked by the troubles on the island.

The population, as at present constituted, consists of five classes:—1. Natives of Spain—many of whom sought Cuba as office holders, while others were industrial immigrants. 2. Cubans of Spanish descent. 3. Whites of other origin. 4. Negroes of pure and of mixed blood. 5. Laborers from Eastern Asia. As regards the original Indian population, it had probably disappeared by 1700, and perhaps considerably earlier. There are one or two villages in Santiago de Cuba whose inhabitants are claimed to be of Indian descent, but this claim lacks evidence, and it is questionable if any trace of Indian blood runs in the veins of these people.

Negro slavery has existed in Cuba since its earliest days, the negroes taking the place of the rapidly vanishing aborigines. The laws of Spain controlling these people have not been severe, each slave had his own cabin and patch of ground and was allowed certain hours for home tillage, and he was given the opportunity of purchasing his freedom. Law, it is true, has not very well controlled the actions of the slaveholders, and the negroes have often been subjected to harsh treatment; yet there has long been a class of free negroes, who have during the present century increased with considerable rapidity. In 1810 the island held about 110,000 free negroes to 212,000 slaves. At the census of 1867 there were 248,703 free negroes to 344,615 slaves. The act of gradual emancipation of 1870 and the treaty of 1878 added largely to the number of free negroes, and in 1879 the blacks numbered 287,827 free to 171,097 slaves. At the date of the census of 1887 slavery was at an end, the negro population (all free) being 485,187, something over one-fourth the total population. These include, as in the United States, all that have negro blood in their veins, though they may be three-fourths or even in a larger proportion white.

The manumitted negroes do not take kindly to small farming, and few of them have places of their own, they preferring to work on the sugar plantations or as laborers in the cities and towns. The mulattoes usually reside in the cities and follow some skilled occupation, being engaged in the manufacture of shoes, cigars, or clothing, in carpentry, and in other artisan labors.

Of the Cuban whites a considerable proportion, perhaps one-fifth, are natives of Spain. Members of this class, under the Spanish dominion, held all official positions of any value. The colonists from Spain have the credit of being far the most industrious people on the island, the next in order being the intelligent and educated Cubans, largely of recent Spanish descent. The enervating climate of the island seems to have taken the disposition for hard work out of those of native ancestry and given them a hereditary love of ease.

Cuba has only a small population of whites of other than Spanish origin, perhaps not more than 10,000 in all. There is still another class of inhabitants, the Asiatic coolies, imported principally from China, whose lot is far from a satisfactory or agreeable one. The first of these, 679 in number, were brought to Havana in 1847, and they have since been added to until they number perhaps more than 30,000; the actual number is unknown. Coolie labor is not called slavery, but is in some respects worse than slavery. The coolie is not a native of the soil like the negro, with his home and family relations and his assimilation to his master in language, religion, and customs, but remains an alien, bound to work a fixed number of years for small pay. No women being brought with them, these Chinese laborers have no domestic life, and the only interest their employer takes in them is to get from them all possible labor. The result is frequently a physical wreck, worn out by hard work and change of climate.

The following table shows the numbers and density of population in the several provinces at the date of the most recent official census, that of 1887:

Provinces.	Inhabitants.	Square Kilometres.	Density.
Pinar del Rio. . . .	225,891	14,967	15.09
Havana	451,928	8,610	52 49
Matanzas	259,578	8,486	30.59
Santa Clara	354,122	23,083	15.34
Puerto Principe . . .	67,789	32,341	2.10
Santiago de Cuba . .	272,379	35,119	7.76
Totals	1,631,687	122,606	13.31

EDUCATION.

The leading educational institution in Cuba is that known, under the Spanish *régime*, as the Royal University of Havana. Its official report of the date of 1890 shows a division into the five departments of Philosophy and Letters, Medicine, Pharmacy, Law, and Science, there being eighty-six professors, including assistants, and 1046 students. The cornerstone of the buildings now occupied was laid in 1884. Each of the six provinces has its separate collegiate institute, whose power of conferring degrees is limited to that of bachelor or licentiate. These had a total of 2909 students.

There is in addition an Havana School of Painting and Sculpture, with 454 scholars, and a Professional School of the Industrial Arts, with fifty-three. The arts of common industry would not, from this statement, seem to be in much favor among students as compared with the fine arts. In 1895, the public or municipal schools held 36,747 scholars. A law was passed in 1880 making education compulsory, but judging from the above figures no attempt has been made to put it into effect. While the proportion of school children to the total population in the most favored division of the United States is about one to four, and even in Spain one to nine, that of Cuba is one to twenty-five, showing that there must be a large percentage of illiteracy in the island. Of the small sum appropriated for education out of the revenues, none has been applied in aid of the common schools, which are sustained by municipal aid. The education to be obtained in them seems to be of a very elementary kind. The number of private schools approaches that of the public ones, these schools being credited with 28,249 pupils. They include the various institutions of private benevolence which add instruction to their other duties.

V. CENTRES OF POPULATION.

HAVANA, THE CAPITAL CITY.

San Cristobal de la Habana, to give the full Spanish name to this picturesque and important city of the American tropics, is admirably situated for commerce, lying as it does on one of the finest harbors of the world, with noble entrance and deep and spacious interior. The vessel approaching Havana passes through a channel nearly 1000 feet wide and more than 4000 feet long, free from bar or rock, and emerges into an ample bay, dividing up interiorly into three distinct arms, and capable of sheltering in its broad expanse a thousand ships, and of protecting them from any storm less violent than a hurricane, while the water is deep enough to permit them to moor close to the wharves. A lofty lighthouse rises on the left of the entrance, which is defended by a series of fortifications, some of them famous for their antiquity. On the east side of the entrance are the celebrated Morro Castle and the fortress of San Carlos de la Cabaña, the first of which, also entitled the Castle of the Three Kings, dates from 1589. Opposite, on the west side, stands the Castillo de la Punta, a much smaller fort than the Morro, but of equal antiquity. Fronting the entrance channel for a distance of 800 yards extends the Cabaña fortress, its barracks ample enough to give accommodation to 4000 men. Farther inland on the bay side is Casa Blanca, another

CENTRES OF POPULATION.

old fort, east of which, on a hill one hundred feet high, is a redoubt named San Diego. On the most westerly of the hills curving around the city stands the Castillo del Principe, a conspicuous fortification. The Castle of Atares, on one of the inland bays, dates from about 1763.

The Morro is a substantial stone fortress of the old style, with thick and solid walls and a deep dry moat, and is quite capable of holding its own against old style guns. How well it would withstand the battering of modern rifled cannon is another question. No trial of it was made in the late war. The Cabaña fortress is the largest on the island, and is claimed to be one of the best in the world. It is built on a precipitous bank that rises directly from the water-side, enabling it to overlook the town and command most of the bay. Built, like the Morro, of solid stone, it has the appearance of immense strength, while its great length gives it an enormous capacity for mounting guns. More ancient still than the Morro and the Punta is the Castillo de la Fuerza, built in 1538 by Fernando de Soto, while governor of the island, to protect the city from its piratical enemies. It is now within the city streets, and presents an interesting example of a mediæval fortress, retaining much of its original form of a star-shaped, bastioned fort.

The city of Havana lies on the west side of the bay, fronting its waters and those of the entrance channel, while it has another front facing the ocean, along whose waters it extends for some distance. It is low-lying, but presents an attractive and picturesque appearance to the approaching stranger, with its bright-colored walls, its red-tiled roofs, and the green of its trees, under the glare of the tropical sun. No other city in the Western world presents so oriental an aspect. The throng of shipping in the spacious bay adds to the beauty of the scene, the ships from far-off ports being added to by numbers of local trading vessels and hundreds of passenger boats, with particolored sails, in constant motion about the bay. These look strange to unaccustomed eyes, with their awnings supported by a basket-like frame-work, and add their share to the picturesqueness of the scene.

The bay of Havana has an extreme length of three and a half miles and a maximum width of one and a half miles, while the available extent is something over one mile in length and less than one mile in width. It branches into three principal coves, while there are many small indentations. Its greatest depth is forty feet, but vessels of over twenty feet draught are restricted to a comparatively limited space. On the east side of the bay is the commercial suburb of Regla, notable for its *Depositos Mercantil*, immense warehouses of solid stone for the storage of sugar. These consist of a long series of one-storied buildings of great height, the heavy iron beams and corrugated iron of the roof being supported by numerous pillars of iron. They stand on the bay shore, their doors opening on substantial wharves, and have few rivals for capacity and systematic management. Another of the attractions of Regla, at least to the Spaniard, is its famous bull-ring, where numbers of bulls and horses are annually sacrificed on the altar of Spanish taste. At some distance from Regla, on the same side of the bay, stands the old town of Guanabacoa, of some 30,000 population, which dates back to 1554, and was originally an Indian village. Its principal modern attraction is the Santa Rita mineral baths, claimed to have performed remarkable cures. The waters, which are cool and pleasant to the taste, pour out of a rocky basin, and are so fully impregnated with bitumen, iron, potash, and magnesia that the mineral substances form a thick layer upon the surface.

Havana, a city peopled by more than 200,000 souls (perhaps 300,000, if all the suburbs be included), popularly consists of two widely different sections, the city within and the city without the walls; though little trace of walls is to-day to be seen. The walls which enclosed the ancient city were completed in 1702, but were almost entirely demolished in 1863, the streets having long before spread far beyond them. The old city lies close to the harbor, and is made up of streets so narrow as to render wheeled traffic within it the reverse of convenient. These contracted streets are normally dirty and insalubrious; the drainage being anything but scientific, and the badly-kept pavements so impregnated with filth as to be sickening to the senses of a foreigner. The Cuban nasal organ is native to the situation and not easily disturbed.

The lot of the foot-passenger in the old town is not an agreeable one. The narrow streets are abundantly occupied by vehicles, while the sidewalks, where any exist, are so narrow that it is no easy matter for two persons to pass. One must brush the wall and the other perhaps be forced off the narrow flag-stone into the street. But he can step into its muddy midway only at imminent risk of being run into by some hasty carriage or other vehicle. Many of the streets are so narrow that it is impossible for two vehicles to pass each other, so that carriages and carts can only move in one direction, directing signs being placed at the street corners.

One advantage of these narrow streets is that they aid in keeping out the hot beams of the tropical sun. This is helped by bright-colored awnings, which cross from roof to roof at intervals and throw downward a grateful shade. Below, in the business thoroughfares, extend rows of stores, with handsome windows and their shelves almost upon the streets, most of their goods being displayed in the broad windows. For signs they do not trust to a mere name and number, but present some striking title and design, such as " The Green Cross," " The Nymphs," " The Looking-Glass," " The Golden Lion," " Diana," " Virtue," and other curious names.

In the new town modern ideas about city building have largely prevailed, there being many wide and handsome avenues, often fringed with rows of stately palms, and with broad macadamized drives in the centre. These are bordered with leafy gardens and solidly built stone houses, having verandas and flat roofs. Iron bars guard the windows in place of glazed sashes, while the walls are gay with varied bright colors and with decorations in white marble, which is lavishly used in Havana both for shops and dwellings.

The houses are usually one story in height, rarely two, and have broad and massive doors, thickly studded with knobs and decorations, and thick, strong walls, that look as if built for defence against enemies. The prison-like aspect given by the window-bars is relieved by the bright colors in which they are painted. The walls, built of a peculiar porous shell-conglomerate glaringly white in color, are nearly always covered with stucco, whose bright colors of yellow, green, and blue harmonize well with the glowing atmosphere. The dwellings, of combined Gothic and Saracenic architecture, are so constructed as to leave an open square in the centre,—the house being divided into living-room, store-room, chambers, and stable, while the street entrance is usually blocked up in part by the family vehicle. If there is a second story, it is reached by a broad flight of stairs, and contains the sleeping-chambers, opening upon a corridor facing the court.

Havana is to-day, as in the past, a city of smells and noises. Little effort is made at cleaning the streets or draining the houses, and such drainage as does take place pours its impurities into the harbor, which is yearly filling up with foul accretions. Yet for this conversion of the harbor into a filth-pool there seems no excuse of necessity, since the city, lying between the harbor and the ocean, is admirably situated for carrying its drainage into the open sea. The streets, stone paved and abundantly occupied by vehicles, driven often with reckless speed, are a scene of constant rattle, to which the street railway cars add their share. The avenues are abundantly provided with restaurants, cafés, casinos, and club-houses, which are largely frequented, home life being a feature of the north which has little existence among the well-to-do people of this city of the south.

Havana is nowhere surpassed for the number and the beauty of its public parks and promenades. Most prominent among these are the Plaza de Armas, facing the governor's palace; the Alameda de Paula, a bay-side embankment; the Parque Central; and the Paseo de Tacon, whose magnificent drive is shaded by double rows of trees. In addition may be named the Paseo Isabel or the Prado, a long and handsome boulevard; the Campo de Marte, or drill park; the highly attractive Botanical Gardens; and the gardens of Los Molinos, long the suburban residence of the captain-generals. The avenues named, with others that might be mentioned, charm the visitor with their trees, flowers, fountains, and statuary, and with their liveliness, they being almost constantly crowded with handsome open carriages and well-dressed promenaders. Only for "its smells and its noises," as one writer says, Havana would be one of the most pleasing of cities.

Its fashionable driveway, the Paseo de Tacon, is two or three miles long, lined with beautiful villas and rich gardens filled with tropical plants. It has two carriage-ways and two foot-ways, with rows of stately trees between. No other city in America has its equal as an avenue. Opening from it, near its outer extremity, are the Botanical Gardens, adjoining which are the equally beautiful Los Molinos gardens, made free to the public by their late owners, the captain-generals. Those charming places of resort are open day and night, and an evening stroll through their beautiful walks, surrounded by the most exquisite of tropical flowers and plants, is nowhere to be surpassed. The Botanical Gardens contain specimens of almost every plant of the tropics, growing freely in the open air, while in the centre a large stone basin is filled with water lilies, surrounding a rustic fountain made of shells. From these gardens one can stroll into those of Los Molinos, with their great variety of tropical trees and flowers and their magnificent avenue of palms, one of the finest on the island. The place seems a wilderness of blossoms, exotic and native, and possesses an interesting aviary, leaping fountains, and other features of attraction.

One of the most striking objects in a general view of the city of Havana is what has long been known as the Royal Prison, a large yellow building occupying a whole city block. This, built in 1771, forms a hollow square, the interior area being used as a place of exercise for the prisoners. It has cells for five hundred captives and barracks for a regiment, the cells being in the rear and the front occupied by offices and quarters. This massive edifice, in the vicinity of the Punta fortress, fronts on one of the choice avenues of the city, the Prado, a wide boulevard nearly two miles long, whose centre is ornamented with rows of trees and possesses stone seats and a promenade, while a carriage-way extends on either side.

The Prado, starting from the seaside near the Punta fortress and passing nearly in the line of the old city wall, has facing it or in its vicinity the finest buildings and the most attractive portions of the city proper. The fashionable Parque Central, with its adornment of trees, shrubbery, and flowers, and surrounded by handsome, colonnaded buildings, forms an enlargement of this avenue, and is one of the liveliest and most attractive features of the city. Fronting on it are the Hotel Inglaterra, the best and largest in Cuba; the famous Tacon Theatre, the Alibasu Theatre, the Spanish Casino, and other striking buildings, while around it extend open-air cafés, brilliantly lighted by night, and gay as those of the Parisian boulevards. On certain evenings of the week a military band plays here, while crowds of well-dressed people promenade or seat themselves in the neighboring cafés and balconies.

The palace recently occupied by the captain-general faces the Plaza de Armas, and is a large yellow building, two stories in height, the upper floor being supported on the front by open stone colonnades, which give an excellent architectural effect. The central colonnade forms an archway leading into the handsomely-adorned court-yard within.

Of the churches of Havana, some of them imposing in size, others famous for antiquity, the one most likely to attract the attention of the stranger is the Cathedral. This edifice, built in 1724 for a Jesuit college and converted into a cathedral in 1789, is constructed of the yellowish-white calcareous sandstone of the island, but now presents a battered and blackened aspect. The façade, with its pillars, niches, and mouldings, and its two high flanking towers, is peculiar and striking in appearance rather than beautiful. Numerous bells, some of them ancient, hang in the towers, and daily call the worshippers to matins and vespers.

Interiorly the church is attractive, with its richly frescoed walls, its floor of variegated marble, and its lofty dome supported by pillars of marble, while the stalls of the priests are beautifully carved in polished mahogany, the designs being light and graceful. Several beautiful altars stand at intervals around the walls, having pillars, cornices, and mouldings of solid ma-

CENTRES OF POPULATION.

hogany, the prominent parts richly gilt. The grand altar, with its porphyry pillars, its images, candlesticks, and other adornments, is a handsome structure, as is also the choir in its rear.

But the great object of interest has long been the tomb of Columbus, the remains of the great discoverer having, in 1796, been brought to Havana from the city of San Domingo, when the island of Hayti was ceded to France. The urn containing these sacred relics was deposited with great ceremony in a niche in the wall, marked by a marble tablet on which was placed a bust of Columbus, in the costume of his age, but sadly lacking artistic merit. Beneath was an inscription in Castilian, similarly lacking poetic taste. Rendered into English it has the following grandiloquent significance:

> "Oh, rest thou, image of the great Colon,
> Thousand centuries remain, guarded in the urn,
> And in the memory of our nation."

The thousand centuries, however, have proved little more than one century, for in 1898, after the close of the war with the United States, the remains of the great Colon were once more removed, this time back again to Spain, which they had left to cross the ocean in 1536. Cuba, as San Domingo before it, had ceased to be Spanish soil, and the ashes of the great discoverer were restored to that land which had permitted him to die in penury and neglect.

Passing from church to theatre, the most important edifice of this kind is the Tacon Theatre, erected in 1838, and with seats for an audience of about 3000 persons. It is situated on the corner of the street San

Rafael and the Prado or Paseo Isabel, opposite El Louvre, a fashionable café, and while not very imposing on the exterior is handsome within. It has five tiers of boxes, their fronts decorated with gilt lattice work of light and graceful design. The auditorium is of horseshoe shape, the parquette, with seats for 600 persons, being reserved for gentlemen. The ornaments are in excellent taste, the house well lighted, and the whole effect brilliant when the house is crowded with gayly dressed ladies and gentlemen in evening dress.

Other places of amusement include the Payret Theatre, seating 2500, the Alibasu Theatre, the Circo, and the Casino, the last combining amusement with instruction. This edifice, which is one of the institutions of the capital, has facilities for dramatic entertainments,—mainly amateur, for charitable purposes, —and has a handsomely decorated ball-room, where masked balls are occasionally given, and, during the carnival season, nightly masquerade balls are held unsurpassed for gayety and picturesqueness of costume and effect. The Casino also supports a free school for the teaching of French and English and drawing. ing.

Of other buildings of interest may be named the churches of San Juan de Dios, built in 1573, San Agostino, in 1608, Santa Catalina, in 1658, and San Felipe, which has the distinction of possessing a large library. The Belen Church, occupying nearly a whole city block, is perhaps the most attractive of them all. There are many monasteries and nunneries and a considerable number of charitable institutions. These include several hospitals, of which the most important is the Real Casa de Beneficencia, dating back to 1790, and containing an orphan asylum, a lunatic asylum, a poor-house, and an infirmary. To these may be added the custom-house, the exchange, the university, and other public edifices and educational institutions.

In addition to the library of the Church of San Felipe is that of the Royal Economical Society of Havana, which possesses a large number of books, many of them rare, particularly those relating to Cuba. The rooms are open from twelve to three each day, though the books, principally in Spanish, do not present indications of being much used.

The Alameda de Paula skirts the bay shore on the city side, and is a favorite evening resort for promenaders, the ocean breeze giving it a refreshing coolness. It is faced by many handsome buildings, while the water-side is bordered with a continuous sea-wall.

The city is well provided with statues and fountains, one of the most attractive of the latter being the beautiful Fountain of India, on the Prado, opposite the Campo de Marte. This work of art, carved out of Carrara marble, is surrounded with royal palms, and adds much to the beauty of the avenue. The city possesses numerous squares, usually ornamented with palm trees, with a few orange, lime, and banana trees, and the shady Indian laurel.

From the Campo de Marte extends the Calzada de la Reina (Queen's Street), which farther on becomes the Paseo de Tacon, already mentioned, the two being, of an afternoon, the liveliest part of the city, as they form the favorite pleasure drive and promenade. The Calzada de la Infanta leads into a long street, called

El Cerro, which extends to the village of that name, three miles out, and is by many considered the handsomest street of the city. It is lined with attractive modern residences, and large old villas in the midst of beautiful gardens, each house in its way like a fort, with its single story, its unglazed and strongly barred windows, and its vast and massive doorways, studded with brass knobs. The principal entrance opens into a large, cool hall, paved with tiles of marble, while broad archways lead to the rooms adjoining. Within the houses doors are lacking, curtains replacing them in the interior arrangement. The ceilings are very high, and the free circulation of air from the courtyard render these halls the most agreeable part of the house for dining purposes. The *patio* or court-yard is laid out with walks, flowers, fountains, and fragrant bushes, while birds of song or of brilliant plumage hang there in ornamental cages. All the rooms open into it, and an upper gallery runs round it when the house has a second story.

On the right of the Cerro lies a charming place formerly known as the Bishop's Garden, one of whose chief attractions is a superb avenue of mango trees. Here are also some noble examples of the cactus, which often attains a vast size in Cuban soil. There is an alley of palms, over two hundred years in age, and grand in dimensions, and many evidences of former artistic adornment, now in a state of neglect and decay. A small stream of mountain origin flows through the grounds, and affords opportunities for irrigation, cascades, fountains, pools, and swimming basins.

Havana is amply provided with facilities for sea-bathing, in which the sharks that haunt the outer waters are set at defiance. The ocean shore is composed of coral rock, within which, at great expense, basins have been hollowed out, the opening to the sea being too narrow to permit the entrance of any of its dangerous habitants. The basins are from twelve to eighteen feet square and eight feet deep, the water within them averaging about five feet deep. The constant in- and out-flow of the sea keeps the water perfectly pure and crystal clear, except in case of a storm, when the sea breaks over the top in a turmoil of boiling foam, giving the benefit of surf bathing.

Of the hotels of Havana may be named the Hotel Telegrafo, situated opposite the Campo de Marte; the San Carlos, a family hotel near the wharves; the Hotel Pasaje, on the Prado; the Hotel Europa, in the Plaza de San Francisco; and the Hotels Central and Inglaterra, in the noisy quarter opposite the Parque Central. All these houses have restaurants, and are run both on the American and the European plan. Restaurants and cafés, indeed, exist abundantly throughout Havana, whose people live largely out of doors and get their meals abroad.

Of the markets, the most convenient is the Mercado de Cristina, in the Plaza Vieja, occupying a hollow square, whose sides are composed of ranges of stores of all kinds, faced by an arcade. Here may be seen immense heaps of vegetables and smaller piles of all the luscious fruits of Cuba, presided over by the swarthy country people or by dusky negroes in highly varied costume. Berries are lacking. There seem to be none raised on the island, the great heat, as is said, burning them up. Nor is there to be seen the variety of delicious summer vegetables of the north,— onions, cabbages, and sweet potatoes being the principal productions of this kind. The plantain, in common with rice and *tasajo* (jerked beef, or fish), constitutes the principal food of the poor.

The fish market is on the other side of the town, in a large stone building near the bay. The varieties of edible fish are very numerous, more than one hundred, it is said, the best being the *pargo* and the *raba-rubia*. These are scarce except during the prevalence of the winter north winds, when they appear in numbers and are sold at a low price. Among other fish exposed for sale is the shark, offered whole or in sections; the spoiler of the seas being thus made food for man.

Havana is fortunate in its water-supply, a sufficient store of excellent drinking water being brought into the city by means of a fine aqueduct. The water comes from the pure and extensive springs of Vento, about nine miles distant, and is conducted through the city to the fountains with which Havana abounds. There is also an old aqueduct, known as the Zanja, built as early as 1597, and drawing its supply from the river Almandares, an impure source. The city has few wells and cisterns, and nearly all the water used is pure. Ice, made by ice-machines, is supplied in sufficient quantity to be sold at a low price, there being three ice factories in the city. In the interior of the island, where this cooling article is not to be had, porous jars, placed where the breeze favors evaporation from their surface, are employed, and serve admirably to cool the water to an agreeable temperature for drinking.

MATANZAS.

Fifty-four miles east of Havana, at the head of a magnificent bay, lies Matanzas, a city of considerable commercial importance, and the capital of the province of the same name. The bay, while large, lacks depth, and is not suitable for vessels of much draught. It receives the waters of the rivers San Juan and Yumurri, between and beyond which the city extends. It was settled in 1693 by a colony from the Canary Islands, and has to-day a population estimated at 50,000.

Picturesque and verdant hills surround the bay in the form of an amphitheatre, to whose ascending slopes the city extends, while the surrounding country is one of the most fertile and productive sections of Cuba. Built later, and under better supervision, than Havana, this city has escaped the evil of narrow avenues, its streets being wide; while its superior drainage and cleanliness give it a better record for healthfulness than that enjoyed by the capital. The climate is claimed to be specially favorable to those afflicted with throat and lung diseases, also to sufferers from rheumatism and neuralgia, and many invalids of this character seek it for relief.

The most prominent building visible on approaching Matanzas from the water-side is the custom-house, a large one-storied stone building, built a century ago. On the high lands in the rear are visible the country-seats of the well-to-do inhabitants, who from this outlook enjoy a delightfully picturesque view of the city and its wide-spreading and hill-clasped bay. Towering above the city is the Monte de Pan, or Bread

Mountain, a lofty background whose far-off summit serves as a welcome landmark to southward-bound vessels.

The city itself has no special features calling for mention, though it is rather attractive in general appearance. Its chief public square, the Plaza de Armas, is quite pretty with its walks, shrubbery, and flowers, and is surrounded by handsome stores and dwellings, club-houses, and the official residence and offices. The principal church is a large, antique building, with nothing particular to recommend it; and there is a new and spacious theatre and the inevitable bull-ring and cock-pits. The city is well provided with railways, running to Havana, Cienfuegos, Sagua, and Santa Clara. These Cuban roads, American in their equipment and often in their engineers, are fairly well conducted and make reasonably good time.

Beyond the San Juan lies the Pueblo Nuevo (new city), flanked by some handsome country-seats; and beyond the Yumurri is a section of the city known as Versalles. Here, on the edge of the bay, is the beautiful Paseo of Versalles, the favorite evening drive, and on the hills adjoining stand the military hospital and the barracks of Santa Isabel.

Matanzas possesses two famous points of attraction, the valley of the Yumurri and the cave of Bellemar. There is nowhere a lovelier view than the former, which is made up of a broad, circular level area, some five or six miles in diameter, enclosed on all sides by steep slopes rising to the height of five or six hundred feet. Through the centre of this winds the beautiful Yumurri, which reaches the bay through an exquisite cañon about four miles long. Seen from the *cumbre*, or mountain height near Matanzas, this peaceful and verdant valley, with its palm groups and plantations, its groves and dwellings, and with the silvery stream and its tributaries winding through it like glowing threads, presents one of the most charming visions of all the tropic world.

Matanzas has in its vicinity other beautiful views, among the most striking of which is the valley of the Magdalen, as seen from the Hill of Paradise. Here for some fifteen miles between hazy mountains extends a verdant country, with green elevations, graceful groves, and the buildings of many sugar estates, while in the far distance lie the city and bay of Matanzas.

The cave of Bellemar, opened accidentally, not many years ago, by some quarrymen, who fancied they had broken through the earth's crust, reaches a depth of several hundred feet beneath the surface, and has many beautiful stalactitic effects. Its length, so far opened, is about three miles. Of its views may be mentioned the Gothic Temple, smaller but much more beautiful than the similar chamber in the Mammoth Cave, and the Fountain of Snow, a splendid effect of pure white stalactites whose charm it would be hard to surpass. It has, besides its Cloak of the Virgin, its Altars, its Guardian Spirits, its Mantle of Columbus, and such like indispensable requisites of Cuban caves, many of them, unfortunately, the worse for the smoke from the torches of the guides.

Of the hotel accommodations of Matanzas, the Hotel Louvre bears the best record for cleanliness and general attractiveness, combined with high prices for inferior fare, which one must expect everywhere in

Cuba. The rooms are small and the partitions between them do not reach to the ceiling, so that privacy is sadly lacking.—but this also is a desideratum not highly considered in Cuba.

If one desires to visit a Cuban watering-place, the Saratoga of the island, a two-hours' railroad trip towards the interior will take him to the village of Madruga, celebrated for its mineral springs, which are accredited with wonderful curative properties. The village lies in a beautiful and healthful rolling country, and is a fashionable place of resort in the late spring and summer. The waters of the baths are impregnated with sulphur, and with some iron, magnesia, and potassa, and are claimed to be sovereign in their effect on rheumatism, scrofula, paralysis, dyspepsia, and certain other ills.

CARDENAS.

Thirty miles east of Matanzas is Cardenas, built almost directly upon the sea, though a long neck of land to the northwest forms a bay-like enclosure and affords a fair degree of protection to the shipping at the wharves. It is the youngest town of any note in Cuba, dating from 1828, and has a population estimated at about 21,000, its prosperity being due to the great fertility of the back country, for whose products it forms the shipping point. It is called the American city, a large number of Americans being engaged in business here, while the English language is in very common use.

The city is flanked on both sides by mangrove swamps; it standing a few feet above their level and running back to higher ground. It is substantially

CENTRES OF POPULATION.

built, and has its fair share of handsome buildings, while in its centre is a large and tasteful plaza, boasting a fine bronze statue of Columbus. The streets are about forty feet wide, but are unpaved and without sewerage. Yet, despite this and its swampy situation, Cardenas is a healthy city, and generally enjoys the advantage of cool ocean breezes.

It is the centre of a large sugar-producing district, and is also the shipping point for much of the sugar of Havana province. Its bay, which is twelve miles long by eighteen wide, is so shallow near the shore that large vessels have to anchor one or two miles outward. Craft of ten or twelve feet draught can reach the wharves, which are from 300 to 1000 feet in length. The city has an excellent water-supply, though many of the people still use the unwholesome cistern water.

OTHER NORTHERN PORTS.

Sagua la Grande, in the north of Santa Clara province, and 160 miles from Havana, is a town of 14,000 inhabitants, situated on the navigable river of the same name, about ten miles inland from its seaport, La Isabella. It has railway connection with Santa Clara and Cienfuegos, and occasional visits from steamboats, but has nothing to recommend it to strangers. Some thirty-five miles southeastward lies San Juan de los Remedios, an old town, founded in 1545 on a coast islet and afterwards removed inland out of reach of the buccaneers. Its port is Caibarien, about five miles distant, which has a good harbor. Its population is nearly 7500. It is surrounded by a very fertile district and possesses a good trade in sugar.

The city of Puerto Principe has for its port the harbor of Nuevitas, a town of about 7000 population, situated on a fine bay, to which Columbus gave the name of Puerto Principe, now applied to the province. The entrance to this bay is through a narrow channel, four or five miles long, which opens into a double bay, one section being called Nuevitas and the other Mayanabo, and each receiving the waters of two rivers.

The province of Santiago de Cuba possesses several fine harbors on its north coast, its most important port on this coast being Gibara, the outlet of the inland city of Holguin. Here is a capacious bay, though not deep enough to let vessels come up to the wharves, lighters needing to be employed. Plantains, grown abundantly in the interior, are shipped from here in large quantities to Havana. The population is nearly 5000.

Almost due north from the city of Santiago opens the spacious bay of Nipe, one of the most commodious on the island, and the scene of one of the latest naval engagements during the recent war. Its commercial advantages have not yet been utilized. North of it lies the harbor of Banes, an important fruit-shipping point, particularly for bananas, more than 1,000,000 bunches being shipped in some recent years. Pine-apples are also largely grown, 32,000 being exported in 1894.

Still proceeding eastward, we reach the ancient town of Baracoa, the oldest on the island, situated not far from Cape Maisi, its most easterly point. This town, seated on a small, land-locked bay, with narrow entrance, was founded in 1512 by Diego Velasquez, who made it the capital of the island and fixed his residence there. The first cathedral of Cuba, built there in 1518, was subsequently removed to Santiago. Baracoa has a population of about 5000, and is an active shipping point, sending out large cargoes of pineapples, bananas, and cocoa-nuts, the produce of the surrounding country, and also having a good trade in coffee. Back of the town rises an abrupt mountain range, while the adjacent country is highly picturesque, being noted for its caverns, cascades, and curious natural formations. The caves are celebrated for the beauty of their stalactites, and also for the fossil remains found in them. In addition to the bones of the lower animals, they contain Indian remains. The town is unhealthy, malarial fevers being very prevalent; but the interior country is very healthful.

West of Havana, on the coast of Pinar del Rio province, are several good harbors, including those of Mariel, at the northern end of Weyler's famous trocha, Cabañas, and Bahia Honda, the last named possessing one of the finest harbors of Cuba. The surrounding country is very rich in its sugar-cane production.

SANTIAGO DE CUBA.

First in importance among the southern ports of the island is the city of Santiago de Cuba, capital of the province of the same name, and at one time capital of the whole island. This city, whose name is commonly abbreviated by the inhabitants to "Cuba" or "Santiago," was founded in 1514 by Diego Velasquez, and is now credited with a population of about 60,000. It is situated on a fine bay, famous as the place of refuge of Cervera's Spanish squadron, while the city has similarly gained celebrity as the centre of military and naval operations in Cuba during the war of 1898, and as the first port of the island rescued from Spanish rule.

Santiago is backed by a mountain country, and is built on an ascending hill-side, reaching at its highest point a level of 160 feet above the sea, so that from any point are presented superb views of the expanding bay and of the neighboring mountains. The city is regularly laid out, the streets crossing at right angles; though the steepness of those which run back from the harbor, gullied as they are by the frequent rains, interferes seriously with the comfort of the pedestrian. The sidewalks are but ten to fifteen inches in width, and the avenues, once paved with cobble-stones, have long been in an almost impassable condition, while the stream of foul water which flowed down them served the purpose of drainage, but not of cleanliness and immunity from unpleasant odors. It is not to be wondered at that this city has been the central seat of yellow fever, that fatal child of filth and neglect.

In the centre of the city is the Plaza de la Reina (Square of the Queen), a breathing-spot with much beauty of vegetation. On its eastern side stands the cathedral, a handsome stone structure, whose elevated position makes it a very prominent object from the bay. It is the largest church in Cuba, as befits its dignity as the seat of an archbishop's see, but has not been spared by earthquakes, which have injured it so that it needed to be practically rebuilt in the early part of the nineteenth century. Externally it resembles somewhat the cathedral of Havana. Internally, the main aisle, leading to the grand altar and choir, is imposing from the height of its arches and massiveness of its pillars, and there are some richly decorated chapels; but the effect, on the whole, is not very striking. The elaborate ceremonials which occasionally take place here attract people from all sections of the island.

Santiago possesses several spacious two-story clubhouses of some pretentiousness, and a multitude of gaudy drinking-saloons, which in the evening, with their open fronts and their abundant display of looking-glasses, bottles of colored liquor, and general glitter, have a dazzling effect. One would think that the Cubans spent their time in drinking, yet it is rare to see one of them the worse for liquor. In fact, they indulge sparingly in intoxicants, preferring some of their numerous "soft drinks." The houses in the older portion of the city are vari-colored, one-storied stone buildings, of the Moorish style of architecture. In the suburbs are many cheap wooden structures.

The sidewalks are so narrow that one involuntarily takes to the street, a not very agreeable alternative in the past, when these narrow avenues were well carpeted with dirt and filth, and served as open sewers for the conveyance of malodorous waters. Santiago, indeed, has long been famous for lack of cleanliness, though under the vigorous control of General Wood, the American military governor, it has had a thorough cleansing for the first time in its history, a mountain mass of dirt being carted away. The streets are now kept thoroughly clean, all garbage is burned daily, and cleanliness of dwellings and shops is rigidly enforced, whitewash, fresh paint, and disinfectants being freely used. Whether this state of affairs will be maintained by the Cubans if left to themselves it is impossible to say, but they have certainly been treated to a most useful object lesson.

The city is at once very hot and extremely unhealthy. The surrounding mountain country shuts it closely in and keeps off the refreshing sea breezes, while the unhealthfulness is due to the disease-breeding filth which has accumulated for centuries in the bottom of the bay, this being so land-locked that little of the sewage is carried out to sea. The rapid upward slope of the city renders drainage easy, but how to carry the sewage beyond the bay is likely to be a serious and costly matter.

The bay itself is a particularly fine one, about five miles long and three miles in greatest width. The water shoals to ten or fifteen feet at the wharves, so that lighterage is necessary for large vessels. The largest steamers, however, can lie beside the magnificent iron pier of the Juragua Mining Company. The island of Cayo Smith, near the harbor entrance, serves as a watering-place for the best families of the city, and contains many beautiful villas.

There are many attractive drives in the vicinity of this city, one of the most fashionable being that of the Paseo de Concha. An agreeable and not very long drive, over ground that has recently become famous, is that to Morro Castle, at the entrance to the harbor. Morro is a familiar word in Cuba and Porto Rico, meaning no more than a fortification on the summit of a rounded or semicircular hill. The Morro of Santiago is a full century older than the more famous one of Havana, and is a highly picturesque structure, being a yellow, Moorish-looking stronghold, with crumbling, honeycombed battlements, odd little flanking turrets, and grated windows. Beneath it, at the water's edge, the sea has worn a deep cave in the cliffs, whose broad entrance lies beneath a perfect natural arch.

The Morro passed through a baptism of fire from Admiral Sampson's fleet during the siege of Santiago, but with far less injurious effect than was anticipated. Antique and adapted to a former age as it is, it bore remarkably well the fire of the great 12- and 13-inch rifled guns, and emerged not seriously the worse for its severe bombardments.

Other localities which have recently become famous about Santiago are the hill of San Juan and the village of El Caney, both made memorable by the intrepid valor of American troops. In the mountain country back of the city are the rich copper and iron mines, already spoken of, whose yield, freed from the annoyances and crippling exactions of Spanish control, can scarcely fail to become great and valuable.

Eastward from Santiago lies the magnificent bay of Guantanamo, within whose confines the American marines gained their first footing on Cuban soil, and whose waters served as a coaling harbor for the blockading fleet.

The city itself, while small, is charmingly situated, the surrounding mountain country yielding the choicest coffee of Cuba, while sugar is grown in the valleys, and the coast country is noted for its beautiful groves of lemon and lime trees.

Westward, in the deep gulf made by the promontory of Cape Cruz, is the port of Manzanillo, a town of more than 9000 population, with a large trade in sugar, agricultural and forest products, and so situated as to make it one of the most unhealthful towns on the island. Farther west, and due south from Puerto Principe, is the port of Santa Cruz del Sur, a town of about 1000 population, dealing in fine timber, cattle, wax, honey, and other products.

TRINIDAD.

The province of Santa Clara possesses two southern ports of importance, Trinidad and Cienfuegos. The former, lying due south of the provincial capital, is situated some miles inland from the bay, with a mountain background and in one of the healthiest districts of the island. The village of Casilda, on the side of the shallow bay, serves as its port, the city being built inland as a partial protection from the buccaneers of past centuries.

Trinidad, with a population of about 18,000, is one of the oldest towns on the island, dating back to 1514. It was formerly the centre of the coffee trade of Cuba, but has declined with the falling off of the coffee culture, while the more modern Cienfuegos has taken much of its trade. The city lies some six miles back from the coast, on the side of Vijia (watch-tower) Mountain, its elevation above sea-level being from 200 to nearly 400 feet.

The streets of Trinidad, as a result of its antiquity, are nearly all narrow and winding, those on the edge of the town being unpaved. Some of them present a peculiar appearance, with their rough tiled houses and the odd titles given the stores. In the better streets the dwellings are usually large and comfortable, a number of them being quite handsome. Of the pleasure grounds of the city much the most attractive is the Plaza de Carillo, situated centrally and beautifully laid out, its walks being shaded with vines and shrubbery and made charming by a profusion of flowers, while a vine-clad arbor of graceful design occupies the centre of the square.

But the principal charm of Trinidad is the beautiful scenery to be enjoyed from various high points in its vicinity. The easiest to be had, and one of the most charming, is the outlook from the Vijia, whose summit an active pedestrian can easily reach by walking. In all directions, inland and seaward, the views are beautiful, particularly when seen at the rising and the setting of the sun. The people are very hospitable, and the town, in the winter season, is gay and lively. It is very healthful, being swept by both the sea and the mountain breezes. The harbor, while spacious, is shallow, and not well protected from the open sea. Its trade is largely in sugar, there being numerous estates in the vicinity.

CIENFUEGOS.

The magnificent bay of Cienfuegos, or Jagua, to give it its proper name, like several others of the best-known bays of Cuba, has a narrow and tortuous entrance, bounded by green hills, the interior being invisible from the seaboard. The harbor is deep and spacious, admitting of vessels of twelve to fourteen feet draught being moored at its wharves, an advantage over several of the Cuban ports, while its surface is amply sheltered from the winds by the high surrounding hills. At the anchorage for large vessels there are twenty-seven feet of water. Las Casas called it the most magnificent harbor of the world, with its six square leagues of water area. Three rivers empty into it, each navigable for some distance inland, an advantage in view of the usually abominable roads of Cuba.

Cienfuegos, like Cardenas, is called an American city, a large proportion of its 27,000 people speaking English, while the great bulk of its trade is with the United States. The town is comparatively modern, a fact to its advantage, the streets being of fair width and kept in a reasonably clean condition. It lies on a level plot of ground and is a busy and active place, enjoying an excellent commerce.

As elsewhere in Cuba, the houses are one-storied, flat-roofed, and parti-colored, built in the Moorish fashion around an open *patio*, or court-yard, which is usually gay with flowering plants. The city is situated in a region admirably adapted to sugar, some of the largest and finest cane-producing estates in the world being in its vicinity. The result of this and its shipping advantages has been a rapid growth and a large commerce, the export of sugar in a prosperous year being over $9,000,000. Considerable tobacco is also exported, while the import trade is considerable.

The prosperity of the city is indicated by a number of handsome buildings, chief among which is the well known Terry Theatre, adjoining which is the largest and finest plaza on the island. This is adorned with numerous statues and with many ornamental plants. Southeast of the city rise the San Juan Mountains, whose picturesque aspect adds much to the attractiveness of the situation.

Cienfuegos has railway connection with Santa Clara, about forty miles to the northeast, and was the centre of several interesting incidents during the late war, the chief of which was its brief blockade by Commodore Schley during his search for the Spanish fleet. Here, as at Santiago, the depth of the bay and its narrow, hill-bordered entrance, prevented his seeing what lay within.

There is only one other coast town that calls for attention, Batabano, due south from Havana, and notable as occupying the original site of that city. It is little more than a village; its importance lying in its position as the terminus of the south-bound railway from Havana and the starting-point of a number of steamboat lines running to the Isle of Pines, and to Cienfuegos, Trinidad, and other southern ports.

INLAND CITIES.

Of the inland towns of note in Cuba the most westerly is the city of Pinar del Rio, capital of the province of that name, and seated in the centre of the famous tobacco region of the Vuelto Abajo. It is situated 118 miles southwest of Havana and fifteen miles from the southern coast, and has a population of about 8000. The city stands 160 feet above sea-level, on the summit of a hill seventy feet high, and has both railway and highway connection with Havana. It is the most important commercial town in the province, its principal business being the handling of tobacco.

Four miles distant is the small town of Consolacion del Sur, around which are said to be more than 800 plantations of the finest tobacco of Cuba. San Cristobal and Artemesia, towns of a few thousand population each, are important stations on the railroad which traverses the province. Candelaria, six miles from San Cristobal, is of note for its mineral springs and the excellent product of its coffee plantations. Another railway line from Havana runs to Guanajay, twenty-six miles distant, a town of over 5000 population, prettily situated in an active sugar-raising district, and about twelve miles from the sea.

The province of Havana is the most thickly settled district of the island, its towns including, in addition to those mentioned, Guara, Güines, Bejucal, Santiago de los Vegas, and San Antonio de los Baños, of from 5000 to 7000 population each, and a number of smaller size. Of the inland towns of Matanzas province, it will suffice to name Bemba (or Jovellanos), Macagua, and Colon, the latter two surrounded by great sugar estates.

The city of Santa Clara, more commonly known as Villa Clara, lies central to the province of the same name, and is connected by railway with Cienfuegos, Cardenas, and other cities. It is of considerable size, but has no particular pretensions to beauty. Founded in 1689, it has now a population of about 12,000, and lies in the midst of a mineral country, yielding gold, silver, copper, plumbago, and asphaltum. There are indications, also, of natural gas near the city. This place has a reputation for the wealth of its people and the unusual beauty of its women. Situated about 200 miles east of Havana, it forms the present termination in that direction of the railway system.

Puerto Principe was originally located at the site now occupied by Nuevitas, but in 1516 was removed to its present situation, forty-five miles inland, in order to escape piratical incursions. The modern Nuevitas serves as its port, being connected with it by railway. An Indian village named Camaguey previously occupied the site, and it was by this name that the district and city were formerly known, and are still frequently spoken of by the Cubans.

Santa Maria del Puerto Principe, to give it its full name, is the largest inland city of Cuba, its population being over 40,000, and in aspect is the most ancient and quaint on the island. It has narrow, winding streets, many of them unpaved and lacking sidewalks. There are several old churches, a theatre, government buildings, and other public edifices, most of its structures being ancient in architecture. It is surrounded by the largest grazing district in Cuba, and owes its importance to the immense herds of cattle which roam over the adjacent plains. There is also much valuable timber. There is not a hotel in the city, but the people are very hospitable to strangers. Twenty-five miles to the north is the Cubitas Mountain district, the headquarters of the Cuban insurrectionary government.

Of the remaining inland towns it will suffice to name Bayamo, in the province of Santiago de Cuba, near which Marshal Campos suffered a severe repulse at the hands of Maceo, the Cuban general; and Holguin, a city of considerable size in the same province, connected by rail with Gibara, and the scene of the last military event of the Cuban insurrection. It was besieged by Garcia with a large army and vigorously defended by its Spanish garrison after the surrender of Santiago to the American forces.

Bayamo is a very old city, founded in 1551, and is substantially built in the older Spanish style. It has eleven churches, some of them excellent examples of the ecclesiastical architecture of the past centuries.

The population is about 4000. Holguin, of some 5500 inhabitants, lies fifteen miles south of Gibara, on a high plain and in a healthful situation. Founded in 1740, it has the narrow and unpaved streets of the past, generally filthy in condition. It is very favorably situated for the development of the hard-wood industry.

HEALTH RESORTS.

Batabano is the point of departure for the two most celebrated of the many mineral spring localities of Cuba, those of San Diego and Santa Fé. The baths of San Diego, reached by rail from Havana, by boat from Batabano to Dayaniguas, and by volante from the latter place, are situated in the Pinar del Rio province, on the banks of the river Caiguanabo, which from this point takes the name of San Diego. Here is a small, neatly-built town, with numerous hotels, which are crowded during the season. The abundant waters of the springs are conducted into a number of baths, all the springs containing sulphuric and carbonic acids, sulphate of lime, bicarbonate of magnesia, and other mineral substances. The waters, used both externally and internally, are claimed to be excellent for several complaints, to which curative powers the pure hillside air undoubtedly adds. Among the scenes in the vicinity are some interesting caves, and a remarkable archway excavated by the river, 100 feet wide and sixty high, the arch divided by a grand pillar of rock.

Santa Fé, on the Isle of Pines, gains its celebrity from its pure, dry, and balmy air, healthful with the resinous odors of the pine forests, and its mineral springs, which are impregnated with carbonate and sulphate of lime, chlorides of sodium and calcium, magnesia, nitrate of lime, and other minerals. The waters are claimed to be excellent for bronchial and various other affections, and in the coming era of Cuba this locality is likely to become a favorite place of resort for invalids.

Mention has been made of the springs of Madruga and Santa Rita, and we need but speak briefly of those of San Antonio de los Baños, a small but pretty town on the river that drains the celebrated Lake Ariguanabo, about twenty-three miles from Havana. Its health-giving baths have made it a favorite place of summer resort from Havana. The San Vicente mineral springs, also of note, are near the town of Viñales, in the Pinar del Rio province.

VI. MANNERS AND CUSTOMS.
CITY LIFE.

One of the first things to strike the visitor at Havana, on his arrival in that city, is its multiplicity of bells, and the furious clanging with which, every morning, they greet the break of day, rudely dispelling sleep from all but those "to the manner born." From every church-tower they peal forth, not one but many, each doing its utmost in noise-making, until one would think that the whole town was in flames and this the tocsin of alarm. Add to this the lusty crowing of the game-cocks, which are kept in multitudes for gambling purposes, and of the plebeian cocks kept by most families as lords of their broods of fowls, and it becomes easy to understand the hasty flight of the deity of slumber.

In truth, noise is native to Havana. Its streets are paved with stone,—the heat banishes asphaltum as a paving material and the dampness would soon rot out a wood pavement. As the usual condition of the streets drives most of the people—all the ladies—to carriages, the rattle of wheels over the stone pavements is incessant, and one's ears are greeted with a constant din. The two-wheeled volante, once universal, has been succeeded by the four-wheeled victoria, of which there are thousands for public hire about the town, carriages and horses alike often the worse for wear; but prices are reasonable and the vehicles largely patronized. Street-cars also have made their way thither, and add their contingent of noise.

It is rare for a lady to venture abroad except in a vehicle, and walking, for which their tiny feet seem ill adapted, has become almost a lost art with the fair Havanese. In dancing, however, they show surprising powers of endurance, and can severely tax the staying-powers of their gentlemen friends. The Cuban ladies mature early and fade early. Marriage is common at ages at which the girls of the North have still before them years of school life, and their comeliness dies away prematurely. But at their best the ladies of Cuba are strikingly graceful in movement, their forms, though well-rounded, sylph-like in lightness, their voices low and sweet, their deep-black eyes vivacious and sparkling, their whole aspect instinct with charm. At home they dress simply in delicate muslins and linens, but abroad their costume is apt to set those with a developed color taste wild by its bold combinations of glaringly inharmonious hues, while the superabundant use of paint and powder is of no advantage to their beauty.

There is one article of dress without which a Cuban lady would be utterly lost,—the fan. Accustomed to the use of this indispensable requisite from childhood, she becomes strikingly graceful and coquettish in its use. This pretty and costly article, formed of rich materials, is wonderfully expressive in her hands,—an instrument of flirtation that seems fairly to speak in its adroit pantomime, and with which almost every desired phase of feeling may be expressed.

Lacking intellectual pursuits, these ladies fair are apt to spend the day in listless rocking and fanning, varied with gossipy chat and broken by a mid-day siesta, their labors being limited to a little sewing and embroidery. After five o'clock, life on the Pasco becomes animated; the ladies, gorgeously attired but bonnetless, wearing as head-dress only the dark tresses supplied by nature, driving in handsome carriages; the gentlemen on horseback or on foot, the broad sidewalks being filled with well-dressed promenaders. Later on they may resort to the Parque Central to enjoy the music of the military band, and chat or flirt with their admirers, winding up the evening, perhaps, in the mazy circlings of the dance or in their boxes at the theatre or opera.

In the furnishing of the houses the rocking-chair is a necessity of the situation, a well-furnished sitting-room having perhaps a dozen of these cane-seated conveniences. These, ranged, in the usual custom, in two exact lines from the window to the rear of the room, with a woollen mat between them on the floor, present an idea of order that is as inartistic as it may be thought convenient.

The broad, projecting window of Cuban dwellings, reaching from floor to ceiling, with its absence of glass and its cell-like bars of iron, reveals the interior of the dwellings to the passers-by in a way that in colder climes would not be deemed desirable, and in some cases not decorous. A loose lace curtain is sometimes used, but rarely, as the freest circulation of air is demanded; and the ladies of the household do not seem to mind being observed in dishabille. In fact, they come freely to the windows to gaze out or to chat with passing acquaintances, and may frequently be seen, like voluntary captives, "looking through the bars."

Inside the houses doors have no existence, curtains dividing room from room and from corridor. Where privacy is desired, these, usually looped back, are dropped; and it is the custom to speak before venturing to pass a closed curtain. But as the division walls between apartments, in private houses and hotels alike, often reach but two-thirds of the way to the ceiling, actual privacy is a thing out of the question. The need of a free circulation of air overpowers all other requisites in a Cuban dwelling, the people living practically in the open air, and doubtless being the better in health for so doing.

While during the day the coolest rooms of the house are sought by the family and its guests, the flat roof being left to the laundress, at night the roof is the place where all gather to enjoy the cool breeze from the ocean. At this hour the long rows of level housetops, when illumined by the beams of the moon, are cheerful and attractive with their happy family gatherings, peals of gay laughter floating across from house to house, songs, or the sound of instruments making the air musical, and from afar the music of the military band now and then swelling into audible strains. There the people often sit until late at night, smoking, chatting, and enjoying the balmy coolness of the midnight air.

Some other things may be said regarding the Cuban dwellings. One peculiarity, to a Northerner, is that such a thing as a chimney is unknown. It is the constant effort to avoid, not to invite, heat, and for this reason even wooden floors are not in use, the floors being laid in marble or tiles. There is a similar absence of carpeting, beyond the long rug which parts the rows of chairs, and mattresses are rejected for sleeping purposes in favor of stretched canvas beds, with upper and under sheets. But an indispensable requisite of sleeping-apartments is the mosquito netting, if one wishes to enjoy his slumber in comfort.

While the Cuban ladies during the day are homekeepers, the men, as a rule, look upon their dwellings only as sleeping, not as living, places. The average Cuban rarely takes his meals at home, his spare hours being given to his club, while cafés and restaurants flourish under his constant patronage. As a result of this neglect of home life, the domestic virtues are at a low ebb in Cuba. The almost utter absence of books and reading matter, the lack of occupation for women of the higher class, the neglect of their homes by the men, all tend to such a result, and a lowered condition of morals is naturally to be expected under such circumstances.

Business, of course, demands a period of attention; but many dispose of this in the mornings, and spend the remainder of the day in festive relaxation, in the cafés or in worse places, yielding to the enervating influence of the climate and passing their time in lassitude and luxurious ease. Love of music is universal, as with the natives of warm climates generally; and the band concerts at the Plaza de Armas or the Parque Central attract multitudes of appreciative listeners, the ladies in full evening dress, in their carriages or on the seats of the square, the gentlemen promenading and chatting.

At night, in the fashionable drinking-saloons, gather multitudes of the lovers of sport and excitement, drawn thither by the blaze of light reflected by a profusion of mirrors, the noise and vivacity, and the gambling that is to be seen openly and everywhere, —games of dominoes, chess, checkers, or cards going on at which all stake their money, lookers-on as well as players. All classes congregate there, and the gaming continues until late in the night, while drinking is continual, though not usually of strong liquors. Of course, there are cafés which ladies can patronize, and in which ices and sherbets are to be had equal to those served in the United States. The ice-creams, indeed, are not up to the best American standard, but the sherbets, flavored with the luscious native fruits, are delicious. Ladies accompanied by gentlemen visit these places freely. If alone, they are served in their carriages at the door.

Smoking is universal in Cuba, all classes, from the highest to the lowest, constantly fumigating themselves with tobacco, and ladies indulging in cigarette smoking almost as freely as the men. Everywhere and on all occasions the people of all classes smoke, —between the courses at meals, in the office, the street, the café, the theatre, at feasts and at funerals. Gentlemen able to purchase them are said to consume the equivalent of a dozen cigars each day, and the ladies sometimes half that quantity, though of late years the cigarette has largely taken the place of the cigar, and is used to an extent that keeps a large class of the population busy in its manufacture. Snuff-taking and chewing, on the contrary, are very rare, smoke being the favorite mode of disposing of the weed.

In the summer season, those who wish to escape the mid-day heats may make excursions to a number of attractive places in the vicinity, where pure and fresh air can be breathed. One of these is Maricanao, a neat and pretty village, reached by a short railroad journey, and much frequented by those who wish to escape from the city heat to a cooler and more airy situation. There are various pleasant walks, rich with tropical vegetation; while the mineral springs found here furnish another attraction, and surf-bathing may be enjoyed on the near-by sea-shores. About half-way back to Havana is a smaller but not less pretty village, Puentes Grandes, also a place of summer resort. At Guanabacoa, the baths of Santa Rita, of which we have already spoken, attract numbers of visitors.

Those wealthy enough to make longer and more expensive flittings may spend the hot season in cool retreats among the hills, in their comfortable country-houses, or may seek the medicinal waters of San Diego, Santa Fé, or some of the various other mineral springs of Cuba, whose waters are used for both drinking and bathing.

Havana is well provided with facilities for bathing, there being a number of well-arranged private establishments in addition to the sea-water baths excavated from the coral rocks. These are somewhat fairly patronized by the men of the city, though neither men nor women seem overly inclined to indulgence in the bath. As for the Cuban women, it seems to be a question whether they ever bathe at all. Some claim that a full bath with a woman consists in moistening the corner of a towel with rum and rubbing with it hands, face, and neck,—though one cannot help thinking this a libel as applied to ladies of the well-bred class. But it is certain that the Cubans do not practise the personal cleanliness of natives of many other tropical lands.

One thing further needs to be said here of Cuban society, that childhood disappears at so early an age that it can be but half enjoyed. One may observe boys and girls of but ten or twelve years of age dressed like young ladies and gentlemen; walking arm and arm, with a ludicrous aping of the fashions of their elders, in the park paths; or attending balls, their faces painted and their forms bedizened in the Cuban fashion; though childhood is apt to reassert itself by their falling asleep in odd corners during the height of the festivities. Small boys with high hats and evening dress-suits, and little girls in long dresses with low necks, look like foolish masqueraders, while these children are versed in the habits of those three times their age, and are familiar with much that seems foreign to childish life. Indeed, at twelve the women are not far short of the marriageable age; and it is common to find sedate mothers of families at twenty.

Hospitality is a trait for which the people of Cuba receive much credit, and fairly so to some extent, though it takes on strange manifestations that mean nothing but the language of compliment. The fashion is one imported from Spain. When one enters for the first time a Cuban mansion, the host and hostess are profuse in placing all their possessions at his service —without an idea that he will think of accepting the offer. Praise an article, be it ring, picture, or other article of value, and you are at once told that it is yours—though it would be the reverse of good breeding for you to attempt to take the giver at his word. In smaller matters hospitality is not wanting, though one may soon wear out his welcome. Flattery is a very common trait, and profuse compliment to ladies is so freely dealt in that they accept it as a matter of course, knowing well how much it is worth. It need hardly be said that this extravagant outward show is lip service only, and that for truly generous treatment ladies must seek colder climes.

A subject which calls for passing attention is the remarkable development of Freemasonry in Cuba, particularly in view of the active opposition of the Catholic Church to the Masonic brotherhood. In proportion to the population there are more Masons in Cuba than in any other country in the world. This helps to show the slight hold which the Church has upon the Cubans, many of whom, restricted by state enactment to the tenets of one religious sect, have sought Freemasonry as an acceptable substitute. The rites of Masonry gratify the religious instinct inherent in all mankind, sustaining the worship of the Supreme Being in freedom from sectarian trammels; while the aid in times of need extended by the society to its brotherhood has helped largely in making it popular. It has been bitterly opposed by the Church. At times attendance on a Masonic meeting has been deemed a crime equal to that of high treason. Some of the captain-generals, being Masons themselves, have supported the order; others have bitterly persecuted it; but it has survived all opposition, and is a living and important element in Cuban society to-day.

FOOD AND BEVERAGES.

Something has been already said about the Cuban hotels. These we cannot fairly speak of as good, bad, and indifferent, since the first adjective rarely applies in the case of a guest accustomed to northern hotel life. Without further reference to their general accommodations, or lack of accommodation, we shall confine ourselves here to some remarks about what they offer to satisfy the appetite.

It is the custom in Cuba, on rising, to break the fast with a cup of coffee or chocolate, and a roll or morsel of dry toast,—" Coffee with or without milk?" being about the first question one hears after being awakened by the clanging of the bells. Fruit is also used to some extent. Cubans, however, prefer to reserve the fruit to begin their breakfast with, the hours for this meal ranging from nine to eleven.

In the hotels the lower floor is used for the commonalty and for business purposes, the dining-room and parlor for guests being on the second floor, the table well supplied with colored glass, silver, and other table-ware; while the parlor is inviting with its cool-looking floor of marble, its flower-stand, and its easy-going rocking-chairs, in which one may nap at will.

Eggs in some of the many ways in which Cubans cook them form the opening dish at breakfast, stewed tomatoes being poured over them when poached, and boiled rice served with them. One may have his choice of fish, there being many kinds. These are best fried in olive oil, served dry and well browned. Shrimps are abundant, and form a wholesome and favorite dish, eaten with salt or as a salad. The meats follow, being generally, for breakfast, stewed or broiled liver, mutton chops, veal, or beefsteak,—the last forming usually rather poor provender in Cuba. One or two hashes are served, and for vegetables fried potatoes, and fried or roasted plantains or bananas. The sweet potato is of excellent quality. As a relish, watercress, an abundant product of the island, is served. Fruits are usually supplied in profusion, and, as a dish native to the island, guava jelly with cheese, a favorite Cuban relish. The inevitable cigarette and *café solo*, or coffee without milk, conclude the meal.

As for butter, the least said about it the better. The firm, sweet, fragrant butter of the north is alien to the Cuban climate; instead you will receive a soft, yellowish material in a wide-mouthed bottle, of which the sight is likely to quite satisfy the appetite.

Dinner is taken in the evening, after the day's work is over and the torrid heat is modified. It is sufficiently elaborate, but presents nothing peculiar, a considerable variety of soups, fish, and meats being served, with the limited number of vegetables that Cuba can boast,—sweet potatoes, tomatoes, beans, cabbage, and lettuce. Rice, indeed, is the most common vegetable. Then comes a custard or canned fruit,—pastry being rarely served,—followed by coffee and the ubiquitous cigar. A peculiarity is that the entire meal is served at once, with the exception of the dessert,—this alike at home and in hotels,—the custom of serving in courses not having been introduced.

A considerable variety of drinks serve the Cubans as cooling or refreshing beverages, first and most common of all being the *Vino Catalan*, a wine sold very cheaply, and found on every table, whether of rich or poor. At the café it largely takes the place of water. It is a very strong wine, of dark claret color, and is generally diluted. Ale is as common a beverage, of excellent quality, and found everywhere.

Coffee is one of the most common of drinks, with milk on rising, without milk after eating. The national drink of the island is the *naranjada*, or orangeade, a favorite and very agreeable beverage. *Limonada*, or lemonade, is also much used, though usually made from limes. The Cuban chocolate cannot be surpassed. Made of the consistency of thick gruel, and served in delicate little cups, its nutritious quality renders it an excellent thing to take when a long ride is contemplated.

The Cubans are fond of drinking, and drinking-saloons and bar-rooms are everywhere in evidence, where strong liquors are dispensed, gin in particular. This is sold at a very low price, and seems to be drunk freely by the common people; yet the rare appearance of a drunken man goes to indicate that the Cubans are a very sober people.

They have numerous non-intoxicating drinks, of which the most common and popular is made of white sugar and water, with the yelk of an egg. Other popular beverages are *orchata*, a milk-white drink made of almond juice and sugar; *agrass*, a slightly acid drink made from the juice of unripe grapes; *cebada*, or barley-water, and various others. What are known as *panales* are made of the white of eggs and sugar. Two or three of these, placed in a glass of water and allowed to dissolve, with a few drops of lime-juice, make a cooling and delicious drink. A summer beverage is made by adding a little gin to cocoa-nut water, and somewhat stronger drinks by mixing absinthe with water or with aniseed decoction.

STREET SCENES.

For the principal retail business establishments of Havana we must seek certain streets of the old town, Riela, Obispo, and O'Reilly Streets, running to the bay, and Mercaderes Street, crossing these at right angles. Obispo Street is one of the liveliest in the city, its rows of well-filled stores extending from the bay to the old walls; while the bustle of carriages and of people on foot keep it in a state of incessant activity. The shops are usually quite open in front, and with their queer names, the narrowness of the streets, and the colored awnings above, form a peculiar and curious spectacle to foreign eyes.

There are many fine stores for the sale of dry-goods, millinery, china, glassware, jewelry, and other articles of taste and luxury. Silver-ware and jewelry stores are particularly numerous, and present a glittering appearance with their display of well-filled glass cases and of rich wares on the shelves. In shopping, ladies rarely leave their carriages,—goods being brought out to them at the sidewalk, while dress-goods are usually sent to the homes of customers to be examined and selected from. The custom is to ask a price beyond that expected to be paid, which is usually reduced about one-half before the bargain is struck.

One peculiarity of Havana is its mingling of high and low life,—the pretentious mansion often standing at close elbows with the humble dwelling of the artisan, or even the negro hut. In the business quarter a handsome private house may stand beside a shabby-looking warehouse; while people of the best class do not hesitate to live in or over stores or warehouses, a well-appointed dwelling often occupying the second floor of a stirring place of business, entrance being made, perhaps, through the litter of a grocer's shop or other undesirable surroundings.

Within the places of business life often goes on in a wholesomely patriarchal fashion. The passer-by may see the merchant and his clerks seated at their breakfast in full view of the street, the table not infrequently spread in the store itself. About noon business suffers a general interregnum; the hour of the siesta has come, and sleep for an interval seals the eyes of the late active multitude, merchants and laborers, men and women, yielding to the gentle influence of the god of slumber.

Aside from the stores, the streets themselves are full of busy and curious scenes, peripatetic venders taking possession of the contracted avenues, and making the air echo with their cries. Here are the fruit-venders, their horses provided with panniers laden deeply with oranges and other native fruits, whose virtues they vociferously proclaim. After them may come a poultry-dealer, mounted on a donkey between two baskets filled with live chickens, which thrust their helpless heads through the net-work covering and plaintively announce their presence. Here comes a *dulce* seller, basket on head or arm and waiter of sweetmeats in hand, mainly the preserved fruits of the country. Next may appear a Chinaman, a coolie freed from service and now seeking by the sale of crockery to gain money enough to carry him home again. Instead of shouting his wares, he signifies his presence by a sharp, rattling sound, made by dexterously manipulating a handful of plates.

Most singular of these venders is the milkman, who, instead of carting his milk in cans, usually drives the cows themselves from door to door, milking for each customer the quantity demanded, and then passing on to the next. At times a calf follows, muzzled to prevent its interference, while its presence induces the cow to yield her milk more freely. Of course the needs of the calf occasionally have to be attended to. This is a custom imported from Southern Spain and Italy, and one which has the advantage of assuring a fresh, pure article.

Occasionally one of the narrow streets is filled almost from side to side by a deeply-laden donkey, whose head and legs alone appear under its widespreading load of green fodder, brought to the city for horse-feed, and constituting, with corn, the only provender of Havana horses. Oats or other grains are not raised on the island, and the stalks and soft ears of unripe maize and the tender tops of the sugar-cane are alone fed to the equine family.

To return to the subject of Chinese coolies, previously mentioned, it may be said that as laborers they have long since proved failures as plantation hands, and none have been brought to Cuba for several years. They were unsuited to the climate and the service, and during their eight-year term of contract the mortality among them is said to have reached as high as sixty-seven per cent. Of those that survived, many of them became lame, half-starved, ragged mendicants, numbers of them being blind. Those able to work are engaged in cigar-making, keep small stores or fruit stands, or otherwise seek by honest industry to save enough to return to their native land. There are no laundrymen among them, as in the United States, the women of color quite absorbing this occupation.

Aside from the coolies, beggars are abundant, Havana having its small army of them; while the same may be said of all the cities that have grown up under the influence of Spain. These gentry have their harvest on Saturdays. It is the custom for shops and families to supply themselves with a quantity of small rolls of bread baked for the purpose, one being usually given to every mendicant who applies on that day. Carrying a large canvas bag for their gratuities, they usually obtain enough, eked out with other gifts of food, to keep them alive during the week.

Among the habitants of the street, the negro, in every shade of complexion from deep black to dusky white, is always and everywhere to be seen. The free negroes have long been disposed to seek the cities and large towns, where they form a healthy and vigorous part of the population,—often an idle and vicious part. They act as porters, stevedores, and light laborers in various pursuits, the negro women doing all the washing and ironing, and spending a fair percentage of their gains in the cheap jewelry and gaudy attire in which they love to flaunt. Attire, however, is never wasted on their progeny, the negro children of both sexes being left in a state of complete nudity until they are nine or ten years of age. In the country the same practice prevails in regard to white children, while in the hot season laborers generally wear just the modicum of clothing that decency demands.

Sunday is by no means a day of rest and worship in Cuba. Ordinary occupations go on, while the churches are so thinly attended that the services seem performed almost to the empty air. Out-doors all the ordinary sports and amusements are intensified. The day opens with a combined ringing of bells, noise of trumpets, and roll of drums, accentuated by the firing of cannon from the forts. It is the day set aside for the military review, the bull-fight, and the masked ball. The stores are open, street venders are busy as usual, open-air performances of all kinds are to be seen, from the Punch and Judy show to athletic exhibitions and gambling devices of various kinds. Everything seems in full activity except religious observances, which are almost lost in the general attention to secular pursuits. Churches are not lacking; in fact, they are somewhat over numerous; but their visitors are mainly children and negro women, white women being rarely seen, while to Cuban men in general Sunday is but a day of revelry. Only on festive occasions are the churches thronged.

THE GAMBLING PROPENSITY.

The Cubans are born gamblers. In the clubs, the cafés, all places of relaxation, games of chance are in constant activity, and betting is the universal custom. The government, instead of seeking to check this propensity, has taken advantage of it and done its utmost to encourage it. There has long been a government lottery at Havana, with semi-monthly drawings; while the selling of lottery tickets, usually in fractional parts, is one of the recognized and active industries. These are openly hawked in all places of public resort, and the demand seems equal to the supply, since almost every one invests in them, rich and poor, white and black alike. It is customary for mercantile houses to invest a certain sum monthly in these drawings, with the forlorn hope that some time the great prize may be drawn. The story is told that some years ago a number of slaves on a plantation clubbed together to buy a ticket, which drew a prize of $40,000. They bought their freedom, sixteen of them in all. Of these, two returned to Africa, four joined the insurgents in 1870, and the remainder soon killed themselves with dissipation. It is difficult to find any one in Cuba who is the better off for his prizes from the lottery, though for years it has netted the government more than $1,000,000 annually.

It seemed a severe example of tyranny to the good people of Santiago when, in 1898, General Wood, the American military governor, ordered that this open gambling should cease. The people grumbled, but obeyed; only, perhaps, to make up for the deprivation in secret. Once the land is their own there will undoubtedly be open doors to the gambling fraternity again, for the practice is ingrained in the Cuban constitution.

Of the gaming amusements of Cuban cities the cock-pit is one of the most frequented, the love of cock-fighting being as fully developed in the native Cuban as that of gambling. The pit is a circular enclosure, always crowded with eager observers and gamesters, and daily a very considerable amount of money changes ownership in this cruel amusement. The birds are of a native breed, said to be superior to the English game-cock in pluck and endurance.

Cruel as this sport is, it falls below that of the bull-fight, another favorite Cuban amusement, exhibitions being given at Havana every Sunday afternoon. The arena, situated in the Regla suburb of the city, has seats for some 10,000 persons, surrounding a space of about an acre in extent, in which the sanguinary contests take place. These it is not our purpose to describe. It will suffice to say that they serve as occasions to exercise the universal passion for betting, and that money is lost and won freely on the performances of favorite bulls and matadores.

Holy week is the occasion in which religious observance gains special control in Havana,—though the season of serious devotion is followed by an utter wildness of merry-making. The seeming devoutness of the Cubans during this week, from Palm Sunday onward, would go far to convince any one then landing in Havana that he was in a country of earnest worshippers. Solemnity prevails. On Sunday the cathedral is thronged, each person seeking to obtain a branch of holy palm from the priests. On Holy Thursday, as midday arrives, the clanging bells of the churches suddenly cease to ring, and almost in a minute every vehicle disappears from the streets. The garrison, with reversed arms, marches silently through the principal avenues. The flags on forts and shipping are lowered to half-mast, and the churches draped in mourning. On Friday an effigy of the Saviour is solemnly carried through the streets, all who follow uncovering their heads, while devout women frequently kneel in the street as it passes.

On Saturday, at ten in the morning, a merry peal suddenly sounds from the cathedral bells; the other churches follow; solemnity suddenly gives way to gayety, vehicles once more crowd the streets, holiday flags wave in the breeze, the cannon roar from every fort, and madness seems to take possession of the populace.

Money is now spent with unwonted freedom, and all places of public entertainment do a thriving business,—the people having saved up for a season of free spending in carnival week. The public masquerade balls attract multitudes of all classes. Chief among these is that held on Sunday night at the Tacon Theatre, with which the merry-making closes. Here the parquette is floored over and the entire lower floor converted into a grand ball-room. The galleries and boxes are thronged with spectators. Two military bands alternate in playing all night long. Shortly after midnight an emblematic dance is performed by a trained party of men, women, and boys, all masked and in costume. Near morning the affair ends in a lively frolic. There is suspended at a distance above the floor a large paper globe, which blindfolded volunteers, armed with sticks, walk towards and try to hit. Their failures are greeted with shouts of laughter, which are kept up until some one hits the bag fairly, when down come its contents of bonbons, toys, and trinkets amid a general shout of applause and a wild scramble for the prizes. Meanwhile the streets are thronged with maskers and mummers and the wildest license of merriment prevails. On every Sunday afternoon during the carnival and Lenten periods the Prado is filled with a solid line of carriages, occupied by maskers in fancy costumes, and the fun of pelting everybody in sight with flowers, paper rolls, and small bags of flour goes actively on.

RURAL LIFE.

The markets of Havana and the other large cities of Cuba introduce us to a phase of life not native to city streets, that of the *Montero*, or countryman, hundreds of whom enter the city in the early morning to dispose of the produce of their farms or gardens, long lines of mules or horses, their panniers well laden with food stuffs, serving as means of carriage. They bring with them sweet potatoes, onions, and cabbages,—the principal vegetables sold in Cuban markets,—fruits in considerable variety, and *maloja*, or horse fodder, an inferior kind of corn that grows with such lack of labor as to suit the laziness of many of the small truck farmers, and which is not allowed to ripen, but is cut green for fodder.

Let us follow these swarthy-skinned market-men to their homes and observe them in their native atmosphere.

The Montero is none too fond of labor. He may plough a little,—his plough perhaps the crooked stick of immemorial times,—and do some little work in his fields; but he is apt to hire a negro to do the most of this labor, and confine his share of the work to gathering the produce and taking it to market. Cultivation is an easy process; the fertility of the soil can be safely trusted to; little more is demanded than to thrust the seed into the ground and leave the growing of the crop to unassisted nature.

In truth, the fertility of the soil of the Cuban lowlands is something marvellous. While the mountains are mainly composed of coral rock, the soil of the plains and valleys seems largely made up of fossil matter of oceanic origin, and is extremely rich in the vital elements of lime and phosphate,—so inexhaustibly rich, indeed, that fertilizers are rarely used except for tobacco. On some of the old sugar plantations the land has borne the same crop for a hundred years without fertilization.

Provided by nature with such a soil as this, the Montero does little to improve it, satisfied to get through life with the least labor possible. The *estancia*, or market-produce farm, varying from a dozen to over a hundred acres in size, is used largely for growing maloja, for raising poultry, and for pasturing cattle,—chickens, eggs, milk, and cheese being produced for city consumption. Only a small part of the farm is devoted to garden stuff, which cannot be grown successfully without skill and attention, and another section is devoted to melons, plantains, and sweet potatoes, maloja usually occupying more than half the farm.

As a result, though the land is capable of producing the greatest variety and profusion of food stuffs, the city markets are none too well supplied, and much food is imported that might be abundantly produced on the island. No grain is raised except Indian corn, and this mainly to be cut green for fodder. The soil is not suited for cereals; and it is said that there is not a flour-mill on the island, the United States supplying Cuba with its flour. In many of the estancias the business of cultivating the soil is abandoned for that of burning the coral rock of the island into lime, only enough corn being raised to feed the draught oxen used to transport the lime to market.

On the larger estancias fruits are grown in considerable variety, the orange, the lemon, the mango, various kinds of melons, etc., it only being necessary in this culture to plant the seed and pluck the fruit. Nature has made the island a garden, and with careful and intelligent cultivation it could be made to yield a superabundance of fruits and vegetables, but as managed barely enough is grown to prevent scarcity in the neighboring cities.

"The rural population of the island," says a Cuban authority, "has rusticity, but not the boasted simplicity of the European peasant. Our countryman is astute though frank, boastful though brave, and superstitious if not religious. His ruling passions are gambling (particularly at cock-fights, of which he is very fond) and coffee, which he drinks at all hours; his favorite food pork and the plantain, usually roasted."

When in ordinary dress he wears a pair of loose pantaloons, with a leather girdle at the waist, a shirt of fancy colors, his bare feet thrust into slippers, a handkerchief on his head or around his neck, and a broad-brimmed palm-leaf hat. A coat is rarely worn, and the shirt is oftener outside than inside the pantaloons.

The Montero is a born horseman, and never stirs from home except upon the back of his favorite steed. He is accustomed from childhood to the saddle, and there are no better riders anywhere. The Cuban horse is small and delicate of limb, but can carry a heavy weight, and has great powers of endurance. It is docile, eats little, and needs no shelter. It can be thoroughly trusted not to wander away from its master's house. It was to this class of horses that the insurrectionists owed much of their success. They were all horsemen, and as skilful as Indians when in the saddle.

The women deserve the credit of being more industrious than the men, as they have their domestic duties to attend to, and often superintend the farm and weave a little cotton for home use. Sufficient cotton is grown for this purpose; but, though the finest quality of sea-island cotton can be grown at points along the coast, its cultivation has not proved a success. They also prepare from egg-shells Cascarilla powder, so favorite a cosmetic with Cuban ladies that over 100,000 pounds of it are annually consumed.

The woman dresses as simply as the man,—a *camison*, or frock, a kerchief around her neck, and slippers on her bare feet constituting her usual attire. On her head is worn a broad-brimmed straw hat. The children are dressed still more simply, being left in a state of nature until nine or ten years of age. These people marry very young,—from thirteen to fifteen for girls, from sixteen to eighteen for youths. Their families are almost always large, and the chief increase of the population takes place in the rural districts. There is abundant room for them, for nine-tenths of the soil of the island await cultivation.

The dwellings of the rural population are of the simplest kind, being little more than one-story huts, put together with poles and palm leaves, and thatched sufficiently to keep out the rain. Air is welcomed, and if a door is added it always stands open. The floor is often of earth, and the hut contains a living-room and one or two sleeping-rooms, while a roofed passage connects it with out-buildings, where the women perform their cooking and other household labors.

These people differ in their customs, and even in their food, from the inhabitants of the cities. They take but two meals a day; though coffee is inordinately used, being drunk at morning and night and at intervals during the day, particularly when a guest appears. They are freely hospitable, and the guest who is present at meal-time is expected to take a seat at the table without waiting for an invitation. To fail to do so would be an offence.

The morning meal of the small farmer consists of fried pork and boiled rice, with roasted plantains in place of bread. The dinner embraces the same viands with the exception of the pork, which is replaced with beef, roast pig, or game; or, more commonly, with *ajiaco*, the national dish, a favorite stew composed of fresh meat and vegetables of various kinds, with plenty of broth. Rice is cooked in it, and it forms a cheap, palatable, and nutritious dish. Various other savory dishes are used, which need not be described.

Amusements are not wanting to the Monteros. In addition to their favorite cock-fight, they have a goose-fight, not less cruel, in which the sport consists in the effort to pluck the head off a live goose when at full gallop. There are various religious feasts and festivals, celebrated by processions, games, dancing, and other sports. During the carnival, or other seasons of merry-making, it is a common custom, in the Vuelta Arriba, for groups of masked and oddly costumed horsemen to ride through the streets with grotesque antics. Their dances have much in them that is peculiar, many of the old-fashioned customs, long vanished in the cities, being retained.

The rural Cubans are glaringly ignorant. Books

and schools are unknown among them, and the inhabitants of Central Africa are not more lacking in intellectual cultivation. Indolence and ignorance, indeed, are their prevailing characteristics. They are as much addicted as the city people to gambling, but less so to drinking, being in the latter respect very temperate. They seem to have no taste for ardent spirits, the extent of their indulgence being to drink the ordinary claret of the country, and anything stronger is seldom imbibed.

The recent insurrection in Cuba was most severely felt by these helpless country people; the young men joining in numbers the Cuban army, the old men, women, and children being driven under Weyler's orders to the cities, their houses and crops destroyed, and they left to perish in thousands of starvation. Not less than 200,000 of them are said to have met this cruel fate.

Let us now seek the very different scene of plantation life, and observe how time passes in the mansion of a sugar planter. This we find to be strikingly unlike the humble home and life of the Montero. As a rule, the houses of the planters are large and roomy stone mansions, with immense doors and windows, as in city houses, the windows without glass. Tiles of burnt clay or marble cover the floor, and no provision is made for fire, it being a rare occasion when need of this is felt in Cuban air.

In front and rear there are usually spacious piazzas, whose coolness causes them to be frequently used as dining- and sitting-rooms, the sun being kept out by curtains of canvas lowered from the roof. Nearly always the houses are of one story, and every provision is made to insure coolness. There is a large hall, on whose sides are suites of bed-chambers and sitting-rooms, while in the rear is the court-yard, bounded on one side by rooms for servants, offices, etc., on the other, perhaps, by stables, a wall closing the rear. The court-yard in some cases is used for horses and as a playground for children; but more tasteful families convert it into a beautiful garden, planted with fruit trees and with the fragrant flowers of the island.

In these mansions lazy comfort is the rule of the day for the family, easy-chairs being everywhere, in which one can pass the slow hours with a book or a chat, dropping off at suitable intervals into the land of dreams. A game of billiards or of cards can be had for those fond of these amusements, and a gallop around the plantation serves to break the monotony of the day. In this out-door exercise one may see numbers of mills in busy operation, fields of the waving cane spreading far before the eyes, and along the roads bordering hedges of the beautiful *Piña Raton*, or *maya*, which is the fence generally used in Cuba, varied rarely by the Mexican *maguey*, with its broad, saw-edged leaves.

The piña bears some resemblance to the maguey, and grows high, with a thick, strong stem, the leaves being dentated and ending in sharp points. While the outer leaves are of a bright green, those within are of an intense vermilion color, the exquisitely tinted flowers nestling in their centre. Long miles of this bright-colored hedge give a peculiar and pleasing effect to a Cuban landscape.

The ladies of the country mansion, we may say, usually prefer the cities to the plantations, and are apt to visit their country-homes at rare intervals only. A few weeks are passed there in the summer, and generally there is a lively party and a gay frolic at Christmas. When the proprietors are wealthy much style is observed during the presence of the ladies,— the servants being in showy livery, the service elegant, and ladies and gentlemen alike in full dress. But under ordinary circumstances show is dispensed with, and life is passed in the easiest and least troublesome way available,—the ladies indulging in the ease of the rocking-chair, the gentlemen looking after the interests of the estate, or spending their time in sports and amusements.

The estate has, in addition to the mansion, the dwellings of the laborers,—often the rudest of huts,—a hospital for the sick, and various other buildings; most important of which, of course, is the sugar-mill, of which we must reserve a description for a later section.

VII. AGRICULTURAL PRODUCTIONS.

COFFEE.

Cuba, with its remarkably fertile soil, its abundant rainfall, and its tropical climate, possesses vast capabilities in agricultural production, though as yet only a small proportion of its soil has been cultivated, and that in a half-hearted way. With skill, energy, and enterprise, such as may be applied to this rich land in the near future under American influence, its productive powers can be greatly increased, and it may be made one of the garden spots of the earth.

We have already described its varied fruits and spoken of its minor farming operations. It remains to deal more at length with its three leading crops, coffee, sugar, and tobacco, which have formed the foundation of the prosperity of the island and furnished the main elements of its commerce. One of these, coffee, has become, however, largely a thing of the past; its culture having in great part vanished before the competition of Brazil, Java, and other countries which used improved machinery to diminish the cost of production, and of the more profitable sugar culture of the island. The industry received a severe blow from the destructive hurricanes of 1843 and 1846, which brought ruin to many of the estates. These were followed by a long succession of wet years, under which the culture rapidly declined. As a result, coffee was widely replaced by sugar-cane, and the industry has since then languished. Yet the mountainsides and highlands of the eastern section of the island are especially suited to this crop; coffee of excellent quality can be produced, and there seems no reason why this once important industry should not be revived. As it is, the insurrections have aided greatly in checking its progress, and to-day Cuba does not produce enough coffee for its own consumption.

The cultivation of the coffee-plant was introduced from the neighboring islands early in the eighteenth century; though it was not until the end of the century, when the negro revolution in San Domingo drove many of the French planters from that island to Cuba, that it became active. Numbers of these refugees settled in the vicinity of Trinidad and Santiago, where their industry converted long-neglected lands into productive plantations, and for many years afterwards coffee was a very profitable crop.

Its decline is largely due to persistence in antiquated methods of culture and to the exactions of the Spanish government, whose severe tariff charges on exported coffee, and internal taxes on that for local consumption, have discouraged planters and prevented the recovery of the industry. Under new conditions and with skill and economy in its cultivation there seems no reason why coffee should not again become an important crop.

The coffee-plant is an evergreen shrub, which bears oblong berries, green at first, then bright red, and finally purple. Each berry—of about the size of a cranberry or small cherry—contains two seeds, enveloped in pulp; the seeds, when ripe, being semi-elliptical in shape and of a horny hardness. In planting, holes are made four or five inches apart and a number of seeds placed in each. After the appearance of the shoot, which requires about forty days, the plant is kept carefully weeded, and allowed to grow for two years, at which time plants that are thirty inches high are cropped. Fruit first appears at the end of the third year, and becomes abundant at the end of the fourth. Under good conditions, the plants continue in bearing for thirty or more years, though as they grow older they yield well only every alternate year. Coffee is the poor man's crop. It does not need the extensive operations and costly machinery of sugar to be made profitable, and may be raised with profit on small estates. The mountain regions of the Santiago de Cuba province are specially adapted to it, though it extended over much of the island during its period of prosperity. This period ended with the rebellion of 1868, which was largely confined to Santiago de Cuba, and put an end generally to industrial operations in that province. After the close of the insurrection, coffee culture began again in many localities; but the 1895 outbreak completely checked operations, and few, if any, coffee estates now remain.

Aside from its utility, the coffee culture has a reason for existence in the remarkable beauty of the plantations, which the tropics present nothing to surpass. We cannot better show the truth of this statement than in the following extract from Ballou's "Due South:"

"As the sugar plantation surpasses the coffee in wealth, so the coffee estate surpasses the sugar in every natural beauty and attractiveness. A coffee plantation, well and properly laid out, is one of the

AGRICULTURAL PRODUCTIONS.

most beautiful gardens that can well be conceived of, in its variety and loveliness baffling description. An estate devoted to this purpose usually covers a hundred acres, more or less, planted in regular squares of one acre or thereabouts, intersected by broad alleys lined with palms, mangoes, bananas, oranges, and other fruits; as the coffee, unlike the sugar-cane, requires partial protection from the ardor of the sun. Mingled with the trees are lemons, limes, pomegranates, Cape jasmines, and a species of wild heliotrope, fragrant as the morning. Occasionally, in the wide reach of the estate, there is seen a solitary, broad-spreading ceiba, in hermit-like isolation from other trees, but shading a fragrant undergrowth.

"Conceive of this beautiful arrangement, and then of the whole when in flower; the coffee, with its milk-white blossoms, so abundant that it seems as though a pure white cloud of snow had fallen there, and left the rest of the vegetation fresh and green. Interspersed in these fragrant alleys dividing the coffee-plants is the red of the Mexican rose, the flowering pomegranate, the yellow jasmine, and the large, gaudy flower of the penon, shrouding its parent stem in a cloak of scarlet. Here, too, are seen clusters of the graceful yellow flag, and many wild flowers, unknown by name, entwining their tender stems about the base of the fruit trees. In short, a coffee plantation is a perfect floral paradise, full of fragrance and repose."

In addition to the plants named, rice, plantain, cacao, tamarind, and the cocoa-nut palm are planted on the coffee estate, adding at once to the beauty of the fields and the profit of the culture. Along the roadways leading from the dwelling-house through the fields the royal palm and other attractive trees are grown in long, graceful rows, forming in time stately and charming avenues.

The coffee-plant begins to blossom in February, the blossoming continuing through most of the spring. This is the season when the fields display their greatest beauty; the green, waxy leaves, starred with their multitude of white blossoms, extending as far as the eye can reach, while above them tower the banana with its massive green cluster, the cacao with its red and yellow fruit, the rose-tinted pomegranate, the loftier cocoa-nut, with its heavy clusters of nuts, and other fruit-bearing plants, the whole presenting a vision of tropical plenty and luxuriance.

The coffee-berry begins to attain maturity in September, and continues to ripen until November, all the hands on the estate, men, women, and children, now taking part in the picking, in which each has a daily task to perform. About a quarter of a pound per bush is the average yield, half a pound being a large yield. The bags, as fast as they are filled, are taken on mule-back to the coffee-house, where the overseer measures the fruit sent in by each hand to see if the allotted share of work has been performed.

In the process of preparing for market, the pulping-mill is the principal piece of machinery. This consists of a circular canal, with ribbed sides, round which rolls a large wooden wheel, worked by steam- or water-power. The berries are placed in the canal and the wheel is rolled over them, for the purpose of breaking and loosening the rind. The coffee-house, in which this is done, is usually a large frame or stone building.

AGRICULTURAL PRODUCTIONS.

The berries are next placed in a large, dry, stone basin, where they remain for twelve hours, in order that the pulp enclosing the seeds may ferment. Water is then let in, and this substance—a slimy, mucous gum—is washed away. The next process is that of drying. The berries are spread on the *secadores*, or drying terraces, and left to dry in the sun; the process requiring from seven to ten days if the weather continues dry. The secadores are quadrangular stone basins, fifty or sixty feet long by twenty or thirty wide, arranged in terraces on a hill-side, numbering perhaps a dozen in all. They stand about three feet high, and are enclosed by a low stone coping, their plastered floors sloping from centre to sides, that the water may drain off in case of rain.

Should rain threaten, the berries are hastily raked up into a large heap in the centre and covered by a conical shield of thatch or palm leaves, which sheds the water. The same is done at night as a protection from the dew.

When fully dried, each berry is enclosed by a dry and dark-colored pellicle. After the whole crop is dried the berries are placed again in the pulping-mill, whose heavy wheel now cracks the dry skin, the two grains of coffee—the seeds of the plant—being set free. A fanning-mill, like that used by our own farmers, is then brought into use to dispose of the chaff-like skins. Now, for a third time, the grains are put into the pulping-mill, this time to color them,—the color of coffee as we get it not being that given by nature. Lamp-black is added, to the amount of half an ounce to a thousand pounds of grains; or other substances, such as soapstone and white lead, may be used, if a different shade of color is required. This process is called polishing.

The sorting process follows, the coffee grains being poured through a hopper into a circular sieve, made into several compartments of different sized wire-mesh. As this revolves, the grain runs slowly from end to end of the sieve, being assorted in size as it falls through the successively smaller meshes.

Three grades of coffee are thus produced, the most prized being the small round grain, called *el caracolillo*, which resembles the Mocha coffee of Arabia in appearance. While not better in flavor than the other grades, it is more easily and thoroughly roasted and looks better, so that it brings a dollar or two extra per bag. The second grade is called *el primer*, or *lavado*. This is the principal yield, being the large, full-grown berry, the former being a stunted product. The third grade forms the refuse coffee, which is used upon the place or sold at a low price for local consumption.

The coffee finally passes through a careful hand-sorting to free it from dirt, pebbles, and decayed berries, this being done on a long table by negro women. The caracolillo grains are very carefully gone over by a skilled hand. The product, now ready for market, is packed in strong canvas bags, holding about 107 pounds each, and transported to the sea-shore on mule- or horse-back; long lines of animals, carrying two bags each, the head of each tied to the tail of the one in front, winding down the hill-sides with their valuable freight.

The *cafetales* yielding the finest fruit have been those of the Sierra Maestra Mountain region, the Vuelta Abajo district, and the Alquizar and San Marcos

AGRICULTURAL PRODUCTIONS. 131

localities. The culture was continued actively in the specially favorable Guantanamo mountain district when it was rapidly on the decline elsewhere.

Of the other products of the coffee estates the cacao comes next in importance to the coffee. The tree bearing this fruit has something of the size and appearance of a dwarf pear-tree, growing as high as six or eight feet. The fruit is a large capsule, with the singular habit of growing directly on the trunk and the thick branches, the lower capsules even touching the ground. The capsule is well filled with beans, usually about twenty-five to each, surrounded by a sweet pulp of pleasant flavor. In preparing chocolate, the seeds are roasted, crushed, and ground to powder. Chocolate is much used in Cuba as a beverage, and large quantities are manufactured into bon-bons, the favorite confection of Cuban ladies.

The *plantano*, or plantain, forms the bread of Cuba, being eaten roasted by the working-people at almost every meal. There are numerous varieties of this plant, the favorite being the banana, whose palatable fruit is considered the result of long-continued careful cultivation. Another important tree, growing everywhere in Cuba, from the mountains to the sea-coast, is the cocoa, whose fruit and wood alike are of the greatest value and utility. There is no drink more wholesome and refreshing than the milk of the fresh plucked cocoa-nut; while a delicious preserve is made from the pulp of the green fruit. From the juice of the stem the natives make a kind of wine; the fruit yields them their cups, lamps, and oil, and the tree furnishes thatch, brooms, baskets, and other household necessities.

TOBACCO.

Cuba possesses three grades of soil, each suited to one of its three special crops. The richest soil is black in color, and is best adapted to the culture of the sugar-cane, its fertility being so great that artificial fertilizers are rarely needed. The red soil, deriving its color from oxide of iron, is of a lower grade of fertility, and in this the coffee plantations are usually established. Inferior to both of these is the mulatto-colored soil, the one preferred by the tobacco planters, who, however, often mix other soils with it to increase its fertility. Tobacco, as is well known, is exhaustive to land, and the soil needs to be carefully chosen and strengthened; but the cultivation demands less care than in the case of coffee, and no expensive machinery is required as in the sugar production, while the fine quality of Cuban tobacco insures it a ready market at good prices. It is, therefore, largely grown.

The use of tobacco was first observed in Cuba; Columbus, in his second voyage, seeing the natives smoking it, rolled in a leaf somewhat like the modern cigar. "It is said that in this way they do not feel fatigue. These tubes, or whatever we may call them, they call *tabacos*." The Indian name for the plant and leaf was *cohiba*, but the name of the Indian cigar has taken its place.

The cultivation of the tobacco-plant began in the vicinity of Havana about 1580, but the famous Vuelta Abajo leaf was not heard of before 1790. The culture has increased with considerable rapidity and has extended to all sections of the island. In 1827 the tobacco farms numbered 5534, in 1846 more than 9000,

AGRICULTURAL PRODUCTIONS.   133

and in 1862 about 11,000. In 1894 the number was given as 8875.

The Vuelta Abajo region, comprising the western section of the island, yields the finest grade of leaf; but this only within a limited district, of about eighty miles in length by twenty in width. This lies between the mountain ridge and the southern coast, in the district surrounding the city of Pinar del Rio. The widely esteemed quality of the tobacco grown in this region is probably due to some peculiar element of the soil, and perhaps as greatly to the physical conditions of the country. Along the northern border of the district, on which is grown the best tobacco, rises the high Sierra de los Organos, down whose southward slopes the frequent rains give rise to numerous streams, while the surrounding heated waters of the Gulf Stream yield this region a climate peculiarly its own. Elsewhere the tobacco varies in quality, being harsh and strong in some districts, while in others leaf of great excellence is produced.

The restrictions and exactions with which the tobacco industry was long surrounded interfered greatly with its prosperity. Up to 1791 it was controlled by a monopoly called the "Commercial Company of Havana," and subsequently by the "Factoria de Tobacco," whose management was such that only the poorer classes of the population engaged in the culture, the "Factoria" advancing funds for this purpose. After this monopoly was suppressed, the tobacco culture had to contend with the more profitable coffee and sugar industries. Recently it has been seriously affected by the insurrection, Maceo's raid into Pinar del Rio having proved highly detrimental to it.

The tobacco farms, *vegas* in Cuban parlance, are generally situated on the moist margins of rivers or in other low and damp localities, and are usually small, ten acres or more in size, while about as much space is devoted to the growth of bananas and other food plants. These farms are scattered about wherever the soil is richest, the intervening land remaining uncultivated.

The plant, which is not allowed to attain a height of more than six to nine feet, bears oblong, pointed leaves, dark green in color when young, changing to a yellowish green when mature. It has a strong appetite for the mineral constituents of the soil, draining the ground of its nourishing properties and needing constant fertilization.

The tobacco seed is sown in nurseries, from which the young plants are taken in October and November, when three inches high, to bed out in the fields, being planted in furrows two feet apart. They reach their full size in three months, during which the utmost vigilance is needed to guard them against the attacks of destructive insects, which include the green tobacco caterpillar and several others. These enemies need to be fought day and night, the planters, at the opening of the buds, often seeking their foes with lights all night long. Ploughing is also necessary, to keep the furrows clear of weeds.

When the large leaves, generally ten in number, have grown, all the small ones are picked off; and the flower-bud at the top of the plant is also nipped off when it appears, so that all the strength may be thrown into the selected leaves. Suckers sprout out, and these also must be removed. As a result, the strength of

AGRICULTURAL PRODUCTIONS.

the whole plant is thrown into the leaves, which expand under the genial sunshine,—those of the female plant being the largest and the best adapted for the wrappers of cigars.

The leaf is bright green in color until the picking season, when it begins to turn yellow and spotted. In gathering, the stalk is cut into short sections, with two leaves on each. This is for convenience in hanging them over the poles in the drying-house, a leaf depending on each side of the pole. These houses are large, open structures, thatched with palm-leaves, and supplied with rows of poles one above another, upon which the leaves are left about five weeks. When the curing process is completed, the leaves are tied into bundles of about 100 each, which are gathered into bales, usually of eighty bundles, and wrapped in palm leaves. They are now ready for conveyance to the Havana cigar factories or for transportation.

A tobacco plantation has for buildings, in addition to the drying-house, a dwelling, some cattle-sheds, and a few rude huts for the laborers, of whom the largest farms employ about twenty or thirty. Whites as well as negroes are employed in this work. It is estimated that about 80,000 persons are engaged in the tobacco culture in Cuba, the annual crop averaging about 560,000 bales of 110 pounds each.

Tobacco, while secondary to sugar as a crop, is far more profitable in respect to acreage, and has the advantage of not needing large capital for its production. Its cultivation is by no means confined to the special region mentioned, but extends throughout Pinar del Rio, while about half the annual crop is grown in the Vuelta Arriba district. It deteriorates in quality, however, outside of the special area named; though it is claimed for the valley of Manicaragua, in the south central part of Santa Clara province, that " it produces tobacco possessed of all the qualities of aroma, combustibility, elasticity, and fineness of texture equal to that of the Vuelta Abajo tobacco." The soil is said to be almost identical with that of Pinar del Rio.

SUGAR.

The cultivation of the sugar-cane, the most important of the agricultural productions of Cuba, began more than three centuries ago. It is said that the plant was first introduced in 1530, in or near Havana, but that its first profitable cultivation began at Regla, on Havana Bay, about 1595. The culture now extends widely over the island, occupying the broad plains between the mountains and the sea and the fertile valleys between the lateral mountain spurs, a rich and well-drained but moist soil being required. Many of the estates embrace several thousand acres; the total outcrop of any other of the West India Islands not surpassing that of three or four of the largest Cuban estates, while Demerara alone equals Cuba in the use of improved methods of manufacture. Of the other cane-sugar countries of the world, Java alone comes within fifty per cent. of the product of Cuba in normal times. Yet the facilities of the island in this direction are far from exhausted; and it is said that if all the land suitable for cane growth were cultivated Cuba might supply the whole western hemisphere with sugar.

Several varieties of cane are grown in Cuba, the oldest known being the *criolla*, or native cane, a thin, poor, and not very juicy species. The favorite cane is the Otaheite, introduced in 1795, which is large, thick, and rich in juice. Still more recently the Cristallina was introduced, and is preferred by many planters to the Otaheite. The cane varies in color, length of joint, height, and other particulars, not only with different varieties, but also with the character of soil and mode of culture. Its height, while averaging six or seven feet, sometimes reaches twenty. The sugar-cane bears a close resemblance in appearance to Indian corn, being divided, like it, by annular joints into short lengths, long, narrow leaves sprouting from each joint, of which the lower ones drop off when the cane is near maturity. The outer part of the cane is hard and brittle, while the inner is a soft pith which contains the sweet juice. This is very nutritious, and the negroes are particularly fond of it.

In the culture of the cane slips or cuttings are planted, consisting of the top and two or three of the upper joints. These are laid longitudinally in holes and covered with an inch or two of earth. They sprout from the joints, the sprouts appearing in about a fortnight after planting. As they grow, more earth is gradually thrown into the hole until it is completely filled up.

The planting takes place during the rainy season, and the cutting begins after Christmas, and is in some cases continued up to May. When fully ripe, the cane is of a light golden-yellow color, streaked here and there with red, the top dark green with long, narrow, drooping leaves, from whose centre shoots up a silvery stem two feet high, fringed at top with a plume of delicate lilac hue. The outer skin now becomes dry, smooth, and brittle; the cane heavy, the pith of a dark gray, inclining to brown, and the juice sweet and glutinous. A plantation, once laid out, will continue for years by a simple process of renewal, several crops being raised in succession from the same roots. Usually about one-third of the ground is replanted annually. The sugar estate lacks the natural beauty of the coffee plantation, the cane not needing shade, and extending, like our western corn-fields, over broad levels of ground.

Palms and graceful fruit trees, however, are planted around the houses of the owner and overseer, yielding stretches of inviting shade; while the negro cabins are surrounded by plantain and mango trees, and patches of sweet potatoes and yams. Several hundred blacks are employed on the larger plantations, reaching as many as 700 in some instances, though every introduction of improved machinery reduces the number required. In addition, a considerable number of oxen, horses, and mules are necessary, and the running expenses of a large estate are very heavy. The rate of profit, however, has long been large, though it has suffered a serious decline through the recent competition with state-protected beet-root sugar. About twenty years ago there began a strong movement towards the centralization of estates, planters perceiving the value of operating on a large scale. The effect, however, of the destruction of cane and machinery during the recent insurrection has been very serious, if not absolutely ruinous to many of the planters.

The sugar-fields are divided into squares of three or four acres each, with roadways between for the convenience of teams in gathering. Tramways have been laid on some of the large estates, leading to the doors of the grinding-mills. When the cane is ripe for cutting, a sugar estate becomes a scene of the greatest activity. The mill is made ready to devour the product with all possible rapidity, and the hands—men, women, and children—are marshalled in the fields, each armed with a machete, the peculiar Cuban knife. They spread out over the fields and the cutting begins, a first cut taking off the long leaves and the top of the cane, useless except as food for cattle, a second near the root felling the cane. It is left where it falls to be gathered up by the carters, who follow the cutters with their slow-moving carts. These, as they are filled, drive to the mill, emptying their loads under a long shed near the crusher.

Faster than the mill can grind the cane accumulates, a huge heap being made by night. But as the mill runs unceasingly night and day, the sheds are nearly or quite emptied before morning, and the hands are roused at an early hour and sent to the fields, that the greedy maw of the mill may not grow hungry. During the grinding season, in fact, the hands are obliged to work nearly twenty hours out of the twenty-four. They make up for this severe labor, however, during the remainder of the year, when their tasks are comparatively light.

The sugar-mill is the central point of the whole process, and the one whose operations demand the most intelligence and care. It is usually very large, consisting of an immense roof, supported by posts and pillars, with brick pavement and stone stairways. The sides are left open for the free movement of air, so that virtually it is but a great shed. It contains the engine-house, with all the machinery for grinding and boiling, and the purging and drying houses. Some small estates may still employ ox-power for grinding the cane, but in nearly all cases powerful steam-engines are used, attended usually by American engineers. The engineer, in fact, is the most important man upon the place, and must be able not only to keep the engine in operation, but to repair any injuries to the machinery that may take place. This is work that requires an intelligence and mechanical skill which none need look for in Spaniard, Cuban, or negro, and for which high salaries are paid, while the engineer is free to spend six months of the year in "the States."

The cane is thrown from the shed on an endless chain, which carries and feeds it into the strong jaws of the crusher. This consists usually of three huge rollers of solid iron, two beneath and one above, between which the cane passes in a constant stream, being squeezed to the thickness of half an inch between the first two rollers and to a still smaller size between the second pair. The yield of juice is from sixty to sixty-five per cent., or as much as seventy where hydraulic pressure is used. In the latest mills five or more rollers are employed, and the yield of juice is comparatively greater. The refuse cane is delivered into a wooden trough, whence it is taken to serve as fuel under the boilers. In the more recent diffusion process, applied in some localities, nearly the whole of the juice is extracted.

The juice as expressed is a turbid, frothy liquid of yellowish green color, which the hot climate renders liable to quick fermentation. To prevent this it is

AGRICULTURAL PRODUCTIONS.   141

carried to the clarifiers without delay, being filtered or skimmed on the way to remove all particles of pulp and other solid matter. The clarifiers are large kettles heated by steam to a temperature near that of boiling. Milk of lime is added to neutralize the acid constituents of the juice, and the impurities rise to the surface as a thick scum, from which the clear liquid below is drawn off. The clarified juice is next filtered through vats nearly filled with bone-black, and thence carried by troughs to storage-tanks.

Evaporation is the next process. This is performed in vacuum-pans, few planters now employing the old and wasteful open-pan process. The vacuum-pan is an air-tight copper cylindrical vessel, from six to seven feet in diameter, and convex or dome-shaped at top and bottom. It has a double bottom, forming a cavity into which steam is introduced, and also a coiled steam-pipe in the chamber, resting upon the upper bottom. In using the pan an air-pump is employed to exhaust the air from the cylinder, in order that the contents may boil at a low temperature. Three to five of these pans are used, the juice growing thicker in each. The final one of the series is called a "strike-pan."

In the process of evaporation the clarified juice is pumped into the first pan, where the boiling process reduces it to a thin syrup. Thence it goes to the second pan, in which it becomes a thick syrup. If three pans are used the liquid is now conducted into syrup clarifiers, in which the impurities are skimmed off, and is again filtered through bone-black. A third boiling takes place in the strike-pan, from which it is drawn into the strike-heater, a double-bottomed kettle kept warm by steam and in which the crystallization of the sugar takes place.

The process is completed in the purging-house This is a large building, two stories in height; the upper floor being simply an open framework with numerous rows of apertures. In these are set the *hormas*, or moulds, funnel-shaped cylinders which receive the crystallized sugar and from which the molasses drains off into troughs beneath. A layer of moist earth or clay is placed on the top of these receptacles, whose moisture drains through and aids in carrying off the coloring matter. The result is that the cake of crystallized sugar presents a composite appearance,—pure white at top, discolored in its central section, and dark colored at bottom. The molasses, carried by troughs to hogsheads below, is afterwards reboiled, and a common grade of sugar made from it. In some cases the "claying" process is not employed, and the sugar, known as *muscovado*, is of a rich brown color throughout. This yields a better quality of molasses, sweeter in taste, while the more uniform grade of the sugar produced makes it preferable to refiners.

The remaining processes may be briefly described. The drained sugar is exposed in the drying-house to the air and the sun, the forms from the hormas being broken up so that it may be thoroughly dried. It is then taken to the packing-room and poured into the empty packing-boxes, in which the loose sugar is beaten down with heavy packing-sticks, the negroes keeping time with hands and voices. The boxes, holding 400 pounds each, are finally closed, strapped with raw hide, and shipped to market. The process

AGRICULTURAL PRODUCTIONS. 143

of sugar-making, of course, varies somewhat on different estates, but the same general methods are in use on all.

The total production of sugar in Cuba averages, in normal times, about 1,000,000 tons. In 1895 the product was 1,004,264 tons, of which more than three-fourths were consumed in the United States. In the following year it fell off, in consequence of the insurrection, to 225,221 tons, and in 1897 and 1898 suffered a still greater diminution. Under the coming conditions in Cuba this important industry may perhaps be susceptible of a great development, its decline being not alone due to the beet-sugar competition, but to the severe restrictions of Spanish financial methods. With an improved governmental system, the industry may regain its old prosperity.

While the sugar-house has been supplied with the best modern machinery and the most economical appliances, and many miles of railway have been laid to expedite the bringing in the cane from the fields and convey the sugar to market, the field cultivation remains in many respects antiquated. The use of fertilizers has scarcely been introduced; there are no irrigation works of any account; the wooden plough is still often used, and on only a few estates is the ground properly cleaned or sufficiently prepared for the new crop. Much might be saved, also, through the use of cane-cutting machines, if such could be devised; and, in short, much needs to be done in the way of economy and skilful management at the field end of the process.

LIVE-STOCK.

In addition to the cultivated area of Cuba, a large section is devoted to grazing, there being fully 9,000,000 acres of fertile plains, natural pasture lands. These, which extend through all parts of the island, but specially exist in its eastern half, have long been used in the grazing of cattle and horses, which are raised in large numbers. The pasture lands north of Trinidad are so well adapted to horses that it was once a common saying on the island that all the beggars of Trinidad rode on horseback. In the vicinity of Santo Espiritu and extending eastward over Camaguey to Santiago de Cuba province great herds of cattle have been kept, the city of Puerto Principe being a central point in a very extensive grazing district.

In these wide cattle ranges water is usually abundant, Cuba being notable for its multitude of springs and its numerous streams of the purest water. In some localities, however, surface water is deficient, and here deep wells are dug, sometimes as much as 300 feet in depth. From these the water is raised in buckets carried on endless belts over large wheels, animal power being employed in the work.

The Cuban cattle farms are of two kinds. One of these is the open range, where the cattle are left free, getting water from the running brooks, and only looked after at intervals by the Cuban equivalent of the cowboy. The *potrero*, or corral, the usual form, is an enclosed space, encircled by stone walls, in which the cattle are more carefully attended to. The cattle business has been a profitable one, though no care was given to fattening for market, the beeves being sold just as they came from the ranges. The result is that good beef in Cuba is a very rare article.

The immense herds of cattle, spread over vast plains, here and there divided by stone walls, and shaded at points by groves of palm and cocoa-nut trees, formed in past years a spectacle well worth seeing. The number of potreros in 1827 was over 3000; twenty years after they had increased to nearly 4500, and in 1862 to over 6000. In 1894 there seemed a decline, the estimate being 4300; but this reduction in numbers was doubtless accompanied by increase in size. At present there are virtually none, or at least they are unstocked, the herds having been nearly annihilated during the insurrection.

In addition to its excellent facilities for raising cattle, Cuba presents the best opportunities for the raising of hogs, to which no attention is needed, the seeds of the palm tree furnishing them with an abundance of fattening food. Yet, in spite of these facilities, neither cattle nor hogs have been raised in sufficient numbers for the home supply, and for many years past hog products from the United States and dried beef from the Argentine Republic have been among the largest items of importation. The Cuban beef is largely cured by drying it, salted, in the sun. This, known as "jerked beef," will keep for several weeks, and is a common article on the Cuban table.

Some of the finest of the Cuban horses are raised around Puerto Principe. The horse of Cuba, a development of the early Spanish stock, has become a special breed under the influence of the new climatic conditions surrounding it. It is of small size, with a short, stout body, neatly-shaped limbs, intelligent eyes, and a peculiar gait which renders it exceedingly easy as a saddle-horse. It has a thick neck and heavy mane and tail, and in its unbroken state presents a very rough and shaggy appearance.

No horses are easier to ride, the gait being something like that of our pacing horses, though much more easy; and the greatest novice in horsemanship need not hesitate to mount a well-broken Cuban horse. So smooth is the pace that on some horses what is called *el paso guatrapeo* can be performed, the movement being so gentle that the rider can carry a full glass of water at rapid speed without spilling. The endurance of the Cuban horse is also remarkable, a journey of from forty-five to sixty miles being performed day after day without evidence of fatigue, while on forced journeys seventy to eighty miles are not unusual. It is also very gentle in temper, a vicious animal being rare. In fact, the horse is made almost one of the family by the Cuban owner, being kept in the patio in town houses, and almost in the house itself by the country people. It was to the intelligence, docility, and endurance of their horses that the Cuban insurgents owed much of their success during the recent insurrection.

The latest available statement of the number of domestic animals in Cuba dates back to 1891, when the totals were as follows: Cattle, 2,485,768; horses, 531,416; mules, 43,309; pigs, 570,194; and sheep, 78,484. In the raising of these Santa Clara was the most prolific province, and Santiago de Cuba next in order so far as horses and cattle were concerned. These animals to-day have practically disappeared,

AGRICULTURAL PRODUCTIONS. 147

the three years of insurrection, during which Cubans and Spaniards alike freely slaughtered them for food, having nearly exhausted the supply. Yet the pastures remain, and there is nothing to prevent a rapid re-stocking of the island.

Of the animals raised in Cuba, poultry call for some attention, since these are kept in large numbers, not only in the country but by many families in the city, and a large proportion of the people never eat any other meat than poultry and wild game. There is a small wild pigeon which is largely snared and shot for table use, and ducks and other water-fowl abound. The domestic fowl is sold at a cheap rate, but is small and poor, usually very tough, from being killed and eaten within the same hour.

Bees flourish in Cuba, and much honey and wax are used and exported. The honey varies greatly in quality, the best being that produced on the cultivated uplands. In the vicinity of the sugar plantations the bees feed about the mills; and here they are said to prefer the by-product of rum to the sugar and syrup, and often become so intoxicated as to neglect their usual industry.

Along some portions of the coast turtle and sponge fishing are active industries. Large numbers of turtles are taken annually on the coast opposite the Isle of Pines, and these yield tortoise-shell of the best quality. The coast opposite the old Bahama channel is also frequented by these animals, which come ashore to deposit their eggs, and are captured by turning them on their backs, they being unable to regain their normal position. The meat is eaten in the vicinity and the shell carefully prepared for export. Sponges are also taken in large quantities, the fisheries at Caibarien yielding an annual quantity selling at from $300,000 to $400,000, while those at Batabano yield about $600,000 annually. The work is crudely performed, the boats being manned by *matriculados*, or former seamen of the Spanish navy. There are no reef sponges on the Cuban coast, but the finer varieties of sheep's wool and velvet, with some coarser grades, are common.

As regards the fishing industry, we have already spoken of the great variety of edible fish sold in the Cuban markets. They are caught in the surrounding waters and in those of the Bahama Islands, and some of the streams are abundantly supplied; so that it is rare to sit down to a meal in Cuba without fish. The oysters have the property of growing on trees, that is, they cling to the twigs of the mangroves. They are quite small and have the coppery taste of the European oyster.

VIII. MANUFACTURES AND COMMERCE.
CIGARS.

If it be asked, What are the manufactures of Cuba? it might almost be answered there are none. Tropical countries nowhere take kindly to the arts of manufacture. Their inhabitants occupy themselves mainly in stimulating the productive energies of nature, content to exchange the products of the earth for the manufactured articles of the temperate zones. Only in one manufacture is any energy displayed in Cuba, that of converting the tobacco of the country into cigars and cigarettes to supply the great and increasing demand of Cuba and the world. As for the Cuban, he half subsists on smoke; the weed is his companion by day and night, and whatever else is neglected his craving for the narcotic effects of this favorite product of the island soil must be satisfied.

There are no less than 120 cigar factories in Havana of considerable importance and several hundred smaller concerns, many of the large ones being very extensive and employing over 400 workmen each, so that a considerable portion of the working class of the city is thus engaged. Some of the factories are large and handsome buildings, and contain within themselves all the requisites for the handling of their product, including printing-presses for the supply of labels, circulars, and the designs for cigarette paper, a carpenter shop in which the packing-boxes and barrels are made, and other departments, all of which are fitted with the most improved machines.

Though these establishments were nearly all founded by Spaniards, some of the more important of them have fallen into the hands of British and German capitalists, the list of which is said to have been added to since the beginning of the recent war. Of the concerns thus controlled by foreign capital the most important is the Partagas, whose product has a world-wide reputation. This is now in the hands of a London company, with a capital of about $1,500,-000, and has a daily output of about 35,000 cigars and 2,000,000 cigarettes. In addition to its factories in Havana, it owns about 18,000 acres of the best Vuelta Abajo tobacco land. Another corporation known throughout the world is that of Gustav Bock, who recently interested British capital in his enterprise; a company being formed which purchased or leased some ten of the larger establishments of the city. It produces an enormous quantity of goods. A prominent German concern, the H. Upmann Company, is also extensive in its operations; and there are numerous smaller German and French establishments in the city.

In addition to the enormous consumption in the island there is a large export trade,—the cigars exported in 1896 numbering 185,914,000. It must not be imagined, however, that these are all of a high grade, since not only does the product of Cuban soil differ considerably in quality, but much tobacco of foreign growth is imported and rolled into so-called Cuban cigars. In the streets of Havana itself one may find himself buying and smoking a cigar whose visible leaf evidently grew in Northern soil.

Though tobacco in its various manufactured forms constitutes the chief article of Cuban manufacture, there is some activity in other directions. Carriage-making, for instance, is somewhat extensively carried on, to supply the large number of victorias and other vehicles in use. The finer carriages are usually brought from the United States. The business of the harness-maker is similarly active. Other articles of Cuban production include shoes, soap, candles, perfumery, sweetmeats, beer, leather, etc., but in none of these directions is any special activity displayed.

COMMERCE.

A glance at the harbor of Havana, in years of peace and prosperity, yields abundant indication of the activity of Cuban commerce, a large portion of which passes through this port. On entering the harbor one finds himself in a busy scene, ships of all nations lying at the wharves or gliding in and out of the bay, while a fleet of small boats darts swiftly about, carrying passengers or otherwise engaged.

Havana, while the most active, is but one of the many ports with which commerce is conducted, no other island or coast of the world surpassing Cuba in its abundance of fine harbors, most of which are purse-shaped inlets in the rocky coast, with narrow passages through the reef rock. But admirable as they are in situation, little effort to improve them has been made, and even the harbor of Havana has been allowed to fill up with the refuse of the town.

In 1894 the tonnage of Havana and eight other

ports amounted to 3,538,539, carried in 3181 vessels. From Havana about 1200 vessels, steam and sail, clear annually for foreign ports; the trade with the United States alone amounting to about 1,000,000 tons annually. There has been, however, very little commerce with the other West Indian islands, or with the Spanish-American countries except Mexico. It is said that even the Havana cigar is not to be found in any city of the Caribbean islands except those visited by European steamers which touch at Havana on their way to other ports.

In seeking to state the commerce of the island, we find ourselves in something of a dilemma. During the past few years the insurrection, with its basic principle of destruction, has so greatly reduced the output that all figures applying to these years are misleading. If we go back to earlier years, we are obliged to depend upon Spanish statistics, which are far from reliable, and find ourselves in a maze of conflicting statements. And it must also be taken into consideration that these figures belong to a past age, and by no means indicate the commerce the island is likely to possess under its new conditions. There will very probably be a rapid and extensive development in business conditions, under which all the productive energies of Cuba must be greatly stimulated and its exports and imports largely augmented. With these remarks, we may give some of the details of Cuban commerce under the old *régime*.

A British Foreign Office report for the year ending April, 1896, gives the value of Cuban exports as $94,395,536; imports, $66,166,754. Here there was an apparent balance of trade of more than $28,000,000 in favor of the island; but this was more than consumed by the Spanish government, which exacted some $40,000,000 from the colony. Complete statistics of the trade with foreign countries are not to be had, but figures taken from United States consular reports show a striking discrimination against this country in favor of Spain and Great Britain. In 1896 the United States received from Cuba goods to the value of $42,314,383, for which there was returned only $9,632,974. These figures are nearly reversed in the case of Spain, whose exports to Cuba were $33,474,680, and imports from that island $9,681,120. The Cuban exports to Great Britain were $174,187; imports, $5,843,892; exports to Belgium, $208,304; imports, $1,089,239. France, on the contrary, resembled the United States, sending Cuba only $424,600 worth of goods, and receiving in return goods valued at $3,338,900.

The great balance in favor of Spain was due to the colonial policy of that country, which had remained unchanged from the eighteenth century. All freedom of commerce with Cuba was vigorously checked by the aid of heavy discriminating duties in favor of Spain, which were never less than forty per cent., and usually much more. Only through the corruption of Cuban custom-house officials had foreign countries any chance at all to compete with Spain, whose higher-priced and less serviceable goods were forced upon the Cubans against their will. A marked example of the state of affairs is to be seen in the fact that in sending flour from New York to Havana it has always been cheaper to send it first to Spain and have it reshipped from there than to send it direct.

This roundabout policy in favor of Spain will, of course, now be reversed, to the great benefit alike of American shippers and Cuban consumers.

The exports from the United States to Cuba have long been largely food materials,—hog products coming first and flour second. As regards the latter, the true figures cannot be obtained, since probably twice as much flour was sent to Spain for reshipment as was sent to Cuba direct. With the new conditions there will doubtless be a large increase in these and others of the food products of the United States.

The third material on the list of exports from this country was dressed lumber. In view of the vast woodland area of Cuba and the high economic value of many of its trees, this is not likely to continue, since wood-working machinery, with which Cuba can dress her own timber, may be sent instead. A similar change is likely to take place in other directions, the two countries working together in every instance in the way that may prove most advantageous. We give on pages 155 and 156 a tabulated statement of imports and exports to and from the United States in 1893 and 1897, the former the largest year since 1874, while the great falling off in the latter year was mainly a result of the insurrection.

The United States forms the great market for Cuban sugar, of which the local consumption is not more than 50,000 tons, while in 1894 this country took 956,524 tons out of a total of 1,054,214 tons. The total amount received in the United States from all quarters during that year was 1,625,960 tons. The leading shipping ports for sugar are Havana, Matanzas, Cardenas, and Cienfuegos, which do not differ materially in their output. Sagua and Caibarien also ship largely, while Guantanamo, Manzanillo, and Santiago follow in succession. It may be said, in conclusion of this topic, that the cane-sugar yield of the world for 1894-95 was estimated at 3,125,000 tons; beet-sugar, 4,975,000 tons; total, 8,100,000 tons.

Tobacco, the second large product of Cuba, yields in an average year, as already stated, 560,000 bales, of about 110 pounds each, of which half is of Vuelta Abajo growth. Of this product about 340,000 bales are exported as leaf, and 220,000 bales are used by the Havana manufactories, the bulk of whose output is exported as cigars.

Next in importance among Cuban exports to the United States come molasses and fruits, and at a lower level are cedar, lumber, and iron ore. Among the minor articles we may name mahogany, logwood, hides, wax, honey, cocoa-nuts, sponges, and cocoa-nut oil, while there is a considerable variety of products of which small quantities are received.

PRINCIPAL IMPORTS FROM CUBA INTO THE UNITED STATES.

Articles	1893.	1897.
Free of Duty:		
Fruits and nuts	$2,347,800	$154,422
Sugar	60,637,631	....
Molasses	1,081,034	5,448
Lumber	1,071,123	63,670
Dutiable:		
Tobacco, unmanufactured	8,940,058	2,306,067
Tobacco, manufactured	2,727,039	1,971,214
Sugar	....	11,982,473
Iron ore	641,943	475,281
Total	$77,446,628	$16,958,575

PRINCIPAL EXPORTS FROM THE UNITED STATES TO CUBA.

Articles.	1893.	1897.
Hog products	$5,401,022	$2,224,485
Wheat flour	2,821,577	564,638
Dressed lumber	1,095,928	286,387
Coal	931,371	638,912
Corn	582,050	247,905
Potatoes	554,153	331,553
Mineral oil	514,808	306,916
Locomotives	418,776	20,638
Builders' hardware	395,964	49,386
Beans and peas	392,962	276,635
Steel rails	326,654	14,650
Boilers and parts of engines	322,384	35,578
Wire	321,120	35,905
Carriages and street cars	316,045	3,755
Passenger and freight cars	271,571	9,202
Saws and tools	243,544	34,686
Household furniture	217,126	34,288
Leather goods	191,394	39,753
Stationary engines	130,652	1,189
Total	$15,449,101	$5,156,461

FINANCES.

The total value of agricultural property in Cuba, with its appurtenances, was estimated in 1862 at $380,554,527, yielding a net income of ten per cent. The appurtenances included slaves, valued at something over $100,000,000. Since then, in consequence of the insurrection, foreign competition, and emancipation of the slaves, there has been a shrinkage in value. In 1894 the total value of the plantations may have been $300,000,000. To-day it is considerably less. The revenue yielded by the island has varied at different times and under different circumstances. During the insurrection of 1868–78 the financial burdens laid on the people were very severe, the average annual revenue exacted being $41,577,699. In the period between 1878 and 1895 the revenue averaged $33,400,000. This heavy exaction from a population of 1,600,000, made up of customs duties and direct taxes, was not the whole the Cubans had to endure, since considerable sums were wrung from them by official fraud and forced levies, the island having the double task of feeding the Spanish treasury and enriching the horde of Spanish office-holders who filled every lucrative position in the land.

The debt of Cuba—in great measure composed of moneys spent in seeking to keep the islanders in subjection—amounted in the summer of 1897 to the great total of $396,500,000. Since that date the war expenditures of Spain have been considerable, and the present debt is probably not less than $500,000,000, a sum surpassing the total value of the agricultural and industrial interests of the island, and which, if assessed against Cuba, would amount to about $350 per capita of the population, a far larger per capita charge than the debts of any of the nations of Europe. As, however, the United States has refused to assume this debt as a charge on Cuba, and as the Cubans will certainly refuse to accept it, since it was spent in efforts to subdue them, it must become a burden upon the already debt-ridden population of Spain.

Cuba has never had a currency of its own, its monetary unit being the Spanish peso, or dollar, estimated at 92.6 cents in nominal value in United States currency,—not the peseta, worth 19.3 cents, the unit in Spain. The circulation, however, is a varied one, consisting of Spanish, French, American, and Mexican coins, all of which pass current. Before 1892, a five-cent silver coin was the smallest in circulation, but since then smaller copper and bronze coins have been introduced. American and British gold and paper are at a premium above the Spanish gold, and considerably so above its silver, the result being a confusing one to visitors from the United States. The difference has been taken advantage of by astute dealers in the newly occupied cities, and a revision of the circulating medium has become indispensable.

The Spanish one-centen, or twenty-five-peseta, gold coin, of $4.82 legal value, has been inflated by Spanish financial methods to $5.30 in Cuba, and the French louis, or twenty-franc piece, from $3.86 to $4.24. This premium cannot be maintained in competition with American gold, and an order has been issued by the United States treasury department reducing these coins to their legal value. As regards the silver coinage, the Spanish peso, or silver dollar, has been reduced to sixty cents in circulating value, and the smaller coins in proportion, a change which is very likely to force these coins back to Spain, in view of their higher value there. This reduction in the value of silver is likely to cause some temporary difficulty with the laboring population, as the prevailing rate of wages has been one dollar for one day's work. It will not be easy to make the ignorant wage-earners comprehend the higher value of the new dollar.

Cuba has long been inadequately provided with banking facilities, the whole island possessing but two chartered banks, whose head-quarters are in Havana while there are branches in the other large cities.

These are the Banco Español, which has the sole right of issuing circulating notes, and the Banco de Comercio, which has the practical control of the main railway system of the island. Both of these have at times suspended payment, and neither enjoys the fullest public confidence, while their modes of operation have not favored commercial activity.

There is not a bank on the island in which money can be placed at interest, nor a single savings-bank for the convenience of artisans; and banking, as it is understood in the United States, does not appear to exist in Cuba. The nearest approach to it is made by a few large business houses, which do a legitimate private banking business, while the "note shaver" and the usurer exist, seriously to the injury of those to whom financial assistance is indispensable. Nothing is more needed in the island than a progressive and secure banking system, ready to loan money at reasonable rates of interest. Institutions of this kind are absolutely necessary if the island is to make any rapid recovery from its existing state of depression.

THE FUTURE OUTLOOK.

The Cuba of the past and the Cuba of the present and future are two unlike countries. Under the Spanish dominion, severe taxation, trade restrictions, official fraud and peculation, and lack of energy and enterprise ruled supreme. Under the fostering influence of the United States, which may be looked upon as assured whatever the governmental relations of the island may be, these unjust exactions and impediments to industrial activity must largely or fully cease, and opportunities for enterprise be opened which cannot fail to be of great advantage to the people of Cuba, and, reflectively, to those of the United States. Some of the probable directions of this future progress may be pointed out.

Agriculturally, there are abundant opportunities. The coffee industry, to which the eastern end of the island is so excellently adapted, is likely to be profitably revived, its present depressed condition being by no means a necessity of the situation. Under equal conditions, the coffee of Cuba can safely enter into competition with that of Brazil and other countries, it only needing relief from official exaction and intelligent and economical cultivation to regain its former standing.

The tobacco crop has suffered little and can be readily restored, while there is opportunity for a considerable increase of the quantity grown. It is stated that a syndicate of American capitalists has been formed with the purpose of controlling the whole of this industry, not only in the fields, but in the Havana manufactories, the latter with the co-operation of Gustav Bock, the well-known dealer in tobacco and cigars.

The sugar culture has been ruined by the insurrection, crop after crop of cane having been burned, and the buildings and machinery in many cases destroyed. Large capital will be necessary for its restoration, and this is one of the directions in which American capitalists may find a profitable opening for investment. The decline in prosperity of the sugar industry of Cuba, which showed itself years before the insurrection, was not due solely to competition with the bounty-supported beet-sugar of Europe. The business has been wastefully conducted in many instances, the non-resident proprietors being ruined, while it is affirmed that their stewards and superintendents have pocketed enough of the profits to build the modern city of Barcelona.

Even in the case of resident proprietors, the strict economy needed in modern industries has rarely been practised. The finest machinery has been bought and railroad tracks laid to convey the cane to the mills, but this covers only a fourth part of the cost of sugar production, three-fourths being expended upon the field culture. Here there are large opportunities for improvement in the direction of more careful planting, cultivating, and cutting, by the aid of which the product might be increased one-third at the same cost. The planting and weeding are now nearly all done by hand. Harvesting is also done by hand, the machete taking the place of the cane-harvester which American inventive genius can be trusted to construct. With all the leaks of the past stopped up, there seems no sufficient reason why the sugar industry may not again become profitable.

There are also opportunities for intelligent industry in the direction of dairying, cattle-raising, and horse-breeding. The fertile pasture lands, as we have said, are of wide extent, and with more attention to the fattening of cattle for market a larger demand might be created for meat products. As regards the minor agriculture,—that of the truck, fruit, and dairy farms, —the openings for development are abundant. In addition to the home demand from an increasing city population, the United States offers a large market for winter supply, particularly of tropical fruits.

Cuba, much the nearest of tropical countries to

our shores, is capable of being made a veritable fruit garden, being specially adapted to the growing of oranges, pineapples, bananas, lemons, and other desirable tropical fruits. These, with the severe Spanish tariff restrictions removed, may be stimulated to an enormous production. The orange grows everywhere without cultivation, but to compete with that of Florida careful selection and improvement will be needed. The banana is similarly universal, and the pineapple finds favorable soil in the western section and the Isle of Pines. The lemons of the mountain region of Santiago de Cuba are equal to those of Sicily, while the peach and nectarine can be profitably grown. In short, so far as the products of the earth are concerned, Cuba offers a rich field for capital and enterprise.

Another opening for American energy lies in the direction of public improvements, for which there is everywhere a crying need. Here there is likely to be a generous field for engineering talent. The harbors need to be dredged, the cities properly drained, waterworks built for many of them, railways constructed, highways extended, and improvements in other directions made. Spain has for years drained the island of its revenue, ignoring the sadly needed public works and municipal improvements, and Cuba offers to-day a virgin field for the engineer.

Common roads are everywhere required, and hundreds of narrow streams, now crossed by fords, need bridging, the fords being impassable in the rainy season. In addition to the steam-railways, there is an excellent field for electric railways in the cities and their suburbs. Horse railways have long existed in

Havana and some other cities, and foreign enterprise is already engaged in active projects for their extension, in which the electric trolley system will replace the antiquated horse-cars. A Canadian and New York syndicate has purchased these railways and also the ferry line to Regla, and proposes to make considerable improvements in both; also to introduce the electric street railway and electric light into Cienfuegos.

Other opportunities for American skill and capital lie in the direction of supplying new machinery to the revived sugar estates, of water-works for the cities,—few of which are well supplied,—of wharves in the harbors and the dredging of their channels, of developing the iron, copper, and other mining industries, and, most pressing of all, of draining the towns, whose present sewers, where any exist, are mere disease breeders. The old system of dumping filth in the streets was safer than the existing unflushed and abominable drains, and to these is no doubt due much of the fever, dysentery, small-pox, and other prevalent diseases. These rarely appear on the interior estates, and have no proper abiding place in the cities. Correct sanitation will regenerate the island.

The question of labor is a leading one in considering the industrial development of Cuba. The war and the emancipation of the slaves have completely overturned the old labor system of the island, and a thorough readjustment is needed. The negroes, while the hardiest of tropical laborers, are unreliable, and prefer city life to work on the plantations. White labor will need to be depended upon to a much larger extent than during the days of slavery. But additions to the Cuban and Spanish stock of laborers cannot safely be made from the United States, unless from the Gulf region. The men of the North could not stand the summer climate except at large sacrifice of life. If white immigrants are to seek Cuba as laborers, they should come from Southern Europe, and of these there is an abundant supply which can acceptably be deflected from the United States.

For Americans, Cuba offers itself specially as a winter resort for health or pleasure. While its climate is ill adapted to those suffering from pulmonary complaints, it has many sanitary advantages, and the invalids who visit its shores from December to May can scarcely fail of relief and physical aid. Those who have in view merely rest and recreation will find here a country of unsurpassed geniality of climate, picturesque scenery, and opportunities for enjoyment.

To the United States, among the chief advantages of the liberation of Cuba will be a commercial one. Even under the restrictions of the Spanish control, our trade with the island was large. It was particularly so during the years when reciprocity in trade existed. These restrictions removed it must greatly increase, and much of the former sum of imports from Spain will undoubtedly be diverted to the United States. While taking more from Cuba than ever before, our exports thither must be largely enhanced, and the sum of exports and imports approximate far more closely than in the years of the past.

SECTION II.
PORTO RICO.

★ ★ ★

I. HISTORICAL SKETCH.

The island of Porto Rico (Spanish, *Puerto Rico*) was discovered by Columbus on his second voyage, November 16, 1493. Three days later he landed and took possession in the name of Spain. In 1508, Ponce de Leon—the romantic Spaniard who afterwards vainly sought the fountain of youth in Florida—led an expedition to the island, subdued the aborigines, and within the next year or two founded, near the site of the present capital, a village which he named Caparra. This, which still exists under the name of Pueblo Viejo (old town), was soon abandoned by him, and in 1511 he founded the city of San Juan Bautista, since then the capital of the island.

The natives, of Arawak or Carib stock,—probably never very numerous,—suffered the usual fate of the West India aborigines under Spanish control, being enslaved and quickly in great part annihilated. No trace of them now remains, though there are people on the island whose hair and complexion seem to indicate a mixture of Indian and negro blood.

There is little of interest in the early history of the island. Hurricanes, a Carib invasion, and other causes led to its temporary abandonment, and settlement proceeded so slowly that in 1700 there were only a few small towns, the people being thinly scattered over the country. Chief among its troubles were attacks by British and other adventurers. Sir Francis Drake, the most active raider of the Spanish settlements in the New World, captured and sacked the capital in 1595, an exploit which was repeated three years afterwards by the Duke of Cumberland. A Dutch navigator named Baldwin Heinrich made an attack on the Castello del Morro in 1615, but lost his life in the attempt. Later attacks were equally unsuccessful. A large British fleet which assailed the town in 1698 was in great part destroyed by a hurricane; an unsuccessful attack was made by Dutch and British fleets in 1702, —though on this occasion a hurricane destroyed the Porto Rican fleet; and in 1797 Abercromby besieged the place in vain.

Porto Rico, however, does not seem to have been highly regarded by Spain, it being used as a penal settlement, and its inhabitants largely composed of convicts sentenced to hard labor and their military guard. This state of affairs has left its mark on the labor conditions of the island. Of the convicts, many succumbed to the severity of the tropical climate; while those who survived and received their freedom were thoroughly seasoned to the island conditions, and were obliged to continue their labors in the field in order to live. The same was the case with their descendants; the result being that the soil of Porto Rico is in considerable measure cultivated and its sugar made by whites. This enforced object lesson has the one merit of proving that white labor can be successfully employed in the West India sugar industry. But the penal conditions have not been advantageous to the character of the succeeding free population, the great mass of whom continue in the state of besotted ignorance naturally resulting from the judicial servitude of many of their ancestors.

Spain spent no money directly upon the island, whose needs were neglected, and the expenses of its administration met by remittances from Mexico. These were cut off on the outbreak of rebellion in the latter country in 1810, and the finances of the island fell into so desperate a condition that the mother-country was obliged to come to its aid. Hitherto but little attention had been paid to the island by Spain, and, as it was too poor to attract a horde of peculating officials like that which descended upon Cuba, it suffered little from misgovernment, and its people remained loyal to Spain.

In 1815 a decree was published in which the mother-country showed an unusual degree of liberality and political wisdom. As an inducement to colonists, the most favorable terms for settlement were offered, lands being given them and freedom from direct taxes granted. The tithes and some other taxes were remitted for a term of years, including the exportation duties, under whose weight the other Spanish settlements so severely suffered. This decree, while very beneficial to the Porto Rican people, had one ill effect. Under its influence, slave labor was introduced. Lack of capital and the poverty and indolence of the previous settlers had stood in the way of an earlier use of slaves, the result being that the negro population of Porto Rico is comparatively small.

The decree mentioned brought prosperity to Porto Rico, and there began an advance in wealth and population unequalled in degree in any other of the West India islands. It was added to by the insurrections in San Domingo and on the main-land, which drove to Porto Rico many Spanish capitalists of thorough business training and well adapted to develop the interests of the island.

Yet the insurrectionary tendency in Spanish America had its effect upon Porto Rico, where in 1820 an insurrection broke out and a declaration of independence was made. Fighting continued for three years, at the end of which time the supremacy of Spain was completely re-established. A later insurrection—that of Cuba in 1868—gave rise to similar rebellious manifestations; the effect being a measure of reform on the part of Spain,—Porto Rico in 1870 ceasing to be a colony and becoming a province of Spain. Its people were given representation in the Cortes by delegates elected by universal suffrage, and acquired the rights of Spanish citizenship. In 1873 slavery was abolished, and all the negro population became free.

As regards the provincial administration, little favorable to it can be said. The governor-general retained his autocratic powers and continued in military control, while under him affairs were administered by a Spanish oligarchy, like that existing in colonial days. In 1897, when autonomy was offered to Cuba, a similar system was introduced in Porto Rico,—a House of Representatives being elected, a prime minister chosen, and all the forms of a home government established, nothing being wanting but the fact of actual home rule. Tranquil as the people appeared under

Spanish domination, and prosperous as they had become, there would seem to have existed a current of discontent analogous to that in Cuba, if we may judge from the warm welcome which they gave the American soldiers in 1898.

On the 25th of July of the year mentioned the transports bearing the American army under General Miles entered the harbor of Guanica, in the southwestern section of the island, and the village of that name was taken possession of by United States troops. Two days afterwards the harbor of the port of Ponce was entered. Here, instead of the expected resistance, the Americans were received with wild enthusiasm by the people, who fraternized with the soldiers and loudly cheered the American flag.

A similar enthusiasm was shown in the city of Ponce, and in other places occupied by the troops; the demand of the people for the stars and stripes being so great that the stock of flags was exhausted and General Miles cabled home for more. This flattering reception continued as the troops advanced from point to point, the Americans everywhere receiving the warmest of welcomes from the people.

The Spanish opposition was nowhere strong, though it seemed probable that a vigorous resistance would be made at Aibonito, a strongly fortified mountain position in the centre of the island. But before this stronghold was reached, the movement of invasion came to an end, a protocol of peace being signed at Washington on August 12, the news of which reached the front in Porto Rico on the 13th. In the days that succeeded, the feeling of the islanders towards Spain was indicated by violence on the part of some of them towards the Spanish residents, many of whom appealed to the Americans for protection; while the town of Cota was burned and its Spanish citizens were forced to flee for their lives. This feeling may in a measure be accounted for by the recent discovery that the laborers on the large sugar plantation had been kept in a state of peonage, being paid but a pittance for their labor and forced to buy at the worst kind of company store, which gave short weight in everything. None of the pound packages of rice, for instance, weighed more than three-fourths of a pound.

By the terms of the peace protocol the island of Porto Rico was to be ceded by Spain to the United States. A commission was appointed on the part of both governments to arrange for its evacuation by the Spanish troops, and on the 18th of October, 1898, the American flag was raised over San Juan, and the island finally passed out of the possession of Spain.

As the stars and stripes at the hour of twelve rose to the top of the flag-pole over the governor's palace and unfolded in the air, the throng of towns-people, who had waited the event in deep silence, bared their heads and broke into cheers. Salutes were fired from the forts, handshaking and fraternization of soldiers and citizens followed, and in a burst of enthusiasm the island of Porto Rico, for nearly four centuries a colony of Spain, passed under the dominion of the United States, and entered upon a new phase of existence as a component part of the great free republic of the West.

II. PHYSICAL CONDITIONS.

SIZE AND SITUATION.

The island of Porto Rico is of minor importance in dimensions as compared with that of Cuba, having less than a twelfth of its area, though it has six times its density of population. It lies about 500 miles to the eastward of Cuba, the large island of Hayti intervening, between which and Porto Rico flows the seventy miles wide ocean channel known as the Mona Passage. The island lies farther south than Cuba, being bounded by the parallels of 17° 50' and 18° 30' of north latitude. Its east and west boundaries are respectively 65° 35' and 67° 10' west longitude; and it has an area, as at present estimated, of 3668 square miles, somewhat less than that of Jamaica. As compared with the States of the American Union, its area is a fourth less than that of Connecticut and less than half that of New Jersey.

Porto Rico has been spoken of by one writer as the only known island in the shape of a brick; it forming a fairly regular parallelogram, nearly three times as long as it is wide, the sides extending nearly due east and west, and the ends irregularly north and south. The north and south coasts are indented somewhat like the teeth of a saw. The greatest length, from east to west, is estimated at 108 miles, and breadth thirty-seven miles, though no very accurate measurements exist. The coast line is about 360 miles in length.

MOUNTAINS AND PLAINS.

Throughout the length of the island, from east to west, extends a mountain range, of about 1800 feet in average height. Its slopes are so situated that the streams flowing north are much longer than those flowing south. The uplands occur in masses and ridges, presenting no clear arrangement in their general disposition; the chief range lying near the southern coast and ramifying westward into several branches, which end in highlands on the western shores. From near San German, in the southwest, the hill country extends to the northeast corner of the island, reaching its highest altitude in the Sierra Luquillo, in the east, where the Yunque peak is 3609 feet high. These mountains extend laterally towards the south under the title of the Sierra de Cayey. Farther west various names are given to the ramifications of the upland system, there being a ridge, with summits of considerable altitude, near San German, known as the Tetas de Montero.

The forests, which probably at one time covered the entire island, have been reduced until they are now restricted to the higher portions of the sierras, where they play their part in the control of the abundant water-supply. The uplands slope downward in gently rolling divides, or terraces, sinking, as they approach the coast, into wide and well-watered plains, beautiful in aspect, and largely devoid of the fever-breeding swamps which haunt the Cuban coast. Between the hills lie valley lands of remarkable richness, capable of yielding astonishing crops. As a rule, it may be said that the island consists almost entirely of mountains and their sloping descents.

In its general appearance the island is picturesque and beautiful; its fertile and verdant plains, rolling hills, numerous streams, and variety of vegetation producing many engaging landscape effects. In the words of one of its admirers, it is "one of the most lovely of all those regions of loveliness which are washed by the Caribbean Sea; even in that archipelago it is distinguished by the luxuriance of its vegetation and the soft variety of its scenery."

RIVERS AND LAKES.

Porto Rico is exceptionally well watered, it being credited with the large number of 1300 streams, of which forty-six are classed as rivers, the remainder being minor water-courses. Some of the rivers are over sixty miles long, and several of those of the north have been given the grandiloquent name of Rio Grande. The northeast trade-winds, which form the prevailing air currents, part with most of their moisture in the northern hill-slopes; the result being that the lowlands of this region sometimes receive an excess of rain, and are intersected by numerous rivers, perennial in their flow. On the other hand, severe and long-continued droughts occur in the south, where frequently scarcely any rain falls for months. Artificial irrigation is here necessary, and opportunity for it appears to exist in the statement that water may everywhere be found within half a yard of the surface. Yet, so far, irrigation has been carried on with little system or co-operation.

The rivers reach the coast at right angles on all the sides of the island, the more important of them being the Loiza or Rio Grande, Bayamon, Plata, Cibuco,

Manati, Arecibo, Camuy, and Guajataca, flowing northward; the Portuges, Jacaguas, Descalabrado, Coamo, Guamani, and Guayanes, which flow to the south; the Culebrinas, Anasco, Guanajibo, and Mayaguez, emptying in the Mona Passage at the west, and the Humacao, Naguabo, and Fajardo, seeking the waters of the east. Some of these are navigable for six to ten miles for small vessels, though bars at their mouths seriously obstruct navigation.

There are eight lakes, all small, including the northern ones of Martinpiña, Tortuguero, Piñones, and Cano Tiburones; the southern, of Flamencos, Cienaga, and Guanica; and Albufera de Joyuda, on the east. Towards the southwest there are swampy tracts of coast, but the islanders are fortunate in the absence of the stagnant pools which so often vitiate tropical atmospheres, but which here rarely occur. On the other hand, the numerous streams offer exceptional advantages in the way of irrigation and water-power.

ISLANDS.

The political organization of Porto Rico embraces three small neighboring islands, that of Mona on the west, and those of Culebra and Vieques on the east. Mona gives its name to the broad channel between Porto Rico and Hayti, and is precipitous in aspect, perpendicular white cliffs, about 170 feet high, composing its shores. These cliffs are full of holes and contain many caves. The bold headland on the west is topped by a huge overhanging rock, named by seamen, *Caigo-o-no-caigo* ("Shall I fall or not?"). Mona signifies "Monkey," and near by is an islet named Monito, or "Little Monkey."

Vieques and Culebra, in the channel between Porto Rico and the Virgin Islands, are known as the Islas de Paseje. Culebra is about six miles long by three wide, and has 500 inhabitants, who are principally engaged in raising small fruits. Vieques, or Crab Island, the larger of the two, is about thirteen miles from Porto Rico; its dimensions are twenty-one miles by six, and a chain of mountains runs through its length. Almost all the fruits and vegetables of the West Indies can be grown here, the land being very fertile. It has a population of about 6000, and a healthful climate that renders it secure from contagious diseases. There are several ports, including Isabel Segunda on the north and Punta Arenas on the south. These islands constitute part of the new acquisitions of the United States, they having formed part of the Porto Rican dominion of Spain.

HARBORS.

The commerce of Porto Rico is confined to a few harbors, of which the most important are those of San Juan and Ponce. The entrance to the former is a narrow channel with rocky bottom, the entering vessels passing so near the bordering cliffs that it is almost possible to leap ashore from their decks. In the winter months this entrance becomes difficult and dangerous during the prevalence of a norther, when the channel is churned into a seething and foaming mass of waves, into which sailing-vessels can venture only at great risk, and which at times detain in harbor large steamers.

The entrance bluff passed, there opens a broad and beautiful bay, constituting one of the finest harbors in the West Indies. Of recent years, the channel has been widened and deepened until now it has a depth of twenty-nine and a half feet. Dredging has also improved the harbor, the depth at the wharves, formerly from ten to fourteen feet, being now more than twenty-two feet.

Playa, the seaport of Ponce, has a spacious and excellent harbor, capable of receiving and sheltering vessels of twenty-five feet draught. Here the American fleet lay during the invasion of the island by General Miles, after first entering the fine bay of Guanica, on the southwest coast. The latter is an excellent haven, but its usefulness is vitiated by the marsh lands adjoining. On the west coast are the harbors of Cabo Rojo and Mayaguez, the latter accessible only to vessels of less than sixteen feet draught. The bay of Cabo Rojo is nearly round, over three miles wide and sixteen feet deep, with good anchorage. Its entrance is by a narrow channel of some fifteen feet in depth. Aguadilla, in the northwest, has a good shipping trade in agricultural products; it possessing a deep and spacious bay, well sheltered from the trade-winds, though not safe in case of north or southwest winds.

The harbor of Arecibo, on the north coast, is simply an open roadstead, exposed to the full force of the ocean waves, while close in shore, on one side, are dangerous reefs. In loading, goods are taken in flat-bottomed boats over the river bar, thence transferred to lighters, and finally to the vessel to be freighted. Yet, despite these disadvantages, the town has a large shipping trade.

On the east coast are the harbors of Fajardo, Humacao, and Naguabo, the first alone being safe during northers. On the southeast are the small ports of Salinas and Arroyo, the latter the port of Guayama, with a considerable trade in sugar. There are several other small harbors of minor importance, including those on Vieques Island. With the exception of San Juan, the harbors of the island have been permitted to silt up, without effort at prevention, much to the reduction of their importance. As those of the north coast are injuriously affected by the northers in winter, so during the rainy season strong southerly winds often affect those of the south, causing the sea to break with great violence upon the coast.

GEOLOGY.

Little has yet been done in the way of geological exploration of Porto Rico, the only observations of importance being those of the Swedish geologist, P. T. Cleve. He found on the northern coast evidences of a very thick series of limestone strata, which had been denuded and cut through by streams, leaving their remnants as detached limestone hills. These dip downward to the sea at a very gradual inclination. As in the Antilles generally, the high mountains are covered at their summits with limestone, yellowish white in color and very hard, except near San Juan, where it is soft. The fossils found in this rock assimilate it in age with the tertiary limestones of the other Antilles.

These limestone rocks rest on an older formation of conglomerates and metamorphic rock, closely resembling the basic rocks of the hills of Jamaica and of the Virgin Islands. The limestone cover is very probably of coral formation, representing an elevated reef; and coral animals are still actively at work building new reefs along the south coast of the island, about four miles from shore.

In Porto Rico, as in Cuba, there are many caves in the limestone formation, including the grand cavern of Pajita Inlares and the caves of Aguas-Buenas and Muertos. There are also numerous thermal and mineral springs, including those of Coama, Quintana, and various others.

CLIMATE.

The climate of Porto Rico has the warmth accordant with its tropical situation, but enjoys the reputation of being more healthful and agreeable than that of any other island of the group of the Antilles. The mean temperature is about 80° F.; the temperature of San Juan, as indicated by twenty years of observation, averaging 78.9°. The highest temperature reached during this period—on three occasions only—was 99°; the lowest 57.2°. Usually, the midday heat in the warmer months reaches 88°, the temperature sinking to 80° during the night. In the cooler period, the morning temperature may be 70°, sometimes sinking to 60°. The temperature, therefore, varies little throughout the year, and during the warmest season the heats are tempered daily by a cooling north breeze.

In the highland region of the interior the weather is cooler, and sometimes the night chill becomes unpleasant. It is never cool enough for snow, however, and hail is a rare phenomenon. The unpleasant land winds, so constant at night in the other Antilles, are rarely felt here. Of the towns of the island, those enjoying the most temperate climate are the inland ones of Aibonito, Adjuntas, Cayey, Lares, Maricao, and Utuado, situated in the region of the mountains. As in the other Antilles, the warmest weather occurs in June, July, August, and September; the coolest in the three winter months.

The mean monthly temperature of Porto Rico varies no more than six degrees, and the extreme limits are only forty degrees, perpetual summer prevailing. During the rainy season, tropical hurricanes are not infrequent; and at times these have been very violent and destructive. There is an average annual rainfall of 59.5 inches; the driest season being from December to March, the wettest month November, with a rainfall of 7.6 inches. Even during the "dry season" there is sufficient rain for the needs of vegetation.

During the summer months rain often falls in abundant showers, attended by strong winds. The fall is usually between noon and four P.M., a clear and beautiful sunset following. The true rainy season begins in August and continues into December. As October nears its end, east and north winds set in, heavy downpours of rain attending the former, gentle showers the latter. To the abundant rainfall are due the multiplicity of streams and the luxuriance of the vegetation of the north, the fields being often inundated and extensive lagoons formed. But the rain-bearing winds are usually drained of their moisture by the central mountain ridge, south of which little rain falls, the droughts continuing sometimes for months.

Porto Rico, despite the fact that its climate closely resembles that of the other Antilles, enjoys a greater immunity from disease than the neighboring islands, its mortality not exceeding that of some of the healthiest countries of Europe. The fevers and dysentery of the tropics are common, as also pulmonary troubles; but yellow-fever rarely becomes serious. It visits the coast cities, but mostly in individual cases, and gains headway only in certain years when intense heat prevails. But in all cases the natives are largely exempt, the victims being unacclimated visitors. With cleanliness and proper sewerage, now sadly wanting, its occurrence would probably cease.

On the whole, so far as climate and healthfulness are concerned, Porto Rico promises to be a more desirable addition to the United States than any of its sister islands; the best time to visit it being in the drier and cooler months between December and May. The temperature of summer tends to produce debilitating effects, and those who have been ill remain weak, not regaining their strength until removed to the mountains or the north. The inundation of the earth during the rainy season is not conducive to health. But, as a recent visitor says, "Taking the climate all in all, it is not unhealthy; and there is no more danger of fever or sickness in Porto Rico than in the State of Pennsylvania, if a person takes proper care of himself and does not at first become overfatigued."

III. NATURAL PRODUCTIONS.

PLANT LIFE.

Though no obstruction has been placed in the way of the scientific visitor to Porto Rico, but little note of its conditions and productions has been made. Its geology is not well known, its area is merely an estimate, and its flora and fauna await systematic study. This is not in consequence of any difficulties in exploration, but through seeming lack of interest, and the fact that Porto Rico lies out of the usual route of travel. The beauty of the island vegetation has frequently been remarked, and the variety and dimensions of its trees noted, but a full exploration is still wanting. Primeval forests, which once extended over the whole island, still cover the higher elevations, resembling in character those of the other Antilles, yet with a remarkable absence of the epiphytes, or air plants, which usually flourish in tropical forests. This is not due to any lack of moisture; yet of this class of plants there are to be found only a few bromeliads and a stray example of the orchid family.

Baron Eggers, who visited the Sierra Luquillo in 1883, and made what seems the only investigation of the forest vegetation, found there only a single species of palm, growing at high altitudes. There were two species of tree-ferns, and other trees of much beauty and utility. The ortegon of the natives (*Coccolaba macrophylla*) is one of the most conspicuous trees, forming extensive woods near the coast. It bears immense purple spikes, more than a yard long. This tree is confined to Porto Rico and Hayti. There are also a beautiful tillandsia, bearing immense white odorous flowers and silvery leaves, very ornamental in appearance and yielding a timber called *sabino;* a hirtella, with crimson flowers; another species with purple flowers and beautiful orange-hued foliage, and various trees of similarly striking aspect.

Of the useful woods may be named the cedar, of both the hard and the soft varieties, and the West India ebony and sandal-wood, all of which are common. Another common wood, called *ausubo*, is used largely for building purposes. Woods suitable for construction, indeed, are numerous, twenty or more species occurring, known chiefly by native names. So excellent are some of the woods that Porto Rican timber has been largely used in building the royal palace at Madrid, including mahogany, cedar, ebony, ausubo, aceitillo (oil wood), and other varieties.

In addition to lumber trees there are said to be some thirty medicinal plants, eight resinous woods, a dozen plants useful for dyeing and tanning, as many plants used for condiments, and a considerable variety of fruit-bearing trees. Of the latter, one of the most ubiquitous is the cocoa, which grows everywhere in the coast region, however sandy and unfertile. Its nuts are an important article of commerce and home consumption, and the tree itself is put to many uses.

The royal palm seems indigenous here, as in Cuba, and is much used for ornamental purposes. It has also its utilities,—one being the use of the leaf spathes for the roofing, and often the framing, of the native huts. Another palm of striking appearance is the beautiful *oreodoxa*, a tenant of the hills and mountains, where it at times attains the unusual height of 150 feet.

ANIMAL LIFE.

There is nothing peculiar in the fauna of Porto Rico, which presents, indeed, a marked deficiency of native animals. Its largest indigenous quadruped is the agouti, an animal of the size and habits of a hare, a shy and timid creature, inhabiting rocky hill-sides and wood borders. We may name, in addition, the shell-covered armadillo, much hunted for its savory flesh, and among reptiles the iguana, a creature of hideous aspect, but whose savage appearance belies it, since it is naturally timid and only fights when cornered. Unattractive as it looks, it is said to form a delicious dish when stewed. Of wild animals, the only dangerous one is the wild dog, which has escaped from civilization and haunts the forests, making depredations on the farmers' pigs and calves. It hunts in bands, and, though never attacking man, it might kill children if they came unprotected in its way. Wild hogs also are occasionally seen.

The island is fortunately free from poisonous serpents; its one large snake, the boa, being regarded rather with favor than dislike, since it is harmless to man, and is of use as a destroyer of rats and mice. It is from six to twelve feet in length. The insect pests of the West Indies are not lacking, including scorpions, tarantulas, centipedes, wood-ticks, fleas, and chigoes; yet with proper care danger from these may be avoided. A destructive insect is the wood-ant, or wood-louse, which bores into timber and furniture, quickly reducing it to powder. At times, in the history of the island, this insect has proved a serious scourge, and the abandonment of the first settlement, Caparra, was due to its attacks.

Birds are numerous in the mountains, the species including the dove; and along the coast the flamingo is found in great numbers, also the pelican. There are in addition pigeons, parrots, plover, snipe, ducks, and various sea-fowl, and the game birds include wild guinea-fowl and turkeys. The song and plumage birds are not plentiful, there being among them mocking-birds, troupials, wild canaries, and sugar birds; while there are several varieties of thrushes, owls, hawks, kingfishers, etc.; there being in all about 150 species of birds in the island. Among these are a few species of humming-birds, very numerous in individuals, which haunt like flying gems the gardens of the island at all seasons of the year.

Of the fauna of the island, the most interesting form is the gigantic tortoise, similar, except in size, to the land-turtle of Trinidad and the adjacent South American shores. It is said to be closely allied to the huge tortoises of the Galapagos and Mascarene islands. The fresh waters contain few species of fish, but the surrounding seas are rich in edible fishes of every size, shape, color, and quality, which are found in the bays and channels and in the deeper waters, including the anchovy, sardine, eel, shad, sword- and saw-fishes, shark, and various other species.

MINERALS.

The mineral products of Porto Rico have been but little developed, and await fuller research. Gold seems to have been mined by the early Spaniards in placer deposits, and is said to exist in the rivers of the Sierra Luquillo, Corazal, and Mayaguez, but little is known regarding it. The occurrence of mercury is reported by Cleves, and iron has been found in several localities, specular ore on the Rio Cuyul and elsewhere, and magnetic ore at Gurabo and Ciales. Loiza is said to possess as fine iron as that of Cuba. Considerable copper has been found at Naguabo; zinc, rock-crystal, coal, etc., in the Mala Pascua Mountains; grindstone in Moca, granite in Maunabo and Yabucoa, marble in Caguas, Rio Piedras, etc., and plaster and whitestone in Ponce and Juana Diaz. As to the quantity of these metals and minerals and their adaptation to mining operations, the future must tell. At present their richness is an unknown quantity.

There are some natural salt works on the island, principally in Guanica, Coamo, and Cabo Rojo, and salt has been obtained in considerable quantities at these localities. As yet it is the only mineral product.

The Rio Prieto yields large quartz crystals of fine quality, malachite has been found at Rio Blanco, and fine agate at Kaja de Muestos. The other minerals include molybdenite, limonite, magnetic pyrites, epidote, garnet, chrysocolla, and other species. What is known concerning the mineral resources of the island indicates that it may possess valuable resources in this direction.

IV. CIVIL AND POLITICAL RELATIONS.

GOVERNMENT AND RELIGION.

Under the Spanish administration, the supreme authority in Porto Rico was vested in a governor-general, who was also military governor of the island, the troops being commanded by a deputy appointed by him. There was an elective council, to be consulted concerning the government of the island, though possessing no executive authority. Justice was administered by four courts,—one supreme over the whole island and three criminal courts, one each at San Juan, Ponce, and Mayaguez. Minor justices served for local administration of the laws.

The island was divided into seven departments. These, named from the chief city of each, bore the following titles: Aguadilla, Arecibo, Bayamon, Guayama, Humacao, Mayaguez, and Ponce. These embraced in all about seventy villages, in each of which the governing power was represented by an alcalde. The island, as has been already stated, was represented in the Cortes of Spain, and under the 1897 system of autonomy was granted a home parliament. But, as in Cuba, Spain kept a firm grasp upon the reins of power, and these seemingly free institutions were so only in form.

We speak here in the past tense, since the form of government described no longer exists, Porto Rico having passed from the dominion of Spain to that of the United States. The war was succeeded by a temporary period of military rule, until a form of government could be organized in accordance with the liberal institutions of the United States.

As in all Spanish countries, the official religion of Porto Rico is the Roman Catholic, supported by taxation. Ecclesiastical affairs are administered by a bishop, attached to the archbishopric of Santiago de Cuba. This dignitary has the credit of holding the most ancient bishopric in America, the earliest incumbent of the office being appointed at the first settlement by Pope Julius II. The island is divided into many vicarages, and every minor district has its curate. The intolerance shown in Cuba, however, is not quite so fully manifested in Porto Rico, since there is at least one Protestant church in the island, in the city of Ponce, though it is not at present used. It is likely to come into use, and others added, under the influence of American religious liberty.

ROADS AND RAILWAYS.

Porto Rico is better supplied than Cuba with traversable highways, and one is able to travel in parts of the island with some degree of comfort. Chief for excellence among its routes of travel is the military road that crosses the island from San Juan to Ponce, and which is an admirably-constructed turnpike, eighty-five miles long. On a level foundation is laid a thick layer of crushed rock and brick, closely packed and covered with earth. The top dressing is a layer of ground limestone, which has been pressed and rolled until it glistens. In that climate, and with no heavy travel, this forms an excellent and durable roadway.

There are well-constructed roads in other parts of the island connecting the towns, the total length of good highways being less than 250 miles. An effort has been made to encircle the island with a series of highways; this quadrilateral to be connected with a second one inland by transverse roads. But this is far from completed, and most of the interior is only to be reached by bridle-paths, or horse and mule trails, on which travellers must go in single file.

The length of good roadway is likely soon to be considerably increased. Even during the brief period of the war, General Roy Stone was actively engaged in road-building, for military purposes, between Adjuntas and Utuado, and the labor thus inaugurated is sure to be continued.

The construction of railways has been fairly commenced, there being at present 137 miles completed and in operation, while 170 miles more are under process of construction. In 1888, a project was formed of encircling the island with a railroad; a Spanish company being organized, and two years' interest at eight per cent. on the capital being guaranteed by the government. The length of the road was to be 283 miles, of which 119 had been completed by 1892. Since then little has been done, the government having withdrawn its support. The longest section of road is that from San Juan, along the north coast, to Camuy, a distance of sixty and a half miles. Another road from San Juan runs fourteen miles to La Carolina. Of other lines in operation may be named that from Ponce to Yauco, twenty and a half miles, and that from Aguadilla to Hormiguero, thirty-five miles. Some of these better deserve the title of tramways.

CIVIL AND POLITICAL RELATIONS. 189

The length of telegraph now in operation is 470 miles, the wires being under government control. The telephone has been introduced, and is in use in the principal cities. There is submarine cable connection with other West Indian islands.

As regards steamship connection with distant lands, it is at present mainly commercial. There has for years been a line to New York, principally carrying freight. The coasting trade of the island is sadly deficient. There is said to be but one small boat engaged in this trade, quite insufficient in size to take all the freight that is offered, and selecting the smaller and more profitable articles in preference.

POPULATION.

Porto Rico is somewhat closely settled, its population having grown with considerable rapidity during the present century. In 1830 it contained about 320,000 people. These had increased by 1860 to 583,308; by 1880 to 754,313; and at the census of 1887 to 806,708. At the present time the population probably approaches a million, or some 250 to the square mile, making it more densely peopled than any of the West India islands except Barbadoes. For this reason, Mr. Hanna, the American consul in the island, has advised intending immigrants from the United States to stay away, particularizing "such persons as clerks, carpenters, mechanics, and laborers of all grades," there being "several hundred thousand Porto Ricans ready to fill the vacant jobs, and at a low price."

At present there is a remarkably small proportion of foreigners on the island, less than one per cent., nearly the whole population being native. There is another particular in which Porto Rico differs from the West India islands in general,—the white outnumbering the black and colored people. In this respect it is only matched by Cuba.

The natives of the island are usually divided into four classes,—those who consider themselves the superior class, and rejoice in the name of Spaniards; the peasant class, usually called *gibaros;* the mestizo class, of mixed blood; and the blacks. During the period when Porto Rico was a penal colony, many of the military men who formed the colonial garrison married and settled in the island, and it is their descendants who now constitute the upper or Spanish class. Some of these are wealthy and all of them proud, filled with Spanish opinions and prejudices, and manifesting all the stateliness of deportment of the Spanish grandee. From this class come most of the merchants, planters, and professional people of the island.

The lower class of whites constitute the small farmers in the country, and many who in the cities manage to support life by any labor that comes to their hands. They are of old Spanish stock, many of them the descendants of former convicts; but there is some reason to believe that they have become modified by an admixture of Indian blood. Their adaptation to field work under the tropical sun indicates that the whites, despite the prevailing theory, are capable of becoming acclimated to out-door labor in the climate of the West Indies.

The black and colored population forms, with the gibaros, the laboring class of the island. They are in a minority, have been well treated, and seem thoroughly content with their lot, which is more than can be said of the colored people of the other West Indian islands. There is a reason for this in the relations of equality existing between the whites and the negroes. As early as 1830 there were far more free colored people in Porto Rico than in any other island of the West Indies, and for a quarter of a century all the negroes have been free. The gibaro, like the white in any land, is not without the pride of race; but he has not thought of treating his fellow-laborer of dark skin with contumely or contempt. The whole former policy of the island was based upon humane treatment of the slaves, and the good effects of this policy are reflected in the present status of the blacks.

Under the Spanish laws, the relations between master and slave were carefully considered, the hours of labor, quantity of food and clothing, and other particulars being provided for. Owners were obliged to give their slaves instruction in the tenets of Christianity, and humane regulations for the encouragement of marriage were made. As regards punishment, twenty-five stripes were the maximum which could be lawfully given. Of course, such regulations as these are apt to become dead letters unless sustained by the sentiment of the people. Similarly humane laws were passed to regulate the treatment of slaves in Cuba, but they were broken at will. In Porto Rico, on the contrary, good treatment of the slaves seems to have been the general rule, and a feeling of amity is the prevailing sentiment between whites and blacks.

According to the last official census, that of December 31, 1887, the population of the island was as follows:

White	480,267
Colored	248,690
Black	77,751
	806,708
Spanish in descent	800,963
Foreigners	5,745
	806,708
Able to read and write	96,867
Able to read only	14,513
Illiterate	695,328
	806,708

EDUCATION.

The census returns for 1887 just given indicate a very low condition of public education in Porto Rico. In truth, what education exists on the island is almost confined to the higher class,—the gibaros being deplorably ignorant and the negroes, of course, in the same condition. The Spanish government has made some efforts to promote the cause of education. In 1882, it was ordered that a portion of the direct taxes should be applied to the establishment of free schools. A few years subsequently, it appearing that the small farmers and planters lived so isolated a life that their children could not attend school regularly, it was proposed to concentrate these people into agricultural colonies and villages, with a view to the advancement of education.

These measures have had little effect, eighty-seven per cent. of the people being illiterate, despite the fact that on paper a satisfactory provision for education exists. The school system, as organized, provides for three grades of instruction,—primary, secondary, and superior. There seems to be a considerable number of the elementary schools through the cities and the rural districts, while the superior schools number twelve, eight being for boys and four for girls. Boys, indeed, have the best of it; and the women of the island are very generally illiterate.

In addition to the public schools, there are many private schools and seminaries, and the so-called Spanish or higher class pay considerable attention to the education of their children. San Juan possesses a college in which medicine and law may be studied, and a normal school to which students of both sexes are admitted. For those able to read, some literary provision has been made, the island, in 1894, possessing thirty-five newspapers and periodicals. Of these, seventeen were published in San Juan, eight in Mayaguez, and seven in Ponce.

V. CENTRES OF POPULATION.

GENERAL CONDITIONS.

The abundant population of Porto Rico has brought nearly the whole surface under cultivation, and, in addition to the large cities, there are more than fifty towns, the centres of small departments containing from six to thirty thousand inhabitants. The effort of Spain to concentrate the people has been in a measure successful, many of the rural laborers dwelling in towns or villages, whence they proceed daily to the fields. Thus the country, with the exception of the unsettled mountain elevations, presents the aspect of a continuous succession of farms and villages. Some of the towns date back to the era of original settlement, others were founded within the eighteenth century, and a considerable number in the nineteenth, as a result of the rapid increase in population.

The towns present a general resemblance in plan and mode of building, and are closely affiliated with those of Cuba in their narrow streets, central plazas, and gaudily-painted, stuccoed houses. The larger cities are chiefly seaports, and are of sufficient importance to call for a separate description.

SAN JUAN.

The capital and oldest town on the island, San Juan Bautista de Puerto Rico, to give it its full official title, is situated on the north coast, at a point approaching

CENTRES OF POPULATION.

the east end, its location being a long, narrow island which bears some resemblance to an arm with the attached hand. The principal portion of the city is on the expanded area representing the hand, which is about half a mile wide. The average width of the island is less than a quarter of a mile, its length about two and a quarter miles. It is connected with the main-land by a bridge named San Antonio. At its western extremity, it is three-fourths of a mile from the main-land, and ends in a rugged promontory, a hundred feet or more in height.

On the summit of this bluff rises Morro Castle, the principal fortification of the harbor. On a little islet off the mouth of the harbor is the small but strong fort of Canuelo, between which and Morro all ships entering the port must pass. Farther along the shore, connected by a wall with the Morro, is the castle of San Cristobal, which crosses the island, facing both seaward and landward, and forming a part of the city wall. In addition are the outlying forts of San Antonio and San Geronimo, which defend the bridge to the main-land. Inland, sharply outlined against the sky, rises a range of mountains, whose spurs come down in broken hills almost to the sea.

The harbor, which occupies the space between the island and the shore, has been already described. The city itself is ancient in date, having been founded in 1511, immediately after the settlement of Porto Rico, and retains traces of its antiquity, particularly in its walls, which are maintained in their original integrity, and present us with a perfect example of the defences of a mediæval town. The walls, which include in their circuit the fortifications of El Morro and San Cristobal, are in excellent condition, massive and strong, and in places more than a hundred feet high. With their moat, gates, portcullis, and battlements, they form a highly picturesque spectacle. The city has overrun its walls in two localities, called the Marina and Puerta de España, of three or four thousand inhabitants each; and there are two small suburbs on the main-land, San Turce and Cataño, built on sand-spits and surrounded by mangrove swamps. The total population is about 30,000.

The city possesses various relics of antiquity, embracing the fortress of San Catalina, in the circuit of its walls, built in 1534, and the Morro, dating back to 1584. Near the latter is another interesting edifice, the "Casa Blanca," the castle of Ponce de Leon, who was the settler and first governor of the island. It is the largest building in the city, and in it are kept, in a leaden case, the mortal remains of the noted searcher for the fountain of youth.

San Juan is regularly laid out, its streets crossing at right angles, some of them following the length of the island, and others running transversely. They are wider than those in the old town of Havana, two carriages being able to pass each other; but the sidewalks, in places, are only wide enough for a single person. The streets are paved with glazed brick, due to the prevalence of small-pox some years ago, which caused the tearing up of the old, imperfect pavement.

The town, like all those of the Spanish West Indies, has its breathing places, there being four spacious and shady plazas, while there are three streets beautifully shaded by trees,—the Princesa, the Govadonga, and the Puerto de Tierra. There is one agreeable feature not common in the Spanish West Indies; the streets are subjected to a daily hand-sweeping and are kept pleasantly clean. The same cannot be said of the houses, which are as notable for filth as the streets are for cleanliness. The ground floors of the two-story buildings, whose upper floors serve as residences for the more respectable inhabitants, are occupied by negroes and the poorer classes generally, and are frightfully crowded,—a whole family often occupying a single room, divided by a flimsy partition.

The result is the reverse of sanitary, and the city, which from its situation should be healthful, is much the reverse. The basic soil is a rock-like mixture of clay and lime, impermeable by water and furnishing a good natural drainage; but the dense crowding of the people, and their very primitive ideas of cleanliness, invite disease. About 20,000 people, half of them of negro descent, and most of them ground-floor dwellers as described, are crowded within the walls, while the suburbs contain probably 10,000 more.

The deficiency of potable water and the lack of sewerage add to the unhealthfulness of the city. No water has been introduced, and there are no fresh-water wells; so that the people have to depend on rain-water conducted from the flat roofs of the buildings to the cisterns, which occupy the greater part of the court-yards. This water is very apt to become contaminated, and may fail entirely in dry seasons. Vaults occupy the space in the court-yards not taken up by cisterns, and the only drainage is through the sinks and that caused by rains in the streets.

Under these conditions, we cannot be surprised that frequent epidemics visit the town. Only for the strong and fresh trade-winds, and the flow of the sea-water, which sweeps past at the speed of three miles an hour, the city would be unfit to live in. As it is, it swarms with vermin of all kinds, fleas, roaches, and other unpleasant visitants.

There is no excuse for such a state of affairs in a modern city, and it will probably not much longer exist. San Juan is now a city of the United States, not of Spain, and cannot be permitted to maintain its unsavory condition. A plentiful supply of water from without, efficient sewerage, and stringent regulations regarding cleanliness would utterly transform the city, converting it from a plague-spot to a sanitarium. As regards the deficiency of water, an effort has been recently made to overcome it; a contract being made in 1892 with a London company to build an aqueduct from the main-land. The completion of this has been prevented by floods and other obstacles.

San Juan has its fair share of public edifices, more or less attractive in appearance. In addition to the Cathedral, the churches include those of San José, San Francisco, Santa Ana, La Providencia, St. Augustine, and others. Other edifices include the Bank of Spain and Porto Rico, the Hotel Inglaterra, the Jesuit college, the Archbishop's palace, and various buildings devoted to public business, amusement, education, charity, etc. There are many shops and a number of large stores, tastefully arranged and well filled with goods. The port usually contains many vessels, being visited by steam- and sailing-craft of all nationalities.

The benevolent institutions of San Juan include an orphan asylum, an insane asylum, a maternity hospital, the Hospital of Santa Rosa, and the College of St. Ildefonsa for the education of poor children. There are also many social organizations, founded upon a benevolent basis, but whose principal purpose is enjoyment. These embrace the Society for the Protection of Intelligence, the Grand Economic Society, the Friends of Peace, the Athenæum, the Casino Español, the Casino de San Juan, etc.

PONCE.

Ponce, the second city in commercial importance, is situated near the south coast of the island, in a southwest direction from San Juan, with which it is connected by the military road already mentioned. It has a civic population estimated at 22,000, with a large adjacent rural population, while Playa, its seaport, about two miles distant, has about 5000 inhabitants. The latter, lying on the spacious bay of which we have already spoken, contains the custom-house, the consular offices, etc., and is connected with Ponce by a fine highway.

Ponce, which was founded by Ponce de Leon, whose name it bears, on his return from his Florida expedition, is one of the most attractive cities on the island, containing many handsome residences, while it is surrounded by a fertile and beautiful plain. In its centre is a pretty plaza known as Las Delicias, having amid its tropical foliage an ornamental Turkish kiosk. The churches of the city include a cathedral and a Protestant Episcopal church; and there are a number of public edifices, including three first-class hotels, two hospitals besides the military hospital, a home for the old and poor, etc. The theatre, called the Pearl, is the finest on the island, and is handsome outside and attractive within.

The houses of Ponce, built of stone and brick, resemble those of San Juan. Those in the suburbs are usually of wood. The city is regularly laid out, is amply supplied with water by an aqueduct, and the heat of the climate is tempered by land breezes at night and sea-breezes during the day, so that, though it lacks the cool winds of San Juan, its warmth is not oppressive. Its record for healthfulness stands high, being much superior to that of San Juan. In the vicinity are medicinal baths, whose warm waters have a reputation for the cure of cutaneous complaints.

MAYAGUEZ.

This city, founded in 1752, at the point on the Mona Passage at which Columbus is said to have disembarked on his visit in 1493, is the third commercial city of the island, having a large trade in the products of the adjacent fertile regions, and possesses, besides, three chocolate manufactories, whose product is consumed at home. It has a population estimated at 11,000, of whom the larger number is white. Near by is a beautiful plain, in a high state of cultivation, over which flow the waters of the Rio Mayaguez. The climate bears a good reputation, the thermometer never recording a higher temperature than 90° F.

A principal item in the trade of this port is coffee, its annual export averaging 170,000 hundred-weights. The quality is high, the prices obtained being those of the best brands. The lower grades are sent to Cuba. There are also large exports of sugar, pineapples, oranges, and cocoa-nuts, all of which go principally to the United States. The imports of Mayaguez include about 50,000 bags of flour annually, more than a fourth of the total receipts of the island.

OTHER SEAPORTS.

North of Mayaguez, and connected with it by railway, is the port of Aguadilla, a town of some 5000 inhabitants, well shaded by tropical trees, and with a central plaza in four sections, in each of which is a statue in the midst of a pretty garden. Fine grazing-lands surround the place, and sugar-cane, coffee, tobacco, and cocoa-nuts are cultivated in the vicinity. Oranges and lemons are also grown, and fish are abundant. The distillation of rum from molasses is one of the chief industries of the town.

Arecibo, in the western section of the north coast, is a town of about 7000 population, a thriving place with an active trade. Of the unsatisfactory character of its harbor we have already spoken. An extensive sandy beach lies between it and the ocean, through which flows a narrow and shallow stream called the Rio Grande de Arecibo. By way of this stream goods are conveyed to vessels in the roadstead, flat-bottomed boats being employed, pushed by long poles. This slow process, with the subsequent lighterage, is a tedious and expensive operation; yet Arecibo serves as the port of an extensive and fertile district, and has a large commerce. In its vicinity are extensive coffee and sugar plantations, fine grazing lands, etc. The town is built of wood and brick, its streets running at right angles from the central plaza, which is surrounded by public buildings. There are a large church, a theatre, and other edifices of importance.

The cave of Consejo, in the vicinity, is noted for the beauty of its stalactites. The valley of Arecibo River is one of the most picturesque and beautiful in the island.

Of east-coast ports the principal is Fajardo, a town of some 3000 inhabitants, its leading industry being the manufacture of muscovado sugar, and the exportation of sugar, molasses, tortoise-shell, etc. Lumber and provisions are imported from the United States.

Farther south, on the east side of the island, lies Naguabo, a small place of 2000 inhabitants; Playa de Naguabo, of 1500 people, on the harbor, serving as its port. Humacao, nine miles away, the capital of the department, has about 6000 inhabitants. Coffee is a prominent product of the district, and much fruit is grown. Cattle are also plentiful.

On the south coast, in addition to the harbors of Ponce and Guanica, is that of Arroyo, near the east end of the island, and serving as the port of Guayama, four miles inland. It is a small place, yet serves as the shipping point for a fertile sugar district, exporting annually to the United States nearly 10,000 hogsheads of sugar, several thousand casks of molasses, and a hundred or more casks and barrels of bay-rum. Near by are the noted caves of Aguas Buenas, from one of which runs the river Caguitas, after a subterranean flow.

INLAND TOWNS.

Porto Rico, while possessing numerous villages in its elevated interior region,—many of them attractive from their cool temperature and salubrious situation, —has few inland towns of importance. San German, in the southwest, not far from the bay of Cabo Rojo, is one of the principal of these. This is an old town, almost as ancient as San Juan, and is the centre of a district containing some 20,000 people, formerly very productive, but now less so. The town, of about 8000 population, stands on a hill near the river Guanajibo, possesses a seminary, hospital, and other institutions, and has three plazas, on one of which is an antique Dominican convent and a church of some pretension.

Some twenty miles west of Ponce, with which it is connected by railway, lies the town of Yauco, one of the first to be occupied by American troops. Somewhat farther to the east lies Coamo, also occupied by General Miles's forces; and north of Guayama is the village of Cayey, which was about being attacked when news reached camp of the signing of the peace protocol. In the hill country north of these positions is the town of Aibonito, on the military road across the island, which the Spanish forces had strongly fortified. A fierce and sanguinary battle at this point was checked by the news of the protocol.

Among the other highland villages are Aguas Buenas, in the midst of coffee fields and fruit farms; Cidra, notable for its fine forest scenery; and the centrally located Barros, in a coffee and grazing district. Adjuntas, the southern end of General Roy Stone's military highway, has an elevated situation, coffee and fruit farms covering the neighboring ridges and many streams flowing through the valleys. Utuado, at its other extremity, has a similarly attractive mountain situation. Aguada claims an antiquity running back to 1511. It has a large sugar-grinding plant; as also has Añasco, the central point in a very productive region. Bayamon has a small iron-works and a refinery of petroleum, Caguas has lime and marble quarries, and Rio Piedras boasts a health resort known as La Convalecencia. The mountain village of Harmigueros, near San German, is notable for possessing the shrine of Montserrat, once a place of pilgrimage not only for the people of the island, but for those of other islands ranging from St. Thomas to Martinique and Curaçao.

VI. MANNERS AND CUSTOMS.

THE SPANISH CLASS.

The upper class of the people of Porto Rico, who still rejoice in the name of Spaniards, despite the fact that they are the descendants of military settlers of a century or two ago, keep up all the pride of hidalgos, and form a distinctive class of the population which scrupulously avoids any mingling of blood with the gibaros. What wealth is possessed by the natives is in their hands, and they have long sedulously maintained the opinions and prejudices of their Spanish ancestry, so that there is little community of feeling between them and the lower people.

This class is the only one on the island that has anything beyond the merest rudiments of education. The professions and the commercial and planting industries are largely in their hands, and many of them are wealthy, while they are generally well-to-do.

They are a good-looking people, and one that enjoys life to the utmost. The ladies are usually handsome, refined in manners, and amiable in disposition, though living in the seclusion prescribed for the sex in Spanish countries generally. They have regular features, large, swimming black eyes, and bright and alert expression. In form they are small, and are noted for their small hands and feet. In dress they seek to follow the styles of Paris, though usually a year or two behind date.

The men of this class—as, indeed, the islanders in

general, from planter to beggar—are gamblers by nature; the habit being common to all the people, many of whom squander their substance in games of chance. The lottery, cock-fighting, and other gambling devices serve as ready means with numbers of them to dispose of their last dollars. The people, indeed, are fond of amusements of all kinds; steady devotion to business being the one thing to which they are not addicted.

In regard to food and drink, what has been said concerning the Cubans will apply here; though something may be said about their fondness for beer, which they prefer to any other drink. Beer, despite its very high price, is used daily in the house as a tonic before meals; and it is also used at parties and festivals, at the theatres, balls, etc., no other drink being so much in demand. In 1896, there were imported $146,000 worth of bottled beer, to which we may add at least $200,000 worth which is smuggled every year into the island. A brewery on the island, which will probably soon be established by American capital, must, by lowering the price, greatly increase the demand.

THE PEASANT CLASS.

In the country the lower class is mainly engaged in farming occupations, doing no more work than they can well avoid, and living as nearly in a state of nature as the laws permit. Clothing here, as in Cuba, is not wasted on children until they are ten or more years of age. Nature is so prolific that no great amount of labor is needed to obtain the means of living. Those of them who work as laborers on the coffee plantations receive for pay fifty plantains a day. After feeding his family on these, the laborer carries the rest to market, devoting one day in the week to this, and carrying his small stock often as many as twenty miles, as much, perhaps, to enjoy the pleasures of the town as to sell his goods. As regards the condition of the laborers on the sugar estates, we have already spoken.

The farming peasantry, though indolent, are quick-witted and sagacious, fond of eating and drinking, and rather free in their morals. They are natively hospitable, and the traveller can always look for a warm welcome and a share of their best. They live in the simplest manner, their cabins being thatched with palm-leaves and often open at the sides, the mild climate calling for no greater shelter. If there is a door it stands open day and night. They have no dread of thieves, for they possess nothing worth stealing,—two or three bark hammocks, a few pots and calabash shells, some game-cocks, and a machete forming the bulk of their movable property.

The small planters constitute a considerable proportion of the population, and by their pre-emption of the land have prevented it from falling into the hands of the monopolizing sugar planters. As long ago as 1835, there were, according to Colonel Flinter, some 1300 small sugar planters and vegetable raisers,—in his view the best part of the population,—and nearly 18,000 (now about 21,000) small proprietors raising cattle and provisions.

These people he characterizes as resembling the peasantry of Ireland,—ready to fight on very small provocation, yet proverbially hospitable and polite to strangers, with the "remarkable, underlying, inbred Spanish politeness." They are, as we have said, normally indolent; their possessions consisting of a few coffee bushes and a plantain grove, an acre or so in corn and sweet potatoes, a cow, a horse, and other small possessions. Thus provided with food plants that need little care and attention, the gibaro spends most of his time at home swinging in a hammock, smoking, and strumming the strings of his guitar. When he goes abroad, dressed in a clean shirt, cotton jacket, and check pantaloons, his head covered with a wide straw hat, and mounted on a half-fed and overworked horse, with a long sword protruding from his baskets, he is one of the happiest and most independent of beings. Whether his destination be the mass, a dance, or a cock-fight, it is all one to him, each being a pleasant variation from the monotony of every-day life. It is evident from all this that there is much room for improvement in the customs of the gibaro, and this may come with improved education and the stimulus of American education. These easy-going peasantry are now citizens of the United States, which means something more than being subjects of Spain.

A marked change has come over the social condition of the people of Porto Rico since a century and a half ago. Then there were no towns, aside from the few seaports, and the sparsely settled people of the island came together only on feast-days at the central points of their several parishes. Their huts were of the rudest, and the calabash almost their only utensil, an empty bottle being kept as an heirloom in the family. At present more than half the population dwell in towns and villages. and their greater prosperity has enabled them to obtain many more conveniences. What they still need is education, with an

MANNERS AND CUSTOMS.

advanced conception of the needs and dignity of civilized life. In this respect time may bring about a great improvement in their condition and aspirations.

We have already spoken of the status of the colored population of the island, and nothing further seems called for. Both as regards whites and blacks, what has been said concerning the manners and customs of the Cubans applies in large measure to the Porto Ricans, who are of the same race and have been exposed to much the same influences. For this reason it is unnecessary to go here into further detail.

VII. AGRICULTURAL INDUSTRIES.

FERTILITY OF THE SOIL.

Porto Rico possesses a soil of the greatest fertility, equal, if not superior, to that of any other island of the Antilles, and perhaps the best of all for the general purposes of the farmer. None of the islands except Cuba yields as much sugar to the acre, and no other is so widely cultivated or produces such a diversity of crops. While there are extensive plantations devoted to the production of sugar, coffee, and tobacco, the land is not monopolized by these large enterprises as elsewhere, but in great part is held by small farmers, and much of it devoted to the growth of food plants for home consumption.

The soil of the mountain regions consists of a red clay, colored by iron peroxide, while that of the valleys is black in color and less compact in texture. The poorest land is in the coast regions, where there are large tracts of sandy soil. These, however, while not very fertile, are capable of some degree of culture; nearly the whole island, in fact, being susceptible of cultivation. Yet much of the soil is devoted to grazing purposes, there being immense pastures in the northern and eastern districts covered with nutritious grasses.

The forest growth, which once covered nearly the whole island, still extended over a great part of its surface a century ago, the process of clearing not becoming active until within the nineteenth century. Since then the land has been rapidly cleared, it being needed for agricultural purposes by the steadily increasing population. The primeval forest growth is, in consequence, now confined to the summit regions of the mountains. As a result of the recent date of its utilization, the soil retains much of its original fertility, and has not yet begun to demand manures as a requisite preliminary to crop bearing. The provision made by nature during the long centuries of the past still suffices in most instances.

The rapid denudation of the forest-covered land was far from satisfactory to the colonial authorities, who made a strenuous effort for the preservation of the woodlands, passing a law under which every one who cut down a tree was required to plant three in its place. But this edict seems to have become largely a dead letter, the needs of the farmers proving too urgent to be controlled by the wisdom of the legislators.

As the island now appears, with its broad stretches of rich pasture lands, its gently rising mountain terraces, its prolific fertility, and its great variety of tropical scenery, embracing groves of beautiful palms and fruit trees and a multitude of undulating streams, it is unsurpassed in its attractions to the lover of landscape effects and in the abundance of its agricultural possibilities. The latter, however, are far from being developed. The peasant manages to live with as little labor as possible, merely scratching the soil and trusting to its prolific returns to support him almost without work. There are on the island more than 20,000 of these small family holdings, devoted to the raising of provisions and cattle, with perhaps a little sugar; a kind of cultivation not likely soon to exhaust the land, since it does not trespass largely on its powers. No more energetic cultivation than this can be looked for from the small land-holders of tropical islands, with their enervating climates and the ease of living with little labor. While the land is divided as it is at present, even American energy is not likely to stimulate the farming population to greater activity. On the other hand, the increased returns from large landholding and more scientific agriculture might be correlated with a serious diminution of the independence and happiness of the people.

As regards the distribution of the soil for agricultural purposes, the last census, that of 1887, yielded the following particulars. The larger estates numbered 433 devoted to sugar-cane and 361 to coffee. Of cattle farms there were 240; of tobacco farms, 66; of small coffee farms, 4181; and of general farms, 4376. What were designated as small fruit farms embraced the large number of 16,988.

FARM CROPS.

The estates for the cultivation of sugar-cane lie mostly on the lowland plains and the lower slopes of the hill country, and are remarkably prolific in their yield, the annual crop averaging about 6000 pounds to the acre, a yield superior to that of any other of the West India islands with the exception of the best lands of Cuba. The product of sugar per acre is about three hogsheads, and this is obtained without the use of fertilizers. The grinding is done in large mills central to the sugar districts, there being one of these at the village of Añasco, another at Aguado, and others elsewhere, eight such plants being enumerated in the last census returns. Many of the mills of Porto Rico, however, are of the old-fashioned, obsolete character,—the mills varying from the antique bullock-power affair or a small concern run by water-power to the large steam-worked ingenio, with its electric lights and motors, and the latest and best sugar-making machinery. The simplest processes, however, have hitherto been the prevailing ones, and few of the mills are thoroughly modernized in methods. Nothing need here be said concerning the sugar cultivation, as its methods do not differ from those in use in Cuba.

The large cane plantations have been hitherto nearly all owned by Spaniards, many of whom resided in Spain. Year after year these great estates have yielded large crops of sugar at a very low cost in labor; but nearly all of this has been sold abroad, and the great sum of the proceeds retained in Spain. The result has been that the apparent balance of trade in favor of the island has been an actual balance against it, a state of affairs that will now probably be reformed.

Of Porto Rican products, however, the leading one is coffee, to which about 122,000 acres are devoted; while but half of this area, or 61,000 acres, is assigned to sugar, and tobacco, the third important export crop, occupies little over 2000 acres. The weight of coffee sent abroad averages from 25,000,000 to 30,000,000 pounds per annum; the island product being a mild coffee of superior flavor, and one which is in high favor in Spain and Italy and on the island of Cuba.

Coffee, as we have seen in the case of Cuba, demands a more elevated situation than that needed for sugar, the highland clearings, usually above 600 feet of elevation, being given to this crop. The finest plantations are in the south and west of the island. The Arabian coffee does best at a height of from 1500 to 3000 feet; but the Liberian coffee, which has been recently introduced, will grow in the lowlands. The latter variety is more hardy and less subject to the scale insect than the Arabian, and is more prolific, yielding sometimes from three to eight pounds per tree. The ordinary average yield is about one pound to a tree, while the yield per acre varies, according to the number of trees planted and the fertility of the soil, from 600 to 1200 pounds.

The shade deemed requisite for the coffee plant in its young state is obtained from banana, plantain, and other fruit trees, while large trees are planted to protect the tender growth from the wind. As the plants are set out in rows at widths of ten to twenty feet, the spaces between are utilized for the planting of yams, sweet potatoes, and other vegetable products. The coffee trees, if allowed their full growth, will attain a height of from thirty to forty feet. For convenience in picking, they are kept cut down to six or eight feet, as the best berries grow at the top. Vigorous pruning is an advantage, as it prevents the strength being given to wood-making and increases the yield of fruit. It cannot be said that the methods of coffee culture in Porto Rico are all they should be; this plant, like everything grown on the island, being left too much to the care of nature. With intelligent culture, the quantity and quality of the crop might be considerably improved.

Tobacco has hitherto been given comparatively little attention, though it is a crop which grows luxuriantly and yields leaf of good quality, not falling far short of the famous Cuban product. The peculiar soil of the Vuelta Abajo is, indeed, closely simulated in many of the Porto Rican valleys,—a light, sandy soil, rich in lime, potash, and vegetable humus. It is, in fact, not easy to distinguish between Cuban and Porto Rican tobacco, as most of the crop raised here goes to Havana, where it reappears as a constituent of the famous "genuine Havana cigars."

The tobacco farmers of Porto Rico, however, are careless in the curing of their leaf, being too indolent to give it the necessary time and labor. A marked impetus was given to the growth of Porto Rican tobacco by the recent insurrection in Cuba, which cut off the home supply and largely increased the price. To preserve the impetus thus gained, there is needed but industry and intelligence, the use of good Cuban seed for planting, and proper care in raising the plant and curing the leaf. The native indolence needs to be in a measure overcome, and capital and judgment invested, to give the tobacco of Porto Rico a reputation approaching or equalling that of the best Cuban leaf.

Another food plant which can be profitably grown in Porto Rico is cacao, which yields the bean from which comes the delicious and nutritive chocolate. This plant is native to the island, growing well in the coast country, but best in upland valleys from 300 to 500 feet above sea-level. The tree reaches a height of twenty or thirty feet; its fruit pods, which grow directly from the limbs and trunk, containing thirty or forty seeds enveloped in a sweetish pulp. The general cultivation resembles that of coffee, though the trees are slower in reaching maturity, not attaining full bearing under seven years. They similarly need shade and wind breaks. The annual yield varies from two to eight pounds per tree.

The staple food of the laboring population is derived from three plants, of which rice is one of the most important. This is largely cultivated, a mountain variety being raised which grows freely in the central hill country, and has the advantage of needing neither irrigation nor special watering of any kind. Plantain, the second of these crops, is grown everywhere, and, baked in the immature stage, serves as the bread of the people. Yauchia (*Caladium esculentum*) is a root plant, somewhat resembling the yam, but totally different from it botanically. It has an acrid taste, but this is overcome by boiling or roasting.

The other vegetables include the sweet potato, yam, bean, maize, etc., and the fruits are the banana, mango, pineapple, mammee, custard-apple, cocoa-nut, guava, aguacate, orange, lemon, and various others. Guavas are very plentiful and, as in Cuba, are largely made into confections. The orange grows everywhere, almost in a wild state, the fruit being very sweet, with a fine, delicately acid pulp. Lemons are equally abundant, growing wild and ripening the year round. The fruit is small but very juicy. The pineapple grows in an almost wild state, and the island fruits include a variety of cantaloupe which has perhaps no equal in the world in quality and flavor.

Scientific agriculture is almost unknown in the island, particularly in the case of fruit-raising, which has never been an industry, the plants being practically left to grow wild. Fertilizers are unknown; but

AGRICULTURAL INDUSTRIES.

as yet the soil does not demand them, having apparently a recuperative power within itself.

Of plants of possible future industrial value may be mentioned cotton, which was grown to a considerable extent during the American civil war, but is not now an industry, though the cotton-plant may be seen growing wild in many places. It yields a fibre notable for length, whiteness, and tenacity. The leading crops of the island will, of course, continue to be sugar, coffee, tobacco, and rice, and these are likely to become greatly developed and to grow much more profitable in the future.

LIVE-STOCK.

The industries of Porto Rico include cattle-raising, which is conducted on a large scale on the extensive pastures of the island. These, which occur principally in the low plains of the north and east, surpass those of the other Antilles for grazing purposes, being covered with a nutritious leguminous plant called locally *malahojilla* (scientifically, *Hymenachne striatum*), which is of high excellence as a cattle food. The beeves of Porto Rico are, in consequence, much superior to those of Cuba; their meat being consumed not only on the island but exported in large quantities to the Lesser Antilles. St. Thomas, Martinique, Guadeloupe, and other islands are largely dependent on Porto Rico alike for meat and for work-oxen, while some of the cattle are sent as far as Barbadoes. Cuba also receives part of the export. In addition to cattle, sheep and horses are raised, the latter being of a small but hardy breed. Efforts have been made to improve the stock by the introduction of horses from the United States, though as yet with no marked results.

The island has the large area of over 1,100,000 acres devoted to pasturage, while the number of cattle and other farm animals was computed in October, 1896, as follows: Oxen and cows, 303,612; horses, 65,751; mules, 4467; asses, 717; sheep, 2055; goats, 5779; swine, 13,411.

Poultry are kept in large numbers on the farms, being as much in favor as in Cuba. The same may be said of the bee, which takes its place among the most active workers of the land, feeding on its many blossoms, and obtaining a supply of sweets from the sugar-mills. Beeswax and honey rank among the exports.

VIII. MANUFACTURES AND COMMERCE.
ARTICLES OF MANUFACTURE.

The results of the productive industries of Porto Rico, aside from those of agriculture, may be dismissed in a few words. The principal of these arise directly from agriculture, being the production of sugar and molasses from the cane and the preparation of coffee for market. There are also in the cities manufactories of cigars, chocolate, soap, matches, and straw hats. The island possesses a few small iron foundries, and there is a considerable distillation of rum from the molasses yield; but its manufactures, as a whole, are scarcely worth consideration.

San Juan has a few industries, including a small refinery owned by the Standard Oil Company, for the refining of petroleum brought in the crude state from the United States. It also produces on a small scale matches, soap, brooms, trunks, and travelling cases of a cheap kind. There are ice-machines in operation for the supply of the city. Ponce has little that can be called manufacturing, and the same may be said of the other cities. The only artisans, as a rule, are those connected with the building trades, together with tailors, shoemakers, and others engaged in necessary local occupations.

COMMERCE.

The principal exports of Porto Rico consist of sugar, coffee, molasses, cattle, and tobacco. There were exported in 1896, according to a report from the British consul, the following quantities of goods:

Sugar	54,205 tons.
Coffee	26,655 tons.
Molasses	14,740 tons.
Tobacco	1,039 tons.
Cattle	3,178 head.
Hides	169 tons.
Timber	30 tons.

The report of a Porto Rican commercial authority, the "Estadistica General del Comercio Exterior," gives for 1895 the following list of values of the principal exports and imports:

EXPORTS.

Articles.	Value.
Coffee	$8,789,788
Sugar	3,747,891
Tobacco	646,556
Honey	517,746

IMPORTS.

Articles.	Value.
Rice	$2,180,004
Fish	1,591,418
Meat and lard	1,223,104
Flour	982,222
Olive oil	327,801
Cheese	324,137
Vegetables	192,918
Jerked beef	133,616
Other provisions	171,322
Tobacco (manufactured)	663,464
Wine	305,656
Soap	238,525
Iron	224,206
Coal	119,403

MANUFACTURES AND COMMERCE.

The countries engaged in this commerce, and the value of articles received from and sent to each, were as follows:

Country.	Imports.	Exports.
Spain	$8,572,549	$5,824,694
Great Britain	1,765,574	1,144,555
United States	1,506,512	1,833,544
Germany	1,368,595	1,181,396
France	251,984	1,376,087
Cuba	808,283	3,610,936
Lesser Antilles	1,709,872	625,010
Other countries	371,485	828,709
	$16,354,854	$16,424,931

If, now, we consider the trade with the United States alone, we find the exports from Porto Rico during the fiscal year ending June 30, 1896, to have been as follows:

Sugar	81,582,810 pounds	$1,707,318
Molasses	2,256,073 gallons	520,275
Coffee	159,649 pounds	24,101
Fruits and nuts		10,079
Perfumery, cosmetics, etc.		8,784
All other articles		26,099
Total		$2,296,656

Imports of Porto Rico from the United States:

Breadstuffs (flour, corn, etc.)	$521,357
Provisions:	
Hog products	599,513
Butter, cheese, etc.	27,447
Beans and peas	44,244
Wood (manufactured):	
Boards, joists, shooks, etc.	251,635
Household furniture	16,518
Other articles of wood	11,472

Coal	$78,625
Candles	4,188
Carriages, street cars, etc.	7,879
Chemicals, drugs, and dyes	56,184
Cotton fabrics	26,543
Flax, hemp, jute (manufactured)	18,497
Oils	30,732
Paper and paper goods	15,423
All other articles	236,504
	$1,946,761

Of the various classes of goods received from commercial nations by Porto Rico in recent years, the United States ranked first only in the classes of provisions and wood and its manufactures. In the class of hardware and machinery it was second to England and Germany, except in scales and boilers, in which it stood first. In paper and books it was somewhat surpassed by Spain. England and Germany far surpassed this country in metals and manufactures thereof, except in the items of wire and tinware. In oils, drugs, and chemicals the United States ranked next to Spain; but in earthenware, stone, glass, and porcelain it occupied only the fifth or sixth place, Germany and Spain being in the lead. In cotton, hemp, jute, and manufactures thereof this country occupied an insignificant position, except in the item of cordage, England and Spain leading. Its trade in wool and woollen goods was as nothing compared with England and Spain, and in silk goods with France and Spain. In the items of leather and grease Spain had nearly the entire trade, while in miscellaneous goods the only American trade of any importance was in jewelry, rubber, oil-cloth, and artificial flowers. Codfish, one of the principal food substances imported into Porto Rico, is received mainly from Nova Scotia, whose dealers find it their best market, many of them taking their pay in molasses.

FINANCES.

The island of Porto Rico, previous to its change of relations to Spain from a colony to a province, was using American currency; but shortly afterwards the Spanish government, finding the value of silver coin declining, decided that it would be profitable to meet its obligations in Porto Rico in this depreciated silver. Mexican dollars were employed for this purpose, by the use of which the currency, by 1878, was brought to a silver basis, the gold and the Spanish dollars disappearing. The heavy payments for crops made a redundant currency, a large portion of which was shipped away.

The most recent dealing with the currency was in 1895, when the Spanish government took up all the Mexican and Spanish coins in circulation, substituting for them coins prepared expressly for the island. These bear on one side the Spanish coat of arms and the words "Isla de Puerto Rico," and on the other the face of the boy king of Spain. They include the *peso*, corresponding in appearance with our dollar, and smaller coins equivalent to forty, twenty, ten, and five cents, with minor copper coins.

These coins represent little more than their bullion value, the Spanish government having made no attempt to maintain their face value, and they pass freely at the rate of $1.75 for $1.00 in American coin, while exchanges have been made at two for one. This coinage aggregates 6,000,000 pesos, while the banks of the island have added to it about 1,000,000 in paper, partly at par with the silver and partly at a discount. But this has no general circulation. The rate which has been fixed by the United States for the Spanish peso in Cuba—sixty cents as compared with the American dollar—has been also established as a standard of value for Porto Rico.

The Spanish system of taxation needs a radical change, and it will undoubtedly be necessary to remit some of the unpopular taxes now prevailing, and raise a considerable share of the revenue by taxes upon spirits and tobacco, now scarcely taxed at all. A tax on spirits would cause no hardship to the people, and in connection with the remission of other taxes would prove a popular movement.

There are only five banks in Porto Rico, of which San Juan possesses two. Private banking houses do a large share of the business, all the leading mercantile houses engaging in foreign banking. The Spanish Bank (Banco Español de Puerto Rico) is the largest institution of the kind, and has facilities extending over the whole island. The second in importance is the Banco Territorial y Agricola. Ponce possesses the Deposito y Ahorro Ponceño. All these do a safe and good business. There is a savings-bank in San Juan, the Ahorro Colectivo, which consists of a co-operative society, its purpose being to educate the working-class in the principles of economy.

The normal rate of interest in the island varies from ten to fourteen per cent., and a loan at nine per cent. is considered very low. Mortgages, when all taxes, charges, and fees are paid, cost almost twenty per cent. to negotiate; and some planters are now paying nearly fifty per cent. on mortgage loans, through various exactions. The taxes laid on agriculture under Spanish rule amounted to from seventeen to twenty-five per cent. of the profits of the planters. Under all these burdens the planters made money, and, if relieved of these unjust exactions, there seems no reason why they should not become very prosperous. The island of Porto Rico has entered upon a new and promising stage of its existence, and as a part of the United States, with just laws and intelligent enterprise, we may safely look for a great development of its resources and a marked increase in its prosperity.

FUTURE PROSPECTS.

By the terms of the treaty signed December 10, 1898, Porto Rico was definitely ceded to the United States and ceased to be a province of Spain. This change of ownership has made a radical change in its commercial relations, putting an end to the preferential duties under which its industrial dependence upon Spain was maintained, and permitting the establishment of equitable commercial regulations. Under the new conditions, the United States must gain a much closer business relation with Porto Rico—now a part of itself—than heretofore, receiving a larger proportion of its exports and sending it a fuller supply of bread-stuffs and manufactured goods. More liberal educational institutions cannot but have their effect in reducing the deep ignorance of the people, and with education must come new wants and demands and increased energy and intelligence in production.

Engineers and representatives of capital have already sought the island in numbers, with the view of building new railroad and electric lines, and making other improvements; while the agents of American business houses are actively on the lookout for trade. Agencies for lumber firms, glass manufactories, and other industries have been established in the principal cities, and there are excellent opportunities for the profitable investment of capital alike in agriculture and manufactures.

The great demand for beer, even at its former high rates, has been mentioned, and breweries will undoubtedly be among the first of the new industries of the island. Tanneries are also likely to be established in view of the large cattle product. Those now existing produce only the poorest quality of sole leather, soft leather being imported mainly from France. Tanneries using improved methods and machinery would soon control the leather trade of the island, which is capable of being largely developed.

Nearly all shoes are imported, and shoe factories would prove profitable investments. The same may be said of cotton- and paper-mills, glass works, and several other manufacturing industries. Steam laundries are needed in the large cities, the prices now charged for hand-laundry work being very high. Ice plants are needed, there being none at present except in San Juan, Ponce, and Mayaguez. The high price charged for ice almost prohibits its use.

Candles are used only by a portion of the inhabitants, the poor people preferring the cheap cocoa-nut oil to candles at five cents each. Those now used are imported from Spain and Belgium, and a candle factory on the island would reduce the price more than half. Lumber machinery is greatly needed, building operations being very expensive from the fact that planing, grooving and sawing of lumber are now all done by hand. There is an abundance of fine building and cabinet woods, but much lumber is imported, wood-working machinery being almost unknown upon the island.

The same may be said of bricks. Splendid brick clay is to be found everywhere, principally red and yellow in color; yet at present there are only a few brick-works, and these very primitive in their methods. The bricks made are of the roughest kind, and are concealed in buildings by plaster and painting. American pressed bricks would be highly appreciated.

Such are some of the needs of the island in relation to manufactures. It will undoubtedly continue mainly agricultural, the bulk of its manufactured goods being imported, and the demand for these from the United States will no doubt largely increase under the new tariff regulations, while cheapened goods cannot fail to add greatly to the total demand.

SECTION III.

HAWAII.

★ ★ ★

I. HISTORICAL SKETCH.

In January of the year 1778, the Resolution and Discovery, the exploring ships of the famous Captain Cook, first came in sight of the outlying islands of the Hawaiian group, and were visited by the wondering natives in their canoes. There is reason to believe that Spanish navigators had visited these islands at a much earlier date; but they kept their discoveries to themselves, and the islands now for the first time became definitely known to the civilized world. His discovery proved a fatal one to Captain Cook. The visitors were looked upon, at first, by the natives as gods, but were soon found to be men, who treated them and their religion with indignity, going so far as to burn their idols. As a result, a controversy arose, which ended in the death of the discoverer, who was stabbed by one of the incensed islanders.

The Hawaiians were found to have made some progress in government, each island having its king, who ruled with despotic sway. Another step in political organization was soon to be made. Vancouver, one of Cook's companions, returned to the islands in 1792, and found Kamehameha, a subordinate chief on his former visit, now ruler over the whole island of Hawaii. In the following years this ambitious chieftain, a man of decided warlike genius and force of character, inspired his people with his own sentiments, and invaded and made himself monarch of the whole island group.

Alert of mind and keen of wit, the new monarch induced Vancouver to build him a vessel on the European model, to which in the succeeding years he added numerous others, obtained fire-arms from the trading whites, drilled and trained his men, and easily overcame his brave but less progressive opponents. He organized a standing army, built armories and batteries, and erected at Honolulu a strong fort mounted with heavy guns.

The Hawaiian king used his absolute power wisely and well. Under his strict rule anarchy was repressed, theft and oppression were prohibited, and peace and security assured; the conquered chiefs being kept at his court, nominally as counsellors, really as hostages for their good behavior. The arts of peace—as agriculture, commerce, and the useful handicrafts—were fostered; horses were introduced, and the Hawaiians soon became bold and skilful riders; trade with foreign lands was encouraged, the king deriving his revenue largely from the active commerce in sandalwood.

White men were encouraged to settle on the islands; Kamehameha, while keeping up the native customs himself, providing European houses and furniture for his foreign guests, among whom were several physicians and many artisans. His own subjects were induced to study the arts of the whites, and numbers of them became expert as carpenters, coopers, blacksmiths, and tailors.

Among the visitors were no missionaries. Vancouver had made earnest endeavors to instruct the natives, and had been requested by the king to send them religious teachers from England. But this request was not complied with, and the natives remained idol-worshippers until after the death of their conquering monarch in 1819.

Yet, though Kamehameha maintained the old rites, the people had for years been losing faith in their wooden gods, and in the repressive custom of the *tabu*, so wide-spread in the Pacific islands. Under this custom, any article declared sacred by king or high-priest dared not be touched on peril of life. In particular, women were prohibited from eating at the same table with men, or even from eating the food left unconsumed by men. They were also forbidden to eat meat. The punishment for breaking the tabu was death, often with torture.

The decease of Kamehameha was followed by a remarkable event. Liholiho, the new king, a weak man as compared with his father, was associated in the government with Kaahumanu, the second wife of Kamehameha, and a woman of decision and resolution. The whites violated the tabu with impunity, and induced native women to do so with them; yet the gods took no heed of this desecration. Kaahumanu thereupon, losing faith in the old custom, determined upon a decisive act, and with some difficulty induced the vacillating king to accede to her wishes. A formal feast was given, to which some of the high chiefs were invited. As soon as the meats prepared for the men were cut up, the king bade his astonished attendants carry some of these doubly-forbidden viands to the tables reserved for the women, and even seated himself among them and ate with them. Cries of amazement succeeded. The shout, "The tabu is broken!" resounded on all sides. Several chiefs, who had been previously won over, followed the king's example, and the tidings of the radical act spread rapidly through the kingdom. The high-priest, who supported the king, resigned his office; the king announced that both idols and priests were abolished, and the wooden gods, which for ages had been worshipped, were hurled from their high estate and committed to the flames.

This act, of a people spontaneously abandoning its ancient religious faith, without instigation from abroad, was one without precedent in the history of mankind. The Hawaiians left themselves by their own act without a religion, and celebrated with a jubilee their deliverance from an oppressive superstition. Their radical act was not accomplished without opposition. The party of the priests flew to arms and fought for their gods. A pitched battle succeeded, the last on the islands, which ended in the defeat of the idolaters and the suppression of idolatry.

This loss of a religion was quickly followed by the advent of a new one. In 1820, a par'y of missionaries, coming from the United States, reached the islands. They found a virgin field for their efforts, and at once went earnestly to work. In addition to their religious teachings they established schools, and with such effect that in less than forty years the whole people were taught to read and write, to cipher and to sew.

The nearly naked and sensual savages of the preceding era adopted clothing and strict marriage rites, accepted Christianity, and became educated and civilized, a remarkable change coming over them within a century's extent.

In 1824, the new king, crowned as Kamehameha II., set out on a voyage round the world, stopping at Rio Janeiro, and reaching London, where both he and his wife took sick with measles and died. His brother, a boy of ten, succeeded as Kamehameha III., Kaahumanu ruling as regent. Under the succeeding kings the precedent established by Kamehameha I. was maintained, a woman continuing to hold the second place in the government, her assent to all public acts being necessary.

The succeeding events in Hawaii had largely to do with the efforts of the missionaries to maintain the puritanical code of morals they had instituted, and the attempts of dissolute settlers and visiting sailors to undo their work and bring back the old easy virtue of the Hawaiian women. Dissensions also arose with some Roman Catholic missionaries who had made their way into the islands. The result of the latter difficulty was a visit from the French frigate Artemise in 1839, whose commander, by threats of bombardment, forced the government to consent to the teaching of Catholicism, and also to the admission of French brandy,—the introduction of ardent spirits being prohibited by law.

The odd mixture of religion and brandy thus forced upon the people had its immediate effect in inundating the islands with fire-water and restoring the old evil of general intemperance. This the government now sought to restrain by a system of licenses, whereupon another man-of-war appeared with new threats and demands.

A British frigate, the Carysfort, appeared in 1842, whose commander, on pretence of British interests being injured, indulged in such severe demands and threats that the helpless government offered to cede the islands to Great Britain, though under protest against the injustice of the proceeding. The result was deplorable. All legal restraint upon the evil disposed was at an end, and for five months drunkenness and immorality ruled supreme.

This painful state of affairs continued until July, when Commodore Kearney arrived from the United States, and at once issued a protest against the seizure of the islands and treated the chiefs as independent princes. Immediately afterwards, Admiral Thomas, a British naval commander, reached the islands and put an instant stop to the proceedings of the captain of the Carysfort, reinstating the king in authority in the most formal manner. The date on which this took place, July 31, 1842, was from that day forward celebrated as a day of national thanksgiving and rejoicing.

Meanwhile, the Hawaiian monarch had sent commissioners to England and France to represent the interests of the kingdom at the courts of those countries. The final result was a formal recognition by England and France of the independence of the Hawaiian Islands, and an engagement never to take possession of any part of their territory. This ended the difficulties, though at subsequent dates French frigates made offensive demands.

During this period an important change had taken

place in the Hawaiian government. Up to 1839 it continued an absolute despotism. But in that year the king, yielding to the earnest persuasions of the American missionaries, came to a radical decision, signing a Bill of Rights for the people. On the 8th of October, 1840, a second step was taken,—a constitution being given under which a system of legislative government was introduced. There were to be, in addition to the king, a House of Nobles of sixteen persons, five being women, and a Council of seven representatives. Later constitutions and codes of law were adopted in 1845 and 1852, all under American influence, and each making the government more democratic than before.

Kamehameha III. died in 1854, after a reign of thirty years. He was succeeded by his son Liholiho as Kamehameha IV. He died in 1863, and his brother ascended the throne as Kamehameha V. With the death of the latter, at the close of 1872, the line of the Kamehamehas became extinct. It rested with the legislature to elect a new sovereign by ballot, and Prince Lunalilo, a stepson of Kamehameha V. and a choice favorite of the people, was elected. Unfortunately, he had a passion for drink, and intemperance carried him off after a year's reign, another high chief, Kalakaua, being elected to succeed him.

Under the new monarch the finances fell into a state that seriously demanded reform, and in 1887 the king dismissed his cabinet and granted a constitution which still further curtailed the power of the crown, the House of Nobles, formerly appointed by the king, being now elected by popular vote.

Kalakaua died in 1891, and was succeeded by his sister Liliuokalani. During the reign of Kalakaua the number of foreigners in the island had largely increased, owing to the progress of sugar culture, and many of them, principally Americans, took part in the government. This state of affairs was not satisfactory to the new queen, who had ambitious views, and she sought to set aside the provisions of the constitution. Ministers were appointed by her in disregard of the vote of the legislature; the interests of the planters were imperilled, and she finally attempted to annul the constitution and restore the old power of the crown. Among her purposes were the establishment of the Louisiana lottery upon the island and the importation of opium, as revenue measures, and in disregard of the fact that they had been constitutionally forbidden on account of their deleterious effect upon the people.

These illegal measures aroused the foreign element in the state and gave rise to an insurrectionary movement which resulted in the dethronement of the queen in January, 1893. A provisional government was formed; United States marines and sailors were landed to protect the lives and property of Americans, and steps were taken looking towards the annexation of Hawaii to the United States. A treaty for this purpose was negotiated and sent to the Senate, but it was withdrawn by President Cleveland before action had been taken upon it, and the project came to an end.

The party of the queen sought to restore her to the throne, but failed; and a subsequent insurrection in 1895 led to her arrest and temporary imprisonment. She left the islands in 1896. A republic was proclaimed on July 4, 1894, under the presidency of Sanford B. Dole,—of American descent, though born on the island,—who had been at the head of the provisional government. The next event of importance occurred in 1897. William McKinley having succeeded Grover Cleveland as President of the United States, a new treaty of annexation was prepared and presented to Congress. Action on this was delayed until 1898, when, during the Spanish-American war, the treaty was adopted in Congress by joint resolution, and was signed by the President and became law on July 6. The act of annexation was completed on August 12, 1898, when the American flag was raised over the government buildings at Honolulu, and Hawaii became a definite part of the United States.

II. PHYSICAL CONDITIONS.

GEOGRAPHICAL RELATIONS.

The group of islands with which we are now concerned, named the Sandwich Islands by Captain Cook, in honor of the Earl of Sandwich, first lord of the British Admiralty, but known in America by the name of the principal island of the group, Hawaii, stands almost alone in the north Pacific Ocean, at a considerable distance north of the great Polynesian Archipelago, which stretches over so vast a width of the southern seas. Intermediate between America and Asia, Hawaii is 2100 miles distant from California and 3400 from Japan, while Alaska lies 3000 miles to the north and New Zealand 3800 miles to the south. The city of Sydney, Australia, is nearly 4500 miles distant, and Hong-Kong, China, is 4950 miles away. The group thus occupies a highly important position in the pathway of the rapidly growing commerce of the Pacific, and must prove of the utmost value to the merchantmen of the coming age, on their way between the busy ports of America, Asia, Australia, and the multitudinous Polynesian islands.

The Hawaiian group consists of twelve islands, most of them small, and four of them barren and uninhabited. There are in addition many islets, mostly barren rocks. Like Cuba and Porto Rico, the group lies just within the tropics, its northern boundary being 22° 16′, north latitude. On the south it extends to 18° 55', north latitude, while it is bounded east and west by 154° 40' and 160° 30', west longitude. The total area of the group is estimated at 6740 square miles, an area about 1000 square miles less than that of New Jersey. Of this area the large island of Hawaii occupies nearly two-thirds, the others being much smaller.

The general direction of the group is in a line from southeast to northwest, Hawaii occupying the most southerly position. Twenty-five miles to the northwest of Hawaii lies Maui, a few miles distant from whose western coast are the small islands of Lanai and Kahulaui, and nine miles from its northern end the long, narrow island of Molokai. Twenty-three miles northwest of the latter is Oahu; sixty-seven miles from which, still to the northwest, is Kauai. The final island of the group is Niihau, fifteen miles west of Kauai. The four uninhabited islands are named Nihoa, Kaula, Lehua, and Molokini, to which some add Leyson Island, lying 800 miles to the west. The following table will give a conception of the comparative dimensions of these islands:

Islands.	Length. Miles.	Width. Miles	Approximate Area. Square Miles.
Hawaii	100	90	4210
Maui	54	25	760
Kahulaui	12	5	63
Lanai	20	9	150
Molokai	35	7	270
Oahu	35	21	600
Kauai	30	28	590
Niihau	20	5	97

GEOLOGICAL FORMATION.

Geologically, the Hawaiian Islands differ radically from those we have hitherto considered, they being volcanic in origin, or only to a minor extent coralline. They owe their existence to a remarkable exercise of the earth's igneous agencies, which are still actively at work, for the volcanoes of Hawaii are without parallel upon the earth in size and energy. As a consequence, the rock structure is volcanic, being mainly composed of successive layers of lava, while the soil is made up of disintegrated lava, scoria, and sand of volcanic origin.

Yet the coral-reef builders, so multitudinous and active in the Pacific waters, have had a share, though a small one, in the formation of these islands, whose shores are to some extent bordered by reefs, double in some instances. These appear only along a portion of the coast lines, and are of much smaller extent than those bordering the islands of the South Pacific. Ledges of compact limestone are found at a height of 100 feet above sea-level, indicating ancient uplifts, due, perhaps, to volcanic forces.

As may be judged from the igneous origin of the islands, they display a great poverty in mineral species, their rocks being made up of the products of eruption and coral growth, and consisting of basalt, lava, coral-rock, and sandstone. On the tops and in the interior of the mountains there is a variety of trachyte, and the bulk of the mountains seems made up of phonolites and graystones, forming a complete series from basalt to trachyte. The sands and sandstones owe their origin to disintegrated coral rock. The scanty list of mineral substances includes sulphur, pyrites, common salt, sal ammoniac, hematite, quartz, felspar, gypsum, copperas, nitre, limonite, hydrochloric, sulphuric, and sulphurous acids, and a few others, all of volcanic origin.

MOUNTAIN SYSTEM.

The Hawaiian Islands are generally of considerable elevation, and they possess mountain peaks of great height. While Niihau is generally low, though with high cliffs on its eastern side, the small neighboring island of Lehua has an elevation of 1000 feet, and the upland region of Kauai constitutes a table-land of 4000 feet in height, reaching the sea on the west in a precipice 2000 feet high. In the centre of the island rises a basaltic mountain 5000 feet high.

Oahu is traversed by two parallel ranges of hills, separated by a low plain. Of these the eastern range is much the longest, and is greatly broken, lateral spurs extending inland with deep ravines between them. On the ocean side a nearly vertical wall of rock extends for thirty miles without a break. The highest point on the island is the peak of Kaula, 4060 feet, in the western range.

The long, narrow extent of Molokai is traversed by a ridge of hills, with lateral spurs inclosing ravines. There are some lofty broken peaks at the western end, the greatest elevation being 3500 feet. Maui is made up of two mountains, connected by a sandy isthmus, so low that a few feet of subsidence would convert the island into two. The lowest of these peaks, that to the southeast, is 5820 feet high. Haleakala, the northwest mountain, is a nearly extinct volcano of extraordinary dimensions, which has an elevation of 10,032 feet. Of the two small neighboring islands, Kahulaui reaches an elevation of 1130 feet, and Lanai has a mountain 3000 feet high.

Hawaii, an island of irregular triangular shape, with sides eighty-five, seventy-five, and sixty-five geographical miles in length, is almost wholly made up of the sloping sides of its four volcanic peaks, though at places bold cliffs, 1000 to 3000 feet high, front the sea. These peaks comprise Mauna Kea (13,805 feet) on the north, the highest elevation in the Pacific Ocean; Mauna Loa (13,675 feet) on the south; Mauna Hualalai (8275 feet) on the west; and Mauna Kohala (5505 feet) on the northwest. From these lofty heights the land slopes gently down on all sides towards the coast, while between them lies a plain of many square miles in extent. The sides of Mauna Kea are rent by numerous deep ravines, in which flow streams, eighty-five in number, at depths of 1800 to 2000 feet. As the intervening ridges reach the coast in high precipices, this part of the island cannot be traversed without great labor and difficulty, it being necessary to descend into and ascend from the ravines by narrow and dangerous paths.

VOLCANOES.

Though the Hawaiian group is of volcanic origin, most of its volcanoes have become extinct; the only active ones remaining being those on the island of Hawaii; though nearly all the islands possess craters, some of which appear to have been active at a recent period. The tremendous agency by which these islands were elevated acted in a line extending southeast and northwest; some writers maintaining that the first and most vigorous force was exercised in the southeast, yielding the great elevations of Hawaii; while others hold that volcanic action began in the northwest, its energy culminating in Hawaii, and successively dying away in the other islands.

Extinct volcanoes, of every age, size, and shape, are common throughout the group; and the small island of Molokini is merely a low-lying crater, with one side open to the sea. Of these ancient volcanoes much the most remarkable is Haleakala, on Maui, which forms a great dome-shaped mass of ninety miles circumference at base and rising with a gentle slope to its summit, where is presented the most stupendous crater upon the earth. This immense cavity has a circumference of eighteen or twenty miles and an extreme depth of 2720 feet, its area being about sixteen square miles. At intervals over the bottom rise sixteen cones from 500 to 600 feet in height; and there are two great gaps in the crater walls through which vast floods of lava seem to have poured at a comparatively modern date.

Of the mountain elevations of Hawaii, Mauna Kea (White Mountain), the loftiest of all, is extinct as a volcano, all its lavas being ancient. The summit of Mauna Hualalai is covered with craters 700 to 1000 feet wide and 300 to 500 deep, with vertical walls. On the sides of the mountain are more than 150 volcanic cones, and the mountain was in eruption as late as 1801, when a flood of lava made its way to the coast, where it filled up a deep bay.

Mauna Loa (Long Mountain) is still an active volcano, pouring out at intervals of a few years vast floods of lava, which occasionally reach the sea, at a distance

PHYSICAL CONDITIONS. 243

of many miles. On its lofty summit is a circular crater, perfect in outline and 8000 feet in diameter, its walls being nearly vertical, with a depth of from 500 to 600 feet. The eruption of 1843 discharged a mighty flood of fiery lava, which formed three streams five or six miles wide and more than twenty miles long. In that of 1859 the flow continued for two months, and a river of liquid rock, from one to five miles wide and of considerable depth, followed a winding course of fifty miles in length, ending at the sea.

The most stupendous of existing volcanoes, however, is that of Kilauea, a mountain sixteen miles to the southeast of Mauna Loa, and much less elevated, its crater being 4400 feet above the level of the sea. This huge depression is oval in shape, with a circumference of nine miles and a depth of 500 feet. Its lava-covered floor is broken by a second depression, approaching a mile in width, and, when empty, of about 1000 feet in depth. This great lake-like cavity is usually well filled with liquid lava, the fiery flood at times occupying its whole extent, boiling and tossing in lurid waves, and sending up fierce jets of smoke and flame. It rises and falls, at times ascending high enough to overflow the wide crater-floor above, and at others sinking to the bottom, in some connection of sympathy with the eruptions of Mauna Loa. On some occasions it seems drawn off by a subterranean channel.

Such an event took place in 1840, the bed of the crater sinking 300 feet, while the lava flowed underground to the district of Puna, where it burst out in a flood from one to three miles wide and from twelve to two hundred feet deep, destroying forests, plantations, and villages, and finally leaping into the sea from a height of fifty feet, in a magnificent fire-cataract a mile in width. For three weeks this gleaming cascade continued, the ocean boiling and raging beneath it, while myriads of dead fish floated on the waves and the glare was visible a hundred miles at sea.

In 1868 a similar event took place from the crater of Mauna Loa, the earth quaking and quivering as the river of lava followed its subterranean channel and finally burst out on a wooded hill at Kahuka, 3800 feet high. Here it rent a fissure nearly a mile long, from which the crimson flood shot upward in an extraordinary fountain to a height of 500 or 600 feet, sending up vast columns of fiery lava and red-hot rocks 100 tons in weight. Thence the glowing stream rushed onward to the sea, finally pouring over a precipice 500 feet high in a frightful cataract of fire half a mile wide. By this eruption, 4000 acres of valuable pasture land were buried under barren lava, and a much wider area of fine forest was destroyed. A similar event, though on a smaller scale, took place in 1866.

These few instances will serve as examples of the wonderful character of the Hawaiian volcanoes. Other eruptions have taken place since the dates given; and in 1877 the lava flood seems to have reached the sea under ground, causing a submarine eruption in which flames and jets of steam burst upward from the sea, while lumps of pumice-stone were thrown up and floated on the waves.

PLAINS AND VALLEYS.

The Hawaiian Islands possess little that can properly be called lowlands, the mountains in many cases sloping down to the sea-coast, or reaching the sea in lofty headlands. In some localities plains extend from the mountain foot, while valleys and ravines lie between the lateral spurs, and there are elevated plains in the interior. The great plain lying between the volcanoes of Hawaii has served as a field for the outflow of lava, being intersected by streams from the three neighboring volcanoes. One of the most attractive of the valleys is that of Nuuana, running up from Honolulu into the hill region, and with its grassy slopes, its luxuriant foliage, its bridged rivulets, its beautiful views, presenting a most charming aspect. It is a favorite ride for the residents of the capital, and from its summit yields a magnificent outlook on the opposite side of the island. There are other delightful valleys on Oahu, which present a rare combination of peaks, cliffs, ravines, cascades, and rich vegetation.

Kauai, of whose lofty table-land we have spoken, possesses numerous deep valleys, whose woods and water-falls give them a highly picturesque aspect. In one sea-shore locality of this island exists a hill of calcareous sand which has attracted much attention from the curious sound it makes when disturbed, a sort of barking noise, from which it has derived the title of "barking sands."

Niihau is the least elevated of the islands, two-thirds of its area consisting of a low plain, whose surface is made up of an uplifted coral reef and material washed down from the mountains. It is mainly devoted to grazing.

Something here needs to be said of the lava which makes up so much of the surface of the Hawaiian Islands, varying from that which has become decomposed into soil and that still fresh from recent outflow. The latter is confined to Hawaii, and is divided into three classes, according to its surface aspect. The *pahoehoe*, or velvety lava, has a smooth surface, rising into billowy masses and greatly folded and contorted, due to its flowing down gentle slopes and twisting around or heaping over irregularities of surface. The *a-a*, or cinder-like lava, on the contrary, is very hard and rough; its surface presenting a multitude of upright, rugged, sharp points that render it almost impassable. It closely approaches in appearance a heap of furnace cinders. It arises, perhaps, from lava less fluid than pahoehoe, and full of solid points or centres of cooling; its roughness is probably, in a measure, due to the effect of obstructions to its flow, causing the lava to heap up into rugged masses with angles and points of obsidian-like sharpness. The third form is marked by clinkers or scoria, and is rough and covered with fragments. It is found where the lava has passed through woods or been impeded by inequalities in the ground, or broken by the explosion of heated-air cavities in the older lava below. Lava in some form or other constitutes the main element of the surface of the islands, and when in its rough form renders travel very difficult.

The islands are too small to contain any rivers of importance, though some of them are well supplied with streams. Those which flow down the deep ravines of Hawaii have been mentioned, some sixty reaching the sea in the district of Hilo. There are also

PHYSICAL CONDITIONS.

numerous permanent streams on Oahu, which, descending from the highlands, form cascades and water-falls, and with their numerous branches give excellent opportunity for irrigation.

A phenomenal feature is the remarkable salt lake named Aliapaakai, four miles from Honolulu and one mile from the sea. It is oval in form and about a mile in circuit, occupying, probably, the remains of an ancient crater. Its general depth is but eighteen inches, and it forms a natural evaporating-pan for the production of salt, which at times collects upon its surface with sufficient thickness to bear a man's weight. It seems to be connected with the sea, there being a hole in its centre to which no bottom has been found, while its level seems slightly affected by the tides. But the mystery is that its surface stands several feet above sea-level, being sustained in some manner unknown.

HARBORS.

The principal harbor of the Hawaiian group is Honolulu, on the southwest coast of Oahu, which is formed by an indentation of the coast, protected by a broad coral reef. The harbor is a spacious one; but its use by large vessels has long been limited by the depth of the channel through the reef, which was formerly but twenty-two and a half feet. As a result, vessels of greater draught had to lie in the outer roadstead, where good anchorage is to be found, except during the prevalence of a south wind, or *kona*. The harbor has been greatly improved of recent years by the cutting of a channel through the reef, 200 feet in width and thirty in depth at mean low water. The inner harbor affords abundant space for shipping, and has been dredged to a depth of twenty-eight feet for more than 500 feet along the Pacific Mail dock.

There are other accessible harbors on the island which might be made use of if necessary, especially that formed by the estuary of Pearl River, closed outwardly by a coral reef over which only small vessels can pass, but deep and commodious enough within to shelter all the vessels of the Pacific. A channel cut through the reef would open the way to a harbor much more capacious than that of Honolulu, from which it is but six miles distant.

Pearl Harbor was granted by the Hawaiian government, in 1884, to the United States as a coaling and repair station for American vessels, and was considered preferable to that of Honolulu for naval purposes. It has, however, not yet been rendered available by cutting a channel through the reef.

The island of Maui has its harbor at Lahaina, a roomy and sheltered roadstead at present but little visited, but formerly the place of call for whalers when they formed the leading agencies in the trade of the islands. Hilo, on the east side of Hawaii, forms the port of that island; though it is little more than an open roadstead, a coral reef, with entrance channel, affording partial protection. In addition to the Hawaiian harbors, the roadsteads in many places yield good anchorage, free from danger of hidden rocks, and with favoring winds during the greater part of the year.

CLIMATE.

Tropical as is the situation of Hawaii, its climate seems rather to belong to the temperate than to the torrid zone. While generally warm, it is highly salubrious; the great healthfulness of the islands being probably due to the fresh and pure breezes which seem to blow continually from one quarter or other. The temperature is remarkably equable, and the weather so uniform that the natives have no word in their language to express that which is so common a subject of conversation elsewhere. Americans and Europeans can work, as is proved by the fact that they do work, in the open air at all seasons of the year. This cannot be said of other countries lying in the same latitudes. At Calcutta, for instance, which lies farther north than any Hawaiian island, Europeans find it impossible to perform hard physical labor.

The mean annual temperature of Honolulu is about 75° F., the mean of the coldest month being 62°, and of the hottest month 81°. The diurnal range of the thermometer is twelve degrees. During twelve years, the extremes of temperature in the shade were 90° and 53°. The seasons correspond in date with our own,—January being the coldest month, June the warmest.

For those who desire to escape from the summer warmth, the mountains are everywhere near at hand; an hour's ride from the capital up the Nuuanu Valley bringing one into a region of cooler air and more bracing wind. Mountain Retreat, at an elevation of 3000 feet above Lahaina, has a temperature varying from 40° to 75° F.; and at Waimea, Hawaii, is an average temperature of 64°. Rains are very frequent on the mountains, and on the upland region of Kauai, at 4000 feet elevation, fires are required even in midsummer. Snow is constantly to be seen on the lofty peaks, and has given its name to Mauna Kea, or White Mountain. It is to the trade-winds that Hawaii owes its salubrious and agreeable climate. For nine months of the year, from March to November, these blow steadily from the northeast; the wind being softened and made equable by its passage over 2000 miles of ocean. It is not always mild and gentle. At times it grows tempestuous; but it is always full of the essence of healthfulness.

On the leeward side of the islands, where the trade-wind is broken by the mountain heights, there is a refreshing alternation of land and sea breezes; the land breeze, or *mamuka*, sometimes descending the mountain sides with such violence as to do much damage to buildings and shipping.

During the winter months the winds are uncertain, there being at times calms of several weeks' duration. Occasionally there comes a damp, briny wind from the south, now bringing heavy rain, now a close and stifling air. The Hawaiians call this "the sick wind," rheumatism and influenza coming with it. Fortunately, it is exceptional; and the winter season is usually marked by cloudless skies and a dry and bracing atmosphere.

RAINFALL.

The fall of rain is in a considerable measure confined to the windward side of the islands, the mountains largely draining the winds of their vapor, so that they have little left for the leeward shores. In consequence, much less rain falls on this side of the islands than on the opposite, and the sky is usually cloudless. Here, indeed, there is not enough rain for agricultural purposes, and irrigation needs to be resorted to, while the persistent sunshine renders the climate somewhat enervating.

The vapor brought by the trade-winds is condensed by the mountain masses, showers and mists being habitual in their summit regions, while the two lofty peaks of Hawaii are rarely free from a belt of cloud. Rains here are very frequent, and the east side of the islands generally is abundantly watered. Hilo, for instance, on the east coast of Hawaii, has an annual rainfall of eighty inches, and sometimes more than twice that quantity; while Honolulu, on the southwest coast of Oahu, has an average fall of about thirty-eight inches.

The most disagreeable season of the year in the leeward districts comes at the time of change of the monsoon, or rather during its interruption, when violent winds sweep through Honolulu, and rains of tropical fierceness fall. These do useful work in flushing the streets, and the winds aid in purifying the air, while the storms are not ungrateful breaks to the long intervals of settled calm.

DISEASES.

Though the native population has decreased at a very rapid rate during the past century, this is not due to any normal unhealthfulness of the islands, but to diseases brought by the whites, such as measles, influenza, dysentery, small-pox, and others, which have swept over the islands like devastating epidemics, and have had much to do with the rapid decrease in population. The most dreaded disease of the island, the terrible leprosy, is also of foreign introduction, probably brought in from China. The first case was discovered in 1853, and by 1864 it had become alarmingly prevalent; its rapid spread being due to its contagious character and the carelessness of the people.

The policy of isolating lepers was adopted by the government in January, 1865, and in the autumn of that year lands were purchased on the north side of the island of Molokai for a leper settlement. This district is a peninsula, surrounded on three sides by the ocean, and on the south shut in by a precipitous mountain, 2000 to 3000 feet high. The law of isolation was strongly opposed, and was not carried into effect until 1873. All who show the least symptom of leprosy are now removed thither, and one might spend his life in the remainder of Hawaii and never see a leper.

Aside from these introduced diseases, which may be largely eradicated by sanitary precautions, the islands are markedly healthful, and the genial climate of Honolulu and other places on their shores is found highly favorable to invalids suffering from pulmonary complaints.

III. NATURAL PRODUCTIONS.

FOREST AND FRUIT TREES.

The approach to the isles of Hawaii from the western or leeward side gives one a conception the reverse of that looked for from tropical islands. Instead of a riotous luxuriance of verdure, the traveller sees heaps of arid hills, rugged and repellent, looking hot and red in the sunlight, and with scarcely a trace of green except in their gorges and ravines. After landing at Honolulu, one still sees in the distance the same aspect, that of bare, red and yellow, lifeless slopes, lava-covered, yielding only a dry, parched vegetation, on which cattle will not feed except in case of need. All looks grim and forbidding, and strangely unlike the ordinary appearance of the isles of the tropical Pacific.

The conception thus received is a misleading one. On the opposite or rainy side of the island there is an abundance of vegetation, and forests clothe the mountain slopes to their summits; while even on the arid side many of the valleys and ravines are rich with tropical verdure. Of the forest trees, the most striking indigenous form is the *kukui*, or candle-nut tree, with its silvery foliage and its masses of white blossoms. Its nuts have very oily kernels, which are strung together and converted into candles by the natives, each nut kindling the next as it burns down.

Another interesting native tree is a species of the pandanus, or screw-pine, which here grows luxuriantly, attaining a height of twenty-five or thirty feet, and bearing great whorls of long, drooping leaves and an abundance of large, heavy fruits. These, shaped like the pineapple, are made up of sections of a rich golden color, containing an edible pulp. Sandalwood, which was once a plentiful product of the islands, has been practically exhausted. It had the ill fortune to find an active market and to yield much of the royal revenue, and was cut with such wasteful improvidence as to destroy the supply. The cocoa-nut palm, that universal tenant of the tropics, is found abundantly in the region of the coasts.

In ascending from Hilo to the crater of Kilauea the traveller passes through a typical Hawaiian forest, here four miles in width, made up of the trees named, together with the *koa* (acacia), of great industrial value from its hard, heavy, and handsomely grained wood; the hibiscus, with its bluish-green foliage and lemon-colored blossoms; two native species of palm, and numerous ferns, including five species of tree ferns, some of them with stems twenty feet in height. Orchids, so plentiful in parts of the tropics, are here rare, only three species having been found.

The flowering shrubs and fruit-bearing trees include, in addition to those named, the *ohia*, the pink-blossomed Malacca apple, which bears a juicy and pulpy but insipid fruit; the *mairi*, a very fragrant plant; the *ohelo*, the shrub whose juicy and agreeable berries have long been sacred to the goddess of the volcano; the wild plantain, and various other shrubs and trees.

An unusual diversity of parasitic plants is found among the trees of the forest, among them the great birds'-nest fern, which may be seen snugly niched in the upper boughs of the pandanus and other trees, beautiful with its bright glossy fronds. Vines are innumerable, and succeed in rendering it a somewhat difficult operation to traverse the forest, tangled lianas of all kinds growing in bewildering abundance. One of the most notable is the *Ie*, which trails over the highest trees, hanging in twisted and contorted festoons, and bearing its foliage in large tufts. In the centre of each tuft are several scarlet buds, surrounded by a group of scarlet leaves, the whole having the effect of a large and beautiful blossom.

Fruits, native and introduced, are numerous and abundant. Strawberries and raspberries grow plentifully on the highlands, large of fruit, but less luscious than our home product. The bread-fruit, plantain, and banana are common, the last existing in some sixty varieties in different sections. The mango grows well, but its fruit is not a success, being poor in pulp and with a turpentine flavor, perhaps due to lack of care in selection and culture, since the introduced mango of Tahiti and the Philippines is a delicious fruit.

Some exotic growths have thrived inconveniently well. The guava, for instance, grows wild in the forests, and forms impenetrable thickets which cover large tracts of country. Another introduced plant, the lantana, has become a veritable nuisance. This plant, an admired and delicate hot-house treasure in colder climates, grows here so profusely as to form dense thickets, forbidding passage by their thorns, and has become so thoroughly at home that it seems impossible to eradicate.

Among the plants introduced from America is the prickly-pear cactus, which now covers abundantly the waste spaces in the arid west, with whose barrenness its aspect is closely in keeping. Australia has furnished the eucalyptus, which has flourished so well as to have become a feature of the landscape. Another of the widely present exotics is the bean-bearing algaroba, or carob-tree, introduced by the French missionaries, and now forming welcome forests on the lava-strewn slopes. It is about the only plant that takes kindly to the lava, in which it roots and over which it flourishes and multiplies. It has, in consequence, been designated a "blessing of the wastes."

Among the fruit-bearing plants may be named the papaya, with its bright yellow fruits, of the size of a muskmelon, edible either raw or cooked, and making delicious pastries; the orange, lime, citron, fig, custard-apple, rose-apple, and others of foreign origin, but many of which grow here like natives of the soil.

In certain sections of the islands marvels of vegetable growth may be seen. Maui, for instance, possesses what is claimed to be the largest apple-orchard in the world. This is a wide-spreading forest of ohias (the native or Malayan apple), which stretches over the Koolau wilderness from the mountains to the sea, and in the blossoming season is gorgeous with its pink and rosy hues. These trees are from forty to fifty feet in height, and from July to September are loaded with red and white fruit, which has the peculiarity of growing on the trunk instead of the boughs, each apple attached to the bark by a delicate twig. For miles along the sides of the mountains may be seen this broad forest, the trees deeply laden with their beautiful fruit, which in shape more resembles the pear than the apple. The skin is thin and tender, and the fruit exceedingly juicy and agreeably cooling, though its taste is insipid. Mr. Whitney, in his "Hawaiian Tourist," says of this remarkable fruit forest:

"The crop of these apple-orchards, which nature has planted so gorgeously in this wild and solitary waste, would fill a fleet of a hundred steamers, for the orchards stretch over a country from five to ten miles wide by twenty long, and many of the largest trees bear at least fifty barrels each. The fruit furnishes the traveller an excellent repast, appeasing both hunger and thirst. So far as now known, no commercial use can be made of the ohia, as when ripe it cannot be kept more than four days."

In addition to this native apple is a native peach, which grows well and bears fruit in two years from the seed. It is much smaller than the American peach, but is very sweet and juicy, and is excellent for pies and preserves. It might, perhaps, in a few years' culture be greatly improved. The American peach can be grown at elevations of 4000 feet. The Avocado pear, usually called Alligator pear, grows well, and bears fruit of splendid quality in from three to five years from seed. The fruit is much esteemed, and a small quantity has been shipped to California. This is expensive, as it needs to be carried in cold storage; yet what reaches there in good condition sells readily at high prices.

Another marvel of the islands is the semi-wild coffee, a plant which we are accustomed to think of as solely a subject of culture, but which has spread until it forms great forests in Kona, on the western side of the island of Hawaii. Here the berry-bearing plant extends for miles over the rough mountain-sides, the berries, when ripe, being diligently picked by the Japanese, and piled in bags on the road-side, to be conveyed by pack-donkeys to the coffee-mills. Sterile and barren of aspect, Kona seems naturally adapted to the coffee-plant, which roots readily in holes broken through the lava to the soil below, where it grows freely and yields fruit in abundance.

The wasteful cutting of sandal-wood and the injury done by wild cattle to the young plants have proved serious to the forest growth in some localities of the islands, Maui having been denuded of its forests through these destructive processes. As a result, the lava dust rises in such clouds from its barren slopes before the winds as to interfere with navigation, hovering, during a brisk gale, like a dense fog miles distant from the shores of the island.

USEFUL PLANTS.

The Hawaiian Islands possess three indigenous plants of such great utility to the inhabitants that some special mention of them is demanded. These are, to give them their native titles, the *kalo* or *taro*, the *wauti*, and the *ti*. The first of these, known usually as the taro (*Colocasia esculenta*), is the invaluable native food staple, and is so exceedingly productive, if carefully cultivated, that it is said a taro-pit a few yards long will supply food for one man throughout the year. It is eaten in its simple cooked state, but the Hawaiians prefer it in the peculiar form known as poi, of which they are so fond that some of them have objected to leaving their native land on the plea that poi could not be had abroad.

The plant is grown in pits or beds, kept very wet; the edible portion being its large beet-shaped root, one of good average size being a foot long by six inches in thickness. There are said to be twenty-eight varieties grown on the islands, their color varying from white to pink. The growing plants, each rising from its own little hillock of clay above the mud and water of the pit, are as unpleasant as rice to cultivate, though a field in full leaf presents a pretty effect.

To prepare the taro-root for food, it is baked in underground ovens. It may be eaten in this form or the cooked root prepared for poi, which is done by pounding it with a stone pestle, in a wooden bowl or on a scooped-out board. The work is exhausting, the root being waxy and close-grained, and is performed by men.

The substance thus prepared is known as *pai-ai*, and may be kept for months in its dry state, being packed in dracæna leaves. It is converted into poi by adding water and kneading it into a smooth paste, which is then left for several days to ferment. This gives it a slightly sour but rather agreeable flavor. The eating of poi is an art difficult to acquire, and only to be performed gracefully by one "to the manner born." A finger is dipped into the bowl and is drawn out thickly coated with the highly adhesive paste, which is given a peculiar twirl and then sucked from the finger. This is one-fingered poi. Another method, known as two-fingered poi, is more difficult to acquire. A fastidious eater need not object to sharing the bowl of poi with others, as no particle that has once touched the finger can escape to mingle again in the general mass.

Wauti, the second of the useful plants named, is the paper mulberry (*Morus papyrifera*), which furnishes the natives with clothing as the taro does with food. The fine and beautiful cloths for which the islands were formerly famous were made from the inner bark of the young shoots. The osier-like plants were cut when ten or twelve feet high, and the inner bark separated by careful and delicate processes and made into *tapa*, or native cloth, by beating with a mallet. The mallet had different patterns carved on its four faces, so that by its use several varieties of cloth could be produced. It was also printed in beautiful colors, derived from earths and plants. This cloth was fashioned into the *pau*, or woman's garment, which reached from the waist to or below the knees; the *maro*, the narrow cloth worn by the men round their loins; the sleeping-cloths of the chiefs, etc.

The third plant mentioned, the ti (*Dracæna*), serves various useful purposes. Its leaves are used in thatching houses, and, woven by their stalks, were formerly used by the islanders to form a short cloak for mountain journeys. Food is wrapped in its leaves for cooking in the underground Hawaiian oven, and these tough leaves are used variously for wrapping purposes. The tree is planted as a hedge, and its porous, starchy root is baked and eaten. From the sap an intoxicating drink is made, a fiery and unwholesome beverage.

A more potent drink in its peculiar way is that made from the *Ava* (*Piper mythisticum*), whose preparation by chewing the root and steeping the masticated pulp in water is not very enticing to European tastes. The effect of drinking it is rather stupefying than inebriating; and the government has sought, though not very successfully, to suppress the use of this disgusting and injurious drink. The sale of intoxicating liquors is forbidden by law, except in Honolulu; but, as may be seen, the natives contrive to evade this restriction.

NATIVE ANIMALS.

The indigenous fauna of Hawaii is a small one. The mammals include a small rat, a lean, long-headed pig, and a small dog with erect ears. There are also mice, and a bat which has the unusual habit of flying by day. These were the forms found there by Captain Cook, though some of them may have been introduced by earlier visitors. There are two native reptiles, small lizards, which are abundant. The native insects are not numerous in species, though they include some which are very injurious to vegetation, particularly the *pelau*, a caterpillar.

The island had of old the fortune of being free from poisonous or noxious animals, with the exception of centipedes, and these were small in size and not numerous. But civilization has brought its nuisances in the form of vermin of various kinds, as fleas, mosquitoes, roaches, etc., and the Hawaiians can no longer boast of freedom from annoyances of this character.

There is a considerable variety of birds, including the domestic fowl, which is apparently indigenous, wild ducks, snipes, and plovers. Wild geese are abundant in the mountain regions, but do not come down to the coasts. The singing-birds are few in species, one of them with a very sweet note, resembling that of the English thrush. Other species are notable for the great beauty of their plumage. Among these are a small paroquet of glossy purple color; the tropic bird, from whose beautiful feathers was formed a fan carried as one of the insignia of the king and chiefs; and a woodpecker, bright with its plumage of yellow, red, and green, and from whose feathers were made the brilliant cloaks and helmets of the chiefs.

Still other birds yielded their bright plumes for these purposes, there being one sacred to royalty, the Oo, a species of honeysucker peculiar to certain mountain districts, glossy black in color, but remarkable for possessing a pair of tiny golden feathers, one under each wing. These birds are now very rare, though they were not injured in obtaining their much-prized feathers, being caught by an adhesive bird-lime, and set free after being robbed of their yellow gems.

The feathers are only an inch long, sharp-pointed, and very delicate. Of these the great war-cloak of Kamehameha I. was composed. This superb mantle is four feet long and eleven and a half feet in width at the bottom, and contains all the feathers gathered by eight or ten preceding chiefs. It is still preserved as a precious relic of old Hawaiian days.

The seas around the islands contain many edible fish, in the taking of which the Hawaiians are very expert. It is one of their customs to take the fish alive and preserve and fatten them in tanks or ponds. So daring are they in the water that they do not hesitate to attack the shark; making, indeed, an amusement of this dangerous exercise, evading and taunting the man-eating fish, and finally killing it with a dagger-thrust.

In former times the dog and pig of the islands were not only used for food, but were esteemed especial delicacies, and were the greatest dainties that could be served at the royal tables. The dog in particular was the favorite of the epicure,—nice, little dogs these, carefully fed on poi, and of the size of a terrier. Their flesh was deemed superior to pork or kid, and a certain number of dogs were exacted by land owners as part of the rent of their lands. Mr. Ellis speaks of having seen nearly 200 dogs cooked in one day; and mentions a royal banquet in which 400 baked dogs were served up, with hogs, fish, and vegetables in abundance.

INTRODUCED ANIMALS.

During the past century various foreign animals have been introduced, some of which have greatly flourished. Vancouver introduced cattle in 1792, and these in time became so numerous that thousands of wild cattle roam at large through the forest belt on the lower mountain slopes. These, increasing at first under state protection, have grown so fierce that the natives hold them in wholesome dread, and avoid their haunts in the forests, where they are said to do much damage to the timber. They had no sooner become numerous than shooting-parties were organized by white men and brown alike, and since then beef has become a common article of diet.

In addition to the wild cattle, great numbers are kept on ranches, some of which are more than twenty miles long; the owners possessing nominally from 10,000 to 15,000 head of half-wild animals, which at some period of their existence are corralled and branded with the owners' marks. In this work many of the Hawaiians are engaged, they being daring horsemen and as expert as cowboys with the lasso. The cattle are a degenerate breed, and crossing with finer stock is highly desirable.

The horse is another introduced animal which has increased with great rapidity, and numbers of which have returned to the semi-savage state. They are so numerous in some of the islands as to be a plague, breaking fences and treading down crops, and otherwise rendering themselves objectionable. Yet their abundance has given rise to a passion for riding among the Hawaiians, men and women alike, though the wild and furious barebacked horsemanship of the past has been somewhat toned down under more civilized conditions. A people whose former delight was in war, who love to plunge down water-falls and swim through the fiercest surf, and who attack the shark as an amusement, is one likely to yield bold riders, who would seize on such a new muscular exercise with avidity. The horses themselves are small, lean, sorry-looking creatures, which sadly need replacing with better breeds.

In addition to their cattle ranches, the islands have their sheep-runs; and deer have been brought thither and set free in the forests of the island of Hawaii, with a hope that they will increase as cattle have done. To hunt the deer in the forests of lava-covered Mauna Loa will be a new and exciting form of sport for whites and Hawaiians alike. Wild pigs are numerous, and boar-hunting has become one of the sports of the islands, often a dangerous one. The dog has also resumed its original wildness, and in times of dearth is dangerous in some of the mountain regions, where it has become almost as savage as the wolf.

Various species of foreign birds have been introduced, and these, like the foreign plants, bid fair to replace the native species. The house sparrow from Europe and the turtle-dove and the maina from China are almost the only birds to be seen in and about Honolulu, and the native species are growing somewhat difficult to find.

IV. CIVIL AND POLITICAL RELATIONS.

TERRITORY OF HAWAII.

The government of Hawaii (or Hawaii-Nei, to give the group its native title) has passed through the several phases of an absolute monarchy, a limited monarchy, a provisional republic, and a constitutional republic, and is now a possession of the United States. The bill for its organization (brought before but not passed by the Fifty-fifth Congress) proposes to give it a territorial government, under the title of the Territory of Hawaii, with a governor appointed by the President and the requisite heads of the several departments of public works, public instruction, finance, etc.

This bill provides for a legislature of two houses, consisting of a Senate of fifteen members and a House of Representatives of thirty members; voters for representatives being required to be "able to speak, read, and write the English or Hawaiian language;" and voters for senators, in addition, to possess a specified amount of property. All persons who were citizens of the Republic of Hawaii on August 12, 1898, are to become citizens of the United States, with the privilege of suffrage under the qualifications above named. Senators and representatives must have resided for three years in the Hawaiian Islands.

The provisions regarding citizenship exclude Chinese and Japanese laborers, who constitute a large part of the population of the islands, from that right, these not having been "citizens of the Republic of Hawaii." The laws of the United States concerning immigration extend to the islands, Chinese being excluded, and also Japanese brought in under contract by the sugar planters. These regulations will render necessary some new method of procuring the requisite labor.

POPULATION.

Captain Cook, on his visit to the islands in 1778, estimated the population at 400,000. This, while largely a guess, was perhaps not greatly in excess of the actual fact; for there was undoubtedly a rapid decrease in population previous to the arrival of the missionaries in 1820, when but about 140,000 people were found on the islands.

Three causes of this depopulation are assigned. One was the sanguinary wars of conquest of Kamehameha I. A second was the practice of infanticide. The third was the effect of diseases brought by the whites and acting with terrible effect upon a people to whom they were new. As the years went on the depopulation continued. In 1832 the natives were estimated at 130,000; in 1836 at 108,000; and in 1850 at 84,000. In 1872 the census gave a total native population of 49,044; in 1878, of 44,088; in 1884, of 40,014; in 1890, of 34,436; and in 1896, of 31,019. There have been for many years several thousand inhabitants of part Hawaiian blood; but the full-blooded natives threaten to become extinct before many more years have elapsed. Of the three causes assigned for this decrease two no longer exist, infanticide and war being at an end, while the introduced diseases are less fatal than of old. The chief cause of decrease at present seems to be the small birth-rate; the majority of families having no children, and few more than two or three. And children are greatly neglected by their mothers, who seem more tender of dogs and other pets than of their offspring. Thus, though open infanticide is at an end, practical infanticide seems to exist, and unless a stronger maternal instinct can be awakened in the Hawaiian women the race seems doomed.

As the Hawaiians have vanished, whites and Asiatics have gradually taken their place. In 1878 the islands contained 5916 Chinese, 1276 Americans, and 2338 foreigners of other origin. The development of the sugar-cane culture in the succeeding period gave rise to a rapid increase in the foreign population, the census of 1890 giving the following statistics:

Hawaiians	34,436
Half-castes	6,186
Whites	21,119
Chinese	15,301
Japanese	12,360
South Sea Islanders	588
Total	89,990

Of these the whites are credited with the following origins:

Born in the islands	7,495
Portuguese from Fayal	8,602
Americans	1,928
British	1,344
Germans	1,034
Norwegians	227
French	70
Other nationalities	419
Total	21,119

CIVIL AND POLITICAL RELATIONS. 269

The latest census, that of September 27, 1896, yielded the following results:

Hawaiians	31,019
Half-castes	8,485
Japanese	24,407
Chinese	21,616
Portuguese	15,191
Americans	3,086
British	2,250
Germans	1,432
French	101
Norwegians	378
South Sea Islanders	455
Other nationalities	600
Total	109,020

Of the total here given, 72,517 were males and 36,507 females; the latter being in great measure restricted to native and half-caste women and whites of island birth. The occupations of the population, per the census returns, were as follows:

Laborers	34,438
Agriculturists	7,570
Fishing and navigation	2,100
General industries	2,265
Commerce and transportation	2,031
Liberal professions	2,580
Miscellaneous	4,310
Without profession	53,726

The inhabitants were distributed over the several islands in the following proportions: Oahu, 40,205; Hawaii, 33,285; Maui, 17,726; Kauai, 15,228; Molokai, 2307; Niihau, 164; Lanai, 105. The last two contain only herdsmen, and Kahulaui is uninhabited.

EDUCATION.

It is to the earnest labors of the missionaries that Hawaii owes its excellent system of public elementary education, one of the most complete anywhere to be found. As long as forty years ago there was scarcely a child on the islands who could not read and write; and a stringent system of compulsory education now exists which reaches all the children of the islands, those of the towns and of the rural districts alike. There are schools all over the islands, and no child of school age is permitted to be absent from school except under some satisfactory excuse.

The government schools are numerous and are very good, all Hawaiian children being educated at public expense, unless they are in some endowed or other private institution. The native is imitative and quick to assimilate, and makes satisfactory progress until a certain point is reached, when the limit of his intellectual powers seems to be attained. Only exceptionally can he be carried beyond this limit. The English language is everywhere taught, there being very few schools in which the Hawaiian dialect is retained. In consequence, it is rapidly dying out and threatens soon to vanish.

There are many endowed institutions for the education of boys and girls, chief among them being the Kamehameha schools, founded by a descendant of the royal family. In these a nominal fee is charged, and industrial training is added to the school education, the boys being taught various trades and the girls the arts of house-keeping.

The truant-officers do not find their duties arduous,

CIVIL AND POLITICAL RELATIONS. 271

as the Hawaiian children are ready and willing to attend school. The government schools were made free in 1888, with the exception of two in Honolulu and one in Hilo; and since then there has been marked progress in education, the number of school-houses having increased, and a uniform course of study, American in origin, being adopted. The number of pupils in 1887 was 5679. In 1894 they had increased to 8050, and in 1896 to 12,612. Of these, 7405 were Hawaiians and half-castes, 4177 whites (largely Portuguese), 740 Chinese, 261 Japanese, and 29 South Sea Islanders. The teachers are well paid, the salaries ranging from $600 to $1000, or more, per annum.

RELIGION.

Religion has the same freedom in Hawaii as in the United States, and had so previous to the overthrow of the monarchy. Nowhere else have the labors of the missionaries been so completely successful; this being in great part due to the remarkable abandonment of their system of idol-worship by the natives themselves, leaving the missionaries a virgin field in which to work. Among the natives the Protestant doctrines most widely prevail, the Congregationalists being the principal sect. There are hundreds of churches with native Hawaiian pastors, while the Roman Catholic congregations are under French and German priests.

At the last census the religious status of the population was as follows: Roman Catholics, 26,363; Protestants, 23,373; Mormons, 4886; Buddhists and other Asiatic faiths, 44,306; doubtful, 10,192.

Of the ancient Hawaiian deities, there was one

whose worship in a measure survived the overthrow of idolatry, and superstitious fear of whom is not yet quite extinct. This was the famous Pele, the dreaded goddess of the volcano, to whose wrath the terrible outbursts of lava were believed to be due. The great crater of Kilauea was the dwelling-place of this wrathful divinity, who, with her attendant demons, bathed and sported in its fiery waves; while the thread-like, silky filaments blown by the wind from the tossing lava are still known as Pele's hair.

When Mr. Ellis visited the volcano in 1822, he found that the people who had forsaken the gods of the low country still held the deity of the crater in awe, and none dared taste of the sacred berries, which grew abundantly from the decomposed lava, without first throwing a branch loaded with the juicy fruit into the crater as an offering to the goddess. The worship of this deity received a fatal blow in 1824, when Kapiolani, a princess converted to Christianity, visited the crater, ate the sacred berries without the customary offering to Pele, and defied her wrath by hurling stones into the burning lake. Nothing happened to her, and the spell of superstition was broken, though a shadow of the old fear still exists. The favorite votive offerings to Pele were white chickens, and these are said to be still occasionally offered in secret to the dread deity. Other offerings are also at times made by superstitious travellers; the worship of this one relic of the ancient Hawaiian pantheon being thus in a half-hearted fashion kept up, even by those who deem themselves good Christians.

PUBLIC WORKS.

The character of the Hawaiian soil and surface lends itself well to the art of road-making, and a number of very good roads exist in the islands and are kept in excellent condition. This is rendered necessary by the heavy loads which are drawn over them. There may be seen great wagons loaded with wood or cane, or huge logs drawn by from six to twelve or more yoke of oxen, ponderous weights for which only a solid road-bed would suffice.

The mountainous character of the interior of the islands and their small dimensions render any considerable extension of railroad building impracticable; yet some good progress has been made in this direction. The Oahu Railway and Land Company ran its pioneer passenger train on September 4, 1889, and the road was formally opened for business on November 16, carrying hundreds of people free from Honolulu to Halawa. It has since been extended to Waianae, a length of line, including sidings, of 38.5 miles. This is a well-built, single-track road, supplied with rolling stock of American manufacture, and kept in good running order. The equipment consists of five locomotives, fourteen passenger and one hundred and thirty-two freight cars, and its business has steadily grown. In 1897 it carried 85,596 passengers and 66,430 tons of freight. Mr. B. F. Dillingham, the projector of the road, expects eventually to carry it around the entire island of Oahu.

There are two other railroads on the islands, one on Maui and the other on Hawaii. That on Maui is thirteen miles long; its trains making regular trips from Wailuka to Paia, but with poor accommodations for passengers, as there is but little passenger travel on this island. The sugar from a number of large plantations is conveyed by this road to Kahului Bay, three miles from Wailuka, and goods in return are carried inland.

The island of Hawaii has about twenty miles of railroad. A line extends from the steamboat landing at Punaluu to Pahala, the starting-point of the stage-line to the volcano of Kilauea. This road ascends through a difficult country, and winds back and forward, passing over deep ravines by tall trestle-work bridges. It is crooked but picturesque, and is provided with good accommodation for passengers; its principal business being to carry tourists to the volcano, which is by its aid rendered much more accessible.

These public railroads are supplemented by plantation roads, with which nearly every large sugar estate is provided. They extend from all parts of the plantation to its central point, the mill; and in some cases a single road connects several plantations. These roads are supplied with small, light rails, connected often by cross-ties of iron, so that they can be taken up and moved with little expense, the track being shifted as desired and cane planted where the cars had run. Their cars carry the hands to the fields and home again, bring cane to the mills, and are used in a dozen ways to lessen labor and expense. The engines are small but of good pulling power, and are kept busy during the grinding season in drawing great loads of cane to the mill.

American enterprise, to which these roads are due, is also displayed in the street railways, of which there are a number of miles in Honolulu. Horses and mules furnish the motive-power for the street-cars, and are likely to do so for several years yet, since the company controlling the roads refuses to put in an electric system in response to the public demand. In this connection reference may also be made to the electric light, which was introduced into the capital by the recent government, and is in use on some of the large plantations.

Travel in Hawaii demands steamship rather than railroad lines, inter-island commerce being a necessity of the situation. In the days of native supremacy, the double canoe served the purposes of travellers. It was succeeded in later years by sailing-craft, and the steamer followed in due time, the Kilauea, the pioneer boat, being run at a loss by the government. But the traffic demands grew rapidly, and a transportation company was formed, which bought the Kilauea, and between 1877 and 1884 added the Likelike, the Mokolii, the Lehau, the Kinau, and the Kilauea Hou (New Kilauea). In 1890, the Hawaii, built for the sugar-carrying trade, and the Claudine, a large and handsomely appointed passenger-boat, were added.

The Wilder Steamship Company, which runs these boats, now devotes the large steamers Kinau and Claudine to regular passenger traffic, the others being used as freight boats, but occasionally carrying passengers. The Kinau makes regular trips between Honolulu and Hilo, stopping at intermediate ports. The Claudine runs from Honolulu to the ports of Maui.

The inter-island traffic has increased so greatly that still another company, the Inter-island Steamship

Navigation Company, has successfully engaged in it; the boats of this company making their trips on the opposite side of the islands to that pursued by the Wilder Company boats. This company put on its first steamer, the James Makee, in 1879. It has since added the W. G. Hall, Mikahala, Iwalani, Kauai, Ke Au Hou, Waialeale, and Kaala. The business of these two companies may be estimated at $1,000,000 per annum, and is constantly increasing.

Hawaii possesses a well-developed system of irrigation, which the necessities of sugar culture have rendered indispensable on the leeward sides of the islands, with their paucity of rainfall. The numerous mountain streams furnish a good supply of water for this purpose; the application of which has had a striking effect upon the aspect of the islands, changing the barren, lava-strewn wilderness in many places into a paradise of luxuriant foliage. Honolulu is abundantly supplied with water from large reservoirs constructed in the mountain valleys, whence pipes convey the water to all parts of the town. To provide an additional supply, many artesian wells have been sunk.

There has been a considerable development of the telegraph, which is extended widely over Maui and Hawaii, and runs all round Oahu. The total length of line is about 250 miles. Hawaii and Oahu have submarine connection, and all the islands are soon to be connected by wire. The telephone has been introduced into Honolulu and come into very general use there, nearly every family having a telephone connection. It is also wide-spread over the islands, the sugar estates usually having telephone connection with the towns. Even on the lip of the lava pit of Kilauea is a telephone station, from which visitors to the crater may notify the people at the volcano house above at what hour they wish dinner to be ready. The Hawaiian postal system is active and increasing. In 1895, the letters sent and received amounted to 3,978,880.

V. CENTRES OF POPULATION.

HONOLULU.

Honolulu, the capital of the Hawaiian Islands, presents a very attractive appearance to the traveller approaching from the sea. Diamond Head, an extinct volcano, lies like a crouching lion in the path, passing which the island city breaks into view, beautiful in its background of picturesque hills, its abundant vegetation, deep blue skies, and warm tropical sunshine. On entering the harbor a scene of activity appears, numbers of vessels lying at anchor, while the canoes of the natives—each a hollowed-out tree kept from upsetting by an outrigger—dart in a lively fashion from point to point.

Honolulu is a creation of the foreigner, and contains representatives of every travelling nation, the American everywhere in the lead. In 1815 it was a mere fishing village on a sandy plain, whose only vegetation was a fringe of cocoa-nut trees along the shore. In that year, John Young, an American sailor who had been taken prisoner by the Hawaiians, and whose ability had raised him to the position of governor of the island of Hawaii, advised the construction of a fort at this point to command what was apparently the best harbor on the islands. The fort was built under his directions in 1816, and made a work of considerable size and strength. In 1820 Kamehameha II. moved his court from Hawaii to Oahu, and made Honolulu

CENTRES OF POPULATION.

the capital of his kingdom. It is now the metropolis of the islands, and has grown until in 1896 it had a population of 29,920.

Honolulu presents nothing of the imposing, though it possesses much of the attractive, many of its residences being converted into little paradises by their wilderness of tropical verdure. The government buildings are handsome, and on a very extensive scale considering the small size of the country. They contain a library and a museum, of which the former is well supplied with books relating to Hawaii, and the latter possesses many interesting relics, including weapons and utensils of various kinds. Prominent among them are necklaces of hair, each containing a hundred or more of the finest braids, reft not from the brow of beauty, but from the heads of warriors slain in battle. From each depends a curious hook-shaped ornament of polished shell or sperm-whale's tooth, a sacred emblem peculiar to the island, its significance not clearly known.

The King's Palace, a handsome edifice built of volcanic rock, stands in the midst of extensive grounds, with well-kept lawns and flowering trees and shrubs. The Queen's Hospital, with its rare tropical setting, is a thing of beauty of which the islanders are proud. There are other buildings of some prominence, including a number of churches, and the Royal Hawaiian Hotel, the chief caravansary of the islands. Honolulu possesses also five public squares, of which the most important is the Thomas Square, a retreat shaded with tree-ferns and palms, within which of old the royal band made the air of evening musical.

This city is said to possess in all sixty-seven miles

of streets and drives, many of them macadamized and fringed with trees. The streets in the business section of the town are narrow, but in all parts they are scrupulously clean, dust being kept down by frequent and careful sweepings. The streets are panoramas of life and color, business of all kinds going on actively, while the stores make an excellent display of desirable wares. In the Chinese quarter are rows of small shops, dealing in a variety of goods, among them Chinese and Japanese curios and Hawaiian antiquities, of which the latter were probably made by the venders themselves, though they are offered as genuine antiques.

A single bank serves all the present financial needs of the city; but insurance agencies flourish, there being nearly thirty of these devoted to marine, fire, and life insurance. Freemasonry has long flourished in the islands, the capital containing thirteen lodges of the Order, of which King Kalakaua was a member of high rank.

A few words in relation to the markets of the city may be of interest, the fish market being specially peculiar in its viands, since the chief of these is the cuttle-fish, or octopus, the eight-armed sea monster otherwise known as the devil-fish. This repellent creature is a favorite article of the Hawaiian cuisine, as it is of the Japanese, and is to be seen here in all its sizes and varieties. The large ones are cut up and sold in sections, while those of intermediate size are displayed alive, with their writhing snake-like arms. Diminutive forms of the same tribe may be bought by the dozen. The Hawaiian native does not hesitate to eat these alive, asserting that a live cuttle-fish is a greater delicacy than the best oysters. Fish are often eaten raw, and seemingly enjoyed.

There are various edible fish offered for sale, together with spiny sea-urchins, oysters, limpets, crabs, cray-fish, and several varieties of sea-weed, eaten either raw or cooked. The fruit market is well supplied with watermelons, large and juicy; bananas, oranges, cocoa-nuts, figs, Avocado pears, and pine-apples of inferior flavor.

Honolulu is a foreign city in more respects than one. Built and largely inhabited by foreigners, it owes its chief charm—the luxuriant foliage which converts it into a paradise of beauty—to foreign plants, vitalized with the water brought by the skill of foreign engineers from the mountain streams. The deficiency of rain has been made good by irrigation, which has converted the site into a blooming garden, rich with the foliage of imported plants.

In the words of C. F. Gordon Cumming, "A multitude of pleasant two-storied bungalows are embowered in gardens brilliant with flowering shrubs, and by the richest trees of the tropics. Beautiful passion-flowers and starry clematis, orange venusta, and bougain-villeas, with their rich masses of magenta foliage, climb in profusion over the verandas and droop from the roofs,—which indeed they almost conceal. Heliotropes, roses, and geraniums well repay the care bestowed upon them. Golden allamandas and rosy oleanders, pure white trumpet-flowers, scarlet and yellow hibiscus, and fragrant gardenia are among the commonest shrubs, while starry white lilies grow in rank profusion, as does also a fragrant and beautiful white cactus, the night-blooming cereus, which creeps unheeded over rough stone walls and banks. Overhead the feathery tamarind trees form a soft veil of the lightest lace-like foliage, or large glossy-leaved india-rubber trees throw their cool, dark shadow on smooth green lawns; and mango and bread-fruit rank as handsome foliage trees, though their fruit is not to compare with that of the Southern isles. Norfolk Island pines and date-palms both grow luxuriantly, also the magnolia and eucalyptus."

The most beautiful of these ornamental trees is the royal palm, which reaches perfection in Hawaii, and adorns nearly every lawn in the city. The Hawaiian dwelling is a one-storied edifice, with verandas front and back, and sometimes on the sides, and wide doors opening into parlor, dining-room, and other apartments. The walk from the street is paved with heavy slabs cut from the trunks of the pulu fern trees, which form a soft and fine-wearing pavement. The tree does not suffer from the wound, since this quickly heals. On either side of this walk are rows of bright-leaved plants, beyond which on each side extends the profusion of bloom above described, while in the gardens grow bananas, oranges, dates, figs, and a dozen other tropical fruits. Shade is supplied by the banyan, the bamboo, the tree fern, and other tropical trees, forming shady and inviting retreats during the midday heat.

Honolulu has its striking surroundings. Overlooking the town is a steep hill of volcanic scoria, reddish brown in color, with a crater at the top known as the Punch-Bowl. A little farther away is the Diamond Head promontory, red and lava seamed. It is about 760 feet high, and contains an extinct crater 700 feet in depth. Its days of power are gone, and it is now crumbling away under the assaults of wind and rain.

Three miles from the city, and between it and Diamond Head, lies the pleasant sea-side village of Waikiki, which the citizens seek in carriages or street-cars for the enjoyment of surf-bathing. It presents a succession of handsome private villas, surrounded by gardens; while bathers find there an excellent beach, clear water with smooth bottom, commodious bathhouses, and good bathing temperature from January to June. The sharks which haunt most of the coast rarely or never cross the reef at this place.

Back of Honolulu, ascending into the mountains, is the beautiful Nuuana Valley, which ends in a great cleft in the mountain ridge known as the Pali, and yielding a magnificent view of the verdant eastern side of the island. This valley is luxuriantly green to within two or three miles of the town, and is bordered by numbers of handsome villas. The rain-clouds passing through the cleft pour their refreshing waters along its course, shedding their last drops on the streets of Honolulu with such parsimony that some streets are rainier than others, and irrigation from the water-pipe and artesian well is necessary for the garden vegetation of the town.

HILO.

Hawaii possesses few towns besides the capital, the only one of importance being Hilo, the port of Hawaii Island. This town has original features of its own; an air of novelty being given by the great palms which adorn the court-house square, and the quaint and picturesque streets, which display a marked variety in architecture and occupants, the people being a mixture of Asiatics, Polynesians, Europeans, and Americans. There are three public edifices,—the court-house, custom-house, and post-office,—and in addition an excellent library.

The town is marked by a luxuriant profusion of foliage, the constant heavy rainfall causing a prolific growth of all kinds of trees and shrubs. The headland which aids in forming the harbor is crowned with cocoa-nut trees, and the streets are flanked with palms, bamboos, and other tropical growths. The town slopes gently back from the shore of the bay, which is enclosed by a crescent-shaped beach, said to be the most beautiful in the Pacific. At its outer extremity is Cocoa-nut Island, which charmingly completes the curve with its verdant covering of tall and graceful cocoa-nut palms.

The humid air and over-abundant rainfall of Hilo give an extraordinary profusion to its vegetation, the dwellings being almost buried in their luxuriant gardens and the flowering vines which clamber over sides and roofs. A like tropical luxuriance marks the country in the background, the surrounding hills being covered with dense forest, while in the vicinity are miles of sugar-cane plantations. There are many beautiful water-falls, caused by the descent of the numerous streams from the higher levels into deep and difficult ravines.

The American predominates in Hilo, as in all the centres of population of the island; but occidental activity is not a characteristic of the town, whose polyglot population seem to think that the chief end of life is to do nothing with the least possible effort.

LAHAINA.

The village of Lahaina, on the western coast of Maui, was once the capital of that island, the residence of its king, and the chief city of the Hawaiian group. Here were the royal palace, the American and British consulates, and streets and harbor marked by bustle and activity. It was the commercial as well as the political capital, and a place of call for the whaling vessels, which here obtained their supplies, frequently paying for the same with blackfish oil. Long after Honolulu had become the leading city, Lahaina continued the whalers' port, the captains preferring it from the fact that their men could obtain no liquor there, the sale of spirits being restricted to Honolulu. During this period the whaling fleets brought the principal business to the islands, and were a valuable source of revenue to the government.

The place has long since fallen from its high estate; the palaces of the kings and chiefs have sunk into decay, and the merchandise warehouses have disappeared. Commerce has fled to new scenes, following royalty, which long since deserted Lahaina in favor of Honolulu, and left the latter a deserted village, destitute even of a hotel.

There is a sugar-mill here, the cane being brought from fields four or five miles away. For two miles along the shore the village spreads, in a grove of bread-fruit, cocoa-nut, mango, tamarind, orange, and other trees, beauty having stayed when royalty fled away.

KAILUA.

Of the other villages of the islands it will suffice to speak of Kailua, on the shore of Hawaii, at the foot of the volcano Mauna Hualalai, whose last eruption took place a century ago. This place was once a royal residence of the kings of Hawaii, and later a favorite country-seat of royalty. A large old stone building is pointed out as the former palace. At Keauhou, six miles south of Kailau, is a spot of historic interest, that in which the great discoverer, Captain Cook, met his death, and where a monument has been erected to his memory. It is a plain obelisk of concrete, with an inscription and a surrounding of chains and old cannon.

VI. THE PEOPLE OF HAWAII.

THE NATIVE POPULATION.

The Kanakas, to give the native Hawaiians the title applied to them by the whaling crews, are a very interesting people. In race they belong to the Malayo-Polynesian stock, and may be classed among the finest of the Pacific peoples, bearing a close resemblance to the New Zealanders in stature and in their well-developed and muscular limbs. The mass of the people are of moderate stature, but the chiefs and the women of their families are of unusual height. Their color is a reddish-brown, resembling that of tarnished copper. They have a broad face, with thick lips and somewhat flattened nose, while the beard is thin and the hair, usually raven black, is straight, or in some cases wavy. They are more hardy and active than the peoples living nearer the equator, due perhaps to their salubrious climate and the comparative sterility of their soil, which renders necessary some degree of industry in the cultivation of their food plants. Yet the country people take life very easy, little exertion being necessary to obtain the means of subsistence.

They are a good-tempered and light-hearted race, given to mirth and laughter, fond of pleasure, and of the most genial disposition. Friendly and forgiving, the Hawaiian meets every one with a smile, and is genuinely hospitable. He is free from malice, harbors no treachery, and is natively simple-minded, kindly, and benignant. Though seemingly unfit to conduct business, he makes a faithful and trusty employee, and there is no occupation on the islands in which he is not engaged.

In former days the only dress worn by the men was the *malo*, a narrow strip of cloth wound round the loins and passed between the legs. Women wore the *pau*, a short petticoat made of *tapa*, the bark of the cloth-tree or paper mulberry, and reaching from the waist to the knees. And this scanty attire was thrown off without hesitation when they wished to indulge in their favorite exercise of swimming. The habits of the people were very licentious, female virtue being an unknown thing; while the common practice of infanticide, particularly of female children, had a serious effect on the numbers of the population.

These former social conditions have largely disappeared before the efforts of the missionaries. Men now wear a shirt and trousers, and those of the better class use the full European dress; while the women all wear the *holoka*, a loose garment, white or colored, which reaches from the neck to the feet. The head is covered with a colored handkerchief, or a straw hat is worn. Both sexes delight to adorn themselves with flower garlands and necklaces of colored seeds. Some of these garlands, or *leis*, are very pretty, being made of small roses, oleanders, jessamines, or other flowers, strung into a thick rope of bloom. They may be made of feathers, or trails of some green vine may be gracefully twined round the hat or worn round the throat. The bright blossom of the scarlet hibiscus is much worn by men, while others make a more durable garland by stringing together the orange-colored sections of the fruit of the screw-pine. This pretty custom adds much to the picturesqueness of the native attire.

Kind and genial as is the Hawaiian, he is remarkably brave and daring, his favorite sports being of a character whose danger would repel most people. In the old days of war the Hawaiians fought with the greatest courage, some of their battles lasting for days, and ending in the annihilation of the defeated party. Their expertness with the javelin was remarkable. One of their games consisted in throwing spears at a warrior, whose skill was shown in his catching the first in his hand and with it warding off the others. King Kamehameha I. would permit six spears to be thrown at him at once, all of which he caught or avoided.

Their ordinary amusements were of the same dangerous character. After the introduction of the horse, a wild passion for riding gained control of the people, and both sexes took delight in dashing wildly through town and country, without thought of danger. The women rode astride, wearing over their holokas a gay riding-dress, which consisted of a strip of crimson, purple, or yellow calico twisted round the body and with its ends flying in the breeze. Riding astride is still the fashion for women in Hawaii; while the men engaged on the cattle-ranges are as skilful horsemen and as expert with the lasso as our own cowboys of the West. The saddle used is the high-peaked Mexican affair, to which huge wooden stirrups are attached.

It is in the water, however, that the Hawaiian has long shown the greatest intrepidity, the perilous pastime of surf-swimming having been for centuries the favorite national sport. It was after a day of storm, when the surf came rushing inward in tremendous billows, that the native most delighted in braving the fury of the waves. Though the great green billows might be rushing in like wild horses and breaking on the beach with overwhelming violence, the Hawaiian, carrying his surf-board,—a carefully prepared wooden plank,—did not hesitate to plunge into the seething surf.

Diving beneath the first wave, he rose beyond it and swam out to meet another, through which he again plunged, and thus dived under wave after wave until he reached the smoother water outside. If he should miscalculate by a second of time, he would be caught and dashed shoreward by the surf, with imminent risk of being flung headlong on the rocks. But failure was rare, the swimmer having gained skill through practice from childhood.

The outer waters reached, the most exciting time came. Lying flat on his board, the swimmer launched himself on the highest wave, and was carried ashore at race-horse speed. He might be caught by a following wave or fail to keep his plank at the right angle, in which case he was likely to have to swim for his life, sometimes being compelled to abandon his trusty board. But if all went well he was carried smoothly and safely shoreward, the most skilful standing upright on their boards and shouting with glee and triumph as they were borne to the beach. Surf-riding, however, appears to be obsolete, and a surf-board is to-day a very difficult thing to obtain.

Not only men, but women and boys, were remarkably expert in the water, and the boys of Honolulu are to-day always ready to dive after a flung coin, usually catching it before it reaches the bottom. It was not only in the ocean that the Hawaiian swimmers exhibited their daring. They did not hesitate to trust themselves to the dashing waters of cascades, darting in glee down the shooting and seemingly death-dealing liquid. Even the long flumes which carry water from the hills to the sugar-mills are made use of by the workmen to save a walk, and a young married couple is said to have made their wedding-trip to the coast down one of these flumes.

The fearlessness of the Hawaiian boatmen makes them indispensable in the traffic along the coast. Many of the landings are very dangerous, and the boats which carry passengers or freight ashore from the steamers are always in peril of being upset by the waves or crushed on the rocks. Yet the boatmen are so skilful that it is a rare event for one of them to be drowned. They swim like fish, and the capsizing of a boat is a matter of small moment to them, while the imperilled passengers are usually safe in their hands. The indolence of the native ends when he has occasion to go to sea. In his light canoe he makes his way daringly through the surf, deftly using his paddle to avoid the beach-combers, and quickly passing the danger-line into the open waters beyond.

We have already spoken of the contests of these bold swimmers with the sharks of the coast. When the shark turns to snap at his intended victim the native dives, and the great jaws come emptily together. A skilful dagger-thrust may end the contest, or the Hawaiian may be armed only with a piece of sharpened iron eight or ten inches long, which he thrusts into the monster's mouth as it opens to seize him, the jaws being propped open by the iron and the great brute rendered helpless.

Dancing is one of the amusements of the people, the favorite performance being a voluptuous dance called the *hula-hula*, which consists of movements of the body timed to a doleful music, the feet taking little part in it. The usual costume is a short skirt made of grass, the upper body adorned with flower garlands. Nude dancing, formerly common, is prohibited by law, though still occasionally performed.

As regards the industrial occupations of the Hawaiians, their employment as boatmen is but one out of many, they being engaged in a great variety of occupations. Among them are many blacksmiths, carpenters, painters, machinists, engineers, and teamsters. Others serve as clerks or book-keepers, or as editors, school-teachers, or clergymen. Their occupations include cattle-raising and sugar-planting, while they fill most of the clerical positions under the government. The pressmen and compositors in the printing-offices are mainly natives; they are employed in the telephone offices, and the heavy work in iron foundries and in the loading of vessels is almost wholly done by them. Considering that less than a century ago they were in their pristine condition of semi-savagery, their progress has certainly been phenomenal.

The language of the Hawaiians, now rapidly dying out, is a branch of the widely-diffused Malayo-Polynesian tongue, which is so similar throughout that peoples as widely separated as the Hawaiians and New Zealanders can with some difficulty understand each other. It is a soft and harmonious form of speech, largely vocalic in structure, the only consonants being *k*, *l*, *m*, *n*, and *p*. These with the five vowels, the gently aspirated *h*, and the vocalic *w*, make up the alphabet in use. *R* and *t*, formerly used, have been suppressed in favor of *l* and *k*, the word *taro*, for instance, becoming *kalo*. What little is left of this language must soon vanish in view of the common teaching of English in the schools.

DWELLINGS AND FOOD.

The houses of the natives were formerly mere huts of grass, their roofs being thatched by and their walls made of dried grass. Wooden houses are now used in Honolulu and most of the country districts, the grass house being rarely seen. Large and substantial dwellings would be none too safe in a country subject to earthquakes, and of little utility for a people whose mild climate tempts them to live mainly out of doors. What little cooking is needed is done outside. The oven consists of a hole in the ground, in which a fire is lighted and stones are heated. The fire being removed, the food is wrapped in leaves and placed in the hole beside the hot stones, where it is covered up and left to the cooking process. The houses are principally utilized for sleeping, the whole family being stretched upon the floor and covered with a broad sheet of *tapa*, or native cloth.

The taro tuber, as already stated, serves as the principal article of food, either cooked or formed into the favorite edible poi. The sweet potato, yam, breadfruit, cocoa-nut, banana, papaya, and other food-stuffs and fruits serve to vary the diet. The edible dogs, formerly the favorite food viand at a Hawaiian high feast, were carefully fattened on poi, and were baked in the manner now employed in baking pig and fish, a method which has received the praises of all epicures who have tested the result.

This method is the common one of cooking with heated stones. The pig is slain and dressed, and is then rubbed upon the hot stones until the hair comes off. The body is filled with heated stones, placed in the *imu*, or earth-oven, and covered with hot stones and taro and banana leaves. The excavation is then closed with earth and the meat allowed to roast and steam for hours. The result is a thoroughly well done, crisp, and juicy roast pig.

A *luau*, or native feast, is one of the great occasions in Hawaii. The natives of that country are credited with cannibalistic feasts in olden times; and it is said that when the question of how they should dispose of the corpse of the great Kamehameha came up, some one calmly proposed that they should eat it. There is the best of reason to believe, however, that all this is a calumny, and that the Hawaiians were never cannibals. Their feasts have a decidedly civilized flavor. A luau is a sort of combined picnic,—some parties providing the poi, others the meats, others the fruits, others the *kulolo*, a pudding made of grated cocoa-nut and taro, and others the *poi-palau,* a compound of poi and sweet potato. *Limu,* a fresh-water moss, is a favorite relish, as also is the candle-nut roasted and salted.

The meats are cooked in the imu in the method described, the fish and pieces of beef and pork being wrapped in young taro leaves, which absorb their juices, tough ti leaves being bound round the whole. Nothing can be more delicious than meats hot from the imu, while the taro leaves yield a delicate form of spinach. Slices of cooked taro and other vegetables, fruits, and bowls of poi form the remainder of the feast.

When the meal is ready, the participants in the feast sit or squat around the matting on which it is placed, and each proceeds to eat with no other aid than that of his fingers, while mirth and good humor prevail. A luau used to be given in honor of every important event, followed usually by hula dances and other festivities.

INHABITANTS OF FOREIGN ORIGIN.

As has been already stated, the Hawaiian population has rapidly decreased since the period of Captain Cook's visit to the islands, and this decrease still continues. It may end in a complete disappearance of the race, the few survivors being swamped by intermarriage. This decrease has been ascribed to immorality, infanticide, and the introduction of foreign diseases. The women are less numerous than the men, and the married ones have few children, the majority of them having none. The maternal instinct seems largely lacking, and children are greatly neglected.

The decrease in population due to these causes has been made up in part by the importation of foreign laborers. Chinese came at first in large numbers as plantation hands, principally after 1875. Later, to supply the increasing demand, many Portuguese were brought from Madeira, and a small number of Polynesians were introduced from other islands. Within the more recent period Japanese have been brought in under contract, until they have surpassed the Chinese in number, while at present the laboring population, of Chinese, Japanese, and Portuguese, is double that of the full-blooded Hawaiians. The remaining population is principally composed of Americans, British, and Germans, the Americans being in the lead.

The importation of foreign laborers was largely a result of the disinclination of the natives to plantation work. The same difficulty arose with the Portuguese, who preferred work of other kinds, and sought openings for employment off the plantation. Even the Chinese, who were expected to solve the difficulty, have branched off into various other occupations, many of them engaging in market-gardening, while others bought up the swampy tracts of land and converted them into prolific rice-fields. Their skill and industry have enabled them to produce such crops of rice, fruit, and vegetables as Hawaii had never before seen.

The plantation laborers are principally Chinese and Japanese, brought over under contract; their wages at present twelve to fifteen dollars per month, of which they send home to China or Japan every cent they can possibly save,—and these Asiatics can live on what would be speedy starvation to a white man. Cheaply as the Chinese can live, the Japanese coolie is said to surpass him in the art, and, small as are his wages, he manages to obtain food and clothing and send home for future use nearly the whole sum. It is said that some of the lower-class Japanese live on one dollar per month, their diet being rice and water and their dress cast-off clothing. The planters usually furnish huts for their laborers and medical attendance when they are sick, but nothing more. The Portuguese and Hawaiians are better paid than the Orientals, receiving from sixteen dollars to eighteen dollars monthly.

The contract-labor system was established in the days of royalty, and was solely a governmental affair; the Japanese government hiring laborers to the Hawaiian government, which in turn hired them to the planters for a fixed period and a stipulated sum. The laborer had no voice in the matter, and during the contract period was virtually a slave, an attempt to leave the plantation being followed by severe punishment.

The new status of Hawaii, as a part of the United States, puts an end to the bringing in of laborers under any such system. The introduction of Chinese labor is positively forbidden under any circumstances, and no Japanese can be brought in under contract. These immigration laws form an awkward problem for the sugar-kings to handle, in view of the steady drift from plantation life of the present laboring population. Just how the difficulty is to be overcome does not clearly appear, unless it be by the introduction of negro labor. "The negro might cost a little more," say some of the planters, "but he is capable of doing more work, and such a change is likely to be profitable."

The Americans and Europeans form the governing, planting, and mercantile classes, and to their enterprise and capital are due all the steps of progress and industrial development to be seen. Of the American residents of the islands a very considerable proportion were born there, being the descendants of the early missionaries who, through the influence of the American Board of Missions, were induced to settle permanently in the islands, as centres of good influence with the people. These islanders of foreign paternity now number nearly 8000, and form a solid basis for the new status of Hawaii as an American territory. A large increase in this American population is likely to take place under the new condition of affairs, and a marked development of the resources of the country may be confidently looked for.

VII. AGRICULTURAL INDUSTRIES.

GENERAL CONDITIONS.

The islands which an immigrant desiring to engage in agricultural enterprises would find of most interest are four in number,—Hawaii, Maui, Oahu, and Kauai. Of these, Hawaii, with its copious rains on the windward side and variety of soil and climate, is full of promise, particularly in sugar and coffee production. The Kona district has an extended reputation for the excellence of its coffee, which some claim to equal or surpass the best Mocha or Java. Numerous sugar plantations have been established here, while there are several hundred coffee-planters, owning from 200,000 trees to one or a few acres. Thousands of acres lie uncultivated, awaiting capital and enterprise.

The same may be said of Maui, on which, also, thousands of acres lie fallow. It has its sugar plantations and coffee lands, the latter having been just opened up. The western slopes of Haleakala, the main mountain, are covered with small farms devoted to potatoes, corn, beans, and pigs. Oahu is rich with opportunities to the investor. Its railroad line opens up rich coffee and farming lands, and, if extended round the island, as proposed, must bring into cultivation its many fertile valleys. Kauai, the "Garden Island," as it is called, is very well watered and luxuriant in vegetation. At present it is largely devoted to sugar-cane, though there is considerable rice grown. Coffee has been tried and failed; but this was through lack of judgment, and there is much land likely to be suited to this crop.

SUGAR PRODUCTION.

Captain Cook and his successor Vancouver were particularly impressed, in their visit to the Hawaiian Islands, with the extraordinary luxuriance of the sugar-cane and its unusual sweetness. Stalks of it were seen twenty feet in height, while it was found growing freely in every valley of Kauai as if it were native to the soil. It was probably introduced by some earlier visitors centuries before; but the genial climate and the rich soil furnished by the disintegrated lava seem to have brought it to a perfection nowhere else attained, and to a richness in sugar reached in no other lands.

The cane was everywhere cultivated in the rude fashion of barbarian agriculture; its sweet pith being a favorite with the islanders, whom it served both for food and drink. Early in the nineteenth century, foreign visitors, chiefly Chinese, tried to produce sugar from the cane, using primitive methods; but the first intelligent effort was made by the American firm of Ladd & Co., who purchased a tract of land at Koloa, on Kauai, in 1835, planted it with cane, and erected the first sugar-mill on the islands. Horses or mules formed their motive-power, water-power being afterwards used, and finally steam. Stone and wooden rollers were first used to grind the cane.

This pioneer enterprise has been succeeded by a large number of plantations, many of them of immense extent. There are said to be about seventy of these monster plantations on the islands, worth more than

AGRICULTURAL INDUSTRIES.

half a million of dollars each. Of these plantations, that at Sprecklesville, on Maui, is not only the largest in Hawaii, but is said to be the largest in the world. It embraces 40,000 acres of cane, and is owned by two sons of Claus Spreckles, the Californian sugar-king.

With the production of sugar in Hawaii was closely associated the question of irrigation, much of the land on the leeward side of the mountains lacking the degree of rainfall needed by the cane, though their surface layer of red lava dust was capable, by the aid of water, of being made highly fertile. The richness of the disintegrated lava is said to be due to the presence of a very large proportion of phosphates and nitrogen, and to this is due also the permanence of its fertility. When, after yielding many crops, the generous soil shows signs of exhaustion, its fertility can be restored by sprinkling it with the ashes of burnt weeds and refuse cane. The cane from the crushing-mills thus becomes the natural manure for the fields, giving them back their lost potash. The volcanic soil has the further advantage of yielding good natural drainage.

The cane found growing by Captain Cook has been replaced by the best varieties from other sugar-growing countries, different canes being used in accordance with the difference in soil and altitude. The irrigation works consist of great flumes, or wooden aqueducts, which cause the water of the mountain streams to spread over the lowland plains. By this free use of water a wilderness of red dust has been converted into fertile fields of cane, whose green expanse is visible not only on the low coast lands but on the mountain sides. The flumes which convey water to the lower fields serve a second useful purpose, the cane from plantations on the higher grounds being floated by them to the crushing-mills in the valleys below. In this way the cut cane is sometimes transported by water for a distance of several miles,—a great saving of labor. The workmen, as already stated, occasionally save themselves a down-hill walk by taking passage in this water-carriage, in company with the cane, or the logs for fuel which are sent down in the same way.

The cane, after its water-carriage of miles to the mill, is delivered on the carrier leading to the crushing-rollers, while the water, after having done its duty, falls through an open grating, and is carried onward to irrigate fields at a lower level than the mill. It may be said that this ingenious method of cane transportation is only applied under favoring conditions, the railway being the usual method of carrying the cane.

The aqueducts used to water the arid fields are extensive and needed much engineering skill in their construction. The district of Makawao, in Kauai, with its great width of arable land, is irrigated by a conduit thirty miles long, descending at a slight grade, nowhere more than twelve feet to the mile. Numerous ravines needed to be crossed by the aid of large pipes, in which the water-pressure was so great that it taxed the resources of the engineer to provide the necessary resisting power. At the Maliko gulch, 500 yards wide, the pipes are carried to the bottom of the ravine and up again on the other side. These works give fertility to the plantations on the mountain side, and irrigate an expanse of several thousand acres of former desert in the plain below.

The plantation at Ewa, on Oahu, is irrigated by

water drawn from artesian wells of inexhaustible yield. The water is pumped up into stand-pipes, from which it is conveyed in conduits to the different sections of the great plantation, every portion of which receives just the necessary quantity of moisture. Thousands of acres of land are watered by these great works, the life-giving streams being carried for miles in every direction.

No small amount of skill is needed properly to distribute the water to the hills of cane, the fields being a net-work of flumes and ditches, through which the water flows. The canes are planted in short rows, separated by little ditches, in which the water is allowed to stand at a depth of several inches for a day or two at a time. Each row is opened in succession with the hoe, the water let in, and the ditch then dammed up, the water being allowed to soak slowly into the ground at the roots of the plants.

The remarks here made apply to the western sides of the islands. On the eastern or rainy sides irrigation is not called for, the rainfall being often over-abundant. The moist atmosphere checks rapidity of growth as compared with the dry and sunny regions, and the cane may make no more progress in twenty months than it does in twelve months in irrigated fields. In the elevated fields, slowness in maturing is correlated with greater density of product and much superior yield of sugar.

The sugar-planter is not without his enemies, especially rats and worms,—the former gnawing the cane for its sweet pulp, the latter boring into and riddling it internally, so that a seemingly sound cane may be a honeycomb within and all its sugary juices gone.

The rat is the most persistent enemy of the planter; his ravages causing great loss in cane and considerable expense in endeavors to circumvent him. In Jamaica, where the rats proved an equal nuisance, numerous expedients were from time to time vainly adopted. Cats were first tried, but were worsted in the fray. The ferret was then introduced, but yielded to the attacks of the chigoa-flea, an enemy to all imported animals. The Cuban ant, a useful rat-destroyer, was next tried, and also the great Agua toad. These were serviceable, but the rats increased; and it became necessary to employ rat-catchers, with their troops of terrier dogs, their traps, and poisons. All these methods proved useless, and finally the Indian mongoose was introduced, the natural foe of rats and snakes. This proved effective, and the rats almost disappeared, districts which were formerly abandoned in despair to the devouring rat being again brought under cultivation.

Rats are as destructive in Hawaii as in Jamaica, and the rat-catcher has long been one of the most useful characters on the islands. With his little corps of twenty or thirty terriers he is able to make havoc in the army of rodents, and in a few days may for the time being clear a plantation of these pests. The mongoose was introduced about 1880, and proved a very effective ally of the planters, increasing in numbers at a rapid ratio and quickly making havoc among the rodents.

The mongoose has one weakness,—it loves eggs and poultry. The rats destroyed, the new animals became something of a pest in turn, giving their attention to the poultry yard. It is claimed that they are less destructive in this direction than the rats, and that, being easily caught, one or two dogs suffice to clear a plantation of these inconvenient allies. However that may be, the poultry-raisers have gained legislation in their favor, and a law was passed in 1892 for the destruction of these foreign rat-killers.

The yield of sugar by Hawaiian cane is large, averaging four to five tons per acre, and reaching under favorable conditions eight or more tons. The cane needs about twelve months to reach maturity in irrigated fields, and the cutting and grinding begin in January and continue to June. No description of the process of sugar-making is here called for, as this process has been fully described under the head of Cuba. The methods pursued in Hawaii do not differ from those of Cuba.

The crushing apparatus in some of the Hawaiian mills is of unsurpassed effectiveness. From three to five crushing-rolls are used in the Cuban mills, but the great Ewa mill on Oahu has no less than nine rollers, working on improved plans, and crushing the cane so thoroughly that it leaves the rolls in rags and powder. The dry product, empty of every vestige of juice, furnishes the only fuel used in the mill.

In some of the mills the diffusion process of extracting juice from the cane replaces the crushing one. The latter, however, is usually preferred. More juice can be obtained by diffusion, but the juice from the crushed cane yields more sugar. The Ewa mill yields 93.08 per cent. of the total juice, and the gain in sugar is eight per cent. over that yielded by the diffusion plant at first employed.

The process of skimming, boiling, and liming does

not need to be again described. It will suffice to say that the thickening syrup, when finally drawn from the vacuum-pans, is run off into the centrifugals, which resemble circular churns with wire screens. These are made to revolve at an extraordinary rate of speed; the result being a separation of solid and liquid, the syrup being thrown through the wire screens and leaving dry sugar behind. This, still hot, is drawn off into bags and conveyed to the warehouses. The boiling of the syrup is repeated until all the sugar it contains is extracted, each new boiling yielding sugar of a lower grade.

The sugar product of Hawaii has steadily increased for many years. In 1860 the export was quoted at 1,144,271 pounds. In 1877 it had risen to 25,575,965 pounds, and in 1881 to more than 88,000,000 pounds. The later crops are estimated in tons, that of 1891 being 146,174 tons, and that of 1897, 248,555 tons. The 1898 crop has been estimated at 248,576 tons, of which there are apportioned to the island of Hawaii 126,737, Kauai 51,864, Maui 41,047, and Oahu 28,929 tons. Nearly 70,000 persons—men, women, and children—are engaged in the sugar culture in some capacity.

COFFEE CULTURE.

Coffee finds itself much at home in Hawaii, especially in the island of that name, where, in the Kona district, it has spread into forests of semi-wild plants. These we have already described. It would not be easy to find a more barren and sterile soil than that of Kona, yet here the coffee-plant flourishes, being often, as is said, "planted with a crowbar." That is, a hole is driven through the crust of lava rock, and the coffee-twig, dug up from the forest, is planted in the soil below. Here it grows and bears luxuriantly.

The soil of the Puna district is similarly lava-covered, Kilauea having long poured her floods of liquid rock over its surface. Yet coffee thrives here, and of a quality nowhere surpassed. Some of the plantations contain from 25,000 to 60,000 trees, there being over fifty plantations where there was dense forest a few years ago.

The soil of Hawaii is of a dark chocolate or reddish-brown hue, the darker being the best adapted to coffee. Being of volcanic origin, its fertility varies according to the degree of disintegration of lava and the quantity of decomposed vegetable matter. When the ground is covered with broken A-a lava the soil is very rich. Stones in coffee land are of utility as an aid to drainage, but are not otherwise necessary.

The coffee crop succeeds best at a height of from 500 to 2000 feet, though there are thousands of fine trees at sea-level. These, however, are more subject to blight than those at a higher altitude. 42° F. is the lowest temperature the coffee-plant will bear, and from 48° to 80° is thought to be the best for successful culture. Wind is its worst enemy, and wind-breaks of some kind are necessary, the banana and the castor bean being among the plants used for this purpose. As regards shade, which is thought so important in Cuba, opinions in Hawaii differ, some planters shading their plants, others exposing them freely to the sun.

The first coffee sent from Hawaii to the United States was the ill-cleaned, poorly-cured product from the semi-wild trees. Even in that condition it attained a reputation for excellence which stands the planter in good stead to-day. With careful culture, the coffee grown here should attain a high standing. The delicacy of its aroma is beyond question; while it ranks as a specialty, being somewhat unlike the Central American and South American coffees in flavor. Although Hawaiian coffee has been grown and marketed for years, its cultivation on an extended scale and on scientific principles has been only recently attempted, and the full result cannot yet be stated.

Of the Hawaiian coffee lands, the government holds 76,000 acres, which are open for sale. The whole extent of coffee lands is about 200,000 acres, of which 178,000 are in Hawaii, 14,000 in Maui, 3500 in Oahu, and 1500 in Kauai. Much of this is as yet inaccessible from lack of roads. The government lands can be obtained at an annual rental of from one to two and a half dollars per acre, or can be leased at eight per cent. on a valuation of five dollars per acre, with privilege to purchase at that price. Homesteads are limited to eight acres at nominal cost, the purpose of the government being to prevent large corporations from obtaining control.

In the year 1896 there were about 10,000 acres planted in coffee, the great bulk of which had been very recently cleared. In 1898 there were 222 plantations in all, of which 193 were on the island of Hawaii. As may be seen, the industry is still in its infancy. The coffee is subject to injury from blight and insects, though as yet no serious trouble has been experienced. The prevailing labor on the coffee plantations is Japanese, the laborers being paid from twelve dollars to fifteen dollars each per month, without board. The planters, however, prefer Chinese laborers, as they are more tractable and need less overseeing. The labor problem, indeed, is a question of serious import, the native Hawaiians not liking field labor, and much preferring employment on the cattle ranches. The question of picking the coffee remains to be solved. Native women and children may perhaps be employed, though there are certain obstacles in the way of this.

No description of the modes of coffee culture and preparation for market is here necessary, as these do not differ essentially from the methods pursued in Cuba, as already described. The two crops above named—sugar and coffee—are the leading plantation products of Hawaii, the government lands, estimated at 1,782,500 acres, being thus divided:

Coffee	76,270
Sugar	25,626
Rice	977
Grazing	451,200
High forest	681,280
Rugged mountains	227,000
Barren lands	300,000
Homesteads, government interest in	20,000

It is estimated that in all there are 2,000,000 acres of grazing and 290,000 of arable soil on the islands. The upland soil is generally thin and poor; but at the bases of the mountains, where abrasion, disintegration, and accumulation of vegetable mould have gone on for ages, there are extensive fertile tracts, while the thinner soils yield an abundance of fine pasturage.

OTHER AGRICULTURAL PRODUCTS.

Rice comes third among the agricultural products of Hawaii, there being over 8000 acres devoted to this grain, of which two-thirds are in Oahu. This culture gives constant employment to about 2500 persons, while 1500 more are employed during the harvesting season. The annual product of rice paddy is about 18,000 tons, yielding when milled about 12,000 tons or 240,000 bags of rice, three-fourths of which are needed for home consumption. The rice is raised from Carolina seed and is of excellent quality.

Most of the rice land yields two crops a year, each crop averaging a ton and a half per acre. The land is carefully levelled, and terraced so that it may be flooded with water, with which it is covered to a depth of from half an inch to three inches. Before harvesting, the water is drawn off and the ground allowed to dry.

This is an industry with which the Chinese and Japanese are thoroughly familiar, rice cultivation being the form of agriculture to which they are specially accustomed at home. As a result, as has been already stated, the Chinese have taken very kindly to the raising of rice, and many waste regions of swamp land have been converted by them into prolific food-bearing fields.

Next in importance among the commercial agricultural products of Hawaii is the banana, to which many large plantations are devoted. In 1894, there were exported 123,000 bunches of this fruit; though the distance of foreign markets stands in the way of an active development of this industry. It is said that an acre of favorably situated land will grow a thousand banana plants, yielding annually ten tons of fruit. The sweet potato, another of the leading food products, flourishes on surfaces of lava which are almost destitute of soil, and can be counted on to yield, in good locations, about 200 barrels to the acre. As for its humble associate, the white potato, of foreign introduction, it will grow anywhere, demanding no care and attention beyond that of planting. Of the ubiquitous taro, the basis of the indispensable poi, it is said that forty square feet of land will supply the food of one man for a year, and that a square mile in taro will support 15,000 Hawaiians.

The indigo plant grows so freely that it has become a troublesome and ineradicable weed, sharing this evil characteristic with the lantana and the guava. It does not repay the trouble it causes, since the indigo yielded by it is of inferior quality. The root of *Tacca pinnatifida* yields a Polynesian variety of arrow-root, and from the crown of tree-fern stems of the genus *Cibotium* is obtained a soft, silky fibre known as *pulu*, which is exported in large quantities to the United States as a material for filling cushions.

Numerous foreign fruit and other plants have been introduced, among which are coffee, tobacco, cotton, wheat, maize, potato, cacao, grape, orange, citron, melon, fig, pineapple, guava, tamarind, and such garden vegetables as the cucumber, bean, onion, cabbage, pea, carrot, turnip, asparagus, lettuce, celery, etc., which are grown in the vegetable gardens of the Chinese. In fact, in the uplands all the products of the temperate zones can be grown.

Several of these exotic plants have proved excellently adapted to the soil and of much economic value. Wheat and potatoes thrive on the uplands of Maui. Tobacco grows freely, though its leaf is of inferior quality. Oranges of fine quality are raised, and in some districts the pineapple grows like a weed, yielding large fruit, though not of fine quality. The watermelon is so prolific that it is almost a drug in the market. The bamboo has been known to grow sixteen inches in a day. Most of the vegetable drugs, dyes, and spices can be raised, and the ramie fibre plant grows luxuriantly, also the Sisal hemp. Only sufficient rainfall is needed to make the soil teem with plenty.

The Hawaiian forests yield many plants of industrial value. Allusion has already been made to the ohia, the ti, and the wauti trees, the widely distributed cocoanut, and the koa tree, which yields a beautiful wood suitable for cabinet-work. There are other valuable hard-woods, and the forests may yet become a fertile source of revenue. Building lumber is transported down the mountains in difficult localities on the backs of strong, sure-footed mules, two of which, going tandem, can carry a log on each side, weighing together 400 pounds or more, along narrow paths and down perilous steeps which seem dangerous to human feet. No vehicle could traverse these difficult paths, and only by the aid of these faithful animals could the lumber of the lofty uplands be brought into use. The irrigation flumes, as already stated, serve a similar purpose.

GRAZING INDUSTRIES.

The native pig, and the ox, horse, sheep, goat, and dog (the native dog has become extinct), introduced forms, constitute the principal large animals of the group, and have increased so abundantly that large numbers of them exist in a state of almost pristine wildness in the uninhabited mountain and forest regions. The wild boar is hunted, while the wild bull

AGRICULTURAL INDUSTRIES.

hunts man, and occasionally with serious results. In certain localities groups of wild dogs are encountered, almost as fierce as wolves if pressed by hunger. Wild goats find themselves at home on the high mountains, and the horse has so increased that in its semi-wild state it does considerable damage to the woods and plantations. The native is poor indeed who does not own a horse, and most of them lay claim to two or three. The wild cattle of the mountains, a very inferior breed, are shot or lassoed for the sake of their hides, of which large numbers are exported, a single island having yielded as many as 11,000 hides in a year. Formerly the natives trapped them by digging pits near pools of water, a practice which proved fatal to Douglas, the botanist, who fell into one of these pools and was gored to death by a bull.

The raisers of sheep are few in number, but some of them own large flocks, and the wool clip is considerable. The island of Niihau, for instance, the greater part of which is a low, grass-covered plain, is mainly used for sheep-grazing. The Gays and Robinsons, owners of the island, have 30,000 sheep, whose wool is not surpassed by the best Australian clip. The island is inhabited only by their employees. The same is the case with the island of Lanai, west of Maui, a region of little fertility and devoted to sheep-raising, the shepherds being its only inhabitants.

The extensive grazing lands on the other islands are largely used for cattle, of which great herds are kept, under the control of the native cowboys, the Hawaiian wild riders, than whom there are none more daring or more skilled in the use of the lasso. The Kanaka herdsman is proud of his accomplishments, and has adopted the broad-brimmed sombrero and the loud jingling spurs of his Mexican counterpart, in which brave attire he delights to swagger through the city streets, to the admiration of the boys.

It is well to say, in conclusion of this section of our subject, that the character of the utilization of Hawaiian soil is largely governed by elevation. It may be divided broadly into four zones. The sugar zone extends from the sea-level to 1500 feet of elevation,—sometimes higher. About half of it needs some degree of artificial irrigation; the remainder is sufficiently watered by the rainfall. The coffee zone extends from a height of 1500 to 3000 feet. A third zone, that of fruit and vegetables, largely overlaps that of coffee, though extending beyond it. The fourth and highest zone, that devoted to grazing, reaches from 3000 to 5000 feet of elevation. As regards the Hawaiian soil, it varies from dark red to light red and yellow shades of color, the dark red being the most, the yellow the least, fertile.

BIRD PRODUCTS.

The ostrich has been introduced into Hawaii, and promises well. In a valley region of Kauai, shut in on three sides by lofty hills and on the fourth by the ocean, is kept a group of these great birds, the property of Mr. Charles N. Cooke, of Honolulu. The valley is sandy, and the birds are as much in their native element as on the Sahara desert. They are carefully fed, ground bones—not overly fine—forming an essential part of their diet. Their feathers are plucked twice a year, the birds being driven into a pen, in which they are securely fastened during the process. Thus far Hawaiian ostrich-farming is an experiment, of which the profits can be told only after a longer interval.

The most interesting industry connected with birds, however, is that of Leyson Island, a lone isle of the Pacific situated some 800 miles west of Honolulu, yet now looked upon as an outlying member of the Hawaiian group, its nearest neighboring land. This island, low-lying and apparently an uplifted coral reef, is of about 100 square miles area, and is the home of myriads of ocean birds, including ducks, gulls, boobies, frigate-birds, and various other species, about twenty-five in all. So numerous are they that they darken the sun when they take to flight, and so tame that they need to be thrust aside in walking, and can be picked up by any one who wishes to make a capture. On the railroad track which has been laid on the island, a man has to sit in front of the car and push the birds with a stick out of the way of the mules, while parties who visit the island are obliged to close their doors or tent-flaps closely at night to keep out the intrusive winged inhabitants.

Leyson Island is sought for its guano, the product of birds which for ages past have lived and died there in myriads. Their decaying remains and the disintegrated coral form a valuable fertilizer, of which hundreds of tons are shipped annually to Hawaii and the Pacific coast. In addition to the guano, the eggs are frequently gathered, cars being filled with them and vessels loaded. But the distance to which they have to be carried renders this industry unprofitable.

At one time an effort was made to utilize the island for the raising of swine. A number of hogs were placed on it, and increased so rapidly that the experiment promised to be a success. But the hog-raiser had not counted upon the buccaneers of the Pacific. Captain Pease, a noted pirate of those waters, being short of meat, swooped down on the island one day, during the absence of the manager and his aids and assistants, killed the hogs, salted down the pork, and sailed away with it in his vessel's hold. Since then the piratical captain has met with a violent death; but the hogs have not been replaced, and the island is left to its native inhabitants, the birds.

VIII. MANUFACTURES AND COMMERCE.

MECHANICAL INDUSTRIES.

Of the manufacturing establishments of Hawaii there is only one to which special attention need be given. This is the Honolulu Iron-Works, which owes its prosperity to the development of the sugar industry, consequent upon the reciprocity treaty of 1876 between Hawaii and the United States. The steady and increasing demands of the planters for improved machinery gave a vigorous impetus to this establishment, which has grown in dimensions and facilities and in the number of its employees until its pay-roll is said to amount to $5000 per week.

It has to import all its coal and iron, which puts it at a disadvantage in competition with iron-works on the continent; but it has the advantage of being on the ground and in position to supply machinery at short notice, which could not be got elsewhere without considerable delay. It possesses also the most recent and powerful machine tools, and during the past ten years has made more than sixty crushing-mills for plantations, with much other sugar-making machinery.

Another large enterprise of Honolulu is the Hawaiian Electric and Cold Storage Company, organized in 1892, and now possessing three powerful engines, of about 1500 horse-power. It runs cars and elevators, has cold-storage and ice-making rooms of over 100,-

000 cubic feet capacity, and is capable of supplying electric light to a city twice the size of Hawaii.

These extensive establishments, due to American capital and enterprise, are the only manufacturing concerns on the islands to which attention needs to be called. There are, of course, numerous minor manufactures, necessary to supply the island demand for articles of immediate consumption, such as clothing, utensils, smith-work, etc., but these have given rise to no establishment on a large scale, and are largely in the hands of the Hawaiians themselves. For instance, out of the 11,135 male Hawaiians over fifteen years of age, shown in the last census, about 1000, or one in eleven, were carpenters. Others of them are painters, blacksmiths, machinists, engineers, etc., a remarkable showing for a people who had scarcely begun to emerge from savagery a century ago.

COMMERCE.

The commercial interests of Hawaii are large and growing, the commerce being very largely with the United States, which receives nearly the total sum of exports. In 1897 the proportion sent to this country was 99.62 per cent. of the whole, of which 96 per cent. consisted of sugar. Our proportion of the imports to Hawaii was considerably less, the United States furnishing 76.94 per cent., while 11.85 per cent. came from Great Britain and her colonies, and the remainder was about equally divided between Germany, China, Japan, and other countries.

The chief articles of export, aside from the overwhelming supremacy of sugar, were hides, wool, rice, coffee, and fruits, the total value of exports being

MANUFACTURES AND COMMERCE.

$16,021,775. The imports amounted to $7,682,628, showing a large balance of trade in favor of the islands. These imports were largely in the lines of provisions, clothing, hardware, machinery, and agricultural implements. The United States has a large proportion of the trade in cotton goods, and a monopoly of that in boots and shoes, felt hats, and the better class of straw hats. Of exported goods, the most marked increase is in coffee, which amounted to $2628 in 1892, $25,063 in 1896, and nearly treble the latter sum in 1897. As yet no large coffee estates have been opened, the industry being composed of a number of small holdings, in addition to the wild, or semi-wild, coffee of the island of Hawaii. The export of coffee in 1897 was 337,158 pounds. Under present conditions, the commerce of the islands is likely to be very largely increased, and the United States to gain a much larger proportion of the import trade than that now possessed.

The leading articles sent from the United States consist of iron and steel, wooden wares, cotton fabrics, fertilizers, breadstuffs, drugs and chemicals, boots and shoes, manufactured tobacco, mineral oil, fish, hay, wine, malt liquors, hardware, and machinery.

Of the Hawaiian exports in 1896, sugar comprised nearly the whole, and all of this, to the value of $14,932,000, came to the United States. The exports of rice to this country amounted to $163,571; of fruits and nuts, to $76,124; of hides and skins, to $65,104; smaller quantities of coffee, wool, molasses, and various other substances making up the total sum. The commerce of 1898 shows a marked increase over that of the two years named, the total value of the exports for that year being $17,346,744; that of the imports, including specie, $11,650,890. Half of this increase was an increase in imports from the United States. The customs duties collected were $896,795, as against $708,493 in 1897.

SHIPPING.

The statistics of shipping for 1897 show a good ratio of increase over the preceding years, 427 vessels, of 513,826 tons, entering Hawaiian ports, as against 386 vessels, of 447,997 tons, in 1896. Of the 1897 shipping, 286 vessels, of 270,045 tons, were from the United States, 141 vessels, of 243,781 tons, from foreign ports. Yet this proportion does not give a correct idea of the actual situation, since the foreign tonnage includes the mail-steamers, mostly British, that stop merely to land the mails and a few passengers and that carry very little freight. Of the 427 vessels, 291, of 215,262 tons, were sailing-vessels, engaged in freightage, and of these 237, of 164,406 tons, were from the United States. The inter-insular traffic in 1896 employed 59 vessels, of 29,024 tons, about one-third of them being steamers, the remainder sailing-vessels.

The steamship lines plying between Honolulu and the United States include the Oceanic Steamship Company, the Oriental and Occidental Steamship Company, the Pacific Mail, and the Oregon Railway and Navigation Company, each with four ships, and the Japanese company, Nippon Yusen Kaisha, with two ships. Most of these vessels touch at Honolulu on their way to more distant ports, at times two or three steamers touching there weekly, at other times ten or twelve days occurring between steamers.

FINANCES.

Until recently, the gold and silver coins of all nations passed current in Hawaii at their real or nominal values, though the Mexican dollar and the French five-franc piece were the leading coins; but since December 31, 1894, only the gold coins of the United States have been legal tender for sums over ten dollars, Hawaiian and American silver being legal tender for smaller sums. Paper money is not in use, with the exception of treasury certificates representing deposits of coin. As a result of this state of affairs, no change in the circulation will be necessary to produce conformity to the new political relations of the country. The silver of Hawaii amounts to $1,000,000, and the whole circulating medium of the islands is estimated at $3,500,000.

Hawaii had a national debt on December 31, 1896, of $4,136,174. Its revenue for 1896 amounted to $1,997,818; expenditures to $1,904,191. The chief sources of revenue were: customs, $656,896; taxes, $706,542; internal revenue, $168,384. The ruling rates of interest range from five to twelve per cent.

The revenue of the islands is likely to increase considerably under their new relations and the growing development of their resources, which are as yet in their infancy. Sugar is the only product to which much attention has been paid, and in whose culture capital has been largely invested. The cultivation of coffee is a rapidly growing industry, and this crop bids fair to gain a large development in the coming years. Other products of commercial value are likely to attract attention. A large area of arable land remains to be utilized; and the early years of the twentieth century will doubtless show so considerable an increase of Hawaiian production and commerce as to make this new accession to the United States one of great and growing value.

SECTION IV.

THE PHILIPPINE ISLANDS.

★ ★ ★

I. HISTORICAL SKETCH.

It is now nearly 400 years since Ferdinand Magellan, on his pioneer voyage across the waters of the newly discovered Pacific Ocean, reached an outlying member of an extensive archipelago to which he gave the name of the St. Lazarus Islands. This event took place on the 12th of March, 1521. Proceeding to Cebu, a neighboring large island of the group, he gained such influence over its ruler as to induce him and his court to accept baptism and to acknowledge the supremacy of Spain, to whose king they took the oath of vassalage.

Magellan, in return, aided the ruler in a war with his neighbors, an act for which he paid severely, being wounded in battle, and dying on March 26, 1521. The alliance with the Spaniards soon came to a violent end, the natives finding reason to distrust their new allies. The leading officers of the expedition were invited to a banquet by the Cebu chief, and were treacherously attacked during the feast and all but one of them killed. The ships left in haste, one of them, the Vitoria, reaching Spain and completing the first circumnavigation of the globe.

From time to time other expeditions were sent to these far eastern waters; one of them, sent by Cortes from Mexico in 1528, taking possession of the Ladrone Islands, the principal member of which has recently been ceded to the United States. The name of Filipinas was given in 1543 by Villalobos to the island now known as Samar, and was applied to the whole group by Legaspi, who conducted an expedition from Mexico in 1564, under orders from Philip II. to "conquer, pacify, and people" this island group. The name "Islas Filipinas," or Philippine Islands, given in honor of Philip II., first appears in a letter of Legaspi's of the date of 1567.

Legaspi, who was appointed governor of Spain's new colony, made a settlement on the island of Cebu in 1565, whence he removed to Luzon and founded the city of Manila in 1571, dying the following year, as the annals say, of disappointment and disgust. The subjugation of the islands made considerable progress under him, and he has since been known as the "Conqueror of the Philippines."

In truth, the true conquerors of the Philippines are acknowledged to have been the Roman Catholic missionaries, who made their way fearlessly among the natives, converted them widely to Christianity, and gained such an influence over them as to keep them in subjection to Spain during most of the time since. "The missionaries were the real conquerors of the Philippines," says Tomas de Comyn; "their arms were not, indeed, those of the warrior, but they gave laws to millions, and, scattered though they were, they established by unity of purpose and of action a permanent empire over immense multitudes of men."

They learned the language of the natives, came into intimate relations with them, and, by gaining an influence over their minds, were enabled to control them through the agencies of faith and superstition.

The history of the islands contains few events of special interest, being largely made up of the annals of a long series of governors, of contests with the natives and the Chinese, and of records of earthquakes, volcanic eruptions, and devastating hurricanes. A fleet of Chinese pirates made a descent upon Manila shortly after its founding, but were repulsed by the Spanish garrison after a desperate assault.

In 1603 occurred a singular event. Three mandarins appeared at Manila, bringing with them a Chinaman who had assured their emperor that the island of Cavité was a mass of solid gold; a story on whose truth he pledged his life. The governor settled the question by conveying the envoys to Cavité and letting them examine for themselves. Soon afterwards a report spread that a Chinese army, 100,000 strong, had been gathered for the invasion of the Philippines, and hasty preparations were made for the defence of Manila, a friendly Chinaman named Eng Kang aiding actively in the work.

The peril was not from the Chinese abroad but from those at home. There were numerous Chinese settlers in Luzon, and a plot, in which Eng Kang was deeply involved, had been organized among them to massacre all the Spaniards on the vespers of St. Francis's day. The conspiracy was discovered, and after some sharp fighting the Chinese were repulsed. They were closely followed in their retreat, and dealt with so sharply that out of 24,000 in revolt only 100 were left alive, to be sent to the galleys. Eng Kang was decapitated and his head exposed in an iron cage.

This disaster did not check the Chinese. Numbers of them continued to seek the islands, and in 1639 another outbreak took place, in which 30,000 of these immigrants were involved. They began a guerilla warfare, causing such devastation that the natives joined the Spaniards against them, and they were subdued with great loss. In a subsequent revolt, this time on the part of the natives, the rebels were induced to surrender under promise of pardon. The result was one with which we are familiar in Spanish colonial history. "The promise was not kept," say the annals; "but the leaders of the insurrection were hanged, and multitudes of the Indians sent to prison."

An event of different character took place in 1645. For two months Luzon was frightfully shaken by earthquakes, during which a mountain was overturned in the province of Cagayan and a town at its foot was engulfed. Torrents of mud and water burst forth in many places, and in Manila nearly all the public buildings were destroyed and 300 of the inhabitants lost their lives. In the whole island more than 3000 perished.

Under the governorship of De Lara, which began in 1653, a series of disasters occurred,—earthquakes, tempests, insurrections, and "a web of anxieties and calamities." Missionaries who were sent to convert the Mohammedans on Mindanao were put to death, many converts turned traitors, and Keuseng, a Chinese piratical chief who had conquered Formosa, sent an envoy demanding the surrender of the Philippines. As he had under him 1000 junks and 100,000 men, his demand created general alarm. All the Chinese were ordered to quit the country, and on their refusal they were attacked and nearly all of them massacred. Keuseng failed to carry out his threats.

For many years following these events the chief matters of interest were the disputes between the civil government and the priests. The archbishops claimed the supremacy of ecclesiastical over civil authority, and long-continued quarrels ensued, which were not all settled without bloodshed. There were similar quarrels between the several religious bodies, the Dominican and the Augustinian friars denying the supremacy of the regular clergy, and resisting the admission of parochial curates.

During the period under review the commerce of the Philippines was strangely conducted. It consisted in the freight of a single vessel, or galleon, sailing annually to and from Acapulco, Mexico, conveying the produce of the islands or goods received from China, and bringing European and Mexican wares in return. Absurd restrictions were placed on merchants, who were obliged to pay $20,000 for the privilege of freighting this vessel, and none could take part who had not resided several years in the islands and were worth less than $8000. Friars, officials, influential women, and others took part clandestinely in the venture, and the goods had to be invoiced at very high rates to cover the expected profits. If they paid high tribute to speculators in Manila, they did the same in Mexico, where thirty-three and one-third per cent. was added to the invoiced prices. Similar conditions controlled the return voyage. The galleon was allowed to bring back only double the value of the cargo she had taken out; but, in order to increase the profits of the venture, the cargo was increased by invoicing it at prices below its value, and roguery of every kind prevailed.

Yet the venture was not always profitable. Occasionally the galleon was lost at sea, and that year loss and sorrow prevailed. In some instances it was taken by the licensed freebooters of other nations. The galleons were four-deckers, of 1500 tons, strongly armed, and commanded by officers of the royal navy; yet they fell an easy prey to the dashing British and Dutch rovers. Drake obtained treasure worth $1,000,000 from one capture, and a successful British cruiser sailed into London harbor with damask sails and silken rigging from its spoils. The Dutch gave still more trouble, their cruisers lying in wait off the coast of Luzon to capture the Spanish treasure-ships. At one time a formidable Dutch fleet appeared off Manila Bay, but instead of besieging the town it hovered about in hopes of capturing merchantmen. In consequence, it was attacked and completely routed by the Spanish fleet.

There were other troubles with the Dutch, and with the English in 1762, in which year war broke out between England and Spain. The first news of this at Manila was the appearance of a hostile British fleet, consisting of thirteen ships with 6830 troops. The city was unprepared for defence and had but a small garrison. The fleet appeared on September 22, and opened fire on the night of the 23d, and the final assault was made on October 5, when the city was taken and given over to plunder by the captors. In addition to the sack of the city, a requisition was made on the authorities for a sum equal to $4,000,000,—a war indemnity that was promised but not paid. The Spanish, under the lead of Simon de Anda, kept under arms in the interior, and confined the British to Manila. One result of their resistance was a massacre of the Chinese, who had conspired to assassinate the Spanish leaders. Anda declared them all traitors, and ordered them all to be hanged; the result being that thousands who knew nothing of the conspiracy were executed.

The British held the city until March, 1764, when it was evacuated as one of the conditions of a treaty of peace, and the authority of Spain was re-established.

In addition to the massacres of the Chinese named, another, in which other foreigners were involved, took place as late as 1820. Yet despite these acts of slaughter the Chinese continued to seek the islands, in which they now reside to the number of 100,000. Of these some 40,000 are in Manila, where they occupy the chief shops and do most of the artisan work.

The political history of the country continued to be a series of revolts, fights, and executions, and of disputes between the friars and the government; while Spain derived so little benefit from the islands that their abandonment was contemplated. De Mas, the historian, tells us, "For more than two centuries the Philippines had been for the crown of Spain a hotbed of so many disputes, anxieties, and expenses, that the abandonment of the colony was again and again proposed by the ministers; but the Catholic monarchs could never consent to the perdition of all the souls that had been conquered, and which it was still hoped to conquer, in these regions."

A monopoly of the tobacco crop was established by Captain-General Basco in 1778, and was maintained for more than a century, being given up in 1882. In 1785 the old system of commerce was replaced by the establishment of the "Company of the Philippines," which was granted a monopoly of trade, the king of Spain having a share in its profits. This monopoly was sustained until 1834, when the increasing demands of foreign nations forced Spain to open the country to commerce, though under severe restrictions. The growth of steam navigation increased the trade of the islands, and the opening of the Suez Canal, which brought Manila within thirty-two days' steam traffic of Barcelona, doubled the commerce, which had reached by the close of the Spanish period an annual total of $30,000,000.

Revolts of the natives have taken place from time to time, those of the nineteenth century occurring in 1823, 1827, 1844, and 1872. The greatest and most persistent of them was that which began in 1896. In this severe outbreak, which continued until near the end of 1897, the hatred of the natives seemed especially directed towards the friars, whom they looked upon as their chief enemies, and treated with brutal cruelty when they fell into their hands.

Spain sought to put down the insurrection in the manner she has elsewhere employed, by cruel treatment and wholesale execution of her prisoners of war, who were publicly shot under circumstances of revolting barbarity. Finding that they could not be subdued by force of arms, the Spanish authorities treated with the leaders, offering a large sum of money to Aguinaldo and his fellow-generals, and promising an extensive system of reforms. As usual with Spain, the bargain was not kept. Aguinaldo and some others retired to Hong-Kong with their share of the subsidy. The leaders who remained in the islands, trusting to Spanish faith, were seized and executed. The promised reforms were ignored, the governor denying that he had pledged himself. As a result of this lack of honesty the rebels were soon again in arms; their anger being particularly directed against the friars, to whose influence they ascribed the dishonesty of the Spanish authorities.

In 1898 came the most important event in the history of the Philippine Islands, the capture of Manila by an American fleet and army and the cession of the entire group by treaty to the United States. The details of this event cannot be given in this brief sketch, and are too familiar to readers to need description. It will suffice to say that an American squadron under Admiral Dewey appeared in Manila harbor in the night of April 30, and on May 1 attacked and destroyed the Spanish fleet. The city was blockaded until August 13, when an assault was made by the army and fleet and it fell into the hands of the American forces.

Meanwhile, on May 24, Aguinaldo and his fellow-leaders returned from Hong-Kong on an American war-vessel and put themselves at the head of the rebel forces, who immediately invested and besieged Manila. Their assaults continued until the capture of the city by the Americans, and they remained under arms during the subsequent period of negotiations between the United States and Spain.

In the treaty of peace, signed December 10, 1898,

the whole group of the Philippine Islands was ceded by Spain to the United States, which country agreed to pay Spain the sum of $20,000,000 as a recompense for improvements made in the islands. The natives, however, continued in arms, under the leadership of Aguinaldo, with the claim that they had fought for freedom, not for a new master, and a demand for independence. The proclamation of President McKinley, under date of December 30, 1898, offered the natives home rule in the fullest sense, giving them a voice in the local government, the right to hold official positions, a fair judiciary, and freedom of speech and of the press; all this under the supreme direction of the United States.

These concessions were not satisfactory to the Philippine leaders; and, as the debate in the United States Senate concerning the treaty promised to end in its ratification, Aguinaldo grew openly hostile, and finally issued a declaration of war against the United States, and made an attack upon the American outposts at Manila on the evening of February 4, 1899. Fighting continued during the 5th and 6th, the result being a defeat of the native forces, which were driven back for miles and suffered severe loss. They continued in arms, however, and on February 22, and subsequently, an effort was made to burn the city, which was set on fire at various points. About the same time two important islands, Negros and Cebu, submitted to the authority of the United States.

Meanwhile, on February 6, the treaty of peace was ratified in the Senate of the United States, and this country succeeded Spain as the ruling power in the Philippines. Great diversity of opinion continued to exist, however, as to whether these islands should be held permanently or only until their inhabitants should prove themselves capable of self-government. This question remains an open one, and military rule will be maintained in the islands until the policy of the United States shall be matured.

II. PHYSICAL CONDITIONS.

GEOGRAPHY.

The Philippine Islands, or the Philippines as they are usually called (Spanish, *Islas Filipinas*), form an extensive group or archipelago lying off the southeast coast of Asia, and separated by the China Sea from China on the northwest and Indo-China on the west, the port of Manila being about 630 miles from that of Hong-Kong. On the east extends a broad stretch of the Pacific; on the north a number of small islands reach out towards Formosa; and on the south lies the great island of Borneo, with which the Philippines have two lines of connection,—a western one by the islands of Palawan and Balabac and an eastern one by way of the Sulu Archipelago. To the south lie two deep ocean abysses, the Sulu or Mindoro Sea, extending to North Borneo, and the Celebes Sea, lying between Mindanao and Celebes, with a width of 300 miles. The Sulu Islands are practically a part of the group, and were included in the cession by Spain to the United States. The archipelago, thus constituted, extends from 4° 45' to 21° north latitude, and between 116° 40' and 126° 30' east longitude, or through a length, north and south, of over 1050 miles, and a width, east and west, of approximately 700 miles.

The total number of islands in the group is unknown. They have never been counted, and the estimates as to their number range all the way from 600

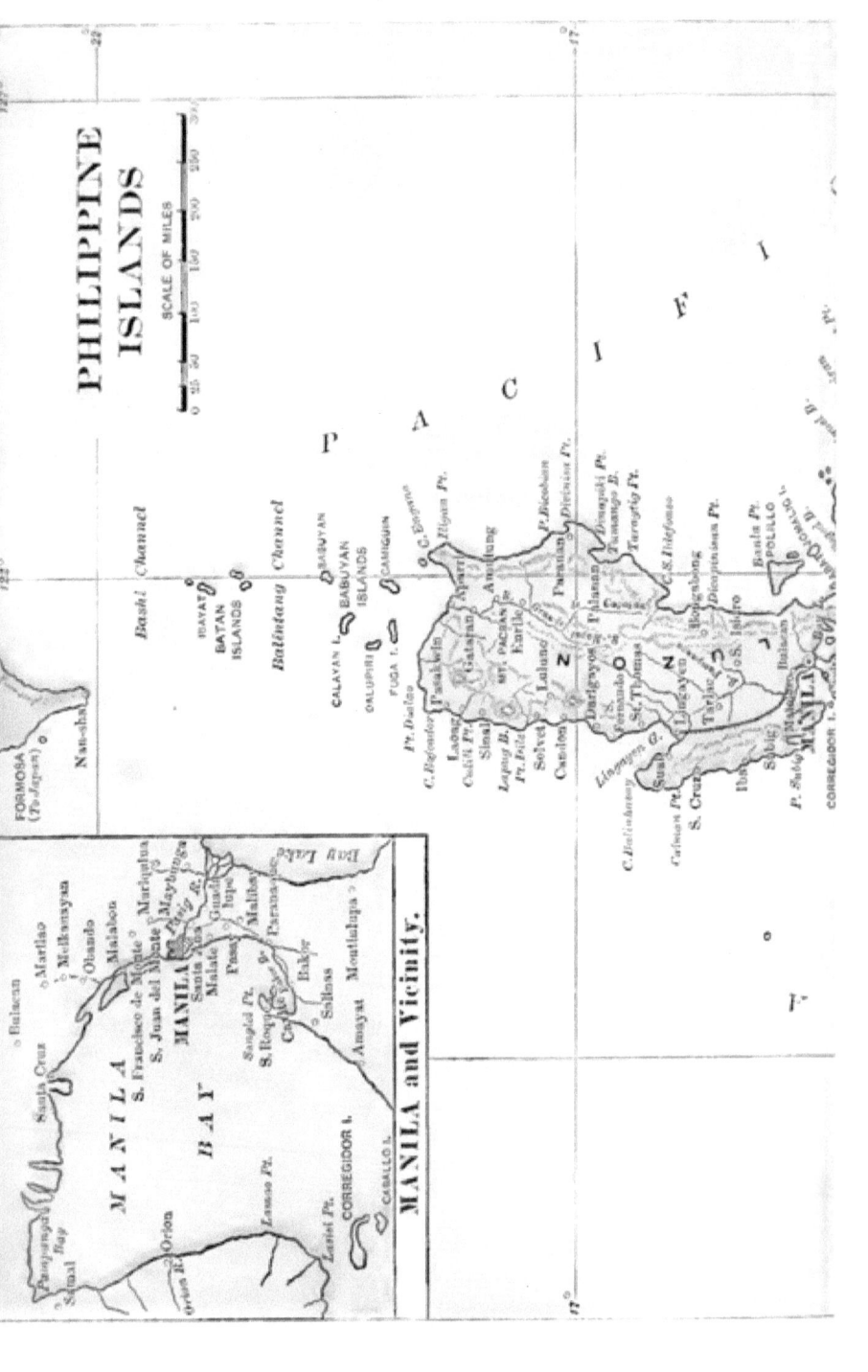

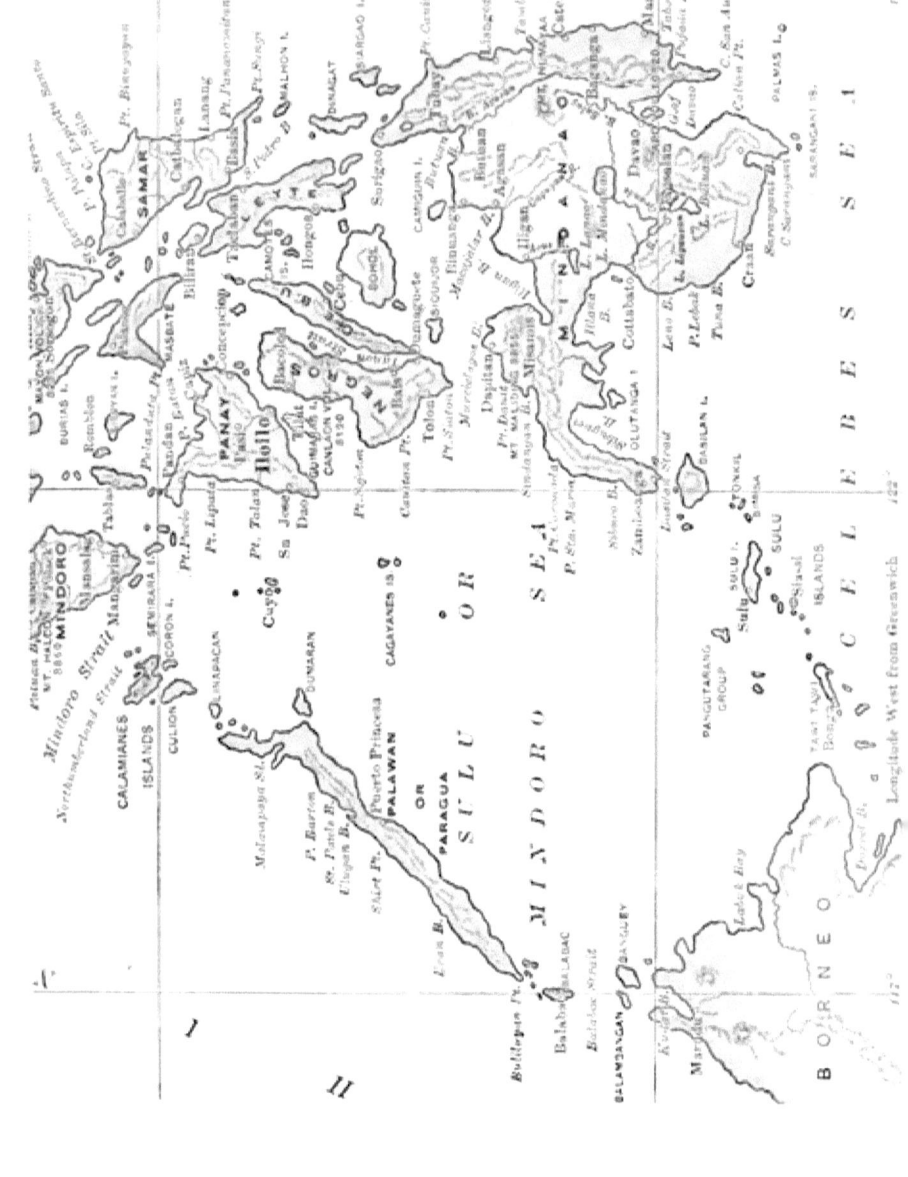

to 2000. The actual number does not probably exceed 1200, if every barren rock be included. The land area is similarly unsettled, a mean between the various estimates being about 115,000 square miles. Numerous as the islands are, the great majority are unimportant in size, many being of minute area, mere rocks or sand-spits, while very few are of sufficient extent to have any geographical or political importance. There are several hundred large enough to be habitable.

The largest two of the Philippine Islands, respectively the farthest north and the farthest south, are Luzon and Mindanao,—the former of 40,885, the latter of 37,256 square miles area. Between these two lies a group known as the Visayas, and embracing a number of islands of considerable size and importance, the largest of which are Samar (5300 square miles), Leyte (3090 square miles), Bohol (925 square miles), Cebu (1650 square miles), Negros (2300 square miles), and Panay (4600 square miles). This group includes in addition several smaller islands of some agricultural importance.

North of the Visayas, near Luzon, lies Masbate (1315 square miles), and farther east the large but little explored Mindoro (4050 square miles). The smaller islands in these groups that call for mention are Guimaras, 215; Burias, 190; Ticao, 121; Tablas, 327; and Sibuyan, 159 square miles; while near Mindoro on its eastern side is the flourishing island of Marinduque, 348 square miles. Two other islands of some importance, Polillo and Catanduanes, lie off the eastern coast of Luzon.

Southwest of Mindoro lie the Calamianes, a great

cluster of very small islands, of which the two largest are Calamian and Busuanga (416 square miles). South of these extends the large island of Palawan or Paragua (4150 square miles), which has the distinction of being one of the narrowest islands for its length in the world. While extending 230 miles to the southwest, it is nowhere more than thirty miles wide, and narrows in some localities to ten miles. It reaches to the vicinity of the north cape of Borneo, from which it is separated by Balabac and some smaller islands and Balabac Strait.

Between Palawan and Mindanao and southwest of the Visayas extends the deep Mindoro Sea, and southwest of Mindanao stretches the Sulu group, practically an extension of its southwestern peninsula. This cluster of islands, known as the Sulu or Jolo Archipelago, lies between the Mindoro and the Celebes Seas, and extends nearly to the northeastern cape of Borneo. The group consists of about 150 islands, with a total area of approximately 948 square miles, the largest islands being Basilan, Sulu, and Tawi-Tawi. This group—formerly, with a portion of northern Borneo, an independent state—was annexed by Spain in 1878, and is now classed with the Philippines. Many of the smaller islands are uninhabited, but the larger possess an industrious Mohammedan population.

As compared in area with American States, the whole group of the Philippines is of nearly the same extent as the New England States with New York and New Jersey. Luzon, the largest island, is of nearly the same size as Ohio. The areas of the principal islands above given are approximate only. They are so stated in Spanish official estimates; but the true areas of most of the islands are far from being known.

GEOLOGY.

An irregular mountain system, known in Luzon as the Caraballos, runs through the central region of each of the larger islands, and the whole group is, as a general rule, mountainous or hilly. Little more than a third of the whole area is arable land. The principal ranges extend in a north and south direction, with a tendency to deflect to the east or west, the system spreading southward in a fan-like shape from Luzon as a radiating point. None of the mountains exceeds 9000 feet in height, with the exception of Apo, in Mindanao, which late observations indicate to be over 10,000 feet high. The other lofty peaks, so far as known, are Halcon, in Mindoro (8865 feet), Mayon, in Luzon (8900 feet), Malaspina, in Negros (8192 feet), while several others range from 6000 to 8000 feet.

Of Philippine geology comparatively little is known, and the geologist has there a very difficult task. As yet there have been few cuttings or excavations to lay bare the structure of the rocks, while much of the surface is covered with so dense a vegetation that there is little from which to draw conclusions. There is reason to believe that much of the archipelago is of recent date, having been uplifted from below the sea-level. The evidences of this are the large tracts of coral reef seen at many points along the shores, and raised beaches of considerable elevation at a distance inland. These contain shells like those now living in the neighboring waters, indicating that they lay beneath the seas at no remote date. Elevation and subsidence seem to be still going on, and the limestone caps that cover some of the islands, as Cebu, indicate that the ocean once flowed where they now stand. The basic rocks of the islands appear to be of old formations, largely schists, and in the north of Luzon granite.

What is now southern Luzon was probably in a recent period a group of separate islands, since the neck of land between several of the southern bays is composed of alluvium, tuffs, and marls, in which modern shells are embedded. Drasche has traced in southern Luzon gneiss and chloritic slates, diabases, gabbros, and eocene limestones, with volcanic minerals and the recent formations above mentioned. In northern Luzon he discovered gneiss, diorite, protogenic and chloritic slates, and an extensive system of stratified conglomerates and sandstones. The more modern rocks traced by him were formations of volcanic origin, tuffs and tufaceous sandstones, banks of limestone, marl, and coral, and the results of late volcanic eruptions, of which there are evidences almost everywhere. The coralliferous limestones—which present the unusual feature of stratification—indicate their late origin by the fact that their corals belong to genera which still exist in the Indian Ocean, and are similar, though not identical, in species.

These sparse results of geological observation are likely to be added to largely under the new political relations of the islands, since scientists will doubtless find better opportunities for observation in the engineering works which will probably be undertaken. A considerable extension of the railroad system is among the probabilities of the near future, and mining operations also promise to be undertaken; these offering opportunities to the geologist as well as to the practical man of business.

VOLCANOES.

Volcanoes have played an important part in the formation of the Philippines, and have left traces of their former activity in all directions. Most of them, however, have long been dead and silent, comparatively few of the once numerous group being now active. Of these the three of leading importance are in southern Luzon—Taal, Bulusan, and Mayon or Albay.

Mayon, the largest and most active of the existing volcanoes, is strikingly regular in form, presenting a perfect cone which rises from a base of about fifty miles in circuit to a height of 8900 feet. It forms one of the most prominent landmarks visible from sea. A constant smoke, sometimes accompanied by flame, rises from its crater, and subterranean sounds, often heard at a distance of many leagues, issue from its depths. Evidences of former eruptions cover the whole country around.

In 1767 this mountain sent up a cone of flame, with a base of forty feet diameter, for ten days, and poured forth a wide stream of lava for two months. A month afterwards came from the crater great floods of water, which overflowed the river channels and did widespread damage. The eruption of 1812 destroyed several towns and was fatal to 12,000 persons, forming deposits near the mountain deep enough to bury the tallest trees. Similar disasters were occasioned in 1867, and several later eruptions have taken place.

In 1876 a terrible tropical storm burst upon the mountain, and the floods of rain, sweeping from its sides the loose volcanic *débris*, brought destruction to the neighboring country, more than 6000 houses being completely ruined. Its latest destructive eruption took place in 1888.

Bulusan, in the southern extremity of Luzon, resembles Vesuvius in shape. After a long period of inaction it began to smoke again in 1852. But the most interesting of the volcanoes of Luzon is that of Taal, which lies forty-five miles almost due south of Manila, and is remarkable as being one of the lowest volcanoes in the world, its height being only 850 feet above sea-level. Another striking feature about it is its location on a small island in the middle of a large lake, known as Bombon or Bongbong. There are traditions—doubtful ones—that this lake, 100 square miles in extent, was formed by a terrible eruption in 1700, by which a lofty mountain, 8000 or 9000 feet high, was destroyed. Evidences of great former eruptions are shown by vast deposits of porous tufa in the surrounding country.

The crater is an immense, cup-shaped depression, a mile or more in diameter and about 800 feet deep. When recently visited by Worcester it contained three boiling lakelets of strange-colored water, one of dirty brown hue, one intensely yellow, and one of a brilliant emerald green. It is still steaming and fuming, and in past times occasionally broke into frightful activity, its three most violent eruptions being in 1716, 1749, and 1754. In the last-named year the earth quaked with the throes of the mountain, and vast quantities of volcanic dust were hurled into the air, sufficient to make it dark at midday for many leagues around and to cover with dust and ashes the distant roofs of Manila. Fluid lava poured into the lake, which boiled with the heat, while vast showers of stones and ashes from the crater fell into its waters.

There are smoking cones in north Luzon and on the Babuyanes group to the north, and extinct volcanoes in many localities. The other islands have their volcanoes. Negros possesses the active peak of Malaspina, and on the island of Camiguin, about ninety miles to the southeast, a new volcano burst out in 1876. In the large island of Mindanao there are three volcanoes, of which Cottabato was in eruption in 1856, and is still active at intervals. Apo, the loftiest of them all, estimated to be 10,312 feet high, has three summits, enclosing the great crater, which is now extinct and filled with water.

Other evidences of volcanic activity are deposits of sulphur, which occurs abundantly in the island of Leyte, the existence of hot springs in various localities, and the earthquakes to which the islands are subject. Of these there are many on record, the most destructive one of recent times being in 1863, when 400 people were killed and 2000 injured, while numerous buildings were wrecked. In 1880 there was great destruction of property in Manila and elsewhere in Luzon, though no lives were lost. In 1675 an earthquake in Mindanao opened a passage to the sea, and a vast plain emerged. These convulsions of the earth affect the style of buildings, which are rarely more than two stories high and are lightly built, translucent oyster-shells being used instead of glass in their windows.

LUZON.

It is impossible in brief space to give any extended idea of the physical conformation of the numerous islands of the Philippine group, and we shall confine ourselves to a concise description of the larger. Luzon, the largest, is composed of a compact northern portion, about 340 miles long, from whose southeast corner stretches an irregular peninsula through a length of 180 miles, formed by a series of mountain ranges. The main trunk of the island is abundantly mountainous, the Caraballos highlands being nearly sixty leagues in length and sending two ranges northward, one skirting the eastern coast, the other keeping twenty-five or thirty miles from the western. Between these two ranges, known as the Sierra Oriental and the Sierra Occidental, lies the basin of the greatest river system of the Philippines, the Rio Grande de Cagayan, which receives numerous affluents from the mountains to east and west, and waters a great fertile valley, 200 miles long by 100 miles wide. Two other large rivers, the Abra and the Agno, rise on the western slopes of the Sierra Occidental and flow westward to the ocean. Smaller rivers and streams are abundant, the island being well watered.

Southwestward from the mountain system stretches a broad extent of lowlands, comparatively flat in surface, and forming one of the richest agricultural regions of the archipelago. It reaches southward to the bay of Manila, and is watered by the lower Agno and its tributaries and the Rio Grande de Pampanga, whose waters flow into Manila Bay by more than twenty mouths, and serve a useful purpose in the conveyance of agricultural produce to the capital. In these lowlands are a number of large lakes.

West of this flat country is the coast range known as the Cordillera de Zambales, whose peaks reach a height of 5000 or 6000 feet, and whose northward termination is in the peninsula which forms the Gulf of Lingayan, while its southern promontory helps to make the bay of Manila.

East and south of Manila Bay the country again becomes hilly, and in parts mountainous, though much of this region is occupied by the large body of water known as Laguna de Bay, or Bay Lake, twenty-five miles long by twenty-one wide, and 350 square miles in area, its outlet being the Pasig River. The depth of this great basin is rarely more than four fathoms. Lake Bombon, from whose centre rises the Taal volcano, is fourteen by eleven miles in dimensions.

MINDANAO.

As Luzon practically bounds the group on the north, so does the other large island known as Mindanao or Maguindanao on the south, though a few small islands lie north of Luzon and the Sulu group extends south of Mindanao. This island is extremely mountainous, its principal range being the Rangaya or Sugat Cordillera, which runs from southeast to northwest, bisecting the island, and curves downward into the great peninsula of Zamboanga, a broad westward bend towards the Sulu Archipelago. At its eastern extremity it bends south to form the peninsula of Butulan.

There are other ranges, one traversing the eastern side of the island from north to south. The lowlands between these ranges contain a number of lakes and are traversed by rivers of more extent and importance than those of Luzon. The Rio Grande de Mindanao follows the valley between the Rangaya and the Tiruray ranges, rising in the north and flowing south and west. It is connected with two great lakes, Ligauasan and Buluan, which practically become one during the rainy season. This stream is navigable as far as Matingcahuan, a distance of seventy or eighty miles.

On the north side of the Rangaya Mountains the river Agus flows from the great crater-lake of Lanao to the sea. Associated with this is a group of small crater-lakes, to which the island probably owes its title of Maguindanao. Its more common title, Mindanao, seems to have a somewhat similar origin, as it signifies "man of the lake." The largest river, the Butuan, or Agusan, is also connected with important lakes. It rises in the Kinabuhan Mountains, within a few miles of the south coast, and pursues a sinuous course northward through the valley west of the range, emptying into Butuan Bay on the north after a flow of more than 200 miles. In its lower course it is navigable for craft of considerable size, but for a few miles only. There are other valleys traversed by streams, as that of the Cagayan. The soil in general, and especially in the river and lake regions, is remarkable for its fertility.

THE SMALLER ISLANDS.

The smaller islands may be more briefly described. Samar, the most easterly with the exception of Mindanao, is separated from the southeastern cape of Luzon by a channel ten miles wide. It is 120 miles long by 60 wide, is hilly, but not mountainous, and is well watered, possessing several rivers of some importance. It contains a very large amount of valuable timber. Leyte lies southwest of Samar, from which it is separated by a narrow but extremely beautiful strait. It is 100 miles long and 30 wide. Southwest of this island lies Bohol, a small island, of compact shape; west of which and of Leyte is the important island of Cebu, the seat of the first settlement in the Philippines. It approaches Palawan in length and narrowness, being 135 miles long while its greatest width is 30 miles. Its chief town, Cebu, is the capital of the Visayas group. This island has no high mountains, though steep and broken hills diversify its interior. Its forests have almost vanished, but the country is difficult to traverse, cultivation being easy only along the coast.

The large island of Negros lies west of Cebu, from which it is separated by a long strait fifteen miles in width. It is mountainous, its highest peak being the active volcano, Malaspina, or Canloon, 8192 feet high. The mountains are richly clothed with forest, peopled by savage tribes; but the lowlands are highly fertile, and Negros is perhaps the richest of all the islands, for its size. It possesses a navigable river, the Danao. To the northwest lies Panay, the seat of Iloilo, the second port of the archipelago. The forests of this island, like those of Cebu, have nearly disappeared, and with them the wild inhabitants, though some may still exist in the high mountains of the northwest. The soil has considerable fertility and much sugar is raised.

Northwest of Panay and south of Luzon, from

which latter it is but ten miles distant, lies the large island of Mindoro, as yet but little known, though the Steere exploring expedition recently made several journeys into its interior. The mountains of its central region contain a number of high peaks, the loftiest being Mount Halcon, 8865 feet high. Extensive grassy plains lie between the mountains and the west coast, while the eastern lowlands are heavily timbered and crossed by numerous rivers. Primeval forest covers most of the surface, within which dwell the Mangyans, a savage but peaceful tribe, which the members of the Steere expedition were among the first to study.

The long, slender island of Palawan, which, with its continuing isles, fills most of the interval between Mindoro and Borneo, is similarly unexplored. A chain of mountains extends through most of its length, though there is said to be a large plain in its northern section. Its streams are necessarily short, its average width being but twenty miles; but there are many of them. Its woodlands constitute its principal wealth, it being rich in valuable woods, such as ebony, logwood, and *ipil*, a very hard wood which can be cut in logs of great length. The soil, though highly fertile, has as yet been little cultivated.

The smaller islands we may dismiss briefly. Masbate, west of Samar, is mainly utilized for grazing, having extensive grassy plains, on which large herds of cattle and numerous buffaloes and horses find pasturage. Marinduque, a small island east of Mindoro, is populous and flourishing, being largely devoted to rice and the hemp plant. The islands of the Sulu group have been industriously cultivated, and Worcester found the forests of Sulu almost entirely composed of fruit trees, the old forest having been cleared away and these planted.

HARBORS.

Chief among the harbors of the Philippines is that of Manila, whose magnificent bay is among the best known and most frequented of the harbors of the eastern world. This beautiful body of water is thirty miles long and twenty-five wide, having a circumference of about 120 miles. Manila lies near its inner extremity. Its great expanse is injurious to it as a harbor of refuge, anchorage being unsafe during a severe storm. It is especially dangerous during the typhoon season, and on more than one occasion large ships have been wrecked almost under the city walls. The shoal water in front of the city prevents the near approach of large vessels, which are obliged to seek shelter at Cavité, eight miles from the mouth of the Pasig River. Vessels of fourteen or more feet draught are obliged to lie out in the bay and discharge part of their cargo by means of lighters before they can enter the Pasig, along which are the principal wharves and warehouses. The Pasig is usually crowded with small vessels. Manila is built on low ground, its highest point being not many feet above tide-water, and is divided into two parts by the Pasig, through which the waters of the large lake, Laguna de Bay, fourteen miles distant, find their way to the bay.

Of the remaining Philippine harbors only two, Iloilo and Cebu, are of commercial importance, these and Manila being the only ports which have any foreign trade. Iloilo, on the southeastern coast of Panay, ranks next to Manila, though at a large remove, in commercial importance. It is situated near the sea-shore, access for small steamers being attained by means of a creek, which has been deepened by dredging. The outer harbor is well protected and naturally good; the island of Guimaras, which fronts Panay at this point, forming a sheltered passage, of from two to six miles in breadth, with deep water and good anchorage. The creek has five fathoms over its entrance bar, and could readily be deepened within by dredging.

The island of Panay possesses another harbor of local importance, San José de Buenavista, the port of the province of Antique. Here a breakwater has been constructed, and whaling and other foreign vessels have long been in the habit of calling for water and fresh provisions. It has little trade, as the surrounding country is thinly settled and undeveloped.

Cebu until recently surpassed Iloilo in commercial importance, but has now fallen to the third rank. It lies on the east coast of the island of the same name, and possesses a good harbor, which needs, however, to be entered with caution, the channel leading to it presenting difficulties. The points of danger are buoyed, and care only is needed for a safe entrance. The principal articles shipped from this port are the neighboring products of sugar, hemp, tobacco, and sapan-wood.

The other ports include Zamboango on Mindanao, Tacloban on Leyte, Sual and Albay on Luzon, and some others of little importance. These are only concerned in the inter-island trade. Zamboango is the most southerly town of importance in the group, being seated at the extremity of the long western peninsula of Mindanao, opposite the island of Basilan. Albay similarly lies near the extremity of the peninsula of Luzon, at the bottom of a deep bay. Sual is situated on the southern shore of the deep Lingayen Gulf, on the middle west coast of Luzon, and at the mouth of the Agno River, a stream of considerable depth, but with a bar at its mouth that prevents entrance from the sea.

None of these ports have other than local importance, though some of them, such as Sual, have possibilities in case of a fuller development of the resources of the islands. There are numerous bays around the circuit of the Philippines, some of which, in the coming future of the islands, may be utilized as harbors. Among these we may mention Subig Bay, which was entered by vessels of Dewey's squadron on its way to Manila, in search of the Spanish fleet. This bay is land-locked, has deep water, and is considered by Admiral Dewey the best harbor in the islands for coaling purposes. In the centre of the north coast, at the mouth of the Cagayan, is an extensive bay, guarded from the sea by a small island at its mouth, its harbor facilities being equal to and safer than those of Manila Bay. Here is the town of Aparri, which in time may become a rival to Manila, being twenty-four hours nearer Hong-Kong and 400 miles nearer San Francisco.

CLIMATE.

The Philippines extend through many degrees of latitude, from near the equator to the vicinity of the tropic of Cancer, and have moreover a considerable diversity of altitude, with the result that there are climatic differences between separated regions. But the characteristics of the climate are in general those of the tropics, there being little to distinguish it from many other places in the Eastern tropics. According to a Spanish proverb, there are "Six months of dust, six months of mud, six months of everything;" indicating that though as a general statement the rainy season lasts one half and the dry season the other half of the year, there are months of uncertainty whether drought or humidity will prevail.

The northern islands lie in the region of the typhoons, and here three seasons are usually recognized, —a hot, a wet, and a dry. The dry season begins in November and extends to February or March. During this period northerly winds prevail, and it is sufficiently cool to render woollen clothing comfortable in the mornings, though it is never cold and there are no sudden changes of temperature. The sky is usually clear and the atmosphere bracing in this season, and to Europeans it is much the most enjoyable part of the year; though there is no season in which men can endure hard physical labor without discomfort from the heat.

The hot season begins in March and continues until June; the heat becoming very oppressive during the latter portion of this period and before it is mitigated by the coming of the southerly monsoon. During May and June thunder-storms are frequent, and are often terrific in violence,—the rains being severe, the lightning fierce, and the thunder deafening. Many lose their lives by lightning-strokes, and houses are frequently swept away by the overflowing torrents.

The southwest monsoon is fully established by June,

bringing with it the specifically rainy season; torrential rains pouring down through the months of July, August, September, and October, with such violence that the low country is widely flooded, rivers overflow their banks, the lakes extend enormously, the roads become generally impassable, and travelling grows difficult and disagreeable. Even in December the effect of these rains shows itself in roads so deep in mud that carriages have to be abandoned and palanquin bearers sink to their thighs in mire.

This is the season of the typhoon, the terrific revolving wind-storm which sweeps all to ruin before it, and which is similar in character to the destructive tornado of our western plains. The force of the wind is such as to uproot the largest trees, unroof or carry away houses, and to imperil the stanchest ships. Vessels are occasionally borne ashore by the waves driven inward before a typhoon, and their bleaching ribs may be seen at intervals in some far inland paddy-field or low-lying farm. Fortunately for the people of the southern islands, the typhoon seldom occurs south of 9° or 10° north latitude.

The close of the southwest monsoon is followed by a period of calms and variable winds, after which the northeast monsoon sets in, with its dry and bracing winds. The mountains affect the seasons,—a high range delaying the wet season for weeks, while the rains begin on the Pacific side of the eastern islands during the continuance of the northeast winds.

These characteristics of the climate apply especially to the northern islands, the southern ones lying below the region of the trades and displaying different climatic conditions. The heat varies considerably in different islands, and no one locality can be taken as typical of the group. As the only careful and continuous observations of rainfall and temperature, however, are those made in the Jesuit observatory at Manila, we must content ourselves with the figures there placed on record.

The mean annual temperature of Manila is 80° F., the thermometer having a total range of forty degrees, from 60° to 100°. It rarely goes above the latter figure. There is no month in the year in which the temperature does not reach as high as 90°, and the mean of the two coldest months, December and January, is 77°. That of the warmest month, May, is 84°. In the winter months nights of reasonable coolness can be looked for; but there is little relief night or day in the hot season, the deep humidity which then prevails adding greatly to the oppressiveness of the temperature.

The average monthly rainfall, as recorded from 1865 to 1896, is for the wettest month, September, 15.01 inches, and nearly as much for July and August. It falls to 7.47 in October, 4.92 in November, and continues low until June, the figures for February and March being respectively 0.47 and 0.65. The total annual rainfall averages 75.43 inches, the range of different years being from 120.98 to 33.65. The greatest monthly fall on record is 61.43 inches in September, while the lowest record for the same month is two inches.

DISEASES.

Very varied opinions exist concerning the healthfulness of the Philippines and the effect of their climatic conditions on white men, these varying from the "lovely" of one author to the "deadly" of another. One says that "for a tropical climate that of the islands may be considered healthful for people of the white race;" another asserts that "the climate of the Philippines is particularly severe and unhealthy," his proof being that of the Spanish soldiers sent there in 1896, twenty-five per cent. died of disease within fifteen months.

Worcester, who had abundant opportunity to judge, ascribes the examples of unhealthfulness to imprudence, and concludes that if one is very careful in his diet, drinks only wholesome water, avoids excesses, does not unduly exert himself, and keeps out of the sun at midday, "he is likely to remain well, always supposing that he is fortunate enough to escape malarial infection."

On the other hand, the story is told that "About eight years ago General-Manager Higgins, of the Manila and Dagupan Railway, having secured a concession from the Spanish government, organized in London a party of about forty Englishmen,—civil engineers and others,—who were to survey the route and build and afterwards assist in the operation and management of the railroad. Mr. Higgins gave special attention to the physical condition of his assistants, selecting only men that he believed could stand the severe climate of the archipelago. To-day not more than half the members of that party are alive."

Malarial fevers are the most constant dangers of the foreigner who in any way exposes himself. Those of milder form may be easily shaken off, if promptly and vigorously treated; but the dreaded *calentura per-*

niciosa is a far more dangerous and malignant diease. It is rapid and violent, running its course in a few hours, and often ending in black vomit and death. Fortunately, it is very local in its occurrence, and the places subject to it are known and shunned as well by the natives as by the whites. Malaria also is absent from some islands, while others are veritable pestholes.

The malarial trouble may be in a measure capable of remedy. Sulu, once a fever centre, was made healthful by General Arolas, who, by filling the low places with coral sand and improving the drainage, nearly put an end to the disease. The same was done at Tataän, in Tawi-Tawi, by cutting off the neighboring forest growth and clearing up the ground. The fever, previously very prevalent, almost disappeared.

But such radical measures must be confined to the towns, and malaria will continue to prevail in the country. So far as the white population is concerned, one serious circumstance is that the climate is especially severe on women and children, a fact which stands in the way of establishing a permanent American or European population. The troubles are mainly malarial and digestive, the danger from epidemic disorders being slight. Small-pox is one of the permanent diseases, but its spread is rarely rapid, and most of the natives have it in childhood.

Cholera occasionally, though rarely, visits the islands. When it does come its ravages are severe, as the natives cannot be induced to take any precaution against it. It is the will of God, they say. A black dog runs down the street and the disease breaks out behind him.

Of the other diseases we may name leprosy, which fortunately is not common, and beriberi, which prevails to some extent. The malignant bubonic plague, so fatal in India and elsewhere in the East, has never established itself in the Philippines. On the whole, aside from malaria, there are no widely prevalent diseases, and most of the deleterious effects upon whites are direct results of the tropical severity of the climate.

III. NATURAL PRODUCTIONS.

FOREST TREES.

The Philippines are exceptionally rich in forests, vast in dimensions and magnificent in aspect, covering immense regions of the islands, particularly in their mountain sections, and containing an unusual variety of valuable timber trees. Forest, indeed, is not everywhere found. Some of the islands, as Cebu and Panay, have been nearly denuded of their trees by agriculturists, and this denudation is still going on, slowly but steadily. The native has no regard for trees. If he wishes to start a farm, he clears a tract of forest of the desired size, burns the felled timber, and plants the ground. In this, however, he is in no sense singular, his method being the same as that employed by the pioneer population of the United States. But the Philippine farmer has one strong enemy to contend with, which forces him to repeat his process of wood butchery. There is a strong, tall grass called *cogon* which in time is sure to invade his farm, and which defies his simple means of eradication. So he abandons the farm to the grass, clears a second tract of woodland, and starts another plantation.

The cogon takes such strong hold that no other plant can compete with it; and this vigorous pest seizes upon vast areas, once thickly forested, now known as *cogonales*. The plant is nearly useless, though not quite so, since it serves for thatch, and its coarse stems are used to some extent for fuel. In its young state it is also used for pasturage, the natives, at the end of the dry season, setting the old grass on fire, and cattle and horses feed greedily on the fresh young shoots which sprout up after the coming of the rains.

The forests, as in the tropics generally, are dense in growth, and possess the usual number of vines, lianas, and thorns, so that passage through them can be had only by the constant use of a heavy machete. Such paths as the natives have made are difficult to traverse except by native feet. They have been worn smooth by much usage, and are slippery after rains, a fact to their detriment when they run along the trunks of fallen trees, as is often the case.

The flora of the Philippines contains nearly 4500 species, belonging to 1223 genera. Of these fifty genera are of ferns, which are very numerous, and there are many handsome orchids. The wealth of the forests in valuable woods is enormous, many of the most useful timber trees being scarcely known outside the islands. More than 200 kinds of wood have been thought worthy of testing in the Manila arsenal, among which are no less than fifty varieties of hard-wood lumber, few of which have been offered for sale abroad. There is a large local use, but as yet Japan and China have been the only considerable foreign users of Philippine timber.

The woods vary in color from the jet-black ebony to the light-hued cedar, and in some cases are proof against the most destructive enemies of building timber. Some of them are specially valuable for underwater construction, as they resist the attacks of the teredo, while others defy the white ant, that most annoying of tropical insects.

Of the hard-woods of the Philippine forests, the best known and most esteemed is the teak-like *molave*, called by the natives "the queen of woods," a heavy brown timber, almost as hard as steel, and of great strength. It resists the action of water for years, is proof against the attacks of the white ant, and is used for all purposes. Its firm surface permits of fine carving.

The *dongon*, another fine building wood, is often substituted for the molave, though not for wharfage, as it does not resist the teredo. There are two others which, like the molave, resist the white ant, the *ipil*, a hard, strong wood abounding in Luzon, and the *yacal*. Both of these are much used for building.

Among the other useful trees may be named the *acre*, an abundant timber, used for buildings and shipping; the *antipolo*, whose light but strong wood is nearly as impervious as the molave; the *bolonguita*, an abundant timber which is used for fine furniture; the *calantas* (native cedar), found throughout the islands and used for canoe-making; the beautifully veined and spotted *camagon*, an easily polished wood which is used for fine furniture; the *guijo*, an abundant wood, whose tough and elastic timber is much esteemed for carriage-wheels and ship-building; and the *lauan*, abounding in the forests, and much used for canoes. It was formerly employed for the outside planking of galleons, as its light, stringy wood did not splinter under the impact of cannon-balls.

Ebony has been found in some quantity, and much

more may exist in the forest depths. Two woods somewhat resembling it are the *mabolo* and the *malatapay*. These are handsome woods, similar in character,—the former black streaked with yellow, the latter black striped with red, and both useful for fine furniture. The *narra* is a strong, hard wood, its color from light straw to deep red, used for cabinet purposes and susceptible of a high polish. The *palo-maria* yields a strong, knotty, and crooked timber, very useful for ship timber. Another tree used for ship timber and building purposes is the *panao* or *balao*, which also yields a resin used for lighting purposes by the natives and the talay oil, which destroys insects in wood. The *bansalque*, or bullet-tree, yields a wood hard enough to be driven like a nail. It furnishes treenails for ship-building and makes splendid tool handles.

The above is far from exhausting the list of useful forest trees, there being numerous others which have been employed for various purposes. The list given, however, includes the best known and most useful, the chief of all being the ubiquitous molave.

Of the native plants growing outside the forests, the bamboo is the most common, the most beautiful, and the most useful. There are no more charming features of the scenery than its graceful bamboo groups, scattered profusely on hills and plains and along streams, their light branches, waving in the smallest breeze, giving perpetual life to the landscape. It supplies the native with nearly all the materials for his house, and for sledges, agricultural implements, bows, arrows, bow-strings, lance-heads, forks, spoons, cups, fences, water-pipes, musical instruments, and a host of other purposes.

Other very useful plants are the canes, rattans, and other branches of the *calamus* family. They grow to a great length, the *bejuco*, or bush-rope, a rattan, being frequently 300 feet long. It is said to be found more than three times that length in Mindanao. These plants are used for ropes and cables, and when split are employed to tie together the parts of house frames, fences, carts, canoes, etc., also for bed-making, chair-seating, and many other purposes. The fibres can be divided into very fine threads, which are woven into delicate textures, some of which, as hats and cigar-cases, are sold at very high prices.

The cocoa palm, common here as everywhere in the tropics, grows on land too poor to bear anything else, each tree yielding an average of twenty nuts a month. These, where water communication permits, are made into rafts and floated to market; otherwise they are hauled on buffalo sledges. The bamboo itself is not of more use to the natives. Every part of the plant is turned to account,—trunk, branches, leaves, fruit alike. The juices yield oil, wine, and spirits. Cables are made from the bark, which is also used for caulking. The trunk often forms the frame and the leaves the roof of the native houses. The leaf fibres are woven into cloth, the fruit fibres made into brushes. The shell of the fruit is made into spoons, cups, etc., the burnt shell used as a black dye, the roasted root as a cure for dysentery.

The *nipa* palm is little less useful to the Philippine native. This common plant grows abundantly in swampy places, and its leaves are widely used for the thatch and sides of houses. Its sap furnishes an intoxicating drink, and strong alcohol, of excellent quality, is distilled from it. The *palma brava* is much valued for the great hardness of its outer wood, which adapts it to pier building, it resisting water indefinitely. By removing the soft inner fibre, hollow tubes of large size, excellent for water-pipes, are made. Another palm highly esteemed by the natives is the *areca*, yielding the betel-nuts so much used for chewing. The tree is a graceful one, which is planted thickly in the villages, each tree yielding annually from 200 to 800 nuts.

FRUIT AND FOOD PLANTS.

Fruits are very abundant in the Philippines, the banana in particular. Of this prolific and useful plant there are said to be more than seventy varieties, the fruit varying from tiny, pear-like specimens to huge examples a foot and a half in length. This everywhere present plant forms one of the important articles of food. The banana of the Philippines, however, does not, as a rule, bear a high record for flavor; and the same is said of the pineapple and the orange, the native orange being very poor and never coming to perfection.

Hardly any of the tropical fruits reaches here the perfection attained elsewhere, except the mango, introduced from the West Indies, which gains an unsurpassed flavor in Philippine soil. The fame of the Manila mango extends throughout the East. The guava, similarly brought from the American tropics, has spread from island to island; birds greedily devouring the fruit and scattering the seeds. The cacao-tree, imported from Mexico nearly three centuries ago, flourishes here, and yields beans of excellent quality in good crops.

Nearly all the Malayan fruits are to be met with, including the jack-fruit, medlar, lanzan, and the much-prized mangosteen, which flourishes in the southern islands. In the extreme south, especially in Sulu and Tawi-Tawi, is found the famous durian, celebrated alike for its disgustingly unpleasant odor and the delicious flavor of its fruit. There may be mentioned in addition the papaw, chico, lime, citron, shaddock, bread-fruit, custard-apple, and tamarind.

The edible vegetables, as in the other tropical islands, are largely composed of roots, some of which grow to an enormous size, weighing from fifty to seventy pounds. The yam and the sweet potato are widely grown and form an important part of the native food-stuffs. The ground-nut is also common. Potatoes and peas are grown to a small extent, and wheat is cultivated in the higher regions. Maize is raised, but does not do well. Other food plants and fruits include the melon, pumpkin, onion, cucumber, garlic, and various other vegetables brought from Mexico and planted in the church gardens, whence they have spread into wider cultivation.

ANIMAL LIFE.

The largest native animal of the Philippines, and the most useful, is the *carabao*, or water-buffalo, which is found everywhere, both as the chief domestic animal of the natives and in the wild state, great herds of wild buffaloes existing in the interior. The tamed animal is the mainstay of the native farmer, being employed in all the labors of the field and in the transport of commodities, which it either carries on its back or draws in wagons.

Muddy water or pure mud is its delight, and it will have its share of this whatever else goes wrong. The worst thing about the buffalo is that it absolutely declines to work at midday if the sun is hot. Its daily mud-bath is also insisted on, the mud drying and caking on its back as an armor against insects. It will go where a horse cannot, but is unsafe to ride, for if urged against its inclinations it is likely to plunge into the nearest mud-bath; and if it should see a tempting slough it is apt to dive into the muddy depths, regardless of what may be on its back.

In its daily labors, however, the buffalo is tractable, and is well treated by the natives, who are obliged to humor its peculiarities, such as its insatiable appetite for mud. Another characteristic of this animal is a prejudice against white men, the scent of an European traveller being sometimes sufficient to set all the buffaloes in a village on the stampede. This, of course, applies to those villages rarely visited by the whites. As a work animal the buffalo is extremely slow in its movements, and lacks the strength and endurance which its bulk promises. But its docility and patience commend it, it being easily guided even by a child.

In his recent visit to Mindoro, Worcester was regaled by the natives with stories of an extraordinary animal called by them the *timarau*, which haunted the depths of the jungles. After considerable effort, he at length found and shot some specimens of this beast, which proved to be a small buffalo different in species from the domestic animal and exceedingly shy and alert. It is very vicious also, not hesitating to attack the much larger water-buffalo, which it kills. It is dangerous for man to approach.

Cattle are raised in large numbers for beef on some of the islands, and bullocks are used in the Visayas as draught animals. They have run wild on some islands, but these do not seem numerous. The horse is claimed to be from Andalusian stock, by way of Mexico, and is a small but very wiry animal, well-formed and sure-footed, and capable of carrying a weight seemingly out of proportion to its size.

There are several species of deer on the archipelago, numerous enough in some places to be hunted for their meat. Goats are common, both their flesh and their milk being prized. Every village of the natives has its swine, and wild hogs are very abundant, especially so in Tawi-Tawi.

The native mammals of the Philippines are very few, these islands being not nearly so rich in species as the neighboring island of Borneo. There are no large carnivorous animals, the order being principally represented by a small wild cat, two species of civet-cats, and the *binturong*. Of monkeys, the *chongo* (*Macacus cynomolgus*) is found in all the islands, and a monkey of pure white color occurs in Mindanao. The lemurs are represented by the strange little Tarsus, and there are two species of insectivora and several rodents, comprising some squirrels, a porcupine, and a few rats. The bats are the most numerous in species, there being twenty or thirty in all, some of them of very large size. Enormous colonies of large fruit-bats exist, which are taken for their fur and are sometimes eaten by the natives.

Birds occur in great abundance, about 590 species being known. Many of these are rare and beautiful. They include pretty little paroquets, several peculiar woodpeckers, and a number of species of pigeons, cockatoos, and mound builders. The principal game-bird is the jungle-fowl, which is very common, and is snared by the natives, either to be eaten or tamed. Other game-birds include fruit-pigeons and large hornbills, with snipe, curlew, and other water-birds.

One species is of considerable commercial importance, the swift, which builds the nest so much prized by the Chinese as a table delicacy. When perfectly clean, these nests are said to sometimes bring more than their weight in gold. They are made from a salivary secretion of the bird, which hardens on exposure to the air into a substance resembling in appearance white glue. The birds build in caves or on the faces of inaccessible cliffs, and those who rob them of their nests do so at imminent risk. They are found in several of the islands, the best being taken on the Peñon de Coron, a very precipitous island in the strait between Culion and Busuanga.

Of the reptiles, crocodiles occur in large numbers in the lakes and streams, and are sometimes of great size. They destroy a considerable number of cattle, horses, and young buffaloes, pulling them into the water when they come down to drink. The natives do not show much fear of them, though man-eating crocodiles in Mindanao prove frequently fatal to the inhabitants.

Serpents are also numerous, some of the species being very venomous. The deadly cobra occurs in Samar, Mindanao, and the Calamianes group, and the loss from snake-bite is serious in some localities. Most to be dreaded is the terrible dehenpalay, whose bite is almost instantly fatal. It is short and slender, and similar to a rice-leaf in appearance. Pythons occur, though rarely large. The small ones are very common, and are dealt in as commercial objects, being sold in the towns to keep about houses as ratcatchers. There are many lizards, among them the gecko, a disturbing creature from its noisy cry. The tortoise is of considerable importance to the natives, who conceal themselves when the animals are coming ashore; then run between them and the waves, turn over on their backs as many as they can, and return at leisure to remove them.

Fresh-water fish are of minor importance, but the ocean species are of great variety and enormously abundant. There are also great numbers of shellfish, including many edible varieties. The pearl oyster occurs near Sulu, and yields fine pearls and beautiful shells; another oyster occasionally yields handsome black pearls. The translucent shell which is substituted for window-glass is obtained from still another species. Some of the mollusks are of enormous size, the *taclova* shells, which are used for baptismal fonts, sometimes weighing 200 pounds.

The usual variety and annoyance of tropical insects exist, among the worst of them being the locusts, which appear in countless myriads every few years, causing devastation to the growing crops, though the natives obtain some recompense by frying and eating the insects. There is a large beetle which is also eaten, and various other insects and larvæ are used as food by the natives.

Fire-flies are abundant and brilliant, and very many beautiful butterflies occur; while there are three species of honey-bees, one of them a large, dark-colored kind which builds great combs on the under side of branches. The honey and grubs are devoured by the natives, and the wax is of value for candles used in religious ceremonies.

The most annoying of the insects is the white ant, a burrowing creature whose destructive powers are almost incredible. Numerous stories of its ravages are extant, one relating to its inroad upon the robes and other fabrics used in the service of the mass. On the 19th of March, 1838, the garments, ornaments, etc., after use in a certain church, were placed in a trunk made of narra wood; and on the following day, some dirt being seen near the trunk, it was opened and examined. Every fragment of the vestments had disappeared or been reduced to dust, except the gold and silver lace, yet not an ant was to be found anywhere in the church, nor a vestige of their presence. Some days afterwards it was discovered that they had eaten a passage through a beam six inches thick.

METALS.

Up to the present time the mineral wealth of the Philippines remains in large measure undeveloped, no systematic workings or explorations having been made. From time to time spasmodic activity has been shown, but nearly every attempt has ended in failure, due principally to lack of capital, and, secondarily, to insufficient means of transportation and difficulty in procuring labor. Of late years more energy in this direction has been shown, the work of exploration having been assumed by a British corporation known as "The Philippines Mineral Syndicate, Limited." which has gone systematically to work and gained some new information concerning the mineral resources of the islands. Of the great number of islands, only about a score are known to contain deposits of valuable minerals, these including most of the large islands and a number of the smaller ones.

As regards gold, greatly varied opinions have been expressed by different authorities, some holding that the Philippines are rich in this precious metal and only await active mining on scientific principles to yield it in large quantities, others doubting the richness of the deposits and believing that the placer-workings were never of much value and have been largely exhausted. The metal was known to exist long before the Spanish period, and was mined by the natives in the primitive and irregular method which they still pursue, a rude and wasteful fashion in which they are apt to lose more than they gather. They have no means of blasting, lacking powder and dynamite, and are ignorant of the process of amalgamation, while the value of pyritic ores is unknown to them.

In consequence, only rich deposits are worked, the gold of the alluvial beds being obtained by the use of wash-boards and flat wooden bowls, in which all the float-gold is lost. The natives work some of the richer quartz veins, the gold-bearing rock being crushed with hammers or ground under heavy stone rollers turned by buffaloes, and then washed to obtain the gold. Their ignorance of amalgamation necessarily causes much of it to be lost. The idea of pumping out the shafts has not developed, the water being bailed out with small water-buckets, which lines of workmen pass from hand to hand. Even in this primitive and wasteful way the natives obtain enough gold

NATURAL PRODUCTIONS.

to pay them for their labor. Nearly all the mountain people of Luzon traffic in gold, which is probably obtained from quartz veins in the mountain region. The alluvial deposits in this island have been prospected by the syndicate above named, and have yielded indications of being rich and extensive.

Gold is not confined to Luzon. It has been found in Mindanao, Mindoro, Panay, Cebu, and the smaller islands of Samar, Catanduanes, Sibuyan, Bohol, and Panaon. Old placer workings exist in Cebu and Mindanao, and rich quartz veins are known to occur in the latter island. Panaon possesses at least one such vein. As for Mindoro, its name is said to come from *mina de ora* (gold mine), and the natives speak freely of places in the interior which are rich in gold. In the interior of Mindanao gold-dust is the instrument of exchange, it being carried about in bags for use in the ordinary purposes of life. The Misamis gold placers in this island are the richest in the archipelago, their yield under the native processes being about 150 ounces per month. Under the new political relations of the Philippines their resources in this direction are likely to be systematically exploited. The placer beds on the Pacific slopes of Luzon are in many cases near the sea, offering facilities for transportation. The introduction of modern methods and machinery might develop an important output of the precious metal in this region and in Mindanao.

Silver occurs on several of the islands, including Cebu, Mindoro, and Marinduque, and platinum on Mindanao, while mercury is thought to exist on Panay and Leyte. Copper occurs somewhat widely, it having been found in Luzon, Masbate, Panay, and Mindanao, though it has not yet been successfully mined by Europeans. The copper ores of the district of Lepanto, Luzon, have been rudely mined by the Igorrote tribe from remote times, they manufacturing their domestic utensils from the copper thus procured. Reports of the richness of the ores have led to several attempts at mining on the part of the Spaniards, but these were individual efforts, much money being spent without providing the necessary machinery or opening roads for the conveyance of the ore. Discouragement has arisen from the rugged nature of the rocks, the density of the forest jungle, and the indolence of the natives; but the principal difficulty in the way has been the lack of capital and of mining experience. A company was formed in 1862 for the working of several mines in Lepanto, the ore of the Mancayan mine yielding over sixteen per cent. of copper, twenty-four of sulphur, five of antimony, and five of arsenic. Copper mines have also been worked at Assit, in Masbate. More energy and better appliances are needed to develop the real richness of the islands in this metal.

Lead occurs in Luzon, Marinduque, and Cebu, veins of galena having been found in Luzon and Cebu in which the lead is associated with a good percentage of gold and silver. There have been mining operations near the city of Cebu. Iron exists in Luzon, Panay, and Cebu, ore of excellent quality, yielding up to eighty-five per cent. of pure metal, having been found in Luzon. But the backward condition of the roads has kept the charges for transportation so high that it has hitherto proved cheaper to import than to mine iron. Many iron-works have been started and abandoned, and cheap carriage must precede any attempt to work these ores with profit. There was actually more activity in iron mining a century ago than there is at present.

MINERALS.

From time to time the discovery of important coal deposits in the Philippines has been reported, its occurrence being recorded in the islands of Luzon, Mindoro, Negros, Masbate, Samar, Panay, Leyte, Cebu, Mindanao, and several of the smaller islands. None of these beds, however, contain true coal, but excellent lignite, highly carbonized, and in very extensive deposits, has been found in Luzon, Cebu, Mindoro, and Masbate. Experiments with this have shown it to answer very satisfactorily the needs of steamers; but it is impossible to make use of it under present circumstances, the veins being situated in localities which are destitute of means of transportation. The highway and the railroad are sadly needed in the Philippines, even if for the exploitation of these rich deposits alone. Systematic exploration is similarly needed, and might very probably lead to the discovery of veins of true coal. In its absence, the lignite of the Philippines cannot fail to be of great value to future commerce in those waters. There are two principal fields of this mineral, one beginning in Caranson, in the south of Luzon, and apparently extending under sea to Samar, and the other in western Cebu and eastern Negros. In the first of these a bed from ten to twenty feet thick, yielding good steamboat fuel, crops out at Gatho, and the second shows a number of beds varying in quality and thickness.

As regards the need of exploration, the story is

told of a vessel which was wrecked on the coast of Mindoro, the captain and crew being forced to cross the island to a port on the east coast. In their journey through the mountains they came across a very rich and extensive outcrop of coal, forming, they said, great ledges, from which thousands of tons had broken off and fallen to the foot of the cliffs. This was reported to the Spanish authorities, and the locality was duly made government property, though nothing further was done.

Of other minerals, the most abundant is sulphur, which is found in Luzon and Biliran, occurring in unlimited quantities in and about the volcanoes, extinct and active, sometimes pure, sometimes mixed with other substances. The crater of the Taal volcano is rich in sulphur, which has been profitably worked. Petroleum has been found in Cebu and Panay, and Mindoro possesses mines of a natural paint, probably composed of red lead. Gypsum occurs on Mindoro and Panay, and excellent marbles exist in large beds on Luzon and Romblon. Some of those of the province of Butaan, of finely variegated color, have been used in the ornamentation of churches, but beyond this no use has been found for them. Kaolin occurs in Luzon. In addition to the mineral deposits are numerous springs of mineral waters, sulphurous and ferruginous; and hot springs, of valuable medicinal properties, occur in several localities. Great virtue is attributed to the waters of Pagsanghan by the people of Manila, and immense throngs gather in the Laguna to drink the curative waters, and join the processions in honor of the virgin patroness of that locality.

IV. CIVIL AND POLITICAL RELATIONS.

GOVERNMENT.

During the Spanish administration, the Philippines, like the other colonies of Spain, were under the control of a governor-general or captain-general, accountable to the authorities at home, but supreme in authority over the islands. He was assisted in his duties by several consulting bodies, including a "junta of authorities," founded in 1850, and composed of the archbishop, general-in-chief, admiral, president of the supreme court, etc.; a junta of agriculture, industry, and commerce, founded in 1866; and a council of administration. His titles covered a page, and embraced all the powers of government except that of authority over the fleet, and partly that over the church. There was a lieutenant-governor, who took his place in case of his death. As his term of office was brief, only three years, he had to press the people hard to obtain the fortune which he went to Manila to seek,—and usually found.

The islands were divided into provinces, each under a military governor or a civilian alcalde, one of whose principal duties was the collection of taxes. The provinces were divided into pueblos (towns or villages), each under the control of a *gobernadorcillo* ("little governor"), who was chosen from the natives or the mestizos, and was an important local personage, as the representative of the provincial governor. This official settled all minor questions arising in his jurisdiction; but his principal duty was to see that the taxes were duly collected and paid over, and he was obliged to make good any deficiency in them. He was required to aid in the arrest of criminals, to assist the friar in church affairs, to attend upon visiting officials, and often to entertain them at his own expense, and at times to travel to the provincial capital on official business, paying his own expenses. In compensation for these various duties he received the diminutive salary of $200 a year, was allowed to carry a cane, and received the title of *capitan*. He could recuperate himself only by "squeezing" his fellow-citizens.

Wealthy men were chosen for this service, if there were any such, and often kept in office for years against their wills. Yet the position was sometimes earnestly sought, the Philippine native dearly enjoying a little show of authority, and often being willing to pay for the privilege.

As for his responsibility for the taxes, he had subordinates in the same position. The towns were divided into groups of from forty to sixty families. *Barangays*, each under a *cabeza*, or native official, whose duty it was to collect the taxes or to pay out of his own pocket all he could not get from the people. This very undesirable position was forced upon the well-to-do inhabitants of the town, who, though nominally elected every two years, were really kept in office while their property held out, financial ruin being a not uncommon end of their official duties. There were other minor officials, while *gobernadorcillos* who had served a term and *cabezas* of ten years' standing formed the "headmen" of the town, who met periodically at the *tribunal*, or town hall, for the discussion of public affairs.

In the words of Worcester, the headmen "assemble every Sunday morning, and, headed by the *gobernadorcillo*, and frequently also by a band playing very lively airs, they march to the *convento* and escort the friar to church, where they all attend mass. Their state dress is quite picturesque. Their white shirts dangle outside of their pantaloons after the Philippine fashion, and over them they wear tight-fitting jackets without tails, which reach barely to their waists. When the jacket is buttoned, it causes the shirt to stand out in a frill, producing a most grotesque effect."

The above description of the governmental organization does not apply to all the inhabitants, there being wandering mountain and forest tribes who have been brought only nominally under control of the established government; while many of the *Moros*, or Mohammedans, of the south have never been subjected to Spanish authority. The Sultan of Sulu is the ruler of all the Moros, though there are two subordinate Sultans in Mindanao who are only nominally subject to him. His court embraces a regent, who replaces him during his absence, a minister of war, and a minister of justice; while there are many *datos* or chiefs. The local village ruler bears the title of *mandarin*.

There was no feature of Spanish rule more provokingly unjust than the administration of *justice*. There were two supreme courts, one at Manila and one at Cebu, and forty-one superior courts, with the requisite number of local courts. The dilatoriness of these courts became proverbial, even in the slow-moving East. The litigant was very likely to be fleeced out of a sum far surpassing the value of the object in dispute before he could escape from the hands of the judges and lawyers, all of whom were sharp on the scent for fees. "Availing one's self of the dilatoriness of the Spanish law," says a recent traveller, "it is possible for a man to occupy a house, pay no rent, and refuse to quit on legal grounds during a couple of years or more. A person who has not a cent to lose can persecute another by means of a trumped-up accusation, until he is ruined by an '*information de pobreza*,'—a declaration of poverty,—which enables the prosecutor to keep the case going as long as he chooses, without needing money for fees."

RELIGION.

Behind, or rather side by side with, the governmental institutions of the Philippines stood the religious, exercising a co-ordinate authority, and, as they came into more intimate relations with the people, acting really as the "power behind the throne." The early treatment of the natives of the Philippines by the Spaniards was far different from their treatment of the American Indians. In these islands the people were not enslaved, and the soldier and adventurer were subordinated by the priest, the small body of troops being accompanied by zealous missionaries, whose purpose was rather to Christianize than to pillage and oppress the natives. The result was that the friars gained in time a paramount influence over the people, all of whom became Christians, with the exception of the wild and wandering tribes, who continue pagans, and the Moros of Mindanao and the Sulu Islands, who are zealous Mohammedans,—though their Mohammedanism is not strictly orthodox. Their *panditas*, or priests, are subject to *cherifs*, hereditary dignitaries who exercise both temporal and spiritual power.

The ecclesiastic administration of the islands consists of an archbishop at Manila and bishops in several other localities, while the several religious orders—the Dominicans, Franciscans, Augustinians, and Jesuits—have convents at Manila and other places. The Jesuits, expelled from the islands in 1768, as a result of the religious dissensions, were restored in 1852, and have now much influence in Manila, though their religious labors are confined to the Mohammedan islands, where they are in constant peril of their lives from the fierce and Christian-hating Moros. The Jesuits are the only learned ecclesiastics in the Philippines, being usually well educated and of good ability, while their special field of missionary labor is notable for an absence of the abuses so common elsewhere.

Unfortunately, the friars of the religious orders, as a rule, have been men of very different stamp from the Jesuit priests. The Austin, Dominican, Franciscan, and Recoleto friars are largely recruited from the lowest classes of Spain, and have no other training than that of the seminary, their lack of secular education leaving them a very ignorant class. These are the people with whom the Philippine natives have come most immediately into contact, who alone have been familiar with their languages, and have acted as the chief medium of communication between the people and the authorities. It has not suited their purposes to have the people speak Spanish, and they have not hesitated to forbid its teaching in the schools. The result has been that the education of most of the natives was confined to the study of the catechism and of a few prayers in their own language. No translation of the Bible has been permitted in the islands.

Many abuses have arisen from this state of affairs. While many of the friars have been moral and well-meaning men, their ranks have included a number of black sheep, there being scarcely any unpriestly fault of which some of them have not been accused, including drunkenness, luxurious living, unchastity, etc. Greed for money has been one of their besetting sins. Their charge for performing the marriage ceremony, for instance, was often so high that many of the people were forced to dispense with this ceremony. In Masbate, as Worcester was told, the priests exacted fifty dollars for burying an uncoffined body and seventy-five if a coffin was used, besides charging a round sum for the coffin itself.

The religious corporations possess large revenues, owning very valuable lands in Luzon, which they rent to the natives on severe conditions. The leases are so cunningly worded that the tenants are at the mercy of their landlords, by whom they are often very unjustly treated. "The Church," says Foreman, himself a Catholic, "as a body-politic, dispenses no charity, but receives all. It is always begging; always above civil laws and taxes; claims immunity; proclaims poverty, and inculcates in others charity to itself."

"The clergy," he continues, "derive a very large portion of their incomes from commissions on the sale of *cédulas*, sales of Papal bulls, masses, pictures, books, chaplets, and indulgences; marriage, burial, and baptismal fees, benedictions, donations touted out after the crops are raised, legacies to be paid for in masses, remains of wax candles left in the church by the faithful, fees for getting souls out of purgatory, etc. The surplus revenues over and above parochial requirements are supposed to augment the common Church funds in Manila. The corporations are consequently immensely wealthy, and their power and influence are in consonance with that wealth."

If the instances of the iniquities of the friars and their oppressive treatment of the people that are on record could be collated, they would make a considerable volume filled with stories of shameful delinquencies. Many men, indeed, have been permitted to hold parishes in the Philippines who would not have been tolerated in Spain, and were utterly unfitted by education and character for the holding of a religious position. Their treatment of the natives has been such as to arouse a bitter hatred against them, evidences of which were shown in the harsh treatment of the friars by the natives during the recent insurrection. Of course, the friars, as a whole, are not chargeable with these faults, but their reputation suffers from the delinquency of many of their members.

The Christianity of the natives is a very superficial one. Of their religious duties, payment of the cash demands of the friars is one of the most rigidly required. As regards actual religion, very little will serve, some degree of outward observance being the main requirement. It is in considerable measure by religious processions that the Church holds its ascendency over the Filipinos, these being the pride and delight of the native mind. On the occasion of the great Church festivals they gather in multitudes, both as actors and spectators. The most brilliant of these are those which take place after sunset, when hosts of persons carry lighted wax candles; the procession being sometimes a mile or more long, while splendidly dressed and richly jewelled images of the objects of veneration are carried in the line. There are numerous bands of music, groups of little girls dressed in white, and everything to add to the attraction of the procession, the different religious orders seeking to surpass each other in display. The images, of life size, and dressed in gorgeously ornamented garments, are borne on platforms carried on the shoulders of their votaries and illuminated by long rows of wax lights on each side of the way.

Everybody takes part in these ceremonials; universal bustle pervades the locality, invitations to feasts are given or accepted, skilled hands busy themselves in making sweetmeats or cooking delicacies, the houses are adorned with flowers and fruits, handsome arches, with variegated lanterns, are erected in the streets, all wear their finest dresses, music is heard everywhere, fireworks are shown, balloons are sent up, and all forms of popular amusement are in full play.

It has been said that it is the policy of the friars to conduct the natives to heaven by a pathway of flowers; but there are thorns among the roses and difficulties on the path, and, despite the efforts to captivate the simple-minded people by outward show, the friars have succeeded in laying up a large debt of vengeance against themselves, if we may judge from recent developments.

The evils which have so long existed in the ecclesiastical administration of the Philippines can scarcely continue under the new dispensation. Hitherto no Protestant church or service has been permitted, but freedom of religious belief is one of the assured results of their passing under the influence of the United States. With vigorous Protestant competition in religious teaching, education deserving of the name, and strict separation of Church and State, a very different state of affairs promises to arise, embracing education of higher grade and religion of a more moral tone than those that have hitherto prevailed.

PUBLIC WORKS.

The Philippine Islands are notable for having almost no public works of any description. Roads are practically unknown. In the Spanish endeavor to subdue the inhabitants, the primary value of highways seems to have been ignored still more here than in Cuba; and those who would make their way inland have usually only the native buffalo tracks to follow or must struggle with primitive nature. To find a road passing inland on which a carriage can travel is a rare discovery. The few roads on which some care has been bestowed average about twenty-five feet in width, some of them being ditched and graded, but very little stone being used upon them. Even the roads leading from Manila are unpaved highways, which become impassable to vehicles in the rainy season. In fact, the streets of Manila itself are little better, being wretchedly paved, if paved at all, and becoming mud sloughs in the rains. In the wet season transportation depends largely on buffaloes drawing rude sledges, a sort of sleighing upon mud.

Spain's hold on the islands has been gained without the use of roads, and the Spaniard confines himself mainly to the coast regions. Other towns besides Manila have what are called by courtesy carriage roads; but these are not only impassable in the wet season, but are apt to be so in the dry, from an unmended washout or a ruined bridge. The roads in general are mere paths on which even horseback travel is next to impossible during the rains, they being a succession of pools and sloughs; while on many of them a horse is at any time useless, unbridged streams being encountered too deep for fording and at times infested by man-eating crocodiles. The water-buffalo can go where a horse cannot; but the peculiarities of this brute, and in particular its love of mud, render it an undesirable riding animal. In short, in Philippine travel, one finds it best to go by water where rivers are convenient; by carriage or on horseback where there is an apology for a road; elsewhere on buffalo-back or on foot. When a traveller has baggage, he is often obliged to depend on coolies for its transportation.

Railroad enterprise in the Philippines has hitherto been confined to the road extending from Manila to Dagupan, 123 miles distant. This is a narrow-gauge road,—the width of the road-bed being three feet six inches, and the engines and cars proportionately small. The road runs northward, its terminus, Dagupan, being on the Gulf of Langayen. It traverses a fertile region,—the first third of the route being a rice-growing district, the second a sugar-cane country, while the final third is more tropical in character, yielding some coffee and minor products, while the cocoa-nut palm is very abundant.

It is not surprising that with this comparatively short railway and with the almost utter lack of practicable roads, the country has not been developed. Overland transportation is almost non-existent, and there is abundant opportunity for the labors of the American engineer if it is proposed to open up the mineral resources of the country or advance its commercial interests. As it stands at present, it presents almost a virgin field to the engineer.

In the direction of water traffic some more enterprise has been shown, and fairly regular steamship communication exists between the more important islands, lines of mail and merchant steamers running with a moderate degree of frequency. Freight charges, however, are very high. To reach islands or ports at which vessels do not call, only the native sailboat is available. This answers the purpose fairly well in good weather, but is not a comfortable or safe mode of travel in case of storm or a high sea.

The telegraph has attained some development, there being submarine communication with Hong-Kong. The cable lands at Cape Bolinao, and is thence carried overland to Manila. The principal towns in Luzon have telegraphic connection with the capital, and there is a cable line, laid by a British company, extending from Manila to Capiz, in Panay, whence a land line runs to Iloilo. It is thence extended to Bakalot, in Negros, round the coast to Escalante, and by sea to Cebu Island, ending at the city of Cebu. The total length of cable and telegraph lines is from 1500 to 2000 miles.

POPULATION.

The population of the Philippines is not known, nothing more than an estimate being practicable. It is usually roughly estimated at 8,000,000, of whom about 5,000,000 are accredited to Luzon, much the most populous island. The population is a composite one, two-thirds of the inhabitants being of Malayan origin, or Indian, as they are often called. In addition there is a large and important half-breed population, born of native mothers and European or Chinese fathers. These *mestizos*, as they are designated, form a potent part of the population. They are especially numerous in Manila, whose estimated 300,000 inhabitants includes 50,000 Chinese and 4000 Spanish half-breeds. Its remaining population is estimated to embrace 200,000 natives, 40,000 Chinese, 5000 Spanish and creoles of Spanish descent, and about 300 whites of other than Spanish origin. The whole European population of the Philippines is estimated at 25,000, principally Spanish, the remainder being mainly English and German merchants.

The large number of Chinese mestizos is due to the habits of Chinese immigrants. Despite the dislike of the natives for the Chinese and the several massacres which they have experienced at the hands of the Spaniards, they have continued to make their way into the islands, in which their industrious, frugal, and persevering habits, as compared with the indolence of the natives, have given them almost a monopoly of the retail trade. In Manila they are everywhere found, and occupy a variety of industrial positions, the merchants among them being supplemented by barbers, tanners, dyers, carpenters, shoemakers, tinsmiths, and other artisans. Their peaceful demeanor and obedience to the laws give their enemies no opportunity to interfere with them, while they rarely hesitate to profess Christianity if they find it will be of any aid in business. Thus they have long been growing steadily in numbers, wealth, and importance.

Yet the Chinese are birds of passage, returning home to be succeeded by others. For some reason no Chinese women accompany them, the women of China showing a remarkable unwillingness to emigrate. Thus among 525 Chinamen in the fortress of Manila in 1855 there were only two women, and the 5055 Chinamen in Binondo included only eight females, all children. It is to this state of affairs that the large mestizo population is due. The dislike of the natives for the Chinese does not seem to be shared by their women, many of them becoming wives or handmaids of these foreigners. Marriage requires a preliminary subjection to the Church of Rome, and as most of the Chinese decline to give up their native faith, their relations with the native women are usually outside the pale of the Church. The Chinese mestizos in the archipelago number more than 200,000, being numerous enough to form separate and very influential communities.

The Chinese were at first restricted by law to agricultural labor. But the dislike felt for them by the rural population, and their invincible tendency to abandon any career for another which seems more profitable, led them to break through this restriction, and they in time gained too assured a position in the towns to be disturbed. Though ready to accept almost any avocation, the business of retail shopkeeping is their favorite pursuit. But within late years many of them have become wholesale dealers and merchants, exporting and importing largely on their own account, and having subordinate agents widely spread through the islands. The Chinaman is a born dealer, cunning, patient, and economical, and many of the Philippine Chinese have grown wealthy through their business talent and activity.

The mestizos seem to inherit the paternal type, their children for generations displaying the Chinese character. None of the natives are so industrious, economical, and, generally, so prosperous. They inherit the speculative spirit of their fathers or ancestors, have gained a large part of the retail trade, and many of them have acquired riches and landed property. They form the middle class of the people, being better educated and more moral and intellectual than the natives, handsomer and better dressed. Some of their women are beautiful. They preserve most of the habits of the natives, but surpass them in enterprise, prudence, perseverance, and devotion to trade and commerce. In short, they are far the most promising part of the native Philippine population.

THE CIVILIZED NATIVES.

The Filipinos, as they are designated by the Spaniards, who constitute the great bulk of the population, are said to comprise more than eighty distinct tribes, each with its special habits. These are scattered widely through the multitude of islands, and of many of them very little is known. The aborigines are believed to be the dwarfish *Negritos*, of whom few now remain, they having been driven into the wilds and largely annihilated by the invading Malays, who now compose the great bulk of the population. The latter, while forming numerous tribes, may be divided into two principal races,—the *Tagals*, occupying the north, and the *Visayas*, of the south. Of these, all those who inhabit the towns and villages profess Christianity, and have long been greatly under the influence of the clergy, who claim 6,000,000 nominal Christians.

Outside the towns, however, religious ordinances receive little attention, and the mountainous parts of the islands are inhabited by wild tribes of pagans. The Tagals form the principal inhabitants of Luzon, preferring its lowland regions, and generally building their pile-supported dwellings near water. They constitute the bulk of the population in the towns of this island, and are also found in Mindoro, Marinduque, and several of the smaller southern islands.

Physically the Tagal is well developed. He possesses a round head, high check-bones, flattish nose, low brow, thickish lips, large dark eyes, straight black hair, and olive complexion. His power of smell is remarkably acute. The natives of this race are devoted to agriculture, rice being their chief crop and means of living; though they are much given to fishing, and keep swine and cattle and great numbers of ducks and fowls. Cock-fighting is their leading passion; they are fond of theatrical entertainments, and have a strong taste and talent for music, being very successful in playing upon European instruments.

Though Roman Catholic in faith, their old superstitions still influence them. They had an alphabet of their own before the Spanish conquest, and still possess some of their ancient songs and melodies. Their language, the Tagalog, has made its way largely through the islands since the Spanish conquest.

The Visayas inhabit all the islands south of Luzon and north of Mindanao, including part of the latter island and of Palawan. The Calamianes, inhabiting the islands of that name, and the Caragus, a coast tribe of eastern Mindanao, are usually classed with them. The Visayas were more civilized than the Tagals at the time of settlement by the Spanish, and lent their aid to the latter in the conquest of the Tagals. They resemble physically the Tagals and the other Malayan races of Luzon, the distinction being in their language. This seems a dialect of the Tagalog, but is rather harsher, and is less copious, refined, and subject to grammatical rules, while it has more Malay words than the Luzon dialects. The languages are sufficiently similar to enable members of the two races to converse with some difficulty. The Visayans furnish a hardy, seafaring race, though with the tendency to indolence shown by the Filipinos in general.

Luzon possesses in its northwest section another civilized tribe, the Ilocanes, resembling the Tagals in appearance and in orderly habits, but differing in dialect. In truth, this is the main difference between the Malay peoples spread so widely through Malacca, Sumatra, and the far-extended islands of the Pacific, from Hawaii to Madagascar; though many of the island Malays have varied physically through intermarriage with aboriginal populations.

The natives so far mentioned, originally pagan, now Christian, are known by the Spaniards under the general title of *Indios*, or Indians, in distinction to the *Moros*, or Mohammedan natives of the most southern islands, an intractable race who have resisted all the efforts of the missionaries at conversion, and who conform more to the general idea of Malays in their fierce, warlike disposition, their seafaring habits, and their tendency to piracy.

The Moros are of late date in the Philippines, which they entered about the same time as the Spaniards, making their way thither from Borneo, and bringing with them the Moslem faith and that unyielding adherence to the doctrines of Islamism which seems everywhere characteristic of Mohammedans. Their route was by way of the Sulu Islands, adjacent to Borneo and only recently attached to the Philippine archipelago.

Landing first in Basilan, they quickly occupied Sulu, Tawi-Tawi, and the smaller islands of the group, and in time made their way by force of arms into Mindanao, spread throughout its coast region, and occupied Balabac and the south of Palawan. In the latter island they first came into collision with the Spaniards, who checked their advance, though they have never succeeded in expelling them from the island.

The Moros are born pirates. The sea, rather than the land, is their native habitation. They haunt the coasts and dwell as nearly as possible in their native element by building their villages over the water, each house erected on piles sunk in the shoal sea. In them we seem to possess a surviving remnant of the Malay sea-rovers who in times past manned their war-praus and went forth to conquer the multitudinous islands of the South Sea. In the Sulus they retain this habit. Moved by a fanatical hatred of the Christians, and particularly of the Spaniards, whom they early learned to hate, they have during several centuries made life anything but safe and agreeable on the northern islands by their incessant raids.

These piratical expeditions became annual events. At the setting in of the southwest monsoon the Moros would launch their boats, seek the central and northern islands, harry the Spanish and native coast towns, and hasten back before the changing of the winds. In these raids they were usually successful and always cruel. Captives were taken by thousands, the men being butchered after having been forced to harvest their own crops for the benefit of the captors, the women and children carried away, the former for the seraglio, the latter to be brought up as slaves.

This state of affairs continued for over two centuries, the Moros not alone attacking the natives, but killing many Spaniards and holding others for ransom. They particularly hated the priests and friars, whom they took every opportunity to capture. All this was not viewed with equanimity by the Spaniards. Many costly expeditions were sent against the Moros, with temporary but no permanent success. At times landings were made and forts built on Sulu itself, the very centre of the Moro power. But they did not remain, the garrisons being in every case slain or driven out by the indomitable Moslems.

Such was the state of affairs until within the past quarter-century, in which the development of light-draught steam gunboats and rapid-fire guns gave the Spaniards at length the advantage over their foes, who continued to use their effective but antiquated steel weapons, the *kris, barong,* and *campilan,* various forms of sword and dagger. Guns they rarely obtained, and used poorly when they did.

Eventually an efficient patrol of gunboats was established, the sea-built villages were shelled and the people driven inland, and no prau was permitted to put to sea without a Spanish permit and a show of the Spanish flag. If encountered without these, it was at once sunk. The town of Sulu was destroyed in 1876 and a Spanish military post established in its place. Other points were taken and fortified, the raids of the Moros were effectually checked, and a sort of armed truce followed, broken at intervals by both sides. Such was the ultimate state of affairs, the Moros practically preserving their independence, but forced to desist from their warlike habits.

These people are highly skilful as boatmen and sailors. Their praus, neatly carved from logs, are of knife-like sharpness in bow and keel, and can be driven through the water with great swiftness. Bamboo outriggers prevent them from sinking even when filled with water. The men are energetic and industrious, —in such work as they are willing to perform,—being free from the listless indolence of the northern natives. They are of medium height and often of superb physical development, always going armed unless prevented from doing so. Their women are exceedingly fond of bright colors, green and scarlet in particular; while their children, though possessing clothes, make little use of them, living more in the water than on land.

What difficulties the Americans are likely to have with these people, in the event of occupation of the islands, remains to be seen. Hatred of Christians is their strongest passion, and they believe that whoever takes the life of a Christian increases his chance of future happiness. If slain while slaughtering the foes of his faith he goes straight to the seventh heaven of bliss. This unpleasant belief at times leads to a bloody result. Some Moro, weary of life, and hopeful of speedy glory in the next world, prepares himself carefully and takes a solemn oath to die killing Christians. Then, hiding about him one of the deadly Moro weapons, he seeks the nearest town. If admitted, he draws the concealed weapon and runs amuck through the street, killing every living being in his path until he is himself slain. At times one of these mad fanatics takes an incredible number of lives before he is dispatched. The news of his death is joyfully received by his relatives.

So fierce and intractable a people as this is not likely to prove easy to deal with. Yet other methods than those of the Spaniards may have better effects. Hostility, treachery, slaughter, are not the best agents with which to win peace and confidence. "If you meet armed Moros outside of the town order them to lay down their weapons and retire; if they do not instantly obey, shoot them." Such was the advice of General Arolas to Worcester, the American naturalist. Worcester, on the contrary, treated them with kindness and confidence, and obtained their respect and trust in return. Probably a general adoption of this treatment would convert the Moros from enemies to friends. What is specially needed is to let their religion alone. To interfere with that in any way would be a sure means of provoking hostility.

THE WILD TRIBES.

The uncivilized inhabitants of the Philippine Islands belong to two widely distinct races, the Negrito aborigines and the Malay invading race. The Negritos are savages of the lowest grade, once wide-spread throughout the islands, but gradually driven back and exterminated by the invaders till few of them remain, and these confined to the most inaccessible regions of Luzon and some other islands. A considerable number of them remain in Mindanao and some in Negros, which derives its name from them. The total number remaining is perhaps not over 25,000.

They are of dwarfish stature, the men averaging four feet eight inches high, and are thin and spindle-legged, with flattish nose, full lips, thick frizzled black hair, and very dark complexion. They wear little clothing, tattoo themselves, have no fixed abodes, and wander through the forests, living on game, honey, wild fruits, roots of the arum, and such other food as they can obtain. They sell wax to the Christians in exchange for tobacco and betel. Their weapons are the bow and arrow, the latter usually poisoned. One of their characteristics is an extraordinary prehensile power in the toes, very useful in climbing. They can descend head downward the rigging of a ship, hanging on by the toes, and can pick up minute objects with their feet. This lowest of the races seems to have been at one time very wide-spread, being found now in widely separated regions, while similar dwarf tribes are numerous in the forests of Africa.

The Negritos are also known as Aetas (in Mindanao they are called Mamanuas), and have mingled to some extent with the Malays and Chinese, there being a number of half-breed tribes. Thus the Itanegs have a mixture of Chinese blood, the Ifugaos of Japanese, the resulting half-breeds being superior in character to the Negritos. The former, according to the friars, only need conversion to make good Indios. The Tagbanuas of Palawan are thought to be a half-breed of Malay and Negrito, being dark-skinned and with curly hair. Though wild wanderers, with little pretence to clothing, they are much superior to the Negritos,—friendly in disposition, less suspicious than savage tribes generally, and possessing that talent for music which is a Malay characteristic. They even possess an alphabet, a simple syllabic one.

Their huts are mere leaf shelters, in which it is impossible to stand erect, and in which fire smudges are kept going to drive away insect pests. Their utensils are a few earthen pots, and much of their time is spent in the forest in search of honey and wax and other useful substances. Polygamy does not exist among them, but child marriage is very common, children being betrothed sometimes before birth,—the proviso being made that they should prove of the desired sex. Their legal system is a simple one. The person accused of a serious crime and his accuser are led to a deep pond, under whose water they dive simultaneously. The one who stays under the longest is believed to have told the truth.

Such are some of the characteristics of one of the half-breed tribes with Negrito blood. In addition to the savages named are a large number of Malay tribes, which differ greatly in character and customs,—wanderers in the forests and on the mountains, some of them fierce and suspicious in disposition, others kindly and trusting. Those who show dangerous hostility to the whites have doubtless good reason for their feeling, and different treatment might in many cases change their attitude, though some tribes in the highlands of Luzon and Mindanao seem natively fierce and warlike. These warlike hill-tribes might perhaps be best disposed of by converting them into soldiers, as England has done with similar tribes in India.

The wild tribes are numerous and possess a considerable variety of languages, the dialects of the separate tribes being usually unintelligible to each other, while sometimes a dialect seems confined to a single family group. The title of Igorrotes or Igolotes, once the name of a single tribe, was gradually extended to include the several head-hunting tribes of Luzon, and later to embrace nearly all the wild tribes of the island. There are said to be several tribes of head-hunters, comprising the Altasanes, the Apayaos, and the Gaddanes. It is stated that a Gaddanes youth cannot hope to win a bride unless he can show at least one human head in proof of his valor.

Of the tribes of Mindanao, seventeen are included among the pagan hill tribes, and most of the smaller islands have interior wild tribes. As we have said, they are by no means all warlike. Worcester, who penetrated to the interior of a considerable number of the islands and came into contact with many of the tribes, had no trouble with any met by him, even those of reputed fierceness. For example, in penetrating Mindoro, he was warned against a tribe of head-hunting cannibals. On meeting this tribe, the Mangyans, he found them the most harmless of people, simple, confiding, and helpful in every way possible to them. They lived the most primitive life, wandering through the forests during the dry season and sleeping wherever night overtook them, under a hasty shelter of palm leaves, and in the wet season building a platform on poles, roofed with leaves of the rattan or palm. The attire of the women was a curious mass of cord, made of strips of rattan, coiled from waist to hips and supporting a clout of bark. The men wore only the clout.

In addition to the wild tribes, there are in the interior of some of the islands lurking bands of *tulisanes*, or bandits, made up of escaped convicts and other outlaws, who form perilous neighbors to the peacefully inclined. Cowardly in grain, their attacks are mainly on the defenceless, while in their difficult retreats they easily keep beyond the reach of the lax authorities.

EDUCATION.

The Spanish have established what bear the name of schools for the education of the Philippine natives, but the name rarely represents the thing, education there being but a travesty of what it is in enlightened lands. Some $40,000 were annually appropriated by the Spanish rulers for the support of the provincial schools, but it cannot safely be said that all this money reached the schools. The school-master has been none too well equipped for his work. Manila possessed a normal school or training seminary for teachers, but its tests were anything but rigid, and its graduates set out upon their work with very little education of their own.

The rate of pay was miserably small, and the drawing of salaries tied up with so much red tape that it cost a fair share of the monthly stipend to get the remainder. This was not all. The teachers were not at liberty to impart what little learning they possessed. The village friars played the *rôle* of school inspectors, and took good care that nothing should be taught of which they did not approve. In particular they laid an embargo on Spanish. It was long ago enacted that the natives should be taught the doctrines of Christianity in the Spanish language, and many decrees have been passed for the efforcement of this law. Even as late as 1887 the governor-general pointedly notified the archbishop that this requirement was not observed. But nothing has been done in the matter. It did not suit the friars that the natives should speak Spanish, and they took excellent care that it should not be taught. Some of the better educated natives might obtain a smattering of this language, with some knowledge of writing, reading, and arithmetic; but education has usually been restricted to the teaching of some of the prayers of the Church and a smattering of the catechism.

When one compares this with the great development of education in Hawaii, through the labors of the Protestant missionaries, it becomes evident that the development of the Philippine intellect has been shamefully neglected. The new owners or guardians of the island will have a largely unworked field, and an opportunity of greatly developing the intelligence of the natives, who are quick to learn and anxious for the opportunity.

The only educational institutions on the islands of

any practical value are those at Manila. Among these is the University of St. Thomas, a Dominican institution, with over a thousand students, and professorships of theology, metaphysics, grammar, canon and civil law, but none of science, modern languages, or the other advanced branches insisted on in recent colleges elsewhere.

Another Dominican institution, the College of San Juan de Letran, has an excellent equipment and a fine museum of history and the arts. It teaches only native youth. Medicine and pharmacy are taught in the College of San José. The Royal Polytechnic Society has for its object the promotion of the arts and sciences. There is a nautical school, an academy of painting, several colleges for women, etc.

Much the best school in the archipelago is the Jesuit institution called the Ateneo Municipal, situated in Manila, and including many able scholars among its faculty. Its scope is one of considerable breadth, including courses of study in many branches, such as mathematics, commerce, modern and ancient languages, history, science, philosophy, painting, and various others. Another important Jesuit institution is the observatory at Manila, which is very well equipped with apparatus, particularly that adapted to meteorological observation and for recording the movements of earthquakes. Skilled and able men are at the head of this institution, whose observations are of great value to merchants in giving timely notice of the approach of typhoons. If necessary, warning of the course of a threatening storm is cabled to Hong-Kong.

V. CENTRES OF POPULATION.

MANILA.

The central fact in a description of the Philippine Islands is the city of Manila, the capital of the archipelago, the centre of Spanish power for the past three centuries, and one of the great commercial cities of the eastern world. This metropolis, situated in north latitude 14° 36′, east longitude 120° 57′, is in effect two cities,—old Manila, the walled and fortified centre of governmental rule, on the left bank of the Pasig River, and Binondo, or New Manila, the business centre, in which the merchants reside and the warehouses are built, on the right of the stream.

The river itself, the dividing line between the old city and the new, forms one of the most active and interesting portions of the whole situation, with its hosts of busy craft of varied size and shape, including numbers of great, square-ended cargo-lighters, forced up the stream by pole-wielding Malays, their sturdy limbs and bodies well revealed by their very scant costume. Steamers, schooners, and other craft from the interior line the banks. Among them are large dug-out canoes, fashioned from tree-trunks, for light freight, and smaller ones with outriggers and shades for carrying passengers. In addition are the ferryboats, which move up and down stream, the whole forming a very animated scene. These boats and the up-river craft are manned by Tagals, the natives who form the great bulk of the city population.

The Pasig, which forms the dividing line of the official and the commercial cities, and the link between the lake named Laguna de Bay and the bay of Manila, is fourteen miles long, averages about 350 feet in width, and varies from three to twenty-five feet in depth. It is crossed by three bridges, one of them a suspension bridge. The Puente Grande, which unites Manila and Binondo, is a time-honored structure, originally built of wood upon masonry piers, and with seven arches of different sizes. Two of these were destroyed by the earthquake of 1824, but they have been restored. The bridge is 457 feet long and 24 wide, and affords fine views of the widely different cities on the opposite sides of the stream.

Manila, the old city, or the citadel, as it is at times called, is a place straitened in dimensions, and surrounded by massive walls, forty feet thick, and about two and a quarter miles in circuit, possessing eight gates, each with its portcullis and a drawbridge crossing the moat without. The latter is supposed to be filled with water from the river, but the sluices have been out of order for years, and the moat is half full of filthy mud, which the authorities dread to disturb lest they should set afloat the seeds of pestilence. Until 1852 the drawbridge between the old city and the new was drawn up every night and the gate closed, as if feudal conditions still prevailed.

The walls, built about 1590, and several times since cracked by earthquakes, are still serviceable against native attacks, but would not stand long against modern armies with heavy guns. Their tops are mounted with cannon two centuries old. The city itself consists of seventeen streets, of fair width and crossing at right angles. These are kept reasonably clean. As little business is done here, few people are seen in the streets, whose monotony and dull respectability form a striking contrast to the bustling activity of the city beyond the stream.

The public edifices, including the city hall, the cathedral, etc., are in a large square, whose centre contains a statue of Charles V., surrounded by a garden of flowers. The cathedral, built early in the history of the city, has been ruined several times since by earthquakes, the last time in 1880. It has been replaced by a new cathedral, built of brick and stone, and the most imposing structure in the colony. It is celebrated for the splendor of its altars and interior decorations. Most of the great religious processions for which Manila is noted begin and end at its doors. Another of the imposing buildings of the city is the archbishop's palace, an extensive though not specially handsome edifice. The oldest church in the city is that of San Francisco. It is under the Franciscans, who have lavished money upon it, its interior being magnificent in decorations.

The palace of the late governor-general is in Malacanan, a suburb of the new city. It is massive in structure and wide in area, but low in elevation. Standing on the bank of the Pasig, it is surrounded by a garden of flowers and fruits famous for its luxuriance. Here grow in rich profusion the most exquisite blooms of the tropical East and the most luscious and attractive fruits. The palace commands a fine view of the city and river, it having a large balcony, from which the governor-general was accustomed to view the yearly boat-race that took place on the king's birthday. In its interior are many evidences of pomp and splendor, including a spacious ball-room where receptions were held, and to which, several times a year, the *élite* of the city were invited.

Other edifices include the mint, museum, university, academy of arts, hospitals, arsenal, prison, barracks, convents, and monasteries. Outside the walls, extending along the bay shore, is the beautiful Luneta, the favorite resort of the aristocracy of Manila. It constitutes a drive and promenade, the carriage road passing each side of and around a slightly raised oval space, with chairs and benches for the people and two stands for bands. Deserted by day, it is thronged in the evening, carriages passing in a constant stream, while equestrians and pedestrians add to the throng.

The Luneta of late years has gained a ghastly repute, a new and popular entertainment being provided there which one would think even Spaniards could not enjoy, though they are said to have been keenly entertained. This was the execution of the prisoners taken during the insurrection. The helpless captives were lined up in numbers on the sea-wall and shot down by soldiers of their own race, at the command of Spanish officers, and seemingly to the high enjoyment of crowds of Spanish spectators, who flocked to the scene as to a spectacle.

While the population of the official city is small, that of Binondo (the new city) and of the suburbs is large, being estimated at from 250,000 to 300,000. The new city is as active as the old one is quiet and dull. Here are the large business houses, the retail and wholesale stores, the commercial warehouses, the bustle of carts and carriages, the constant coming and going which make the life of a centre of commercial activity. There is fairly good wharfage along the Pasig, and numbers of warehouses adjoining the stream, that intended for tobacco being specially extensive. The edifice in which cigars were made for the state during the existence of the monopoly is vast in dimensions, 9000 women having been steadily employed within its walls.

Stone, brick, and tiles form the ordinary building materials of Binondo, though about one-third of the dwellings are the native wooden houses with thatch of nipa palm. The better class of houses follow the Spanish fashion, as seen in Cuba and Porto Rico, having a central patio or court, surrounded by shops, warehouses, stables, and domestic offices, the family occupying the floor above. This is built of wood, the lower story being of brick or stone. A gallery in the interior looking into the patio is a general feature, and a corridor near the street communicates with the apartments. Houses more than two stories high are rare. All the rooms have sliding windows, the small panes being made of flat, half-transparent oyster-shells, through which the full light of the sun cannot make its way.

The apartments are large and are furnished much as in European houses, with mirrors, tables, chairs, sofas, paper on the walls and lamps hung from the ceilings, porcelain flower-vases, etc. Carpets are rare, fire-places lacking; the kitchen, to avoid heat, is separate from the dwelling. The heavy tiles formerly used in roofing have been replaced by galvanized iron, as lighter and less dangerous in the event of an earthquake, a possibility always to be considered. Even in the night attire the earthquake is kept in view, people seeking their couches with sufficient clothing to enable them to make a presentable appearance in the street, if aroused and forced to flee by a midnight shake.

The Philippine bed is an old-fashioned, imposing structure, with its four high posts and substantial frame. The modern springs are replaced by a network of cane, woven as in chair-seats. Lace curtains and mosquito netting depend from above. The bed is composed of a thin sleeping-mat, with a sheet or two, pillow, and bolster, the latter being used to support the body, not the head, and to relieve the hardness of the mat.

The native houses differ essentially from those of the Europeans. The old Malay idea of living over water, still practised by the Moros, appears in dwellings erected on hard ground, the house resting on a number of strong piles set in the ground, which lift it from five to ten feet into the air. The floor is made of strips of bamboo, their rounded sides turned upward and wide cracks between them. Bamboo also forms the framework, tied together with rattan, not a nail or a peg being used. The sides are made of split bamboo, beaten flat in its green state, or more commonly of the stout leaves of the nipa palm, which are also employed for the roof. Swinging shades, which can be kept open during the day, answer for windows. To enter the door a ladder must be used. A single room often answers all the purposes of the household, those of cooking, eating, and sleeping, a heap of earth in one corner serving to build the fire on for cooking, while the smoke is left to escape as it may. In the better dwellings there is a kitchen partitioned off and two or more other rooms.

The streets of Manila are sadly lacking in the requisites of a modern city, being either unpaved or with a weak excuse for paving. Drainage is as sadly needed as paving, there being no satisfactory system of sewerage. The low-lying city is traversed by canals radiating from the Pasig River, and into these the filth of the city, where not heaped about the houses, is thrown or is washed by the rains. In the suburb of Tondo the site is so low as to prevent a free flow of the surface water, which gathers in stagnant pools under the huts during the rains. With the dry season comes the natural result, ill-smelling black mud and fever. There is, however, a good supply of wholesome water for drinking and cooking, the city being provided with a system of water-works. The water is brought from Santolin, on the Pasig River. There are fountains at convenient places for the use of the poor.

There are two lines of street-cars, one following the Escolto, the principal business street, and extending out through the residence part of the city; the other following Rosario Street, reaching the suburbs in one direction, and crossing the Puenta de España to old Manila in the other. Each car is drawn by one horse, and its approach is announced by the sound of a small tin horn blown by the driver. The electric light has been introduced into the city to some extent, and the telephone is also in use.

Along the Escolto are numerous Spanish stores, and some kept by French, German, and other merchants. They are well supplied with European goods.

though the very high import duties under the Spanish administration kept these at a costly figure. Some of the many Chinese shops are also on the Escolto, but the most of them are on neighboring streets, especially the Rosario, which they line from end to end. They offer for sale a surprising variety of goods, and the streets occupied by them are usually thronged with the common people of the city, though white men other than priests and friars are rarely seen among them.

Here one meets hosts of the natives, the poor and the well-to-do, mestizos of Spanish and Chinese birth, sailors, coolies, and all classes, of varied costume and shades of complexion. The Chinese are abundantly represented, each shop having several of them, while outside the doors may be seen their native wives and half-breed children, the boys frequently in Chinese dress, the girls all wearing the native costume. Native merchants usually do their vending in the streets, walking about or resting in the doorways, with fruit, flowers, and other articles for sale. The women are notably erect in attitude, due to the custom of carrying articles balanced on their heads. The hotels of the city have hitherto been nothing to boast of, but they are improving, and are sure to attain a marked development under American control.

Old Manila and Binondo do not constitute the whole city. There are numerous suburbs or wards, fifteen or twenty in number, extending in all directions around the city. Tondo lies on the bay, adjoining Binondo. It is principally inhabited by natives, over 30,000 in number, and, owing to its combustible material, is frequently the scene of destructive fires.

CENTRES OF POPULATION.

From this quarter comes most of the milk used in the capital, and it has some small manufactures.

Two miles up the north bank of the river lies San Miguel, a residence quarter for Europeans, especially Spaniards. Santa Cruz has over 11,000 inhabitants, many of them merchants. Santa Ana is a favorite place of residence for merchants; Pasay is noted for its cultivation of the betel; and La Ermita and other villages are centres of production of the exquisite piña handkerchiefs, which command very high prices. Malate is the seat of many public offices, and the women here are employed in ornamenting slippers with gold and silver embroidery.

Of the suburbs of Manila, one of the most interesting is Cavité, on the bay shore several miles south of the walls of Old Manila, the seat of the arsenal and navy-yard and the port of refuge of large vessels in the event of stormy weather. It contains some handsome residences and fine shops, a theatre, several cafés, and a large cathedral of old date. A fire in 1754 destroyed most of the town, since which date stone and brick have replaced wood as building materials. Its history is of interest, it being deemed the key to the capital, and as such taken by the British in 1763. It was the seat of the most formidable rebellion of the natives before 1896, that of 1872, an outbreak due to hatred of the friars, which ended disastrously for the insurgents. But its most famous event was the attack of Commodore Dewey's squadron upon the Spanish fleet, drawn up across the mouth of Bakor Bay, on whose shores Cavité is situated. Nothing needs to be said concerning this striking engagement. It has become an essential fact in American history.

To return to the habits of the Manila people, it may be said of the foreign residents that the use of the small but sturdy Philippine horse is almost universal. As a rule, only the natives walk; everybody else rides: carriages throng the principal streets, or horsemen dash along, the little but spirited animals being capable of carrying a heavy rider and of racing at an excellent rate of speed. Thousands of carriages traverse the Escolto daily, giving this street a highly animated appearance.

Only on three days in the year are the ponies given full rest from their labors. These are Holy Wednesday and Thursday and Good Friday, on which days the use of carriages is permitted only to the archbishop and the doctors, the church-bells cease their endless jangling, and silence and solemnity prevail. The people are held in the leash, impatiently awaiting the end of the fast. On the first stroke of the bell announcing their release there is a rush to and fro, horses and vehicles suddenly appear in multitudes, and the streets resound again with the clamorous cries of the native venders.

Among the excitements of Manila under Spanish rule were the religious processions, of which each year furnished occasion for several, and which were celebrated with the utmost pomp and display and the greatest freedom of merry-making, dances, songs, music, fireworks, cock-fighting displays, and other entertainments giving liveliness to the occasion. The general character of these processions we have already described.

Among the features of the city may be mentioned the numerous wayside native restaurants, most of them primitive in character, with little more than rice and fruits for sale, which are offered for a mere pittance. For two cents a native can satisfy his appetite, and to these establishments the multitude of cigar-makers and other workmen hasten at noon for a rapid lunch. They are poor, indeed, who need go hungry in Manila.

Other interesting features of the streets are the water-girls, with great rude jars balanced upon their heads, and the pedlers of milk or cocoa. A native funeral is a peculiar spectacle, the hearse a rude wagon drawn by white horses, preceded by a brass band playing a brisk marching air and followed by a long line of carriages. The heat of the climate renders it necessary to have the funeral, as a general rule, on the day of the death. The bodies of the well-to-do are deposited in a vault in the church as long as the privilege is paid for, but the remains are finally dumped unceremoniously into a huge pit in the rear, into which the bodies of the poor go at once. All, finally, come to the pit.

There are several theatres in Manila, but they are very poor concerns. The opera is the most popular form of amusement, and is thronged when foreign celebrities visit the city. The Filipinos are especially fond of theatrical entertainments, and rarely fail to be present in force when any play of interest is offered. Everybody smokes at the theatre, from the fashionable ladies and gentlemen in the boxes to the gallery gods above. Pretty mestizo girls between the acts offer fragrant flowers for sale. A theatre night, when a good company has been secured, is one of the gayest and most popular events known to Manila.

One thing remains to be said of this island capital: it is, in its way, the Venice of the East. The city lies at a considerably lower level than the lake which feeds the stream, and is traversed by numerous creeks and canals, which in the wet season are flooded with water from the overfull Pasig. At that period the water overflows the low-lying suburbs, washing beneath the pile-borne native houses, and boats ply in multitudes through the streets, which are for the time being converted into water-channels.

ILOILO.

Iloilo, the chief city on the island of Panay, has recently risen in commercial importance to the position of the second city of the archipelago, having passed Cebu, which formerly occupied that position. The commerce of the central Philippines is rapidly centring in this place. It is by no means an attractive city, the principal part of it standing on low, yielding ground, formerly marsh land, and the whole town being overflowed during the spring tides. It partly fronts the sea, partly lies on the left bank of a creek. Its population is not large, the narrow tongue of land on which it is chiefly built forbidding extension. Several towns in its close vicinity, Jaro, Molo, and Oton, surpass it in population, having from 15,000 to over 30,000 each.

The streets are unpaved, and are either unpleasantly dusty or muddy, as the dry or wet season prevails. There are a few good shops and some attractive residences, but the public square, once handsomely laid out, has been sadly neglected; there are no places of amusement, and the whole town sadly needs a more progressive element. The traders are mostly Chinese mestizos, many of whom are wealthy.

The commercial interests are conducted mainly by English and German firms, and consist principally in the exportation of sugar, in which Iloilo exceeds Manila. The sapan-wood of Negros and Panay is also shipped from this port. The surrounding country is very fertile and is widely cultivated, its products including tobacco and rice in addition to sugar. But the poor facilities for transportation from the interior interfere seriously with the development of the port.

Iloilo enjoys a more agreeable climate than Manila. This is due to the neighboring island of Guimaras, which is much higher than the coast region of Panay, so that it forms a sort of funnel, through which draws a constant breeze, adding very acceptably to the coolness and healthfulness of the town.

CEBU.

Cebu, the third centre of Philippine commerce, is on the east coast of the island of Cebu or Zebu, as variously spelled. It is a clean, well-built town, with the unusual distinction in the Philippines of having good carriage roads leading from it. How far they continue good is another matter. It has a population of something over 10,000, and is the seat of numerous churches, it being the see of a bishop. In addition to the cathedral, there are several churches of some interest, that of Santo Niño de Cebu being notable as built in honor of the most ancient and famous of the Philippine religious images. The Santo Niño dates from 1565, the year of origin of the city, it being found on the island shore by a soldier, and decided to be an image of the Christ Child fallen from heaven. It is, in consequence, very highly venerated; a festival in its honor being held on January 20, when the image is exhibited, and pilgrims gather from all quarters to see it. It is of ebony, about fifteen inches high, and is half covered with silver trinkets.

Cebu was the capital of the Philippines from 1565 to 1571, and up to 1759 had a municipal government. This was then abolished, as the place possessed but one Spaniard capable of acting as a city councillor, while the mayor had been turned out of office for the not unusual crime of cruelty. The government was restored in 1890. As a commercial centre Cebu is the leading place for the exportation of hemp, and also ships much sugar, most of which comes from the plantations of Leyte, Camaguin, and Mindanao. The character of the harbor we have already described.

OTHER TOWNS.

The remaining towns call for no extended description. There are several hundred in all, including villages, but only a few of them are of any importance. Zamboango, the leading town of Mindanao, on its southwest extremity, is one of the oldest Spanish settlements, having originally been taken and fortified as a convenient base of operations against the Moro pirates of Sulu. The old stone fort, built as a place of shelter for the inhabitants if attacked, still stands. The town is spacious and is kept in a respectable state of cleanliness. Its pier extends out to water of some depth, but not sufficient for large vessels, which have to lie well off shore. Many of the inhabitants appear to be the descendants of slaves escaped from the Moros.

Sulu, once the capital of the Moros, and the central seat of their piratical raids, has of recent years been held by a Spanish garrison, whom the truculent inhabitants of the island have not left in peace. Under the famous General Arolas this place was made a spectacle of "how to do it" for the Philippine Spaniards. He found it a pest-hole and converted it into a place of unusual healthfulness. He built a splendid market, constructed water-works, erected a hospital, and established a free-school system. The fortifications were strengthened by the Moros themselves, they being made prisoners and compelled to work on the ramparts. Since the return of this energetic governor to Spain, the Moros, long cowed by his severity, have regained much of their old combativeness and made some virulent attacks upon the Spaniards.

Capiz, on the north coast of Panay, is a town of some 25,000 inhabitants, seated in the midst of a very productive district, its inhabitants being fairly well to do. They include about 100 Spaniards and a large number of Spanish mestizos, who are wealthy and influential. Large quantities of alcohol, of high grade of purity, are made in its vicinity from the sap of the nipa palm.

Dumaguete, on Negros Island, is a town of about 8000 inhabitants, few of them white. The shops are kept by Chinese. It is in a fertile district, the people are prosperous, and the public buildings large and showy. Bacolod is the capital of this island, and contains, in addition to the church and government house, some handsome residences. It is a coast-town, but the water is shallow and steamers cannot approach within a half mile. Calapan is the capital of Mindoro, which is about all that need be said concerning it. It lies in a region of very heavy rainfall, and has no anchorage, the surf often running so heavily that steamers cannot even land the mails.

Luzon, the most thickly populated island, contains a number of towns in addition to those already mentioned. Majajay, not far distant from Manila, is a picturesque mountain town, with church and convent and many handsome residences. It is surrounded by magnificent scenery, its chief attraction being the waterfall of Botocan, 600 feet high and 60 feet wide. Not far distant, but 1000 feet higher, stands Lugbang, crossed by several canals and surrounded by extensive rice fields.

Lipa, the capital of Batangas province, is a centre of the coffee trade. Many wealthy planters live in the vicinity, and most of its houses are three stories high. Its church and convent are notable buildings. Taal, formerly near the volcano of that name, was destroyed by the earthquake of 1754, and is now built in a hill region, among sugar plantations and great forests. It has a considerable trade, by way of the Pasig River, with Manila, and its streets are lined with modern shops and spacious residences. With its suburbs it has a population of 50,000.

The principal towns of the north are Ilagan, the capital of the tobacco-raising province of Isabella, with between 10,000 and 15,000 inhabitants, and Aparri, at the mouth of the Cagayan River, with 20,000 population and considerable trade. It has some good streets and many handsome houses.

CENTRES OF POPULATION.

Other towns of some importance are Batangas, capital of Batangas province; Santa Cruz, capital of Laguna province; Silan, noted for its religious feasts and fairs; Carmona, Viñan, Tayabas, and Calamba. Near the last is the town of Los Baños, at which are hot springs, credited with value in rheumatic complaints. This place was once a popular resort, and might be made so again. A few miles distant, at an elevation of 1200 feet, is the boiling lake of Natungos, also possessed of excellent curative properties. In the province of Albay, near the volcano of Mayon, are sulphur springs which are celebrated for their curative properties. Here is an excellent location for a sanatorium, awaiting some enterprising American.

VI. THE PEOPLE OF THE PHILIPPINES.

CHARACTER OF THE NATIVES.

The Malay race, wherever found, possesses certain strongly marked characteristics, all of which appear in the character of the Filipinos. The native is a born stoic, a natural fatalist: his stoicism visible in his impassive demeanor and imperturbable bearing, his fatalism in his coolness when exposed to danger, and his daring in the face of overwhelming odds. Well led, he makes a good soldier, though he is averse to discipline. General Gordon speaks thus of the Philippine troops who formed part of his forces in the China war:

"They are a fine, sturdy body of fellows, faithful and long-suffering, bearing hardships without murmurs, plucky and never losing heart in defeat, and considerably superior to the Japanese."

As sailors they have no superior, the Filipinos displaying that instinctive love of the water and inclination for a sea-life which we have already seen in the Hawaiians, and which seem to belong to the Malay blood. For centuries past the wilder spirits of the race have made piracy their occupation, pursuing this lawless avocation with a reckless daring and a bloodthirsty cruelty that long made them the terror of the Eastern seas. These piratical incursions continued, in the case of the Moros, until within comparatively a few years.

But the cruelty of the pirates should not be charged against the race as a whole, any more than we should consider the cruelty of the West Indian buccaneers a general characteristic of Europeans. These pirates were the outlaws of their race, preying upon their own peaceful countrymen, and visiting upon the Spaniards an old debt of vengeance.

The natives are as thorough water-dogs as the native Hawaiians. They are excellent swimmers, and seem absolutely devoid of fear in the boiling surf, in which they disport themselves—men, women, and children—with the wild delight and fearlessness of the Hawaiian surf-riders. Many of them swim with ease for miles, and groups of naked men do not hesitate to plunge, dagger in hand, among a shoal of sharks, which dangerous animals they attack with a fierceness, alertness, and skill that always bring victory to the natives and death to the sharks. As for the boys, they are as alert and skilful as those of the harbor of Honolulu, diving thirty or forty feet for pennies flung into the waves, and rarely failing to bring them up.

Calm and impassive as is the native, he is not secretive, but is more apt to be loquacious. While innately polite, and respectful to superiors, he is curious and inquisitive, being possessed of an eager thirst for information. He has the faults of the half-civilized,—improvidence and shiftlessness, and the indolence that seems characteristic of all tropical peoples, and is an almost necessary result of the enervating climate. The most energetic Europeans involuntarily yield to it after a few years, and it seems inherent in those born to the situation.

The Filipino is a philosopher. He works when he

must, but takes every opportunity to rest. Nature does most of his work, and he has little occasion for active exercise, so that most of his time is his own. His needs are few and easily satisfied, and the fertile soil, warm sun, and moist atmosphere do for him what only hard work can do for the farmer of the colder zones. Laborers on the plantations, therefore, are not to be easily procured, or kept when obtained; a fact which acts as a serious detriment to plantation enterprises in the Philippines. Slaves are not to be had, and the native laborer cannot be trusted. He is unwilling to work without pay in advance, and after receiving his money is apt to refuse to work. The employer has no remedy but through the law, which, under the Spanish system, was so dilatory and expensive that the cure often proved worse than the disease. Yet the difficulty has been partly a result of the situation. Thousands of natives work in the factories of Manila, and hundreds of thousands in the districts where just and humane business methods prevail. The trouble in procuring laborers has doubtless been due as much to Spanish mismanagement as to Malay indolence and lack of good faith.

Yet the Filipino has a reason for his indolence whose force all must admit. One native is quoted by Worcester as having said to his employer, whose service he had decided to quit, "Señor, if you were back at your home in Andalusia, living in a house as fine as any in the province; if your food and clothing were not only as good as any of your neighbors could boast, but were all that you yourself desired; if you had money enough for all present and future wants—would you turn your back up to a sun as hot as this

THE PEOPLE OF THE PHILIPPINES. 419

and work?" Could there be better logic? If there is nothing worth working for, why work in such a climate?

The Filipino morally is a curious compound. While exceptionally kind and gentle in his home relations, he is, like partly civilized peoples in general, apt to be cruel to his foes. Passionate when roused, he can be wrought up by injustice and oppression to a wild frenzy, in which, reckless of life and craving only vengeance, he runs amuck through crowded streets, killing indiscriminately all he meets until slain himself. Fortunately, these frenzied outbursts of the bloodthirst are of rare occurrence. They are similar in character to the outbreaks of murderous religious fanaticism among the Moros, already described.

At home the Filipino is a model. Family affection is strong in his nature, and no people could be fonder of or kinder to their children, who, as a rule, are respectful and well-behaved. The noisy and disrespectful children of American and European cities are unknown in Philippine villages. The old people are venerated and tenderly cared for, while poor relatives may be seen in many households, as kindly welcomed as if members of the family. Indeed, the Filipino is natively hospitable. Guests are always welcomed, and the better class embrace every opportunity to entertain their neighbors or casual visitors.

The character of the people is thus succinctly summed up by a former British consul at Manila, his statement being quoted and endorsed by the American traveller, Dean C. Worcester:

" Rarely is an intertropical people a satisfactory one to eye or mind. But this cannot be said of the Philippine Malay, who, in bodily formation and mental characteristics alike, may fairly claim a place, not among the middle ones merely, but among the higher names inscribed upon the world's national scale. He is characterized by a concentrated, never-absent self-respect; an habitual self-restraint in word and deed, very rarely broken, except when extreme provocation induces the transitory but fatal frenzy known as 'amuck;' an inbred courtesy, equally diffused through all classes, high or low; by unfailing decorum, prudence, caution, quiet, cheerfulness, ready hospitality, and a correct though not inventive taste. His family is a pleasing sight—much subordination and little constraint; unison in gradation; liberty, not license; orderly children, respected parents; women subject but not oppressed; men ruling but not despotic; reverence with kindness, obedience in affection,—these form a lovable picture by no means rare in the villages of the eastern isles."

One hospitable custom is common in the interior. Little bamboo frames may be seen supported by a post or projecting from a window, on which, covered with plantain leaves, is placed a supply of food or fruits, of which any passing traveller is free to partake, paying something if able, but nothing if poor. The bounty is free alike to those able and those unable to pay.

As a rule, the natives are superstitious and very credulous, these qualities having been developed and encouraged in them by 300 years of priestly control. The educated native, however, is an apt convert to the conclusions of modern research, as is attested by numerous instances of men of talent and ability.

The Filipino is rarely humorous and seldom witty.

Though passionate when roused, he is slow to anger; but if unjustly punished, he will treasure up the wrong for years, until an opportunity for revenge is presented. Courageous by nature, he despises cowardice and pusillanimity, and in consequence cordially dislikes the meek Chinaman, who is ready to pocket any insult in his thirst for gain. On the contrary, he has great esteem for the European, in whom he recognizes qualities similar to his own, and whom he will follow into any danger. While easily awed by a show of force, he is best ruled by mild measures based upon justice. He lacks ambition, unless to make a fine display in a procession or other social event; and is sober, patient, and always clean, being as fond of bathing as the Hawaiians. Men and women bathe in the same place, partly clothed. Every village has its bath, where possible; and if water is lacking it will be carried from a considerable distance, through the desire to keep clean.

The native, indeed, seems half amphibious, passing much of his time in the water. He appears insensible alike to the burning sun and the drenching rain, and generally has good health, his medicines being herbs whose usefulness long experience has proved. It has been said of him that he is more of a quadruped than a biped, his large hands and pliant toes enabling him to climb trees easily, and perform other active functions not easy to Europeans.

In the words of Sir John Bowring: "He receives no favors, and cannot, therefore, be ungrateful; has little ambition, and therefore little disquiet; few wants, and hence is neither jealous nor envious; does not concern himself with the affairs of his neighbor, nor indeed does he pay much regard to his own. His master vice is idleness, which is his felicity. . . . .

"He uses no soap to wash, no razor to shave; the river is his bathing-place, and he pulls out the hairs in his face with the assistance of a sharp shell; he wants no clock to tell him of the flight of time, and no table, nor chairs, nor plates, nor cutlery, to assist him at his meals; a *hacha*, or large knife, and bag are generally hung at his waist; he thinks no music equal to the crowing of his cock, and holds a shoe to be as superfluous as a glove or a neck-collar."

One striking characteristic of the Filipino we may extract from the recent work of Ramon Lala, himself of native birth: "As a result of the stoicism of the native character, he never bewails a misfortune and has no fear of death. When anything happens, he merely says, 'It is fate,' and calmly goes about his business as if nothing had happened. Europeans often seem to notice in them what they deem a lack of sympathy for the misfortunes of others; but it is not this so much as resignation to the inevitable. This, it must be confessed, saves them many a bitter pang. The educated native, however, impregnated with the bitter philosophy of the civilized world, is by no means so imperturbable. While more keenly alive to the sufferings of others, he is also more sensitive to his own sorrows. After all, whether he is any happier for his wisdom is a question."

The Filipino enjoys litigation far too much for his own good, and is always ready to go to law. He has some degree of artistic taste, and there are several examples of painters of marked talent, while considerable literary ability has been shown by educated natives. It is in music, however, that he seems most likely to make his mark. Every village has its orchestra, and music is the highest delight of the natives, who will listen entranced for hours together to the playing of their bands.

To quote again from Lala: "All the people are born musicians; even little boys and girls of five or six years of age play the harp, the guitar, or the piano as if by instinct; while their elders show a proficiency that, when their opportunities are considered, is truly astonishing."

DWELLINGS, FOOD, AND DRESS.

We have already described the house of the native laborer of Manila. The dwellings of the poorer people in the rural districts are closely similar, structures of bamboo thatched with palm, and raised on posts five or six feet from the ground. The eaves are broad, and the window openings, destitute of glass or shell, as in the better houses, have palm-leaf shutters hung at the top and propped open during the day. These shed the rain and keep out the sun. At night they are tightly closed. The house has usually two rooms, its furniture consisting of sleeping-mats, pillows, and perhaps a few wicker stools. The kitchen utensils are of the most primitive character, the stove an earthen affair like a brazier, with projecting knuckles to hold the cooking-vessel. Sometimes the space under the house is enclosed by mats; but it is oftener left open, and is used as a storehouse for the water-jars and wash-tubs, the latter hollowed out of a flat block of wood. The house is usually as clean and tidy as constant scrubbing and care can keep it.

A system of reconcentration, somewhat similar to that in Cuba, was practised here by the Spaniards throughout the districts in rebellion. To prevent the native peasantry from giving aid and assistance to the rebels, they were forced to leave their huts, scattered widely over the country, and to assemble in large villages where they could be under inspection and control. Thus we find great groups of small, cheap huts, where the peasants are crowded together far from their tillage grounds. Their domestic arrangements are of the simplest. "The beds of the Indians are merely mats, on which the whole family repose indiscriminately. Here they smoke their cigars, chew their betel, and fall asleep."

The custom of elevating the house is wide-spread throughout the archipelago. The Moros, where possible, build theirs on piles in shallow water. The uncivilized Tagbanuas, of Palawan, perch their small houses high in the air, upon lofty bamboo poles. The more savage natives, of the mountain regions, build mere rude shelters, composed of poles covered with a few palm leaves.

The more prosperous native planter possesses a dwelling superior in size and comfort to that of the poorer peasant; raised like his above the ground, but provided with sliding windows with translucent shell panes, divided into a number of rooms, and the outer walls painted in bright colors and decorated with grotesque carvings. It has more furniture, including chairs and table, a chandelier with globes of colored glass, and some pictures on the walls, which are covered with cloth instead of plaster, as better suited to earthquake shocks.

The marked cleanliness of the people, their constant bathing, washing, and scrubbing, has one good effect, they are much less annoyed by insect pests than in other tropical countries. Mosquitoes are the most persistent, and they seem mild as compared with those of many other localities. Of course, insects and reptiles are numerous; but many of those which infest the houses are harmless, and the little lizards which one sees running over the walls are engaged in the innocent and useful exercise of catching flies and mosquitoes.

Rice is the ordinary food of the natives. It is boiled for half an hour, and capsicum, or chilly, is used as a condiment. They help themselves with their fingers out of a large dish, or sometimes use a plantain leaf for a plate. Around the dish are sauces, into which they dip the *canin*, or boiled rice. Fish, sweet potatoes, and vegetables add some variety to their diet. One writer tells us that " They are great consumers of fish, which are found in immense abundance. After rains the fields and marshes and ponds are full of them. Fish two palms long are often pulled up from among the paddy [rice plants]. As the waters dry up, the fish retreat to any muddy recess, and the Indians catch them with their hands or kill them with sticks." What becomes of the fish when there are no " muddy recesses" it is difficult to say, but they always reappear. after the rains.

The sugar-cane serves the native for sweetmeats, and his two luxuries are the cigar and the betel-nut. In fact, these may be called necessaries, as they are constantly used. The cigarette can be bought at a very low price, and the cost of the *areca*, or betel-nut, is extremely small, so that there is no check to indulgence in these sources of enjoyment.

The betel-nut is used for a double purpose. It dyes the teeth black and imparts a deep red color to the lips,—these being considered marks of beauty by Malay women. And it produces continuous and sustained exhilarating effects, highly agreeable to those accustomed to its use. It causes giddiness to the unaccustomed.

The betel-nut is the fruit of *Areca catechu*. A small quantity of lime is placed on a piece of the nut, and enclosed in a leaf of *siri*, or betel-pepper. This is rubbed violently against the front gums, the teeth being tightly closed. It is then chewed for a moment, and afterwards held between the teeth and lips, while a stream of red saliva flows from the mouth. A small piece of tobacco is often used with the betel.

The dress of the Filipinos is very simple. The men wear a loose shirt or blouse outside of a pair of pantaloons,—the shirt of native manufacture, made of *abaca*, or Manila hemp. The pantaloons are of cotton, white or striped with various colors, and girded round the waist with a kerchief, whose folds serve for pockets. The head is covered with a kerchief or a straw hat, or more commonly with a broad circular cap like an inverted punch-bowl, with a metal spike at the top for ornament. It is made of bamboo, or sometimes of tortoise-shell, and fastened by a ribbon under the chin.

The wealthy wear shirts made of the costly *piña* cloth, handsomely embroidered, and of various colors, bright red being predominant. These sometimes are worth $100 each. A small, exquisitely woven and embroidered piña handkerchief sent to the Queen of

Spain is said to have cost $500. The pantaloons are made of silk. The feet of the peasants are bare, those of the better class protected by sandals. One occasionally sees a mestizo in Manila dressed in an exaggerated European costume, his feet in patent-leather shoes, and a black Derby hat on his head. The hat is particularly prized, and is the first article of European dress adopted by the native.

The women dress as simply as the men, their attire consisting of a flowing skirt of gay colors, with an overskirt of dark color, composed of a square of cotton cloth, wound tightly round the body from waist to knees and tucked in at the waist. A white cotton chemise, low-necked and short-sleeved, covers the body. Outside of this the opulent wear a broad, loose-sleeved jacket of the thinnest possible piña cloth, supplemented, when in full dress, by a large kerchief of the same material. More commonly, however, the kerchief is of cotton and the jacket of Manila hemp. Stockings are not considered necessities of the situation, and the women go barefooted like the men. They wear no hat or other head-gear, their heads being protected by the baskets or bundles which they carry with the utmost grace and ease of motion.

The women of pure native blood are often very comely. They have a wide, oval face, rather flat in profile, a well-formed but broad nose, well-cut mouth and fine teeth, large, dark, and expressive eyes, a strong but small chin, and a low forehead, the sleek black hair being drawn tightly back and twisted into a simple knot. They are far more industrious than the men, and also more cheerful and devout. Morality prevails among them, marital irregularity being almost unknown, though jealousy is a common characteristic of the men.

The women of the better class are proud of their small feet, which, in full dress, they thrust into a heelless slipper, supported by the toes, and shuffled with lazy grace. They even contrive to dance in these slippers, which are often embroidered with gold or silver. The knot of their abundant hair is fastened by a comb and gilded needles, and adorned with a fragrant flower. A white mantle is thrown over it on dress occasions. They have a graceful and rather coquettish walk, and are somewhat given to languid glances of their liquid, lustrous eyes. The mode of embracing is by touching noses, though a kiss often accompanies this act. Their exquisite sense of smell may perhaps have something to do with this custom.

POPULAR AMUSEMENTS.

One favorite form of entertainment in Spain and her colonies, the bull-fight, has never gained a footing in the Philippines. There is, indeed, a bull-ring at Paco, a suburb of Manila, but the people of the better class avoid its shows, and it affords but a sorry spectacle. But gambling of one sort or another is widely indulged in, and the lottery and the cock-fight have long flourished in the land. Games of hazard are prohibited by law, but the lottery, as an institution from which the government gained half a million dollars annually, has been diligently fostered, the tickets being sold not only throughout the island, but even in Hong-Kong and along the coast of China. Many a poor native has spent his last dollar for a lottery chance and gone to jail in default of money to pay his taxes.

Among the games which are not prohibited is one called by the natives *panguingui*, which is played with six packs of cards, five or six persons making a party. It is so popular with all classes that the authorities forbade it during working hours, but permitted it to be played from twelve to two P.M., and from sunset to ten P.M. On festival days there was no restriction.

Kite-flying, a form of amusement introduced by the Chinese, is popular in the Philippines, as are also fire-balloons and other pyrotechnic displays, also of Chinese introduction. Gun-firing, illuminations, and music, the last in particular, are features of all the religious feasts. So much, indeed, is demanded of the musicians that it is stated that they are not admitted to the bands unless they can play eight hours without cessation. Smoking is another Philippine passion, cigars and cigarettes being served at every entertainment and used on every possible occasion.

But the one overpowering delight of the native Filipino is the cock-fight, which may be called the national vice of the islanders, and the custom in which the passion for gambling has its fullest vent. The man is poor who does not own at least one game-cock, which he may commonly be seen carrying under his arm, caressing it and talking to it as if to a child.

The Spanish had laws controlling cock-fighting, but only that they might obtain from it all possible revenue. As a rule, it was limited to Sundays and feast-days, and on these occasions the seats surrounding the *gallera*, or cock-pit, were sure to be crowded. The cocks are not left to depend upon the spurs provided by nature; a keen gaff, two inches or more in length, being tied to the left leg of each, so that chance is as common an element as skill in deciding the contest. The amount of betting has long been regulated by law,—no person being permitted to wager more than fifty dollars on a fight; but to this restriction little heed is paid.

"The Indians," says Buzeta, "have an inveterate passion for the sport, which occupies the first place in their amusements. The cock is the first object of their care, their general companion, which accompanies them even to the church-door, and is fastened to a bamboo plug outside when they enter for the service of the mass. For no money will they dispose of a favorite bird. Some possess as many as half a dozen of these inappreciable treasures, for whose service they seem principally to live."

Bowring says, "It is considered a discourtesy to touch an Indian's game-cock, and permission is always asked to examine a favorite bird. He is the object of many a caress; he eats, crows, and sleeps in the arms of his master; and, whatever else may be forgotten, the cock is in continual remembrance. I have found him celebrated in verse in terms the most affectionate. A cock that has been frequently victorious is subjected to the most minute criticism, in order to discover by external marks what may serve to characterize his merit."

"The traveller," says Worcester, depicting another phase of the situation, "soon comes to detest game-cocks; for he is often compelled to pass the night in the same room with them, and they begin to crow about three in the morning, after which time sleep is impossible."

It is not necessary here to describe a cock-fight. It

is a mode of amusement not restricted to the tropics, and whose characteristics are well known. In betting, the Filipinos fling their money into the cock-pit and pick up their winnings after the fight. There is little desire to claim money not won. That would be a dangerous experiment with the hot-tempered natives.

Of another of the popular amusements, the religious feast-day and procession, sufficient has already been said. There is nothing which the native more thoroughly enjoys; the glitter and garish show of the parade, the music, fire-works, feasts, and other holiday accompaniments, all appealing warmly to his imagination, and forming, doubtless, an essential part of what is spoken of as his religion.

Much as the Filipino loves music, he loves the dance as well, and many of his hours of festivity are spent in the enjoyment of these two elements of delight. In addition to the Spanish dances, there are native ones which are still more enjoyed, dances into which the love sentiment enters as an essential element.

There is a favorite dance in which a girl goes through the whole gamut of the love passion in song and movement, opening with a low and plaintive air, accompanied by slow and simple movements, as if indicative of unrequited love. Then her tones become louder and her movements livelier, the supple curves of her graceful form being warmly significant of growing passion. She feigns anger. She stamps her foot, now petulantly, now angrily, passionate fury showing in the expression of her deep-flushed face. Still she sings as she dances, her voice eloquent with passion, her body swaying backward and forward in rhythmic unison with her song. Her tones of passion, scorn, and defiance finally give place to a note of triumph; her face glows with eestasy, and she bounds forward, her long, loose hair flowing behind her, like a vision of joy. Then slowly her tone sinks to a gentle sound of soft content, and she blushingly withdraws.

A second dance, in which two young men and a girl take part, typifies the old story of jealous rivalry on the part of the men, and of tantalizing coquetry on that of the maiden; all told in a series of dance movements as striking and expressive as original. A stranger might suppose that what he saw was serious earnest, a real drama of the heart, so realistic is the dramatic feeling with which the dance is performed.

These are not all. There is still another native dance, in which a girl and a man take part, of the suggestive and voluptuous character seen in the Hawaiian *hula-hula* and various other dances of tropical lands. It is an exhibition quite out of accord with Western ideas of propriety, but which the natives view as a matter of course.

The Filipinos have their actual dramas, some of them fairly good,—if no high standard is set,—though a very thin texture of plot, if it but cover an abundance of bombast, love scenes, shows of suffering, and other evidences of passion and feeling, is all the native is apt to demand. The *moro-moro* play is a sort of miracle-play, in which the stage is filled with royal personages, chiefs, soldiers, and persons with Biblical names; a tragic show full of murder, revenge, retribution, and all evil acts and passions. With these is mingled a coarse humor, shown by the stage fool and lads who represent women. It is devoid, however, of grossness, —probably the Church sees to that.

THE PEOPLE OF THE PHILIPPINES. 433

There is one characteristic of the native to which some allusion should be made,—the utter ease with which he deviates from the truth and the little sense of moral delinquency which he attaches to falsehood. It will suffice to quote from Worcester's "Philippine Islands:"

"The civilized natives seldom voluntarily confess faults, and often lie most unconscionably to conceal some trivial shortcoming. In fact, they frequently lie without any excuse whatever, unless it be the æsthetic satisfaction derived from the exercise of their remarkable talent in this direction. When one of them is detected in a falsehood, he is simply chagrined that his performance was not more creditably carried out. He feels no sense of moral guilt, and cannot understand being punished for what is not, to his mind, an offence."

The natives usually marry early, the brides being often not more than eleven or twelve years of age. The marriage-day is one of much pomp and ceremony, and is of importance to the priest, who expects a fee large in proportion to the means of the parties concerned.

On the evening before the ceremony the bride and groom go to confession and receive absolution. On the next morning they leave the house of the bride, their relatives following in a long procession. After the saying of mass, the priest places a thick mantle over their shoulders, typical of their bodily union. The ceremony is then performed, the only special feature being that, as the bride and groom are leaving the church, a bowl of coin is handed them. The husband takes from it a handful of coins which he gives to his wife, who on her part returns them to the bowl. This signifies that he presents to her his worldly goods.

They return home to a banquet, at which all the notables of the village as well as the relatives are present, and all the delicacies of the season are served up. Special dances and songs follow. The marriage is always arranged by the parents of the young couple, the father of the groom furnishing a dowry for the bride. The property of the wife is her own to dispose of, the husband having no right of inheritance in it,— a regulation which adds to the importance of the woman's position in the family.

THE MESTIZOS.

The mestizos, or half-breeds, have been already adverted to, and little more needs to be said concerning them, since in most respects they conform in mode of life to the customs of the civilized natives. They are usually the children of Chinese or Spanish fathers and native mothers, largely of the former, though the Spanish mestizos occupy the superior place in the community. The latter are generally handsome, and are more intelligent, enterprising, and energetic than the pure natives, many of them becoming wealthy merchants and attaining positions of influence.

Many of the mestiza women and girls are beautiful, with a soft olive complexion, red lips, pearly teeth, and liquid black eyes. Their hair, like that of the native women, is of a glossy black, reaching frequently to the ground. They are very proud of it, and also of their small feet, when endowed with them by nature. To enhance the seeming smallness of their feet, they often wear slippers much too small for them, and

THE PEOPLE OF THE PHILIPPINES.

leaving one or more of the toes outside. They are lithe and graceful in movement and are famed for their dancing. Those educated in the convent schools are trained in music and possess other accomplishments.

The fair mestizas wear the native dress, the *camisa*, or waist, and the *pañuelo*, or neck-kerchief, being, with those of wealth, made of the beautiful and costly piña, or pineapple silk, which is handsomely embroidered. This dress, with the gay-colored skirt and long train, is very pretty, and is so comfortable in its adaptation to the climate that many of the European ladies wear it as a home attire.

The characteristics of the Spanish mestizo soon disappear if not maintained by admixture of blood in the second or later generations. This is not the case with the Chinese mestizos, whose characteristic qualities are more lasting,—probably from the close affinity of the two races. These half-breeds, known as *mestizo Chinos*, possess a higher degree of intelligence than the natives, and have much of the business shrewdness of their paternal stock. Many of the prominent merchants of Manila are of this descent. They are, however, tricky in their dealings, and are not liked or trusted by the people. "They have the mongrel stamp and a cunning, shifty look." Many of them took part with the rebels during the recent insurrection; a fact which made the high-class natives slow in joining the insurgents; they being strongly disinclined to connect themselves with the despised mestizos, even against the hated Spaniards.

THE MOROS.

The fierceness and love of war of the Moros of the Sulu Islands and Mindanao distinguish them markedly from the much more peaceful natives of the north. The men are of medium height, but are often superb in physical development, and dress tastefully in pantaloons, waistcoat, jacket, sash, and turban. Their pantaloons are skin-tight below the knee and loose above, and are usually of scarlet or some other bright color. Rows of shining buttons ornament the sides. If fighting is expected, this showy garb is discarded for loose black trousers. The mode in which the turban is tied indicates the rank of its wearer.

The women are equally fond of bright colors with the men, and love to adorn themselves with jewelry. They wear the baggy divided skirt everywhere used by Mohammedan women, and a skin-tight waist of bright color, and usually embroidered in arabesque designs. The *jabul*, a long strip of cloth sewn together at the ends, is draped about the body or thrown over the head as a protection from the sun, its end being held under the arm.

Weapons are carried by all males above sixteen, their coats of mail, swords, lances, krisses, and other weapons being all of their own make, an art in which they are very skilful. These are often beautifully finished, and are excellently suited to the purpose designed. Silver and gold are used to inlay the steel, and the hilts are made of ivory or hard polished wood, at times beautifully carved. The art of tempering is thoroughly understood.

The men are often handsome and usually robust

and active. Their complexion is of a dusky bronze, their eyes black and piercing, their foreheads low, the glossy black hair falling in waves upon the neck. Fierce and daring as they are, they are not lacking in caution, being mentally sober and self-contained, while quick in judgment and decision. Suspicion seems an element of their nature, and they are obstinate and vindictive in disposition and merciless in anger.

Slavery has existed among them since the conquest of the land, and by the laws of Sulu not only the debtor, but his wife and children, become slaves of the creditor if he is unable to pay his debt. He can only free them from this fate by the sacrifice of his own life, through joining the *juramentados*, who are sworn to die in killing Christians. The bloody raids of these devoted fanatics have been already described.

The Moros of Mindanao hunt the savage tribes with murderous thirst, eager to win the coveted title of *bagani*, to obtain which the aspirant must have cut off sixty heads. This entitles him to wear a scarlet turban, and only a bagani can become a chief. The Mandayas seek to escape these murderers by building their huts high up among the branches of trees, whence they hurl stones upon their assailants. The Moros in return try to fire their huts with burning arrows. Failing in this, they will climb the tree with their shields locked together above them, and cut down the posts that support the hut in the tree. The captives are then divided among the captors, the heads of the males being cut off, and the women and children carried off as slaves.

The office of chief is hereditary among the Sulu Moros. On the death of a chief, the *pandita*, or priest, chants a requiem, while a gong made from hollowed wood is beaten by the attendants. The people, hearing this alarm sound, rush in, and stamp and shout while the body is sprinkled with salt. A successor is then chosen.

Though the Sulu Islands were annexed to the Philippines and their people subdued by General Arolas, they paid no taxes, and the Spanish government found it wise to pay the sultan a pension of $2400 yearly. In their language, the sultan is the "Stainless One," and is despotic over both church and state. His power is hereditary in his family, an advisory council and ministers helping him in the toils of government. His palace, a large edifice of wood, is in the new capital Maybun, where he lives in state. The vestibule to the throne-room is adorned with an abundant display of the richest flowering plants and shrubs, and servants flit about in gay costumes, offering betel-nut to every one present, from the sultanas to foreign guests, all being seated on embroidered silken cushions scattered about the floor. There are two sultanates in Mindanao, both subordinate to the sultan of Sulu.

In 1885, the governor-general cited the sultan to appear at Manila, that he might be duly invested in his office. He refused to go; a predecessor having obeyed the summons and been made prisoner. In consequence, another chief, Datto Harun, was appointed in his place. The new sultan proved himself a true Moro. General Arolas having returned to Spain and a less shrewd and cautious governor taken his place, the latter unwisely decided to tax the Moros, and ordered them to come to town and pay their tribute. They appeared on the appointed day in considerable force, headed by Harun, and after some hesitation were admitted to the town. Harun came forward, offering the governor a bag of pearls, then, suddenly drawing a *barong*, clove his skull to the teeth. His followers fell upon the soldiers with such fury that only two or three of them escaped. The town was razed to the ground. Thus it was that the Moros paid tax to Spain.

THE WILD TRIBES.

The wild Malay tribes of the interior need no further description than we have already given them, as they mainly differ from the civilized natives in the greater primitiveness of their habits. They present the Malay in his savage, hunting stage as the others present him in his civilized, agricultural stage. Each possesses the Malay character, though in the latter case it has been softened and refined by civilizing influences and by the effects of Christian teaching.

The wild natives remain heathens, possessing various notions derived from their ancestral doctrines. In case of death, the Tagbanuas seek to guard the corpse against a mysterious, man-like creature, called *balbal*, which comes from the Moro country, moving through the air like a flying squirrel. It has curved nails with which it tears up the thatch of houses, and a long tongue with which it can reach down and "lick up" the dead body.

The dead are judged by a gigantic deity named Taliakood, residing in the interior of the earth, who keeps a fire steadily burning. He asks the deceased if he has led a good or a bad life, and is answered, not by the individual, but by a *louse* on his body. If the report is unfavorable, the hapless individual is pitched into the fire and burned to ashes. If favorable, he passes on into rich and happy hunting grounds, where a house and a wife await him. Each person dies seven times in all, going successively deeper into the earth, and each time gaining a happier stage of existence.

The more savage Mangyans appear to be destitute of anything that can be called religion, presenting no evidence of worship of any sort or of any conception of the supernatural. As regards ideas of a future life, they settle it briefly by the statement, "When a Mangyan is dead, he is *dead.*" If they have any religious conceptions, these must be very crude and unformed. Yet they are not immoral. Women are faithful to their husbands, though the idea of modesty does not seem to exist, and property precious to them may be safely left among them without risk of its being stolen.

THE AETAS, OR NEGRITOS.

The Negrito aborigines differ essentially from the Malays in racial characters and customs. They are very dark in color, some as sable as negroes, are dwarfish in size and ugly in countenance, their features being coarse and ill shaped. Their hair is black and curly and closely matted. Mentally they are stupid and undeveloped, apparently incapable of improvement, and lacking in the qualities of judgment and aggressiveness. They go almost naked, and subsist by hunting and on the wild fruits and tubers of the forest, seemingly having little or no knowledge of agriculture. They seem to stand at the bottom of the human scale, and all attempts to instruct them have proved failures.

The weapons of these forest dwarfs are a bamboo lance, a bow of palm-wood, and a quiver of poisoned arrows. In this respect they agree with the pigmy tribes of Africa, who also possess the art of poisoning their arrows. Though mentally deficient, they are physically alert, being remarkably fleet of foot, while they can climb like monkeys.

About fifty families of Negritos usually live together, their life being spent in wandering, and shelter obtained by a simple erection of sloping poles and leaves or rude thatched huts raised on bamboo poles. Fond of tobacco, they obtain it by trading the wax and honey of wild bees with the Malays. Meat they often obtain in another fashion,—swooping down upon the valley and driving off the cattle of the natives into the mountain recesses.

Unlike savages in general, they give tender care to the aged and show much reverence for the dead. Death comes to them early, their age seldom exceeding forty years. The dress of the men consists of a belt of bark fibres, that of the women of a sort of petticoat of the same, unmarried girls wearing a collar of palm leaves, whose ends meet beneath their breasts. They are said to resist all attempts upon their chastity.

Their marriage custom is a curious one, being a form of pursuit and capture. The young man whose advances to a girl have been favorably received by her parents, begins the ceremony by catching her in his arms. She breaks loose and runs, he in hot pursuit; she being several times caught and as often escaping. After this play of struggle and release has been kept up for a time, the maid submits, and is led back in triumph to her home.

The father of the bride now drags the youth up a ladder to the floor of their hut. The mother does the same with the girl. The two now kneel side by side and the father throws over them a cocoa-nut shellful of water. He then bumps their heads together and they are considered man and wife. Their honeymoon is spent in the mountain depths, where they remain for five days and nights, finally returning to village life.

A still more curious marriage custom is described as follows: The youth and maiden are made to climb two slender saplings in close propinquity. These are now seized by an elder of the group and drawn together until the heads of the climbers touch each other. They are now considered man and wife and allowed to descend.

VII. AGRICULTURAL INDUSTRIES.

MANILA HEMP.

Prominent among the products of nature in the Philippines is the valuable fibre known as Manila hemp, yielded by a plant native to these islands and as yet never cultivated profitably elsewhere. The plant in question is *Musa textilis*, a species of plantain that grows wild in many of the islands, and in appearance closely resembles the banana. The banana is taller and its leaves of a lighter green; but the only other visible difference is in the fruit, that of the hemp plant being small and unfit to eat.

This plant is known in the Philippines as the *abacá*. Like all the plantains, it is an herb, not a tree. It dies after once bearing flowers and fruit; but a new plant springs up from the root, reaching an average height of ten feet and an extreme height of twenty feet, with a diameter of from eight to twelve inches. This plant flourishes in hilly situations, sometimes in the thinnest volcanic soil, but will not grow in low, wet lands. Its period of growth is three years, at the end of which time it sends up a central flower-stem.

It is now ready for utilization. The flower-stem is cut away before the fruit appears, and the leaf-stalks—over six feet long—are cut down and torn into strips five or six inches wide. These strips, known as bast, contain the hemp fibre, surrounded by a soft, pulpy substance, which must be got rid of. This is done in a very primitive fashion; the pulp being scraped away with the aid of a dull knife, which is attached by a hinge to a block of wood. The bast is drawn between the knife and the block, a foot-treadle being used to produce the necessary pressure upon the strips. As a result, the pulp and juice are squeezed out and remain on the side of the knife, and the fibre, as it passes through, is wound round a stick of wood.

Little more is necessary. The fibre is still very moist, more than half its weight being water. It is laid in the sun to dry, and left for about five hours, after which it is gathered into bales of about 240 pounds weight, bound with hoops of iron or rattan, and is ready for shipment.

Many attempts have been made to improve upon the native method of cleaning the bast, but none have proved successful,—some of them breaking, others discoloring the fibre, and the best of them being more expensive than the old hand process. Yet the natives are not the most honest of operators. They are apt to leave the bast exposed to rain and air, which makes it more easily cleaned, but weakens and discolors the fibre. They also often use a toothed knife, which fails to remove all the pulp and wounds and discolors the fibre. Properly prepared Manila hemp should be perfectly clean and white, but, as it is sold by weight, the dishonest native seeks to leave some of the pulp so as to make it weigh heavier, without taking thought of its loss in value.

Hemp-growing is the least troublesome form of Philippine agriculture, and gives the best returns in comparison with expense. Considerable capital is needed in starting a plantation, as three or four years pass before any profit can be made; after that the planter can count on an annual yield. There is little risk to be feared, a forest wind-break being left to protect the plants from hurricanes, while they are free from attacks by locusts and most other insects. Their moist stems are an assurance against fire, no ploughing is needed, no expensive machinery is required; it is only necessary to loosen the earth and keep down weeds. An occasional drought is the only enemy the planter need fear.

Yet he suffers severely through the negligence of his native help, the waste being enormous. In some cases the leaf-stalks are cut before they are mature; in others they are left until they rot on the plant. Through this and other forms of carelessness full thirty per cent. of the fibre is lost.

Work on an estate is done on the co-operative plan, the workmen not being paid in money, but receiving half the fibre they clean. They work in couples, and make good wages even for a poor quality of hemp. In addition to the large planters, many natives produce hemp fibre in a small way, selling it to the Chinese dealers. Chinamen also often lease the native lands for a term of years, work them exhaustively, produce poor fibre, and return the plantation ruined for the time being. As a result, the Chinese product is critically inspected before purchase.

The islands of Leyte and Marinduque and certain districts in Luzon yield the finest quality of hemp. The province of Albay, in southeast Luzon, perhaps stands first in quality and quantity, its annual yield averaging about 20,000 tons. The demand for hemp has grown up principally since 1825; before that date the yield was insignificant. In 1840 it reached about 8500 tons, in 1880 about 50,000, and is now perhaps double this quantity.

Manila hemp is used principally in the manufacture of sail-cloth, mats, and cordage. The stout brown wrapping-paper known as Manila paper is made from old rope. A large percentage of the fibre goes to the United States, most of the remainder to Great Britain. In Paris, carpets, tapestry, hammocks, and even bonnets are made out of this valuable material.

A very fine hemp fibre is obtained in small quantities from the edges of the leaf-stalks or petioles, from which a fine, silky material, suitable for dress goods, is woven. On one island this is mixed with the piña fibre and the fabric sold to foreigners for pure piña, whose exquisite softness it lacks.

During the last decade the United States is said to have received fully forty per cent. of all the hemp fibre produced; a single firm in Boston, in the ten years previous to 1898, buying 79,000 tons of hemp, for which they paid an average price of three cents a pound in the Manila market. The total export to the United States during this period was 914,100 tons. This quantity is capable of being greatly increased.

SUGAR.

The poorest sugar in the world comes from the Philippine Islands, though the best might be produced with careful culture and manufacture. The yield is large, but the whole process is slovenly in the extreme, and the sugar produced is coarse in grain and inferior in quality. The culture of the cane extends to some extent through the whole archipelago, but is principally confined to the islands of Negros, Panay, Luzon, and Cebu,—the yellow variety being grown in Luzon, the purple in the southern islands. The quantity yielded for export, after the demands of the islands are satisfied, is about 175,000 tons annually, or about one-sixth the output of Cuba in prosperous times.

Negros, an island of about the size of Porto Rico, possesses the finest region for sugar-cane. The culture began there about 1850, and the yield for export is now about 80,000 tons per annum, though not more than half its area is cultivated. Its sugar is sent to Iloilo for shipment abroad.

The inferior quality of Philippine sugar is due to the conservatism of the natives, who cling to primitive methods, the mills employed being as antiquated as those used in Europe in the thirteenth century. They have rollers of wood or stone, which are turned by buffalo- or ox-power, and fitted with wooden teeth to break and crush the cane. As a result, only about forty per cent. of the juice is extracted. This is boiled in iron pans, yielding a black, pasty mass.

No other colony under European control is so primitive in its methods, many of the sugar lands being held by the natives, who do not care to change from the system first taught them. The province of Batangas, in Luzon, is the most backward. In those of Pampanga, Bulacan, and Laguna the natives own most of the lands, but here many small steam-mills have been introduced. In Negros and Panay, where the culture is much more recent, improved methods have been adopted. Cebu possesses many of the old cattle-mills, though some estates have adopted modern methods. According to the latest available statistics, the islands contain 5920 cattle-, 239 steam-, and 35 water-mills, with only two vacuum-pan works.

In the native manufacture, the sugar, after being brought to the proper density by boiling in open pans, is put into pilons, which are placed over pots, into which the molasses drains slowly and imperfectly. The pilon is a conical earthen jar, holding about 133 pounds of sugar, the molasses draining through a straw filter in a hole in its bottom. It rests on an earthen crock holding twelve quarts.

After the drainage is completed, the pilons are emptied at *farderias*, or drying-grounds; the sugar, varying in hue from light at top to dark at bottom, is cut up and broken and left to dry, and the product is then mixed to obtain sugar of uniform color. The dry sugar shipped from Manila to the United States and England is almost all prepared in this way.

The sugar of Batangas province, the worst produced anywhere upon the earth, is prepared for market in the following manner. The juice expressed in the cattle-mills is boiled in iron pans over a trench in the ground, the sugar and other solid matter combining into a black, pasty mass of repugnant appearance. This is taken from the pans and thrown into the corner of a shed, a mud wall being built before the heap as it grows in depth. This wall is an essential part of the process, for when the sugar is taken from the shed much of the mud of the wall is mixed with it to add to its weight. This delectable compound forms the Taal sugar of commerce, the town of Taal being the mercantile centre of the province.

The sugar, packed in mat bags, is carted to the coast, the molasses dripping from the carts into the

AGRICULTURAL INDUSTRIES.   449

road as they lurch onward. The bags reach Manila in a dilapidated state, and the sugar is there packed into new bags and loaded on board vessel. On reaching Europe, the bags are frequently found to be torn to pieces and the sugar mixed into a solid mass, which needs to be dug out of the hold of the vessel with pick and shovel. The loss is often as much as ten or twelve per cent., which is borne by the several shippers in proportion to their consignment. Near Taal there are many steam-mills and two vacuum-pans and centrifugal mills; yet the natives pay no heed to the example.

In Negros, Cebu, and the Iloilo province of Panay the juice is boiled to a certain density, and the sugar emptied into wooden trays and beaten until it has a yellow color. This forms the "Superior de Iloilo." It is then put in bags and exported without farther preparation. It does not drip molasses like that of Taal, and loses little in weight.

The sugar plantations are generally small, there being less than a dozen in the country with an annual yield of more than 1000 tons of raw sugar. The lack of transportation greatly checks production, and there is abundant opportunity for capital and enterprise to increase very greatly the quantity and quality of Philippine sugar.

Until 1890 the United States imported annually from 50,000 to 150,000 tons of Manila sugar. Much of the product now, however, finds a nearer market. China and Japan having become large consumers, and in 1898 the United States received only about 37,000 tons. There is an extensive refinery in Hong-Kong which takes a large supply.

TOBACCO.

The tobacco plant was introduced into the Philippines by missionaries from Mexico, and has developed into one of the most important crops of the islands. From 1781 to the end of 1882 Spain maintained a monopoly over this product, during which period, in certain districts in northern Luzon, the natives were virtual slaves of the leaf, each family being obliged to produce a certain quantity of leaf annually, failure to do so being followed by severe treatment. If an Indian was caught smoking a cigar made from his own leaf, he was arrested and fined; the fine and costs amounting to about eight dollars for a cigar and two dollars for a cigarette.

Earnest efforts were made to confine the growth of tobacco to certain selected districts; yet, despite all precautions, much tobacco was grown in remote and concealed localities, and those who knew the art could always buy a good cigar for about one-fourth the price paid in a Manila shop. The attempts to break up this illicit growth and smuggling led to many stubborn encounters between the natives and the revenue officers, and the difficulty grew until it led in the end to the abolishment of the monopoly.

Since 1882 the growth of tobacco has been greatly stimulated. The best leaf comes from the districts of Cagayan and Isabella, in northern Luzon, these yielding from 60,000 to 100,000 tons annually. Tobacco is also grown in other parts of Luzon and in Cebu and Panay, there being in all about 60,000 acres under cultivation. The methods of culture and curing do not differ from those in Cuba, and need not be again described.

AGRICULTURAL INDUSTRIES.

Smoking is universal in the Philippines, by natives and foreigners alike; even the savage Negritos have acquired a taste for the foreign leaf, their smoking frequently performed with the lighted end of the cigar in the mouth. Everywhere the fumigation goes on,— except in church. Women smoke as freely as men; Spanish women of wealth and fashion as freely as the wives of the natives. Cigars and cigarettes are sold in the remotest hamlets of the islands as well as in the largest cities, and to all classes of the population, from savage to governor; smoking being the absorbing passion of the Filipinos of all grades and degrees.

There are various views as to the quality of the Philippine leaf. Old residents believe their own tobacco unequalled in quality. Foreigners are sure to prefer the Cuban cigar, of Vuelta Abajo origin, and millions of "Havana" cigars are sold in Manila, every fibre of whose leaf grew in Philippine soil. About equal quantities of Cuban and Manila cigars are produced,—unlike in size and shape but alike in quality and flavor,—the difference being far more a matter of opinion than of fact.

RICE.

The product of the rice fields is that upon which the very existence of the Filipinos depends, rice being the universal aliment of the people, the food substance to which all others are supplementary. Rice, a plant native to the East, has from immemorial time been the leading food-product of Eastern Asia, and has in the recent period extended its range widely round the tropics. It is grown in every island of the Philippines; rice culture being the branch of agricultural industry which the people of these islands, as of China and Japan, best understand and most enjoy.

Rice in the husk is called paddy, in the Philippines as in India, and in speaking of its cultivation this word is very commonly used. More than twenty varieties of this grain are grown, they being divided into the two groups of *paga*, or highland rice, and *macan*, or lowland rice. The former needs no irrigation, and is sown broadcast on the hills, needing only to be hoed and weeded. Sown at the end of May, it ripens in from three to four and a half months, and is harvested ear by ear.

The macan rice is of much the finer quality, the white-grained variety being the most esteemed. It yields twice the crop of paga rice, but only one crop can be grown annually, while three crops of the latter may be raised. Macan rice is sown in June, in a plot saturated with water until it is a mass of mud. After six weeks the plants are pulled up by the roots and transplanted in the fields, which are kept flooded during the growth of the plant. The rains are usually depended upon for irrigation, but where regular irrigation is resorted to two crops can be grown annually, with a much larger percentage of yield.

When ripe each ear is cut separately, and the paddy is heaped into stacks. After six weeks the threshing takes place, either by the use of the flail, by treading, or by driving ponies over the paddy heaps. No machines are in use for husking the grain, this being generally performed in a large mortar, in which it is beaten with a pestle. There is, however, a primitive wooden mill for this purpose, worked by buffaloes, and steam- and water-power are being brought into use.

The rice-growers of the Philippines have many insect enemies to contend with, one of the worst being the locust, in its occasional migrations. Yet the usual product is large, one *quinon* (about seven acres) of land yielding from 250 to 300 *cavans* (about ninety-six pounds each) of rice; which product might be greatly increased with proper irrigation. At present the rains are mainly trusted to. About 250 pounds of rice will serve a family of five persons for a month.

Formerly, rice was the main crop of the Philippines, and was largely exported; Sual being an important port for its shipment to China. Sual is now a mere village, and nearly half the rice consumed is imported. This is due to the extension of the sugar culture, whose larger profits have greatly reduced the growth of rice.

COFFEE.

The culture of coffee was begun early in the nineteenth century, in a little valley in northern Luzon. The plant is supposed by some to have been previously unknown on the island, and to have spread through the agency of a small wild animal, which ate the berries and scattered the seed. As a result it rapidly extended over the whole island, and many of the plants, whose origin is thus accounted for, are still in bearing, thousands of pounds of coffee-berries being gathered from the wild bushes. Others, however, think the plant indigenous.

The culture is now scattered throughout an area of wide extent, and the amount of coffee produced is unknown. Many of the natives have a few bushes in their front yards, shaded by plantain-trees, and yielding perhaps four or five bushels of berries. These are bought by speculators to help in making up cargoes. The merchants of Manila give the preference to the coffee raised in Cavité, Laguna, and Batangas, the last-named province giving the greatest yield. The coffee of Mindanao is sent to market without being examined and sorted, good and bad beans being mingled. The natives buy this at low prices, but it has no European demand.

The coffee of the Philippines has a fine aroma, not equal to that of the Mocha or Java, but capable of being improved by proper care in cultivation. This, however, is rarely given, there being much carelessness in selecting sites, in planting, in pruning, and in preparing the beans for market, good and bad being often left together. The latter is due in a measure to the natives, whose house-plot coffee is poorly prepared.

The plant, as elsewhere, is grown on high ground, and carefully shaded until mature; a coffee plantation in the Philippines presenting the same features of attraction as described in those of Cuba. This is especially the case in the vicinity of Lipa, where there are many coffee estates, and the planters are usually very careful in the culture of the plant and the preparation for market of the bean. The Philippine coffee, like that of other regions, is gathered by hand, and the fruit laid in heaps for a few days before washing. In this way the pulp is largely got rid of. The berries are now placed in a mortar and pounded until the clean beans emerge; these, packed in hemp bags, are sent to Manila for sale.

The Philippine archipelago, from the extent of its highlands and the suitable character of much of its soil, is well adapted to the coffee culture, which could readily be greatly extended. The industry was hindered by the Spanish government, which laid extra licenses on the planting of coffee and a heavy import duty on the machinery which has been of late years introduced to aid in preparing it for market. A release from these exactions will give encouragement to the planters, and doubtless lead to a large increase in the crop.

OTHER VEGETABLE PRODUCTS.

The areca palm is extensively cultivated for its fruit, the betel-nut, which most of the natives deem almost a necessity of existence. It is used to such an extent that Manila possesses nearly a thousand warehouses and shops for its sale, or for that of the buyo or siri leaf in which the betel is wrapped for chewing, and the lime used with it. The buyo palm is largely grown for its leaf, which has a pungent taste, and is not used solely in connection with the betel-nut, but is considered a remedy in some diseases. It is believed to be an antidote to snake poison when bruised and laid on the wound.

Another palm of much economic value is the nipa, a swamp plant which resembles a gigantic fern. Its leaves are used for thatch, and the sap from its fruit-stalks yields a favorite wine. The juice of the sugar-cane is used for a similar purpose, a strong but pure brandy being distilled from it, to whose use the natives are much addicted.

Though the Philippines possess all the important tropical fruits, no attention is paid to their culture, except in the case of the banana, which is kept trimmed and free from weeds. The guava, mango, custard-apple, and many other fruits grow wild on the hills and even within the town limits, and are gathered by the natives as needed. The wild mango of the Philippines is one of the most delicious of fruits, and the same may be said of the durian, if one can endure the odor of putrefying flesh emitted by its outer skin.

The banana grows both wild and under cultivation, seventy-seven varieties being claimed for the islands. In addition to its great utility as a food-plant, it yields a fibre which the natives weave into cloth, and from which they make a coarse paper. The cacao-tree was early introduced from Mexico, and has long been grown in the orchards and gardens of the monasteries, the friars being famous for their chocolate. There is a chocolate factory at Manila for the benefit of those who do not care to prepare this favorite substance for themselves; but in the country the planters usually grow their own trees and have their chocolate-paste made at home.

Aside from the special crops of the island, and the fruits which form an important part of the food products, agriculture has made little progress; and one of our consuls makes the strong statement that there is not a farm in the Philippines which will compare with the worst in America. The culture is of the most primitive kind, the land being ploughed with a sharpened stick drawn by the buffalo, and the lumps broken by a heavy frame with long wooden teeth. Fertilizers are never applied.

The natives, under Spanish regulations, could not own land, but simply held it subject to certain conditions of cultivation. Outside the tobacco districts—in which they were obliged to confine their chief attention to the leaf—they were required to plant useful

AGRICULTURAL INDUSTRIES.

trees, to raise maize, wheat, rye, vegetables, cotton, and pepper, to grow fruit in their orchards, keep all kinds of suitable cattle, and have at least twelve hens, one cock, and a sucking pig. Should they fail in these conditions, the land could be confiscated in two years.

These conditions were not well complied with; some of them were impossible. Maize has been grown to some extent: probably not over 10,000 bushels of unshelled corn per year. This is mostly sold in Manila, boiled or roasted. Some wheat is grown in the hill country. Hay is unknown, animals being fed on fresh grass, a crisp, succulent variety grown in swampy fields and sold by natives in the streets.

Cotton is produced in quantities sufficient for home use. It is easily and cheaply grown, and might be made an important article of export. Indigo plants grow in the greatest luxuriance, needing little labor in their cultivation, and returning large profits on the capital involved. The indigo is famous for its superior quality.

We have already spoken of the products of the forests. Aside from the many valuable varieties of hard-wood lumber, there are other products to which passing reference may be made. Sapan-wood yields a rich crimson dye, which is much esteemed, though less permanent than that of the cochineal. The bark of the dita tree yields an alkaloid resembling quinine in its effects, though not so strong. The perfume called ylang-ylang is made from the flowers of a tree of the same name. The cocoa-palm yields the oil used in lighting houses and streets, for lubricating and cooking purposes. In many provinces the tree is grown for the oil alone, which is used at home or shipped to Europe. In the European climate it becomes solid and is made into soap and candles. There is a large exportation of copra, the dried meat of the cocoa-nut; this amounting in 1897 to 801,437 pounds. This goes principally to Europe, where it is used in soap-making. Another useful tree is the gutta-percha, which is abundant in some of the islands, especially in Mindanao. It has hitherto been little utilized, but might become a valuable commercial product.

LIVE-STOCK.

Little remains to be said concerning the domestic animals of the Philippines. We have already described the buffalo, the favorite working animal of the Philippine farmer, by whom it is almost universally employed. Buffalo meat is valued by the natives as an article of food, but Europeans find it tough and rather tasteless. Cattle are extensively raised on some of the islands for beef; Masbate, for instance, being mainly devoted to grazing. They are of a small humped variety.

Dairying is almost unknown, the Filipinos never eating butter or any other dairy product. As a result, milk is a very scarce and dear article, being used only in a few towns. Fresh butter and cheese are not to be had at any price, they never being made. The only butter used is a very dear article imported from London in bottles. Goats are raised in large numbers, being prized alike for their milk and their flesh. Pigs also are very common, being kept in every native village, while there are large numbers of wild ones.

Poultry are abundant, and the artificial hatching of ducks is a common industry in some localities. Pateros, for instance, a village near Manila, seems to derive its name from its multitude of ducklings thus hatched (*patos*), which are seen in vast numbers along the banks of the Pasig. They are fed on small shellfish found in abundance in the neighboring Bay Lake.

The eggs, as laid and collected, are placed in large receptacles containing warm paddy husk, whose temperature is kept uniform. A canvas covering is spread over the heap, and one man suffices to attend to a large number of frames, from which the ducklings are removed as soon as hatched. They may be seen in hundreds running about in shallow bamboo baskets, waiting to be carried to the river banks. In that climate they need no further care. Along the Pasig almost every cottage with a river front possesses its *patero*, or duckery.

VIII. MANUFACTURES AND COMMERCE.

CIGARS.

Of the manufactures of the Philippines, as in Cuba, tobacco stands at the head, the cigar factories of Manila vying with those of Havana as public spectacles. Binondo, the trading centre of Manila, is the seat of this industry, there being twelve large cigar and cigarette factories, employing about 11,000 hands, besides many small factories. The Compania General de Tabacos has a capital of $15,000,000, and employs nearly 10,000 hands,—6000 on plantations and 2500 men and 900 women in the factories. It produces annually 80,000,000 cigars, 400,000,000 cigarettes, and 5,000,000 pounds of tobacco. There are six other Spanish firms, several German, Swiss, and English, and a number of Chinese.

The factories present a scene of the most bustling activity, with their thousands of operatives, largely young girls. The working hours are from seven to twelve in the morning and from two to five in the afternoon. The hours of work are often followed by a plunge into Manila Bay, where thousands of the operatives may be seen disporting themselves in the surf, diving, tumbling, and shouting like children.

The scene inside the factories is an interesting one, every stage, from the baled tobacco to the finished cigar, being rapidly passed through. Experts separate the leaf into grades of color and quality with remark-

MANUFACTURES AND COMMERCE. 461

able rapidity, and the whole series of processes may be seen in quick succession, till the finished article is packed in cedar boxes, properly labelled, and ready for market. Many efforts have been made to use less expensive woods for cigar-boxes, but nothing seems to supply the place of cedar, which either preserves the aroma of the leaf or adds a flavor of its own.

While the cigars are hand-made, the cigarettes are made by machines, each of which is capable of turning out 12,000 a day. The leaf is divided into many different colors, though only five are known to the trade, —Maduro, Colorado maduro, Colorado, Colorado claro, and Claro. Of these, Spain takes the strong, dark brands; England takes every shade; America prefers the lighter colors. In 1897 the total export of cigars was 156,916,000, in addition to the large home consumption. The leaf tobacco exported amounted to 801,437 pounds.

OTHER MANUFACTURES.

Very little remains to be said about the Philippine manufactures. Manila possesses some industries introduced by Europeans, including a Spanish brewery, a German cement factory, and Swiss umbrella and hat factories, the latter making felt and straw hats. There are a number of rope-factories, worked mainly by hand. A cotton-mill, with £40,000 capital (English) and 6000 spindles, is the most recent addition to the productive industries.

The natives possess few manufactures, though fabrics of several kinds are woven by them on simple hand-looms. These are made of bamboo, and are very numerous, about 60,000 of them being computed in the province of Iloilo, where there is one in nearly every house. They are used for the manufacture of tissues of silk, cotton, hemp, and the exquisitely fine piña, the fibre from which is obtained from the pineapple leaf, and forms a thread so fine that it is necessary to protect it, by the use of a fine gauze, from even the agitation of the wind.

This beautiful tissue is made most largely in the vicinity of Iloilo, and is sent to the capital to be embroidered. It is so costly when finished that for the more elaborate specimens fabulous prices are paid,— one or two ounces of gold, for instance, for a small handkerchief. It forms an essential part of the dress of the richer natives and mestizos.

A texture of less fineness is made from a mixture of abaca and piña fibre, and a very coarse one from abaca. This is used for sails, rough garments, etc. Mats are extensively produced, some of them beautiful, being of various colors and ornamented in gold and silver patterns. In the Philippines all sleep on mats.

Hats of split bamboo are largely manufactured, and the other native arts include furniture-making, wood-carving, the manufacture of wooden clogs, and the production of various other articles of art or necessity. The natives possess the art of softening and manufacturing horn; produce fibre-wrought hats and cigar-cases of various colors, of which the white are the most costly and beautiful; and work skilfully in metal, making chains of gold and silver of great fineness. The skill of the Moros in producing their highly tempered steel weapons has been already spoken of. The tools and implements used by the natives in manufacture are all of the simplest and rudest character.

The women have long, slender fingers, very fine and delicate in touch, and many of the articles produced by them are models of delicacy. These include the piña fabrics, hats, cigarette holders, articles of embroidery, and other artistic products.

COMMERCE.

It was with the greatest difficulty that foreign trade forced its way into the Philippines against Spanish distrust and opposition, which threw every available obstacle in its way. Though constant pressure from without gradually brought about a more liberal state of affairs, useless and obstructive formalities and vexatious delays continued to stand in the way of trade, and the development of the colony seemed an idea foreign to the intellect of the Spanish authorities.

It was not until within the nineteenth century that foreign ships were permitted to enter the waters of Manila or foreign merchants to reside within its walls. Yet the demands of commerce in time put an end to this mediæval policy, and an American firm, Russell & Sturgis, was admitted by favor of the governor-general. Others followed, and to-day there are about twenty British and as many German firms in Manila, with a number of firms of other nationalities.

The great house of Russell & Sturgis long continued at the head of foreign business, and was the mainspring of Philippine enterprise, opening up the sugar culture in the island of Negros, and investing a large sum of money in agricultural operations. It advanced its capital freely to the native planters, who in return victimized the house. As a result, in 1875 the great firm failed, to the amazement and consternation of the people and the wrecking of business for several years. But the minor firms which it had thrown into the shade gradually took its place and business regained prosperity. These, now mainly English, German, and Spanish houses, pursue the same course of advancing money to the natives to aid them in getting out their crops. While this is accompanied with considerable risk, it is justified by the large profits that attend success.

In 1869 a royal decree was passed abolishing export duties and doing away with the severe port charges which had hampered trade. But various vexatious regulations continued, tending to drive foreign trade from Manila, and as late as 1886 the authorities declared foreign trade to be prejudicial to the "material interests of the country."

The conservatism and ignorance of the natives have also stood in the way of commercial progress. They could not be brought to understand that changes in quotations were the result of world-wide influences, but charged them to the caprice and avarice of the merchants, and often lost by withholding their goods to await higher quotations. They had no fixed price for their products, preferring the Oriental system of bargaining. In this they were steadily overreached by the shrewd Chinese dealers, with whom they usually came into contact. The same system was adopted by large mercantile houses, which seldom stated prices, purchasing the produce of the natives through middlemen familiar with their customs and knowing how to deal with them.

In 1891 Spain laid a protective tariff on the Philippine trade; the result being that the bulk of the traffic

MANUFACTURES AND COMMERCE. 465

was diverted to the home country, the Manchester cotton goods, which had been imported in large quantities from England, being replaced by similar goods of Barcelona manufacture. Iron goods and hardware continued to come from Germany and Switzerland, while American trade was principally restricted to flour and kerosene oil.

The trade of the islands may be briefly summarized. In 1841 the total imports were valued at $3,230,000; the exports at $4,370,000. In 1885 the imports had gained the much larger figure of $19,171,468; the exports, $24,553,686. These figures are given in the silver currency of the island, and would need a reduction to accord with standard gold values. The export duties, as reimposed in 1891 and increased in 1896, caused a falling off in trade; while on August 21, 1897, a decree went into effect under which an extraordinary customs duty of six per cent. *ad valorem* was imposed on all merchandise imports.

For a number of years past the trade of the United States with the Philippines has steadily declined. The export trade has always been insignificant, and has of late years continued to fall off. The import trade has suffered a considerable decline, sinking from $10,268,278 in 1888 to $4,383,740 in 1897. In 1896 the imports of this country from the Philippines were nearly confined to sugar and hemp,—sugar, $2,270,902; hemp, $2,499,404; other articles, $212,551; total imports, $4,982,857. The exports included mineral oil, $89,258; cotton goods, $9714; varnish, $1500; other articles, $61,169; total exports, $161,641.

The trade of the Philippines with the several commercial countries is summarized in the following table.

the date of latest full returns for each country, at the time the table was made, being given:

	Exports.	Imports
Great Britain (1897)	$6,223,426	$2,063,598
United States (1897)	4,383,740	94,597
Japan (1897)	1,332,300	92,823
China (1897)	56,137	97,717
New South Wales (1897)	119,550	176,858
France (1896)	1,990,297	389,796
Germany (1896)	223,720	774,928
Belgium (1896)	272,240	45,660
India (1896)	7,755	81,156
Straits Settlement (1896)	274,130	236,001
Victoria (1896)	180	178,370
Spain (1895)	4,819,344	4,973,589
	$19,702,819	$9,205,093

The exports from Spain, which in 1889 aggregated only $890,000, in 1897 reached nearly $8,000,000, principally cotton fabrics. The United States exported, in addition to the classes of goods named, bread-stuffs, chemicals, and iron and steel goods; and imported, in addition to sugar and hemp, cigars, tobacco, woods, hides, shells, coffee, and indigo.

The decline in American influence in the Philippines, from its maximum previous to 1875 to its minimum at a recent date, is doubtless destined to be followed by an important advance as the American soldier is followed by the American merchant and planter. The enterprise of the Americans is already shown in the newspapers published by them, including "The Manila Times," "The Manila American," and "The American Soldier," whose advertisements show that the man of business has followed the soldier into the Philippine capital, and that American push and enterprise are already making themselves felt in the business world. This significant beginning will, no doubt, be quickly followed by an important commercial progress, and the resources of the islands be developed to a degree undreamed of in the days of Spanish control.

FINANCES.

The currency of the Philippine Islands is on a silver basis, no gold having been in general circulation for more than twenty years. In fact, practically the only money in general circulation is the Mexican dollar of a date prior to 1877. In 1897 a local currency of $6,000,000 in silver was coined in Spain and sent to the islands. It was lighter in weight than the Mexican coins, but was quickly absorbed, owing to the scarcity of money. The Banco Español Filipono has issued notes based on silver, which are now outstanding to the value of about $2,500,000.

The original currency consisted of gold coins of the values of one dollar, two dollars, and four dollars, with Mexican and Spanish silver dollars, the latter having a limited circulation. But the recent depreciation in the value of silver caused so rapid an exportation of gold and importation of Mexican silver that the Spanish government sought to check this movement, issuing a decree in the spring of 1898 in which the importation of silver dollars of a date later than 1877 was prohibited. This law had no long life, for the United States quickly succeeded Spain in the islands, and American coin will quickly make its way into the channels of Philippine commerce. After the American occupation of Manila, the banks were given permission to import silver freely, with the result that the rates of exchange soon assumed a more stable basis.

Under the Spanish prohibition of silver importation there was a large fluctuation in the value of coin, the amount of money needed varying in the different seasons. In the height of the sugar season there is a sharp increase in the demand for money. In the off season the demand is light. It was not uncommon under Spanish rule for silver to go to a premium of ten or twelve per cent., which was met by active smuggling of silver into the islands, an industry practised largely by the rich Chinese mestizos. This illicit industry is at an end now that the hinderance to silver importation is removed.

Of the quantity of money in circulation in the Philippines there are no trustworthy estimates. In addition to the $6,000,000 coined in Spain in 1897 and the $2,500,000 of bank-note circulation, there are about $10,000,000 in smaller coins, and probably from $20,000,000 to $25,000,000 in Mexican dollars, making a total of approximately $40,000,000 to $45,000,000.

The question of the future currency of the islands is an important one to business men, and it seems necessary for this to be in silver, which is the recognized currency of the Oriental countries, with which the Philippines largely trade. The natives will have nothing but silver, and will take the depreciated Mexican dollar in preference to the silver dollar of the United States. The soldiers in Manila, who are paid in gold, find it necessary to exchange it for silver at some of the local banks. A special coinage of silver dollars may prove desirable for the archipelago.

Despite the severe taxation and other exactions to

which the Philippine people were subjected under Spanish rule, the crown derived little benefit from this distant colony, the expenses cutting so deeply into the receipts that only a few hundred thousand dollars annually reached Spain. The islands profited no more than the king, very little being spent on public works. If a bridge was needed, the natives of the vicinity had to provide the money to build it. If a road was required, the neighboring people were obliged to open it at their own expense. The clergy and the grasping officials kept the cash that was wrung from the hands of the merchants and laboring population; the officials seeming to have occupied themselves chiefly in robbing the people with one hand and the government with the other. In so doing they sowed a crop of hatred of everything Spanish, whose fruit we have seen in the recent insurrection.

THE FUTURE OUTLOOK.

At present it is impossible to predict the industrial future of the Philippine Islands, since it must depend largely on the relation of the United States to these islands, which is far from clearly defined. Whatever the political connection of the two countries may be, there is the strongest probability that some close relation will exist between them, and that the Philippine industries will be largely under the influence or control of the United States. This country will assuredly be the leading factor in Philippine commerce, and will exert a stimulating influence upon Philippine agriculture and other interests, the capital and enterprise of American citizens making themselves felt widely throughout the archipelago.

The important interests of the Philippines are, as may be seen from the description given, two in character, agriculture and mining,—the former far from fully developed, the latter scarcely developed at all. Preliminarily to the development of these interests one thing is absolutely needed,—improved means of transportation. The highroad and the railroad are the agencies demanded alike for the pacification of the people and the advancement of their interests, and these, the railroad in particular, are very likely to be the first things to which American enterprise will direct itself.

If the islands are once penetrated by railroad lines and supplied with good roads, not only will their agricultural industries be greatly stimulated, but their mining possibilities will be developed wherever any fair promise of profit shall declare itself. In the latter, the scientist needs to precede the engineer, the geology and mineralogy of the land to be closely observed, and the probable output of coal, iron, gold, and other minerals to be studied and tested.

But the present great promise of the archipelago lies in the direction of agriculture, whose possible results, under energetic and modernized methods, cannot fail to prove enormous in amount and highly profitable. One thing, however, needs to be borne strictly in mind. The Philippines are tropical in situation, and have all the defects along with the advantages of the tropics. While possessed of a highly fertile soil, in which useful plants grow luxuriantly under the stimulus of warm sunshine and frequent rains, the effect of their tropical climate on the human population is as enervating as it is stimulating to plant life. Active physical labor can scarcely be looked for in such a climate, and the energies of nature are likely to be vitiated by the lack of energy in man.

A second element of the situation is the little which is needed in such a climate to support life and the slight exertion with which this little can be obtained. The Philippine natives are not likely to work energetically under their warm sun and humid atmosphere, when they can so readily and with so little labor obtain all that their simple life demands.

Only three ways out of this difficulty present themselves, and at least two of them are very doubtful. The one is to raise the intellectual level of the Filipino by education and example and increase his demands in accordance with the development of his intelligence. If he requires more, he will work more vigorously to obtain it. This very problematical solution of the problem may be contrasted with the second one, the free opening of the country to the Chinese, a people whose industry appears unchecked even under the most adverse conditions of nature. Yet to flood the country with Chinese would perhaps cause greater evils than it would cure, and it certainly seems a remedy not to be employed except as a final resort.

The third and most promising solution of the problem would appear to be a reduction of the amount of human labor by the introduction of the most advanced modern methods and the best modern machinery. In the most profitable of the Philippine industries, that of sugar production and manufacture, primitive methods are employed, and the output could be at once more than doubled, with the same or less labor than is now employed, by adopting the methods in use in Cuba and Hawaii. Mechanical power can doubtless be applied effectively to many other of the agricultural products of the Philippines, and with the present sum of labor an output considerably greater in quantity and in many cases much superior in quality could be counted upon.

In the question here considered, the moral element must enter to a far greater degree than it did under Spanish control. It is the duty of Americans to consider the well-being of the people first, and material advantage second; and only where the profit to be derived from the soil coincides with the just treatment and best interests of the Philippine natives should it be considered at all. Profit is a good thing to take into account; human happiness and liberty a better. Both of them will doubtless be considered in our relations with these distant lands and people, since they can readily be made to harmonize if justice and the sentiment of human fellowship be made their combining element.

But speculative suggestions of this kind are of little practical value. The future of the Philippines is a problem which only time can solve. All that can positively be said is that these tropical islands possess enormous productive capabilities, which need only intelligence and energy to develop. Under American influence and control such a development can scarcely fail to take place,—at least to some considerable degree,—and these fertile islands to take a prominent place in the circle of the producing countries of the earth.

INDEX.

★ ★

A.

Abaca, the, 443, 462.
Acacia, the, 254.
Adjuntas, 203.
Aetas, the, 393, 440.
Agno River, 349.
Agouti, the, 38, 183.
Agriculture, 124, 160, 161, 299, 314, 443, 470.
Aguadilla, 176, 201.
Aguinaldo, General, 330, 331.
Aibonito, 169, 178, 203.
Alameda de Paula, 73.
Albay, 349; hemp of, 445.
Albemarle, Lord, 9.
Algaroba tree, 256.
Alluvial deposits, 27.
American commerce, 153-156, 221, 318, 465.
American influence in the Philippines, 466.
American mining companies, 43.
American troops at Havana, 9.
Americans in Hawaii, 297.
Amusements, 120.
Anda, Simon de, 329.
Animals, domestic, 27; of Cuba, 38; of Porto Rico, 183; of Hawaii, 261; of the Philippines, 362.
Annexation of Hawaii, 236.
Aparri, 349, 414.
Apo, Mount, 337, 341.

Apple forest, 256.
Aqueducts, 76, 301-303.
Area of Cuba, 16; of Porto Rico, 171; of Hawaiian Islands, 238; of Philippine Islands, 334.
Areca palm, 361; use of, 426, 455.
Arecibo, 176, 201.
Arolas, General, 413, 438.
Arrow-root, 311.
Arroyo, 177, 202.
Artemisia, 91.
Artesian wells, 303.
Asphaltum, Cuban, 45.
Ateneo Municipal, 398.
Avocado pear, 257.
Awa beverage, 260.

B.

Bacolod, 413.
Bagani, the, 437.
Bahia Honda, 83.
Balabac Island, 336.
Bamboo, the, 312; uses of, 359.
Banana, the, 35, 162, 255, 310, 361, 455, 456.
Banes, 82.
Banks, Cuban, 158; Porto Rican, 223; Hawaiian, 280; Philippine, 467.
Baracoa, 8, 82; anvil of, 19.
Basilan Island, 336, 349.
Batabano, 91; sponges of, 148.
Batangas, sugar of, 448.
Bathing facilities, 74, 102.

INDEX.

Bathing, Hawaiian, 289; Philippine, 421, 425.
Baths of Havana, 74.
Bats, Cuban, 39; Philippine, 364.
Bay of Guantanamo, 87.
Bay of Havana, 64.
Bay of Santiago, 83, 86.
Bayamo, 93.
Beans, Cuban, 35.
Beef, curing of, 145.
Beer, 206, 226.
Bees, Cuban, 40, 147; Porto Rican, 218; Philippine, 366.
Beggars, Cuban, 111.
Bejucal, 92.
Bellemar, cave of, 78, 79.
Bells of Havana, 96.
Bemba, 92.
Beriberi, 355.
Betel-nut, 426, 455.
Binondo, 402; activity of, 403; dwellings of, 403.
Birds, Cuban, 39; Porto Rican, 184; Hawaiian, 261, 265; Leyson Island, 315; Philippine, 364.
Bird's nest, edible, 365.
Bird's-nest fern, 255.
Bishop's Garden, 74.
Boats on Pasig River, 399.
Bohol Island, 335, 345.
Bombon Lake, 340, 343.
Bone-black, 141.
Books, 100.
Borneo Island, 336.
Botanical Gardens, 68.
Bowring, Sir John, 421, 430.
Boys and girls, 103.
Bread-fruit, 255.
Breakfast, Cuban, 105.
Bricks, 226.
British in Hawaii, 233.
British rovers, 328.

British take Manila, 328.
Buffalo, Philippine, 362, 363, 458.
Buildings of Havana, 66, 69-75.
Bull-ring in Cuba, 64, 113; in the Philippines, 428.
Bulusan volcano, 340.
Burias Island, 335.
Busuanga Island, 336.
Butter, 106, 458.
Buyo palm, 455.

C.

Cabaña fortress, 62.
Cabañas, 83.
Cabeza de Barangay, 374.
Cables, submarine, 56.
Cabo Rojo, 176, 202.
Cacao-tree, 35, 131, 215, 361, 456.
Cafés, Havana, 75, 100.
Cafetales, 26.
Cagayan River, 342, 349.
Cagayan tobacco, 450.
Caibarien, 81; sponges of, 148.
Calamianes Islands, 335.
Calapan, 414.
Calcareous deposits, 20.
Calzades, the, 54.
Camaguey, 51, 93.
Campo de Marte, 73.
Canarreos Islands, 24.
Candelaria, 91.
Candle-nut-tree, 253.
Candles, 226.
Canes, 361.
Caparra, 165.
Cape Cruz, 20.
Cape Maisi, 20.
Cape San Antonio, 20.
Capiz, 414.
Captain-general, 11, 49.
Caraballos Mountains, 337, 342.
Carabao, the, 362.

INDEX.

Cardenas, 80.
Cardenas Bay asphaltum, 45.
Card-game, Philippine, 429.
Carnival week, 114.
Carob-tree, 256.
Carriage-making, 151.
Casino, Havana, 72.
Cassava, the, 34.
Castillo de la Fuerza, 63.
Castillo de la Punta, 62.
Cat, wild, 40.
Cathedral of Havana, 70, 84; of Santiago, 84; of Manila, 401.
Cattle of Cuba, 145, 161; of Porto Rico, 217; of Hawaii, 263; of the Philippines, 364, 458.
Cattle ranges, 144; farms, 144.
Cattle, wild, 263, 313.
Cauto River, 21.
Cave of Bellemar, 78, 79.
Caverns, Cuban, 20, 22, 23.
Caves of Baracoa, 83; of Porto Rico, 178.
Cavité, 347, 407.
Cayey, 203.
Cebu, 323, 348, 411; churches of, 412; history, 412; commerce, 412.
Cebu Island, 335; deforestation of, 345, 356; tobacco of, 450.
Ceiba tree, 33.
Celebes Sea, 334, 336.
Census of Cuba, 10; of Porto Rico, 192, 212; of Hawaii, 268, 271.
Children in Havana, 103.
Chimneys, lack of, 99.
Chinese in Cuba, 110; in Hawaii, 280, 295; in the Philippines, 325, 329, 384, 471; massacres of, 325, 327; relations to native women, 385; mestizos, 385; shopkeepers, 386; hemp raisers, 445.

Chocolate, 131, 456.
Cholera in the Philippines, 354.
Christianity in Hawaii, 231; in the Philippines, 376, 379.
Church of Santo Niño, 411.
Churches of Havana, 72; attendance at, 112; of Hawaii, 271.
Cienfuegos, 89; buildings of, 90.
Cigar cases, 462.
Cigar manufacture, 149-151, 450, 460.
Cigars, Cuban, 149; export of, 150; grades of, 150; Philippine, 450, 460, 461.
Cinco Villas, Los, 50.
Cities of Cuba, 62-95; of Porto Rico, 194; of Hawaii, 278; of the Philippines, 399-415.
Citizenship in Hawaii, 266.
Clarifiers, sugar, 141.
Climate of Cuba, 28; of Porto Rico, 178; of Hawaii, 248; of the Philippines, 349.
Cloak, Hawaiian feather, 261.
Cloth, Hawaiian, 260.
Coal in Cuba, 44; in the Philippines, 371.
Coamo, 202.
Coast of Cuba, 16, 25; of Porto Rico, 171, 177.
Coast trade, Cuban, 56; Porto Rican, 189; Hawaiian, 275.
Coastal islands, Cuban, 23.
Cock-fighting, Cuban, 44, 113; Philippine, 429.
Cocoa-nut palm, 35, 131, 182, 254; uses of, 360; oil, 457.
Coffee, 10, 37, 105, 107; gathering, 128; preparing for market, 128, 130; grades of, 130; wild, 257, 453; Hawaiian, 306, 307; Philippine, 453-455.

INDEX.

Coffee culture, 124-131, 160, 213, 299, 307-309, 454.
Coffee lands, 308.
Coffee plantations, 126.
Cogon grass, 356.
Colon, 92.
Colors of houses, 63, 66.
Columbus discovers Cuba, 7; tomb of, 71.
Commerce of Cuba, 151-156; of Porto Rico, 219-223; of Hawaii, 237, 275, 318, 327; of the Philippines, 463-466.
Company of the Philippines, 330.
Compliment, language of, 104.
Concentration policy in Cuba, 12.
Consolacion del Sur, 91.
Constitution of Hawaii, 234.
Contract labor, 296.
Convicts, Porto Rican, 166.
Cook, Captain, 228, 286.
Cooking, 105, 293.
Coolie labor, 60, 110.
Copper, 42, 87, 185, 369.
Copper Mountains, 18.
Copra, 458.
Coral islands, 23; growth of, 27.
Coral reefs, 177, 239, 337.
Cortes, expedition of, 324.
Cortes, representation in, 49.
Cotton, 38, 217, 457.
Cotton goods in Philippines, 465.
Countrymen, habits of, 116.
Courts, Cuban, 49; Porto Rican, 186; Philippine, 375.
Crocodile, 365.
Crops, Cuban farm, 117, 118.
Cuba, names of, 7; invasions, 9; population, 10; oppression, 11; situation, 15; extent, 15; coast and islands, 16, 23; mountains, 17; commercial advantage of position, 17; forests, 25, 32; climates, 28; seasons, 28; rains, 28, 30; diseases, 29; food plants and fruits, 34; animals, 38, 41; metals and minerals, 41; reforms, 48; divisions, 48, 50; government, 49; slavery, 51; religion, 52; roads, 53; railways, 54; steamships, 56; telegraphs, 57; population, 57-60; education, 60; chief towns, 62-95; agriculture, 124; manufactures, 149; commerce, 151; foreign trade, 151; restrictions on trade, 152; value of estates, 156; debt, 157; currency, 157; revenue, 157; future of, 159; public improvements, 162; advantage to United States, 164.
Cuban hatred of the Spaniards, 11.
Cuban landscapes, 26; atmosphere, 30; waters, 30; representation, 49; women, 97; habits of men, 100; area of cultivated soil, 142; pasture lands, 144.
Cubitas Mountains, 19, 93; iron deposits of, 43.
Cuchillas, the, 18.
Culebra Island, 175.
Cultivated plants, 34.
Currency of Cuba, 157; of Porto Rico, 223; of Hawaii, 321; of the Philippines, 467.
Custard-apple, 36.

D.

Dagupan, 382.
Dances, Hawaiian, 292; Philippine, 431.
Debt of Cuba, 157.
Deer in Cuba, 38; in Hawaii, 264; in the Philippines, 364.

ND EX. 477

Departments of Porto Rico, 136.
Depopulation of Hawaii, 267.
De Soto, Fernando, 8.
Dewey, Admiral, 331, 407.
Diamond Head, 282.
Diana Key asphaltum, 45.
Dinner, Cuban, 106.
Diseases of Cuba, 29, 163; of Porto Rico, 179; of Hawaii, 251; of the Philippines, 352.
Districts, Cuban judicial, 48.
Dita alkaloid, 457.
Dogs, wild, 40, 183, 264; edible, 261, 263, 293.
Dole, Sanford B., 235.
Dramas, Philippine, 432.
Dress, Cuban, 98, 118, 119; Porto Rican, 205; Hawaiian, 288; Philippine, 426.
Drinking in Cuba, 85, 100; in Porto Rico, 206.
Drinks, Cuban, 106, 107.
Drunkenness in Hawaii, 232, 261.
Dry season, Cuban, 28; Philippine, 350.
Duck hatching, artificial, 459.
Dumaguete, 413.
Durian, the, 362, 455.
Dutch fleet at Manila, 328.
Dwellings of Havana, 66; of country, 119; of San Juan, 197; of Honolulu, 281; of Manila, 403; of Philippine natives, 423.

E.

Earthquakes in Cuba, 20; in the Philippines, 326, 341.
Ecclesiastical division of Cuba, 50.
Edible roots, 362; bird's-nest, 365.
Education in Cuba, 60; in Porto Rico, 192; in Hawaii, 231, 270, in the Philippines, 396-398.

Eggers, Baron, 181.
El Caney, 87.
El Cerro, 74.
Electric railways, 163.
Elevation of land, 337.
Engineer, sugar plantation, 140.
Estate, Cuban, 121-123.
Eucalyptus, 256.
Ewa, 302, 305.
Execution of prisoners, 402.
Exotic plants in Hawaii, 310.
Export duties, 454.
Exports of Cuba, 153-155; of Porto Rico, 219-221; of Hawaii, 318; of the Philippines, 465.

F.

Fajardo, 176, 202.
Fan in Cuba, the, 97.
Farm crops, 212.
Farmers, 190.
Farming, 456.
Farms, cultivation of, 116; clearing, 356.
Feast days, 431.
Feasts, Hawaiian, 263, 294.
Feather cloaks and fans, 264.
Ferdinand of Spain, decree of, 10.
Fertile districts of Cuba, 21.
Filipinos, character of, 386, 416; demeanor, 417; philosophy, 418, 422; home-life, 419; superstitions, 420; courage, 420; cleanliness, 421; litigation, 422; love of music, 423; progress of, 4
Filipinas Islas, 324.
Finances, Cuban, 156; Porto Rican, 167; Hawaiian, 217; Philippine, 467.
Fireflies, Cuban, 40; Philippine, 366.

Fish-market, Havana, 75; Honolulu, 280.
Fishes, Cuban, 40; Porto Rican, 184; Hawaiian, 262; Philippine, 366.
Fishing industry, Cuban, 148.
Flora, Cuban, 32-38; Philippine, 357.
Flowering plants, Cuban, 37.
Food in Cuba, 105, 120; in Porto Rico, 206; in Hawaii, 280, 293; in the Philippines, 425.
Food plants, 34, 216.
Foreman, John, 378.
Forest, a typical Hawaiian, 254.
Forests, Cuban, 21, 25, 26, 37; Porto Rican, 172, 181, 211; Hawaiian, 253, 258; Philippine, 346, 356-359.
Fortifications of Havana, 8, 62; of San Juan, 195.
Fossil animals, 26.
Fountain of India, 73.
Freemasonry in Cuba, 104; in Hawaii, 280.
French interference in Hawaii, 232.
Friars of the Philippines, 327, 376; character of, 377; abuses, 378; hated by natives, 330, 379; control of education, 397.
Fruits, Cuban, 35, 161, 162; Porto Rican, 216; Hawaiian, 255-257, 311; Philippine, 361, 445.

G.

Cro
Crop anes, the, 395.
Cuba ons, Spanish trade, 327.
   pop ling in Cuba, 101, 112; for-
   situa en in Santiago, 113; in the
   and pines, 428.
   17 in Cuba, 147.

Gardens of Havana 68, 74; of Honolulu, 281.
Geography of Cuba, 15; of Porto Rico, 171; of Hawaii, 237; of the Philippines, 334.
Geology of Cuba, 26; of Porto Rico, 177; of Hawaii, 239; of the Philippines, 337.
Gibara, 82.
Gibaros of Porto Rico, the, 190, 191.
Goats, 364, 458.
Gobernadorcillo, the 373.
Gold in Cuba, 41; in Porto Rico, 184; in the Philippines, 368.
Government, Cuban, 48-50; Porto Rican, 168, 186; Hawaiian, 266; Philippine, 373.
Government lands in Hawaii, 309.
Governor-general, 10, 49, 373, 401.
Grazing plains, Cuban, 164; Porto Rican, 210; Hawaiian, 309, 312; Philippine, 346.
Guana, 92.
Guanabacoa, 44, 102; springs of, 46.
Guanajay, 92.
Guanica, 176.
Guaniguanico Islands, 24.
Guano, Leyson Island, 315.
Guantanamo, 87.
Guava, the, 35, 255, 361.
Guayama, 177, 202.
Guimaras Island, 335, 348, 411.
Gutta-percha, 458.
Gypsum, 372.

H.

Halcon, Mount, 337, 346.
Haleakala volcano, 242.
Half-breeds, Philippine, 384.
Harbor of Cienfuegos, 90; of Havana, 62, 151.

INDEX. 479

Harbors, Cuban, 16, 151; Porto Rican, 175; Hawaiian, 247; Philippine, 347.
Hard-wood timber, 32, 182, 357-359.
Harness-making, 151.
Hats, bamboo, 462.
Havana, settlement of, 8; captures, 8, 9; temperature, 28; situation, 62, 63; defence, 62, 63; bay, 64; suburbs, 64, 65; population, 65; streets, 65-68, 74, 103; odors, 65, 67; old town, 65; new town, 66; houses, 67, 74; noises, 67, 96; parks and gardens, 68, 74; prison, 69; prado, 69; theatres, 69, 71; churches, 70, 72; libraries, 73; El Cerro Avenue, 74; sea-baths, 75, 102; markets, 75; water supply, 76; bells of, 96; street scenes, 108, 109; stores, 109; harbor, 151; shipping, 152.
Havana cigars, 150, 152.
Hawaii, situation of, 237; western side, 253; eastern side, 253; plants, 253; animals, 261; government, 266; population, 266; education, 270; religion, 271; roads and railways, 273; soil, 301, 307, 309.
Hawaiian Electric and Cold Storage Company, 317.
Hawaiian government, 228, 233; independence, 233; legislature, 234; annexation, 235; republic, 235; area, 238; names and positions of islands, 238; geology, 239; mountains, 239, 240; volcanoes, 241; plains, 245; rivers, 247; harbors, 247; storms, 250; rainfall, 250; horsemanship, 264; public lands, 309; herdsmen, 313; industries, 317; debt, 321; revenue, 321.
Hawaiians, race and character of, 287; dress, 288; immorality, 288; daring, 289; surf-swimming, 289-291; boating, 291; dancing, 292; industries, 292; language, 292; dwellings and food, 293; feasts, 294; decrease of, 294.
Healthfulness of Hawaii, 252.
Health resorts, 94.
Hemp, Manila, 443; culture, 444; use of, 445.
Herdsmen, Hawaiian, 313.
Hibiscus, the, 254.
High and low life, mingling of, 108.
Highlands, Cuban, 17.
Hilo, 246, 248, 251, 254; aspect of, 283; vegetation, 284; Americans in, 286.
History, Cuban, 7-14; Porto Rican, 165-170; Hawaiian, 228-236; Philippine, 323-333.
Hogs, 145, 218, 261, 263.
Holguin, 82, 93, 94.
Homesteads, Hawaiian, 309.
Honey, 147, 218, 366.
Honolulu, 229, 245, 247, 249; distances from, 237; hills back of, 253; water supply, 276; aspect of, 278; growth of, 279; public buildings, 279; streets, 280; markets, 280; vegetation, 281; dwellings, 282; scenery, 282.
Honolulu Iron-Works, 317.
Horses, Cuban, 118, 145; gait of, 146; endurance of, 146; treatment of, 146; Porto Rican, 217; Hawaiian, 264, 289; Philippine, 364; in Manila, 408.
Hospital methods in Cuba, 30.

Hospitality in Cuba, 103; in the Philippines, 420.
Hospitals in Havana, 72.
Hotel fare, 105.
Hotels of Havana, 75, 104; of Matanzas, 79.
Hot springs, 46, 341, 371, 415.
Houses, Cuban, 66; colors of, 67; furniture, 98, 99; lack of privacy in, 99; Hawaiian, 293; Philippine, 403, 404, 423, 424.
Humacoa, 176, 202.
Hurricanes in Cuba, 29.

I.

Idolatry abolished in Hawaii, 231.
Ignorance, 121.
Igorrotes, the, 395.
Iguana, the 183.
Iligan, 414.
Ilocanos, the, 388.
Iloilo, 345; harbor of, 347, 410.
Immorality, Hawaiian, 232.
Imports, Cuban, 156; Porto Rican, 220, 226; Hawaiian, 319; Philippine, 463.
Indians of Cuba, 58; of Porto Rico, 165.
Indigo, 311, 457.
Indios, the, 389.
Indolence, Cuban, 100, 116; Porto Rican, 206, 211, 215; Philippine, 418.
Industrial future, 159, 225, 469.
Industries, Cuban, 149; Porto Rican, 219; Hawaiian, 292, 317; Philippine, 460.
Insects of Cuba, 40; of Porto Rico, 183; of Hawaii, 261; of the Philippines, 366, 425.
Insurrection of 1868, 11; of 1895,
12; Hawaiian, 235; Philippine, 330.
Inter-island Steamship Company, 275.
Inter-island traffic, 275, 383.
Interest rates, 223.
Iron ore, 87, 185, 370.
Iron wares, 465.
Irrigation, 276, 301–303.
Isabel Segunda, 175.
Isabella Province tobacco, 458.
Islands, Cuban coast, 16; Hawaiian, 237; Philippine, 334.
Isle of Pines, 16, 24, 32; hot springs of, 46.

J.

Jamaica, rats in, 304.
Japanese laborers, 295.
Jardin el Rey, 24.
Jardinellos, 24.
Jardines de la Reina, 24.
Jardines, springs of the, 22.
Jatibonico River, 23.
Jesuit observatory, 398.
Jesuits in the Philippines, 377.
Juice, sugar-cane, 140.
Jungle fowl, 365.
Juramentados, the, 437.
Jutia, the, 38.

K.

Kahulaui, 238, 241.
Kailua, 285.
Kalakaua, King, 234.
Kamehameha I., 229; II., 230, 232, 278; III., 232; IV., 234; V., 234.
Kanakas, the, 287.
Kaolin, 372.
Kauai, 238, 240, 245, 299.
Kilauea, crater of, 243, 272; eruptions of, 243.

INDEX.

Kite-flying, 429.
Koa tree, 254.
Kona coffee, 299, 306.
Kona district, 306.

L.

Labor, native, 445.
Labor, plantation, 295-297.
Labor question, 163.
Laborers, 139, 418.
Ladies, Cuban, 97, 122; bathing habits of, 102; Porto Rican, 205.
Ladrone Islands, 324.
Laguna de Bay, 342, 347.
Lahaina, 248, 285.
Lake Ariguanabo, 22.
Lake Bay, 342.
Lake Bombon, 340, 343.
Lakes, Cuban, 22; Porto Rican, 174.
Lakes, marsh, 25.
Lakes of Luzon, 343; of Mindanao, 343.
Lala, Ramon, 422.
Lanai Island, 238, 241; sheep on, 313.
Land crabs, 39.
Landscape, Cuban, 26.
Language, Hawaiian, 292.
Languages, Philippine, 388.
Lantana plant, the, 255.
Las Casas, Luis de, 10.
Lava, varieties of, 246.
Lead, 370.
Leather, 226.
Legaspi settles the Philippines, 324.
Lemons in Cuba, 35, 162; in Porto Rico, 216.
Lemurs, 364.
Leprosy in Cuba, 29; in Hawaii, 251; in the Philippines, 355.
Leyson Island, 315.

Leyte Island, 335, 341, 344; hemp of, 445.
Lianas, the, 33, 255.
Libraries of Havana, 72, 73.
Lignite, Philippine, 371.
Liliuokalani, Queen, 234; insurrection against, 235; deposition of, 235.
Lime, the, 35, 127, 256, 362.
Limestone caverns and tunnels, 22.
Limestone rocks, 20, 177.
Lingayen Bay, 349, 382.
Lipa, 414, 454.
Live-stock, 146, 217, 312, 458.
Lizards, 366.
Looms, Philippine native, 461.
Lottery, Cuban, 112; Philippine, 428.
Lowlands, Cuban, 21.
Lumber, 226, 312.
Lunalilo, King, 234.
Luneta, the, 402.
Luzon Island, 324, 335; geology of, 338; description of, 342; lowlands of, 342; natives, 386; towns, 414; sugar, 447; coffee, 453.

M.

Macagua, 92.
Machinery, 161, 163, 471.
McKinley, President, 332.
Madringa springs, 46.
Madruga baths, 80.
Magellan, Ferdinand, 323.
Maine, sinking of the, 13.
Mairi plant, 254.
Maize, 35, 362, 457.
Majajay, 414.
Malarial fever, 29, 353.
Malaspina, Mount, 337, 339.
Malays, 384, 388, 399, 416; wild tribes, 439.

INDEX.

Mammee, the, 36, 37.
Manatee, the, 39.
Mandayas, the, 437.
Manganese, 44.
Mango, the, 36, 255, 361, 455.
Mangosteen, the, 362.
Mangrove, the, 25.
Mangyans, the, 346, 395, 440.
Manila, founding of, 324; taken by British, 328; taken by Americans, 331; temperature of, 352; streets of, 381, 405; Chinese in, 384; schools, 396; divisions, 399; river scenes, 399; bridges, 400; walls, 400; buildings, 401; luneta, 402; population, 402; new city, 403; dwellings, 403; home life, 404; business streets, 405; suburbs, 406; riding, 408; processions, 408; merchants, 463.
Manila Bay, 347; battle of, 331.
Manila hemp, 443-445.
Manufactures, Cuban, 149-151; Porto Rican, 219; Hawaiian, 317; Philippine, 460.
Manzanillo, 87.
Marble, 46, 372.
Marianao, 102.
Mariel, 20, 83.
Marinduque Island, 346, 445.
Marketmen, 116.
Markets of Havana, 75, 76; of Honolulu, 280.
Maro, Hawaiian dress, 260.
Marriage customs, 103, 433, 440.
Marsh region, 25.
Matanzas, 77, 78.
Matanzas, Pan de, 20, 77.
Matanzas province, soil of, 21.
Masbate Island, 335, 346; grazing on, 458.
Masquerade, carnival, 115.

Mats, 462.
Maui Island, 238, 240, 258, 299.
Mauna Hualalai, 242.
Mauna Kea, 241, 242, 250.
Mauna Loa, 241, 242; eruptions of, 243, 244.
Mayaguez, 176, 200.
Maybon, 437.
Mayon, Mount, 337; eruptions of, 339.
Meals, Cuban, 105.
Mestiza women, 434; dress of, 435.
Mestizos, 384-386, 434, 435.
Metals, 41, 367-370.
Metal work, 462.
Milk, 458.
Milkmen, Cuban, 110.
Mills, sugar, 139, 212, 305.
Mindanao Island, 335; volcanoes of, 341; description of, 343; Moros of, 389, 437; tribes of, 395; coffee of, 493.
Mindoro Island, 335, 346.
Mindoro Sea, 334, 336.
Mineral springs, 46, 65, 178, 371.
Minerals, 44, 47, 92, 184, 239, 371.
Mines near Santiago, 87.
Mining companies, 43, 44.
Missionaries in Hawaii, 231, 271, 324, 327; in the Philippines, 376.
Moa cascade, 23.
Molasses, 142.
Molave tree, 358.
Molines garden, 68.
Molokai Island, 238, 240, 251.
Mona Passage, 174; Island, 174.
Money, 157, 158, 223, 321, 467.
Mongoose, the, 304.
Monkeys, 364.
Monsoons, 351.
Monte de Pan, 77.
Montero, the, 116; dress of, 118.

INDEX.

Montserrat, shrine of, 204.
Moro chief, 437.
Moro Moro play, 432.
Moros, the, 375; history of, 389; piracies, 389, 416; hatred of Christians, 390, 392; cruelty, 390; weapons, 391; home life, 391; fanaticism, 392; houses, 424; dress and weapons, 436; character, 437; tax paying, 438.
Morro Castle of Havana, 62, 63; of Santiago, 86; of San Juan, 195.
Mortgages, 223.
Mountains, Cuban, 17, 20; Porto Rican, 172; Hawaiian, 239, 240; Philippine, 337, 342.
Mules, 41.
Music in Havana, 98-100; in the Philippines, 387, 423, 429.

N.

Naguabo, 176, 202.
Native revolts, 330.
Natives, Christianity of Philippine, 376, 379; manufactures of, 461; trade ideas of, 464.
Natural gas, 92.
Negritos, the, 386; character of, 393; description of, 440; smoking, 451.
Negroes, 8, 59, 111, 190.
Negros Island, 332, 335, 345; sugar of, 447, 463.
Newspapers, 193, 466.
Niihau Island, 238, 240, 245; sheep on, 313.
Nipa palm, 360, 455.
Nipe Bay, 82.
Noises of Havana, 67, 96.
Nuevitas, 82, 92.
Nuuana Valley, 245, 249, 283.

O.

Oahu Island, 238, 240, 245, 247.
Oahu Railway, 237.
Observatory, Jesuit, 398.
Officials in Cuba, 11.
Ohela plant, 254.
Ohia tree, 254; forest, 256.
Orange, the, 35, 162, 311, 361.
Orchids, 254.
Ostrich farm, Hawaiian, 314.
Oysters, Cuban, 40, 148.

P.

Palace, Captain-general's, 70.
Palawan Island, 336, 346.
Pali, the, 283.
Palm, royal, 26, 32, 33, 82; uses of, 34, 69.
Palma brava, 361.
Palms, 33, 254.
Panay Island, 335; deforestation of, 345, 348, 356; sugar of, 447; tobacco of, 410, 450.
Pandanus tree, 253.
Papaya fruit, 256.
Parks of Havana, 67.
Parque Central, 69, 98, 100.
Partagas cigars, 150.
Paseo, Isabel, 69, 98; de Tacon, 68-73.
Pasig River, 342, 347; craft of, 399; course of, 400; overflow, 410; ducks on, 459.
Pasture lands, 144, 210, 218.
Patriarchal habits, 109.
Pau, Hawaiian dress, 260.
Pearl oyster, 366.
Pearl River harbor, 248.
Peasants, Porto Rican, 206, 207; indolence of, 211, 215.
Pele, the goddess, 272.

INDEX.

Penal settlement, 166.
Petroleum, 27, 45, 372.
Philippine Islands, discovery of, 323, 329; ceded to the United States, 332; geography, 334; number, 334; area, 335; geology, 338; volcanoes, 339; harbors, 347; climate, 349; seasons, 350; rainfall, 352; diseases, 353; forests, 356-359; fruits, 361; edible roots, 362; animals, 362-367; metals and minerals, 367-372; government, 373; religion, 376; roads, 381; population, 384; tribes, 393; education, 396; tobacco, 450; industrial future, 469.
Philippine soldiers, 416; sailors, 416; swimmers, 417; houses, 423; food, 425; smoking, 425; betel-nut chewing, 426; dress, 426; women, 427; gambling, 428; cock-fighting, 429; feasts, 431; dances, 431; drama, 432; marriage, 433; untruthfulness, 433.
Pigs, Hawaiian, 261, 263; wild, 264; Philippine, 458.
Piña fabric, 462.
Piña Raton hedge, 122.
Pinar del Rio, 32, 91.
Pine-apple, 35, 37, 162, 311, 361.
Pines, 32.
Pirates, Malay, 416.
Plains, 21, 172, 245, 342, 346.
Plantain, the, 34, 131, 255.
Plantation life, 121, 122; railways, 274; laborers, 295.
Plantations, sugar, 300.
Planters, 207.
Planters, houses of, 121.
Playa, 176, 199.

Poi making, 258; eating, 259, 311.
Ponce, port of, 176; city of, 199; industries, 219.
Ponce de Leon, 165, castle of, 196.
Popular divisions, 50.
Population of Cuba, 10, 57-60; of Havana, 65; of Porto Rico, 189, 192; of Hawaii, 266, 267-269; of the Philippines, 384.
Porto Rico, history of, 165-170; prosperity, 168; insurrection in, 168; invasion of, 169; cession to the United States, 170; size and location, 171; mountains, 172; fertility and beauty, 172; rivers, 173; lakes, 174; islands, 174; harbors, 175; geology, 177; climate, 178; temperature, 178; rainfall, 179; healthfulness, 180; plants, 181-183; animals, 183; minerals, 184; government, 186; religion, 187; roads, 187; railways, 188; population, 189, 192, 194; classes, 190; education, 192; cities, 194; villages, 203; customs, 205; towns, 208; soil, 210; forests, 211; scenery, 211; farm crops, 212; manufactures, 219; commerce, 219-223; finances, 223; future prospects, 225-227.
Portuguese in Hawaii, 295.
Postal system, Hawaiian, 277.
Potatoes, 311, 362.
Potrillo, peak of, 20.
Poultry, 41, 147, 218, 458.
Prado, the, 69.
Prickly pear, the, 256.
Priests in the Philippines, 327.
Prison, royal, 69.
Processions, religious, 379, 401, 408.
Provinces of Cuba, 48, 51.
Public works, 162.

INDEX. 485

Puerto Principe, 82, 92; cattle of, 144; horses of, 145.
Pulu fibre, 311.
Puna district, 243; coffee of, 307.
Punch bowl, the, 282.
Punta Arenas, 175.

R.

Railways, Cuban, 54, 162; Porto Rican, 188; Hawaiian, 273; Philippine, 382, 470.
Rainfall, Cuban, 28, 30; Porto Rican, 179; Hawaiian, 249, 250; Philippine, 351, 352.
Raspberries, 255.
Rats, 261, 304.
Rattan, uses of, 366.
Reconcentration, 12, 424.
Reforms, promised, 11.
Regla, 64, 114, 163.
Religion in Cuba, 52; in Porto Rico, 187; in Hawaii, 230-232; in the Philippines, 376.
Religious orders, 377; revenues of, 378.
Religious processions, 379, 401, 408.
Representation in Cuba, 49.
Reptiles, 38, 261.
Revenue, Cuban, 157.
Revolts, Philippine native, 330.
Rice culture, 35, 216, 309, 425, 451-453.
Rivers, Cuban, 21, 22; Porto Rican, 173; Hawaiian, 246; Philippine, 342, 343.
Roads, Cuban, 53, 162; Porto Rican, 187; Hawaiian, 273; Philippine, 381.
Rock basis of Cuba, 27.
Rocking-chairs, Havana, 98.
Rocks, Philippine, 338.
Roof, life on the, 99.

Rosario, Falls of the, 23.
Rose-apple, 36.
Royal palm, 26, 32, 33, 182; uses of, 34, 69.
Running amuck, 419.
Rural population, 116-121, 206-209.
Russell & Sturgis, firm of, 463.

S.

Sabana Camaguey, 24.
Sagua la Grande, 81.
Sagua la Grande River, 22.
St. Lazarus Islands, 323.
Salt lake, Hawaiian, 247.
Salt production, 46, 185.
Samar Island, 335, 344.
San Antonio de los Baños, 92, 95.
San Antonio River, 23.
San Cristobal, 91.
San Diego springs, 46, 94.
San German, 202.
San José de Buenavista, 348.
San Juan, hill of, 87.
San Juan Bautista, 165; harbor of, 175, 177; schools, 193; description of, 194-196; industries, 219.
San Juan de los Remedios, 81.
San Juan y Trinidad Mountains, 20.
San Vicente, 95.
Sandal wood, 254, 258.
Sandwich Islands, 237.
Sanitation, lack of, 30.
Santa Clara, 92.
Santa Clara province, 21, 146.
Santa Cruz del Sur, 88.
Santa Fé hot springs, 46, 94.
Santa Rita mineral springs, 65, 102.
Santiago de Cuba, settlement of, 8, 17; blockade and capture of, 13; mountains adjacent to, 18; cleaning of, 30; location, 83;

streets, 84, 85; cathedral, 84; saloons, 85; sanitation, 86; bay of, 86; Morro Castle, 86; mines in vicinity, 87; gambling prohibited, 113.
Santiago de Cuba province, 18; copper of, 42; iron, 43; coal, 44; mineral wealth, 47; coffee, 126; live-stock, 146.
Santiago de los Vegas, 92.
Sapan wood, 411, 457.
Sapodilla, the, 35.
Scenery, Cuban, 26, 30; Matanzas, 79; Trinidad, 89.
Schools, 60, 61, 193, 270, 396.
Sea-bathing, 74.
Seasons, Cuban, 28; Porto Rican, 179; Hawaiian, 250; Philippine, 350.
Serpentine rocks, 27.
Serpents in Cuba, 38; in Porto Rico, 183; in the Philippines, 365.
Sewerage, 67, 163.
Shark killing, 262, 291, 417.
Sheep raising, 41, 264, 313.
Shellfish, large, 366.
Shipping, Cuban, 152; Hawaiian, 320.
Shipping ports, 154.
Sibuyan Island, 335.
Sierra de Cubitas, 19, 43, 93.
Sierra Luquillo, 172, 181.
Sierra Maestra, 18, 20, 43, 44.
Silver, 42, 369, 467.
Slavery in Cuba, 42; abolition of, 51; in Porto Rico, 167, 191; in the Philippines, 437.
Slaves, 8; join rebels, 51, 59; treatment of, 191.
Small-pox, 354.
Smoking in Cuba, 101; in the Philippines, 425, 429, 451.

Snakes, 38, 183.
Soil, fertility of, 21, 116.
Soils, Cuban, 27, 132; Porto Rican, 210; Hawaiian, 301, 307, 309, 314.
Solenodon, the, 38.
Spain, barbarity of, 12; war with, 13; policy of, 13; cedes the Philippines, 332.
Spanish class, Porto Rico, 190, 205.
Spanish farm laws, 456.
Spanish settlement at Cebu, 324; at Manila, 324.
Sponges, Cuban, 147.
Spreckles, Claus, 301.
Springs, mineral, 94, 95, 102.
Star-apple, 35.
State dress, Philippine, 375.
Steamship lines, 56, 189, 274, 320, 383.
Steere expedition, 346.
Stores of Havana, 66, 67.
Storms, 28, 179, 251, 350, 351.
Strawberries, 255.
Street railways, 55, 163, 274.
Street scenes, 199, 406, 409.
Streets of Havana, 65, 74.
Sual, 349.
Subig Bay, 349.
Sugar, manufacture of, 141-143; exports to United States, 154, 305.
Sugar-cane, culture of, 136, 137; cutting and grinding, 139; crushing, 140-142; cultivation, 143, 160; in Porto Rico, 212, 213; in Hawaii, 299-306; in Philippines, 446-449.
Sugar-mills, 139, 212, 300.
Sulphur, 341, 372.
Sulphur springs, 437.
Sultan Harun, 437.

INDEX.

Sultan, Moro, 375, 437.
Sulu, 354, 413.
Sulu Islands, 334, 336, 346, 375, 437.
Summer resorts, 102.
Sunday in Cuba, 111.
Surf-swimming, 289-291.
Sweet potato, 35, 76, 116, 216, 310, 362.
Swine, 315, 364.

T.

Taal, 414.
Taal sugar, 448.
Taal volcano, 340.
Tablas Island, 335.
Tabu, the, 230; overthrow of, 234.
Tacloban harbor, 348.
Tacon theatre, 71, 115.
Tagals, the, 386, 387, 400.
Tagbanuas, the, 394, 424; religion of, 439.
Tamarind-tree, 33, 35.
Taro plant, 258, 311.
Tawi Tawi Island, 336.
Taxes, Philippine, 374, 469.
Telegraph, 57, 189, 276, 383.
Telephone, 189, 296.
Temperature, Cuban, 28; Porto Rican, 178; Hawaiian, 249; Manila, 352.
Territory of Hawaii, 266.
Theatres of Havana, 72.
Ti-tree, 260.
Ticao Island, 335.
Tierro Adentro, 50.
Timarau, the, 363.
Tobacco, Cuban, 21, 37; culture of, 132-136; use of, 149; exports of, 155; development, 160; Porto Rican, 216; Hawaiian, 311; Philippine, 330, 450, 460.

Tobacco region, 50.
Tondo, 406.
Towns and cities, 62-95, 194, 208, 278, 399.
Trade-winds, 250.
Traffic, inter-island, 275, 383.
Transportation, 53, 383.
Travel, Cuban, 53; Philippine, 382.
Tree ferns, 254.
Trees of Cuba, 26, 32; of Porto Rico, 181; of Hawaii, 253; of the Philippines, 356-359.
Tribes, Philippine, 375, 386, 387, 394.
Trinidad, 8, 20, 88; horses of, 144.
Trocha, the, 19, 20.
Tropical climate, effects of, 471.
Truck-growers, 116.
Tulisanes, the, 396.
Turquino, peak of, 18.
Turtles, 147, 184.
Typhoons, effects of, 351.

U.

United States' sympathy with Cubans, 12; war with Spain, 13, 169, 331; trade with Cuba, 154-156; with Porto Rico, 221, 222; with Hawaii, 318; treaty with Spain, 331; trade with the Philippines, 449, 466; relation to the Philippines, 469.
University of Havana, 60; of St. Thomas, 398.
Utuado, 203.

V.

Vacuum-pans, sugar, 141.
Valley of Yumurri, 78; of the Magdalen, 78.
Valleys of Hawaii, 245.

INDEX

Vancouver, 228, 230.
Vegetables, garden, 35, 311.
Vegetation, Cuban, 30.
Vieques Island, 175, 177.
Villa Clara, 92.
Village headmen, 374.
Villages of Porto Rico, 203; of the Philippines, 424.
Visayas island group, 335.
Visayas, the, 388.
Volante, the, 53.
Volcanic structure of Hawaii, 239.
Volcanoes, Hawaiian, 241-244; Philippine, 339-341.
Vuelta Abajo region, 50, 91; tobacco district, 133.
Vuelta Arriba region, 50.

W.

Waikiki, 283.
Walls of San Juan, 196; of Manila, 400.
War cloak, Hawaiian, 261.
War with Spain, 13.
Water buffalo, the, 382.
Water supply of Havana, 76; of San Juan, 197; of Honolulu, 276.
Wauti-tree, 260.
Wet season of Cuba, 28; of Porto Rico, 179; of Hawaii, 250; of the Philippines, 350.
Wheat, 311, 362.
White ants, 367.
White labor in Porto Rico, 166.

Whites in Hawaii 229, 235.
Wild animals, 312, 364.
Wild cattle, 263.
Wild dogs, 183, 264.
Wild tribes, 393, 439.
Wilder Steamship Company, 275.
Windows, Cuban, 98; Philippine, 403.
Winds, prevailing Cuban, 29; Hawaiian, 249, 250.
Wine-drinking, 106.
Winter resort, Cuba as a, 164.
Women, Cuban, 119; Hawaiian, 288, 290; Philippine, 427, 434, 463.
Wood, General, 85.
Woods, Cuban, 32; Porto Rican, 182; Hawaiian, 312; Philippine, 357-359.
Worcester, Dean C., 353, 375, 419.

Y.

Yam, the, 34.
Yauco, 203.
Yellow fever, 29.
Ylang-ylang, the, 457.
Young, John, 278.
Yumurri Valley, 78.

Z.

Zamboango, 348, 412.
Zamboango peninsula, 343.
Zapata marsh, 25.

THE END.

www.ingramcontent.com/pod-product-compliance
Lightning Source LLC
Chambersburg PA
CBHW051200300426
44116CB00006B/385